Design for the Changing Educational Landscape

The whole landscape of space use is undergoing a radical transformation. In the workplace a period of unprecedented change has created a mix of responses with one overriding outcome observable worldwide: the rise of distributed space. In the learning environment the social, political, economic and technological changes responsible for this shift have been further compounded by constantly developing theories of learning and teaching, and a wide acceptance of the importance of learning as the core of the community, resulting in the blending of all aspects of learning into one seamless experience.

This book attempts to look at all the forces driving the provision and pedagogic performance of the many spaces, real and virtual, that now accommodate the experience of learning and provide pointers towards the creation and design of learning-centred communities.

Part 1 looks at the entire learning universe as it now stands, tracks the way in which its constituent parts came to occupy their role, assesses how they have responded to a complex of drivers and gauges their success in dealing with renewed pressures to perform. It shows that what is required is innovation within the spaces and integration between them. Part 2 finds many examples of innovation in evidence across the world – in schools, the higher and further education campus and in business and cultural spaces – but an almost total absence of integration. Part 3 offers a model that redefines the learning landscape in terms of learning outcomes, mapping spatial requirements and activities into a detailed mechanism that will achieve the best outcome at the most appropriate scale.

By encouraging stakeholders to create an events-based rather than space-based identity, the book hopes to point the way to a fully-integrated learning landscape: a learning community.

Andrew Harrison is a researcher and consultant with experience in many aspects of space use. In 2011 he set up Spaces That Work, an independent consultancy specializing in learning environments. Before that he was Director of Learning and Research at DEGW, leading major research projects in the UK and internationally. These included Sustainable Accommodation for the New Economy, supported by the European Commission, Spaces for Personalized Learning for the UK Department for Children, Schools and Families, and Project Faraday, which developed new space and experience models for the teaching of secondary school science in Britain. He has also led projects exploring the impacts of technology and pedagogy change on school and higher education institution design, including work internationally for the Aga Khan University, the University of Central Asia, Aalto University in Finland and the Dublin Institute of Technology.

Les Hutton is a writer, editor and copywriter with experience in education, management, commercial property and architecture. Publications include *Architectural Knowledge*, *The Distributed Workplace*, *The Responsive Office* and *Working Beyond Walls*. He was the founder editor of *Facilities* magazine and has written extensively on the UK and international real estate market.

Design for the Changing Educational Landscape

SPACE, PLACE AND THE FUTURE OF LEARNING

Andrew Harrison and Les Hutton

Routledge
Taylor & Francis Group

LONDON AND NEW YORK

First published 2014
by Routledge
2 Park Square, Milton Park, Abingdon, Oxon OX14 4RN

Simultaneously published in the USA and Canada
by Routledge
711 Third Avenue, New York, NY 10017

Routledge is an imprint of the Taylor & Francis Group, an informa business

British Library Cataloguing in Publication Data
A catalogue record for this book is available from the British Library

Library of Congress Cataloging in Publication Data
A catalog record for this book is available from the Library of Congress

ISBN: 978-0-415-51757-7 (hbk)
ISBN: 978-0-415-51758-4 (pbk)
ISBN: 978-0-203-76265-3 (ebk)

Typeset in Officina Sans Std 9/12.5pt
by Fakenham Prepress Solutions, Fakenham, Norfolk NR21 8NN

Printed in Great Britain by Bell & Bain Ltd, Glasgow

MIX
Paper from
responsible sources
FSC® C007785
www.fsc.org

Contents

Contents

Acknowledgements

The dominant theme to emerge from these pages is that space, place and learning have become inextricably bound up with each other into a blended whole which is beginning to achieve a critical mass of importance across society. In great part this spatial world view is the legacy of almost 30 years of discussion and shared information with colleagues at the international architects, DEGW, and in particular Frank Duffy, John Worthington and Despina Katsikakis. We would like to record and acknowledge both their professional rigour and personal generosity of access to a wide range of new ideas, many of them instrumental in the formulation of our own thoughts.

DEGW was a rich centre of enquiry about the workplace in all its manifestations and as a forum for innovation will be sorely missed. Many of its values, fortunately – and certainly its chief quality,

intellectual curiosity – are present in the work of the worldwide diaspora of DEGW people who continue to find new ways to describe, analyse and systematize the built environment, among them the business strategists and designers of Strategy Plus, our colleagues at Spaces That Work and Tom Weaver, whose assistance was especially invaluable at the early stages of this book's development.

We would also like to acknowledge the contribution of clients who have provided us with the opportunity to get to know their institutions and work with them to address issues of academic mission, pedagogy, space and technology. Everyone at the institutions illustrated in this book deserves our thanks for their generosity and support with photographs, illustrations and project information.

Introduction

This book attempts to look at all the forces driving the provision and pedagogic performance of the many spaces, real and virtual, that now accommodate the experience of learning – from purpose-built school and higher education buildings to museums, galleries, hotels and conference centres – and by means of this examination provide pointers towards the creation and in particular the design of learning-centred communities.

It is our belief that this move to putting learning at the centre of our lives is well advanced and universally observable across the learning landscape at all scales and in all societies. There is no doubt, however, that the overwhelming weight of academic evidence for this phenomenon lies in a relatively small handful of territories worldwide – the UK, the US, Scandinavia, Australia and New Zealand – and deals disproportionately with formal, mandatory education at the expense of compelling new narratives involving business and cultural spaces.

We are unapologetic about concentrating on the findings that have emerged from this narrow band of academic and organizational enquiry – particularly the astounding ten-year period in the UK when the debate about learning and space reached a sustained fever pitch before collapsing with the arrival of the 2008 world economic crisis. This coincides intellectually, geographically and chronologically with our main (though not sole) areas of experience and expertise but it is also sufficiently suggestive of innovations in educational space worldwide to claim universal significance – to justify our concentrating on the mass of data to emerge from such initiatives as the Building Schools for the Future programme and the blizzard of higher education research conducted during the course of 2006.

We must similarly justify our delimitation of our conceptual framework. Because we are fundamentally concerned with design, aiming to provide designers, procurers and users of space with the means to effect useful change in their own sphere of influence, we take a place-based approach to this learning universe. And because our purpose in looking at these places is not primarily to systematize (although that is an essential and rather neglected first stage) but to assess their performance as a necessary precursor to prescriptive action, we must acknowledge that this transformational imperative inevitably privileges certain spaces at the expense of others: classrooms will always command more of our attention than hotel conference centres and coffee shops.

The learning environment is not alone in having to deal with this opening up – and, critically, running together – of possibilities. It is taking place in organizations of all sorts – part of a wider pattern in which the whole landscape of space use is changing: the hybridizing of space, the dispersing of work, the annexing of non-traditional spaces or the freedoms and constrictions that come with new technology and the blending and layering of virtual and physical work arenas. The learning environment is, though, we would contest, in the front line of these volatile developments, as we illustrate in Part 1, in which we look at the entire learning universe and track the way in which its constituent parts came to occupy their role, assess how they – individually and collectively – have responded to a complex of drivers and gauge their success in dealing with renewed pressures to perform. We show the gap widening between what learning space could support and what it in fact does support, during the course of which two things become clear: the costs of the loss of transformative potential are rapidly becoming economically insupportable and societally damaging; and a piecemeal response, however reflexive, is damned to fail both case-by-case and systemically.

What is required is innovation within the spaces and integration between them. Part 2 looks at the many examples of innovation in evidence across the world – first in schools, then the higher and further education campus and finally in business and cultural spaces. It finds and celebrates many examples of best practice, fewer – though shining – examples of innovation, and almost no strategic vision at the level of the community or city. The innovation that is taking place is happening at different rates in different institutions, as organizations have responded to changing imperatives and to some extent met them – but the response is undeniably piecemeal. It is notable that while there has been a great deal of innovation within building types – and a lot of talk about shared community resources and partnerships – there is little concerted effort to take an overview about holistic learning and remarkably little concentration on the spatial implications of any cross-cultural partnering that does exist – in short, an absence of integration.

We cannot, of course, impose a culture of integration where none exists, but in Part 3 we offer a model that encourages stakeholders to redefine the learning landscape – their learning landscape – in the widest and most generous way possible: to enter into a briefing process that takes into account in the first instance the activities required by the total learning community and only then negotiates the square foot utilization of budgetary and departmental allowances. With its unbounded view of learning requirements, this process allows stakeholders to look at learning outcomes in much the same way as strategies evolved over the past decade to deal with distributed work patterns in the commercial and corporate workplace. Using existing tools to make their decisions on desired outcomes less subjective, this model allows providers to map spatial requirements and activities into a detailed mechanism to achieve the best outcome at the most appropriate scale.

We have uncovered many instances worldwide of integrated learning strategies between institutions, some examples of business–academia collaboration, and there has undoubtedly been innovation in terms of sharing of community learning resources. There has been some use of university facilities by schools and some shared curriculum work and even the creation of neighbourhood schools as hubs – the 'nexus' centres in post-Katrina New Orleans, with schools at their core but providing a resource for the entire community (CELE 2010).

What there has not been is a general acceptance, unprompted by the upheavals of nature that – in learning as in so much else – interconnectedness is the reality from which we diverge at our cost. By encouraging educators to withhold the rush to provide physical accommodation until an entire learning strategy is in place – by creating an events-based rather than space-based identity – we hope to point the way to a fully-integrated learning landscape: a learning community.

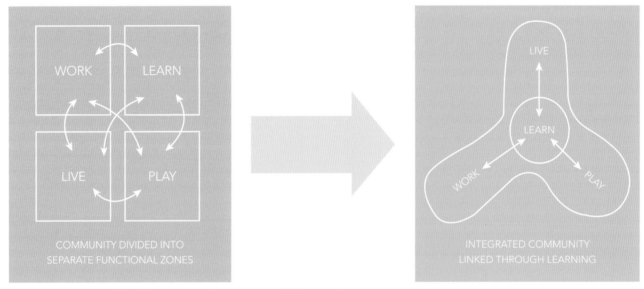

Figure 0.1 Learning is the hub of the community. Source: Harrison 2007/Steve Smith

PART 1

Learning space

CHAPTER 1
The learning universe

Learning takes place throughout our lives and across the physical and virtual communities we occupy: as an activity it can be encountered in an enormous range of spaces, from purpose-built school and higher education buildings to museums, galleries, hotels and conference centres (Figure 1.1). This is an extensive portfolio across a rapidly changing landscape. Both the scale and the speed of change ask designers the hard question: is it possible to create space for learning that will be responsive, resilient and well designed – or is it already too late to do more than passively acknowledge this change in status and circumstance?

Because we are fundamentally concerned with *design*, this book takes a place-based approach to this learning universe, while acknowledging that the activity can be free-floating and virtual. Our purpose in looking at these places is not primarily to systematize, although that is an essential and rather neglected first stage (Temple 2008: 229–41), but to assess their performance as a necessary precursor to prescriptive action. We also acknowledge that the aim of this book is to provide designers, procurers and users of space with the means to effect useful change in their own sphere of influence – and this transformational imperative inevitably privileges certain spaces at the expense of others.

Three major space groupings emerge from the baggy portfolio covered in Figure 1.1. The first place is the school building, the core space of which, the classroom, at one time adequately defined the activity – teacher at the front, children facing – and now does not (Figure 1.2). The second is the complex of spaces and activities that make up a further and higher education campus – lecture rooms and classrooms, libraries, student centres, sports facilities (Figure 1.3). This is no longer a remote, hermetic space but an accessible, permeable space with deep roots in the wider

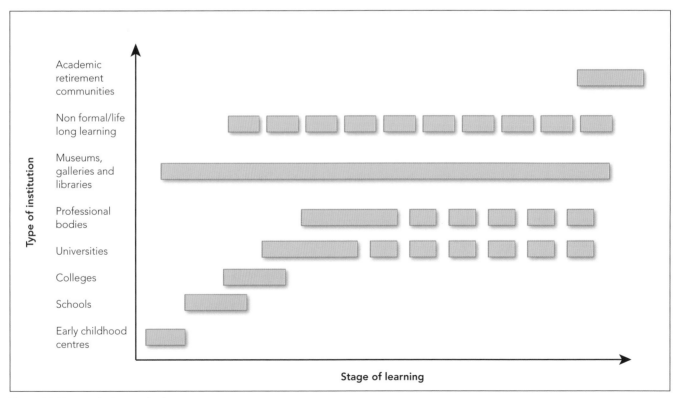

Figure 1.1 Mapping the learning landscape

Figure 1.2 School buildings: Chantry High School, Ipswich. For decades the classroom was no more than a teacher and an audience and a single acceptable configuration: learning styles – and spaces – are changing

Figure 1.3 The university campus: Aga Khan University, Karachi, Pakistan. The type of further and higher education accommodation that used to be enclosed and exclusive and is now a focal point for the whole community

Figure 1.4 Business and cultural spaces: Turku City Library, Finland. The public library: the space is disarmingly similar but its use has utterly changed. Now the library has the capacity to be a learning hub for the entire community

community – and deep economic obligations: these places have to exist as rigorously and accountably in the real world as any commercial workspace. This extension of once-restricted services and obligations is taken much further in the final category – those spaces above, below, within and beyond traditional learning spaces that nevertheless must be planned for, designed and assessed in terms of performance: just like any learning space, any workplace (Figure 1.4).

All these spaces – school, higher and further education and the new ancillary learning spaces, including virtual learning environments – emerged piecemeal over time in response to a number of long-term drivers, and betray their disaggregated origins in their haphazard suitability for current – let alone future – learning needs. Do we – put simply – know enough about this landscape to prepare ourselves for the changes it must face?

In July 2006, Paul Temple undertook a literature review of learning spaces for the Centre for Education Studies at the University of London

aimed at informing 'the future design of learning spaces, in order to facilitate the changing pedagogical practices needed to support a mass higher education system with its greater student diversity. It was anticipated … that issues arising might include the implications for learning space of changing student demands, new pedagogies and technological advance' (Temple 2007: 4). In this he makes the point that the design of learning spaces has been 'a continuing occupation' in the schools sector – and he cites Clark (2002) – whereas several standard texts on teaching and learning in higher education (e.g., Light and Cox 2001) 'do not mention the nature of learning spaces, even in passing' (Temple 2007: 10). He traces the causes of this divergence of interest – for the 'long-standing and continuing tradition in the UK and elsewhere, of applying an education-centred philosophy to the planning of school buildings (DfES 2002: 7)' – to the start of publicly financed education in Europe in the later nineteenth century (Temple 2007: 57).

The connection between building design and educational theories and methods received 'special emphasis in the post-1945 national school building programmes, where standardized, innovative school designs were created, for reasons both of cost-effectiveness and to allow new pedagogic methods to be readily applied (Maclure 1984)'. Furthermore, he adds, 'there was been a tradition in school pedagogy of careful observation of the differences that school designs and classroom layouts make to student behaviour and work (Loughlin 1977)'. 'This level of detailed observation and reflection on the micro-organisation of teaching spaces', he asserts, 'is largely absent in the higher education literature' (Temple 2007: 57). More recently Barrett et al. (2013) conducted a study to look for evidence of the demonstrable impact of school building design on the learning rates of pupils in primary schools. The study, 'A holistic, multi-level analysis identifying the impact of classroom design on pupils' learning', developed hypotheses as to positive impacts on learning for ten design parameters within a neuroscience framework of three design principles. These were tested using data collected on 751 pupils from 34 varied classrooms in seven different schools in the UK:

> The multi-level model developed explained 51 per cent of the variability in the learning improvements of the pupils, over the course of a year. However, within this a high level of explanation (73 per cent) was identified at the 'class' level, linked entirely to six built environment design parameters, namely: colour, choice, connection, complexity, flexibility and light. The model was used to predict the impact of the six design parameters on pupils' learning progression. Comparing the 'worst' and 'best' classrooms in the sample, these factors alone were found to have an impact that equates to the typical progress of a pupil over one year. It was also possible to estimate the proportionate impact of these built environment factors on learning progression, in the context of all influences together. This scaled at a 25 per cent contribution on average.

> This clear evidence of the significant impact of the built environment on pupils' learning progression highlights the importance of this aspect for policy makers, designers and users. The wide range of factors involved in this holistic approach still leaves a significant design challenge.
>
> (Barrett et al. 2013: 1)

In 2011, the fourth compendious Organisation for Economic Cooperation and Development (OECD) study of exemplar buildings, *Designing for Education* (OECD 2011), was overwhelmingly schools oriented, drawing evidence from 28 countries and 60 recently built/refurbished education facilities only seven of which are further or higher education establishments rather than schools (Box 1.1). Yet in the introductory chapter of the book, Alastair Blyth, acknowledging the schools slant of traditional reporting by the Centre for Effective Learning Environments (CELE) and its precursor, the Programme on Educational Building (PEB), heralds a more recent concentration on further and higher education: 'higher education facilities became a concern as a university level education became almost universal and problems developed in relation to managing large university estates, catering for greater student numbers and managing greater varieties of courses on offer' (OECD 2011: 17).

In its coverage of learning space in our third grouping, however – the rising presence of place without space, virtual/distributed learning and of space ungeared to established institutions – the literature is distinctly spottier. None of the exemplar spaces in *Designing for Education* (OECD 2011), for example, is a non-formal or informal learning environment (OECD terminology for these third stream locations: Box 1.2): these are covered in another OECD report (OECD 2010) – 15 years after OECD education ministers agreed to develop strategies for 'lifelong learning for all' (OECD 1996).

SCHOOLS

In the UK, eight clearly identifiable phases can be observed in the development of publicly provided education over more than 150 years. At each stage, the design and provision of school buildings have emerged from a potent mix of policy, economics, demographics and changing learning and architectural theory.

The burst of elementary school construction that followed the 1870 Elementary Education Act, for instance, seems, at this distance, to

---

Box 1.1 Further and higher education exemplars

Cork Institute of Technology, Ireland; MAD-faculty, KHLim–PHL Belgium; The Saltire Centre, Glasgow Caledonian University, United Kingdom; Sino-French Centre, Tongji University, China; Bâtiment Atrium, Université Pierre et

Marie Curie, France; Stephen M. Ross School of Business, University of Michigan, USA; Akademia Muzyczna im. Karola Szymanowskiego, Katowicach, Poland.

Source: *Designing for Education* (OECD 2011)

Box 1.2 The learner's perspective

From the learner's standpoint, formal learning is always intentional – their explicit intention is to gain knowledge, skills and/or competences. This would include learning that takes place inside the initial education and training system, and also workplace training by their employer. Informal learning is often referred to as learning by experience or just, experience. The simple fact of existing, this view holds, constantly exposes the person to learning at home, at work and during their leisure time. This definition – with a few exceptions (Werquin 2007) – is fairly consensual.

Source: OECD (2010: 2)

be a monolithic process designed to meet the provisions of the Act – but 'it disguised a wide variety in both internal organisation and external architecture' (Seaborne and Lowe 1977: 22, quoted in Woolner et al. 2005: 7). In its provision for free elementary education, this vast Victorian building programme was as complex in its origins as the post-war building response to free, universal secondary education in the wake of the 1944 Butler Education Act: free, as in non-fee-paying, but at a heavy cost to losers in the Burt 11-plus IQ lottery that determined their place in the UK's tripartite system of education that operated between 1944 and 1976.

> Long after the 1944 Act, its chief political architect Rab Butler wrote of how important it was to 'ensure that a stigma of inferiority did not attach itself to those secondary institutions ... which lacked the facilities and academic prestige of grammar schools'. But how could it be otherwise? Grammar schools had, in general, three times more money spent on them; they had the best teachers, the best facilities.
>
> (Benn 2011: 42)

The Butler Act itself, of course, was the end-product of a long and iterative programme: the 1902 and 1903 Balfour Acts had transferred control of state schools from school boards to country and borough councils and begun the process of 'regularizing arrangements previously made by some boards, especially in cities, to go beyond "elementary" education' (Saint 1987: 36). The provision of secondary schools remained haphazard and inadequate through the Acts of 1918 and 1921, the initial Hadow Report in 1926, followed by further reports in 1931, 1933 and 1938, reviewing the whole structure of English schooling and informing the spirit of the Butler Act.

In Andrew Saint's estimation, the English post-war school-building movement that followed the Act can advance bold claims both for its aims and its achievements. 'Alone in Britain, without exact parallel in other countries, its proponents grasped the chances for social development implicit in modern architecture since the 1930s and succeeded in applying its principles in such a way as to benefit a whole nation' (ibid.: 225). He sees the aim in terms of lofty architectural commandments:

> Firstly, they held that everything about architecture and building ought to be submitted to the test of the most searching, rational scrutiny. Secondly, the benefits of a better architecture had to be conferred evenly upon the whole population, not reserved for one small segment. Thirdly, the methods of architecture had to be intensely cooperative and collaborative. From a combination of these tenets sprang a fourth. Buildings were to be the embodiment of a continuous, developing process between architect, client, user and maker.
>
> (ibid.: 225)

This 'austere code', he asserts, formed the bones of a movement that achieved great things for the nation's children:

> Against a shifting backdrop of urgency, opportunity, shortage and stringency, [the school-builders] helped to develop policies and means of construction which housed a whole generation of children in state schools to a far higher standard of accommodation and services than anything thought imaginable before the war. There was no 'double-banking' of the kind common elsewhere [splitting the curriculum into morning and afternoon sessions], no child turned away for want of a school place. The schools built were neither temporary nor identical. They could expect a medium- or long-term life-span, and they were tailored to the different local wants and aspirations of teachers and education authorities. Some were original and handsome, others were not special to look at, but most were practical. Imaginative practicality, in so far as such generalizations can be made, was the distinguishing mark of the post-war British school.
>
> (ibid.: 225–6)

Would this forgiving assessment be the generally held view by 2004, when the Labour government launched its Building Schools for the Future (BSF) programme, acknowledging the poor standard, condition and relevance to changing circumstances of England's secondary schools and aiming to refurbish or rebuild all 3,500 of them over a 15-year period at an anticipated budget of £45 billion (DfES 2004)? (Or 2010, when the Coalition government's education secretary, Michael Gove, scrapped it and replaced it with a more limited capital investment programme?)

The poor state of the UK school building stock – and, to a lesser extent, the poor match between the space and its current uses – was no secret. Between 1997 and 2004/5, the Labour government increased capital investment in school buildings from £700 million to £3 billion per annum (DfES 2003a), in an informal programme using Private Finance Initiative (PFI) as a funding mechanism, in which the private sector provides the capital funding, and also builds and (mostly) operates the facilities under a 25 to 30-year contract. A significant number of primary and secondary schools in England were built during this period, often in bulk schemes. Northamptonshire Group Schools Project 2, for example, encompassed five new build secondary schools, six new build primaries, and 30 extensions or refurbishments (Partnerships UK). These schemes were driven very strongly by the need to replace 'unfit' school buildings, and although they were to be educationally fit for purpose, too, innovation was not on the agenda.

Scotland was at the same time engaged in a similar programme, using Public Private Partnerships (PPP) as the main method for building new schools, starting in 1998 with ten projects containing 74 schools with a capital value of £535 million (Scottish Government 2010). The first schools were completed in 2000 and the last in 2005. The second round, announced in 2001, eventually involved 28 projects with a capital value of £2.8 billion and contained 213 schools, completed between 2004 and 2012/13 (SPICE 2011). Here, too, the dominant need was the replacement of ageing building stock, but there was also a focus on the possibilities of good architecture in unlocking the school building as a place for learning:

> all agree that it's not simply the classrooms and assembly halls that matter. It is also important to consider those forgotten spaces such as the corridors where pupils can spend up to 20 per cent of their school day. Outdoor areas, particularly playgrounds, also emerge as an important but too often forgotten school area. When children are asked what would make the most impact on their school, 'social spaces' is the most popular answer.
>
> (The Lighthouse 2008)

The lack of focus on teaching and learning innovation within school building projects that came with PFI schools changed with the introduction of the Building Schools for the Future programme, which aimed to ensure all English schools 'had facilities of 21st-Century standard' (DfES 2004c: 1), and, more importantly, had the goal of transformation of education.

The aims, as in the post-war programme, were ambitious. The children were to be given state-of-the-art computer technology and a modified school layout to exploit it:

> Instead of sitting in a class, filled with a line of wooden desks facing a teacher firmly ensconced in front of a chalk board, they might perch in Wi-Fi enabled 'learning hubs', using their own laptops to carry out their own independent research. And for the multi-billion pound investment to be sustainable, the new facilities had to be flexible, as no one could predict what education would be like 50 years ahead.
>
> (BBC Education 2010)

By 2009, the BSF timescale had been extended to 18 years and the cost had risen to £52–55 billion, largely as a result of the need to accommodate the Labour government's commitment to academies, special education needs (SEN) schools, voluntary aided schools and carbon reduction measures (Mahony et al. 2011). This was an investment in the school capital on a par with the enormous Victorian and post-war building sprees.

The state of dilapidation went beyond the superficial peeling paint and worn flooring to serious leaks, unopenable windows, headache-inducing 100 Hz fluorescent lighting and uncontrollable lighting (Winterbottom and Wilkins 2009: 63). The original consultation document clearly expressed a statement of value: 'school buildings should inspire learning. They should nurture every pupil and member of staff. They should be a source of pride and a practical resource for the community' (DfES 2003a: 3).

Equally clearly, the building stock fell far short of this aim. But as the Select Committee asked in 2007 (DfES 2007: 2), was BSF the best way to spend £45 billion on education?

A concentration on economic value rather than pedagogical worth runs through assessments of the BSF programme, the largest school building programme in history in terms of capital, and the most ambitious in terms of timelines: 'there is no project like it anywhere in the world. Not since the huge Victorian and post-war building waves has there been investment in … school capital stock on this scale, and of course the potential for new ways of learning has moved on considerably since then' (E&SC 2007: 12).

From the beginning, BSF struggled with its ambitious timelines. There were numerous challenges associated with the scale of delivery, and criticism of the procurement techniques used that led to some bidders losing many millions on lost bids (including one company, Skanska, losing £5 million on one bid alone).

When the Conservative–Liberal Democrat coalition government was formed in 2010, one of the first announcements was that Building Schools for the Future was on hold, indefinitely, while it was reviewed. Concerns were cited about the costs involved in a time of austerity, that there were significant issues around implementation (Mahony et al. 2011: 350), and that the original programme was too design-led and schools too 'bespoke' (DOE 2011), with Education Minister Michael Gove attacking the architectural profession, 'claiming those working on the BSF programme were "creaming off cash" and that creating schools should not be about making "architects richer"' (*Building Design* 2010). In July 2010, he controversially axed the national school rebuilding programme for England because it was 'wasteful and bureaucratic' (BBC Education 2010).

One of the core criticisms of Building Schools for the Future – the lack of definition of the concept of 'transformation' of education – was addressed by the Scottish government by its insistence on a curriculum review before launching its replacement schools programme for the Public Private Partnership programme in June 2009:

> A fundamental change is under way in Scottish education – a holistic approach to more effective learning and teaching. Curriculum for Excellence is already driving changes to the concept of the school – its purposes, functions, design and the way spaces are used. In turn, the buildings, the physical environment and facilities must themselves also be drivers of change. They need to be more than just passive or responsive, to be used and adapted. They need to inspire and challenge both learners and teachers to think in new and imaginative ways about the surroundings within which learning takes place, indeed about the very 'how' it takes place. Buildings can and should be real catalysts for creativity.
>
> (Scottish Government 2009)

The Scottish Executive commissioned a programme, Building Excellence, to explore in depth the link between the Curriculum for Excellence and the design of new schools. This had similarities to the National College BSF Leadership Programme in England, aimed at educating school leaders about school design to inform briefing and improve the quality of learning space provided:

> Curriculum for Excellence does not necessarily demand radically different designs for classrooms or schools, but it does offer the opportunity to think about how spaces are perceived and whether they are being used effectively. By recognising that

learning takes place throughout the school and beyond, the boundaries between the traditional teaching environment – the classroom – and the rest of the school building and grounds become blurred.

> (Scottish Government 2007)

A project funded by the Scottish Executive, Senses of Place, explored design themes, such as 'big spaces' and 'learning communities' (The Lighthouse 2006) and provided a series of workshops that schools and architectural practices could run in tandem to improve the quality of the brief (http://www.scotland.gov.uk/Resource/Doc/920/0049729.pdf).

Wales had a later start than England or Scotland in redesigning schools, launching its 21st Century Schools project in late 2009 to replace decrepit infrastructure and positively enhance teaching and learning. Early project documentation focuses in depth on procurement details, but is vague about the specifics of educational vision, aiming only to have 'a more flexible approach to the nature and location of places where the whole community can learn' and 'to ensure that changing approaches to teaching and learning can be reflected in up-to-date facilities' (Welsh Assembly Government 2010). The economic difficulties meant the project was frozen for a number of months, and faced scaling back and cuts during 2011. The first wave of schools, worth £1.4 billion, was announced in December 2011 and was expected to be spread over seven years (BBC Wales 2011).

In Australia, the Building the Education Revolution (BER) programme was created as part of an economic stimulus package by the Rudd government in 2009, with three main sub-programmes (BER 2009):

● 'Primary Schools for the 21st Century' (P21 – $14.2 billion): provision of new and refurbished halls, libraries and classrooms.

● 'Science and Language Centres for 21st Century Secondary Schools' (SLP – $821.8m): provision of new and refurbished science laboratories and language learning centres.

● 'National School Pride program' (NSP – $1.28 billion): provision of new and refurbished covered outdoor learning areas, and sporting facilities.

The programme has funded around 24,000 infrastructure projects for approximately 9,500 schools across Australia, although this is clearly focused on micro-project refurbishment of facilities as opposed to educational innovation. BER has been heavily criticized for offering poor value for money and delivering buildings of poor quality (Klan 2011), as well as failing to provide the necessary revenue funding to operate the newer facilities (Ferguson and Owen 2012).

Certain states – such as Victoria – already had a strong recent record of educational transformation, underpinned and illustrated by planning principles (Fisher 2005) and case studies, such as the Australian Science and Mathematics School. The educational vision in Victoria was centred on the planning for an evaluation of Principles of Learning and Teaching (PoLT), using the concepts of 'wellbeing', 'student engagement', 'learning for life' and 'global impact', measured across key spaces: administration; learning commons; learning studios (technical and specialist spaces); and non-formal learning spaces (Fisher 2007).

In the US, Sweden and the UK, the last two decades have seen the establishment of autonomous schools operating free of many local governing structures. There has been no single school building programme as yet in the highly federated US – with its federal regulations, state regulations and 16,000 school districts – although President Obama proposed a $25 billion school modernization programme in 2011 as part of the American Jobs Act, to improve 35,000 schools and upgrade them to twenty-first century standards (White House 2011). As with Australia's BER, this will aim broadly to cover a wide number of schools, and although the Department of Education claims the 'investments will give American students the edge they need to prepare for the 21st century economy and compete with students from around the world' (US Department of Education 2011), there is no strong educational vision, as yet, behind the proposals.

In the US, charter schools are mainly not-for-profit, although they may be run by for-profit management organizations such as EdisonLearning and National Heritage Academies. Despite an otherwise only relatively piecemeal investment in school buildings, many innovative approaches have occurred through the charter school system, with exemption from school design codes freeing schools to be set up in factories or offices. Over 1.4 million students were educated in charter schools in 2008–9 (NCES 2011).

In January 2011, California introduced a Schools of the Future (SOFT) initiative, focused on the reform of the schools building programme and the design of high-performing, greener schools. In part this was a response by State Superintendent of Public Instruction Tom Torlakso to a reluctance by policy makers to invest in infrastructure in the face of the economic recession: 'It makes no sense to teach the next generation of California's students in facilities that are relics of the past, powered by energy sources that are out of touch with our state's renewable future' (CELE 2011). The framework on which SOFT acts emerged from a roundtable event bringing together architects, educators, policy makers and practitioners. It recommends that participants should:

- design for the educational programme
- design for adaptability
- promote health and sustainability
- enhance safety and security
- connect to the community
- support a small school culture
- accommodate student diversity
- support the teacher as a professional.

Sweden set up 'free schools' in 1992 (Hlavac 2007) – a form of charter school – by creating a universal voucher system. The government funds vouchers and parents can choose whether to spend them on state schools or 'free schools', creating competition in the education system by enabling greater choice. Here the free schools *can* be for-profit. It is argued (Sahlgren 2010) that the profit motive creates greater competition, which in turn creates 'better' results. Opinion is, however, starting to shift, with the high-profile publication of research claiming private sector operators had increased segregation and not improved standards, and that evidence showing competition is good lacked credibility due to grade inflation (Orange 2011). As in the US, 'chains' of free schools are run by for-profit providers, such as Internationella Engelska Skolan and Kunskapsskolan.

In opposition, the UK Conservative Party studied the Swedish system in depth, and after its 2010 election victory began implementing free schools in the UK. They bear similarity to charter schools in the US, as they are, currently, not-for-profit, although they can be run by for-profit enterprises such as EdisonLearning or Kunskapsskolan. They also benefit from the relaxation of many of the building regulations that prescribe the form and function of a school, so that free schools, like charter schools, may be set up in warehouses or retail spaces. Educational innovator Stephen Heppell welcomes this: 'Shops are big agile spaces, DDA compliant with ventilation and car parking, food and security already provided in a town centre. Your homebases could be the Burger King unit or Clinton Cards' (*RIBA Journal* nd). (In 2012 Clinton Cards went into liquidation.)

FURTHER AND HIGHER EDUCATION

Further and higher education space (Box 1.3) also evolved to a leisurely timetable, only intermittently – the post-war population boom – responding to greater urgency. Temple notes that 'some writers have argued that the university campus, in the sense of a

Box 1.3 Further and higher education

Further education (FE) – called continuing education in the US – in the UK and Ireland refers to post-compulsory education (in addition to that received at secondary school). It is distinct from the education offered in universities (higher education: HE). It may be at any level above compulsory education, from basic training to Higher National Diploma or Foundation Degree. HE is education at a higher level than secondary school, usually provided in distinct institutions such as universities. FE in the UK therefore includes education for people over 16, usually excluding universities. It is primarily taught in FE colleges (which are similar in concept to US community colleges, and sometimes use 'community college' in their title), work-based learning, and adult and community learning institutions. This includes post-16 courses similar to those taught at schools and sub-degree courses similar to those taught at higher education (HE) colleges (which also teach degree-level courses) and at some universities.

defined area within which a university is physically located, is a thing of the past: the learning spaces of the future will be found in workplaces, shopping centres, cultural venues and so on, taking advantage of advances in ICT (Harrison and Dugdale 2003)' (Temple 2007: 25.)

In 1997, Peter Drucker had been confident (*Forbes* 1997) that: 'Thirty years from now the big university campuses will be relics. Universities won't survive. It's as large a change as when we first got the printed book.' He went on to compare higher education to the US healthcare system, noting that its cost had risen just as fast and suggesting that such totally uncontrollable expenditure, without any visible improvement in either the content or the quality of education, indicates that the system is rapidly becoming untenable and that higher education is in deep crisis. He highlighted the impact of changing technology on the university estate: 'Already we are beginning to deliver more lectures and classes off campus via satellite or two-way video at a fraction of the cost. The college won't survive as a residential institution. Today's buildings are hopelessly unsuited and totally unneeded.'

But Temple acknowledges that while 'the campus as a learning space appears from time to time in the literature ... it is under-conceptualised' (Temple 2007: 25) and quotes Strange and Banning: 'among the many methods employed to foster student learning and development, the use of the physical environment is perhaps the least understood and the most neglected' (2001: 30). He also quotes a bold conceptualization by Edwards, taking a long view of the intimate connection between the design of space and the idea of the university:

> Taking a broad sweep of nearly a thousand years of university construction, it is possible to draw one significant conclusion. Of all building types none more conspicuously links new ideals of design and innovative technologies to the mission

of development than the university. The exacting agendas of intellectual inquiry, of scientific experiment, and refined taste, are historically to be found in the design of many university buildings. For example, the sense of scientific rationalism is embodied in built form in the ancient universities of Oxford, Cambridge, Paris, Bologna and Turin. The ideals of democracy find expression in the layout of universities from Virginia to Cape Town ... the campus has never been an ordinary place.

(2000: 150)

For almost as long as there have been universities there has been discussion about the nature of the university, its role in society and its future. In 2010, Mike Neary (Neary et al. 2010) set out to provide a vocabulary and framework within which that future could be discussed – based on the idea of the university as an ideal: a common assumption in the development of thinking about universities (Delanty 2001).

This was an important undertaking, because it acknowledged that what distinguishes the university as a public institution is the extent to which its essential nature is underpinned by idealism – and that responsibility for guardianship of that ideal lies with the academic community.

In the UK, Gordon Graham warned that 'British universities have been guilty of a failure to redefine their identity in a new, diverse world of higher education ... The most essential task is to recreate a sense of our own work by refashioning our understanding of our identity – our understanding of what the word "University" means' (2002: 199).

This rethinking of the idea of the university is necessary in the light of the monumental changes that are taking place in society – including the impacts of globalization, the proliferation of information technology including the internet, changing demographics of the learning population, changes in government policies including fee structures for students and the support of research and teaching in publicly funded institutions. In addition, student expectations about the learning experience are changing (student as customer, student as producer) and the blurring of learning, living, working and leisure within many people's lives is having a huge impact. From an institutional point of view, resources are becoming scarcer and many universities are facing increased competition and pressures in a global educational market where students can choose where, how and when they want to learn.

In 2006 alone, four major reviews of further and higher education space addressed this scarce resource. The Institute of Education in the UK was commissioned by the Space Management Group (SMG) to investigate the impact on space of future changes in higher education (SMG 2006b: 17). JISC (rebadged from Joint Information Systems Committee but still championing digital technology) published a guide to twenty-first-century learning space (JISC 2006). In the US, the director of Educause, Diana Oblinger, published her ground-breaking book *Learning Spaces,* emphasizing 'the power of built pedagogy (the ability of space to define how one teaches)' (Oblinger 2006: part 1). In Scotland, the Scottish Funding Council (SFC) commissioned AMA architects and haa designers to identify and carry out a study of learning space types in further and higher education (SFC 2006).

In his 2007 review, Paul Temple (2007: 5) stated that there is a broad acceptance in the literature that the design of the 'the learning landscape', around the campus and within buildings, can help to create a sense of belonging, as well as facilitating peer-group discussion and thus informal learning. These social features of higher education appear to be bound up with student retention and progression in complex ways. Many of the physical features thought to support these benefits are small-scale and low-cost and *'clear technical recommendations are needed on the best ways of providing such features in different university settings'* (ibid.: 5 – his italics).

He went on to say that the creation of more flexible teaching and learning spaces, capable of being laid-out in different ways, and better micro-design (e.g., of seating and other furniture) are further examples of responses to new pedagogic require-ments. Impressive new buildings are, on their own, no guarantee that improved learning will be achieved; although they may be useful in marketing terms, by helping to brand the institution (ibid.: 7).

He was equally ambivalent about the quality of research on the impact of new learning spaces on learning outcomes:

A substantial proportion of the literature on higher (and other) education space issues makes unsupported, or at best, anecdotal claims about the benefits of new designs or new configurations of existing space. Where they are presented, empirical findings are often flawed, as they either tend to report changed student attitudes (rather than learning outcomes), or, where learning outcomes are reported, they fail to take account of observer effects of various kinds. The difficulties in designing research that can distinguish inputs to learning from the physical environment from inputs arising from other sources are formidable, and do not appear so far to have been seriously addressed ...

... newly-designed learning spaces are usually described in positive terms in the literature, as encouraging informal student and student–staff contacts, therefore supporting social cohesion and thus (it is assumed) learning. These accounts usually fail to describe the impact on academic staff time (as ready student access to teaching staff is assumed), or to assess the costs with regard to floor space utilisation. No rigorous evaluations have been found of the improved learning said to result from facilities of these types.

(ibid.: 6–7)

Rigorous studies *have* been undertaken by some institutions seeking to evaluate the impact of new approaches to learning and teaching combined with innovative learning spaces. In the US, evaluations of the SCALE-UP (student-centred active learning environment for undergraduate programmes) spaces in use found that student ability to solve problems was improved, conceptual understanding increased and attitudes improved. Failure rates were reduced by nearly three times compared to a traditional section of physics (Oblinger 2006).

Dori and Belcher reviewed the performance of physics students taught in media-rich technology enabled active learning (TEAL) classrooms and found that they performed significantly better than control groups in terms of improved conceptual understanding and overall course performance. They concluded that 'The technology-rich engagement atmosphere and the group interactions enabled the high achievers to blossom while teaching their peers. This setting also facilitated upward mobility of the intermediate and low achievers, thereby reducing failure rate and obtaining overall better results' (Dori and Belcher 2004: 243–79).

Temple (2007) suggests that changed physical design features on their own may not be enough to achieve improved learning outcomes: a change in the whole pattern of university organization may be needed to make the new learning spaces work properly. He also wonders whether space design, based on ideas about improved student learning, is driving a wider, possibly unanticipated, set of organizational changes including how the university is organized, the location of academic and administrative offices and the way in which faculty engage with students (ibid.: 48).

A common theme in discussions of innovative learning spaces is that students will take more responsibility for their learning – they will have more choices about where to work, how to work, and with whom to work. Temple also notes that it is possible that, while this may suit some students, others might prefer a more structured environment and set of choices (ibid.: 48). Certainly it is clear that spatial innovation is only effective if it is combined with timetable innovation and the development of appropriate teaching skills to take advantage of the capabilities of the spaces and the technologies on offer.

The Learning and Skills Council (LSC) was a rare example in the UK of systemic innovation in further and higher education – a quango set up in April 2001 under the Learning and Skills Act 2000 to replace England's 72 Training and Enterprise Councils (TECs) and the Further Education Funding Council for England. It was sponsored until June 2007 by the Department for Education and Skills (DfES), charged with managing the programme to refurbish and rebuild FE college buildings round the country, and by 2006 had an annual budget of £10.4 billion. Its abolition was announced in March 2008, with funding responsibility for 16–19 year olds to be transferred to local education authorities and funding for adult learners in further education colleges to come under the control of the new Skills Funding Agency. A report by the Public Accounts Committee (PAC) in July 2009 stated that: 'The council behaved recklessly by approving too many projects and allowing colleges' expectations of financial support to outstrip what it could afford by nearly £2.7 billion' (Edward Leigh MP, Chairman of the PAC, 29 July 2009). By March 2008 a total of £4.2 billion of projects had been approved 'in detail', including grant support from the council of £1.7 billion and about half of the estate had been renewed. It had approved 'in principle' 79 college projects and left them beset with 'considerable uncertainty' (PAC July 2009).

In higher education there has now been considerable interest in the development of learning spaces (Oblinger 2006; JISC 2006; SMG 2006b; SFC 2006; Neary et al. 2010), if a great deal less in evaluating the impact of these spaces on learning outcomes. So how is Drucker's 1997 prediction of imminent extinction of the university campus faring?

Not extinction, perhaps – but we are undoubtedly entering a period of transformation, and this will affect every square metre of the university estate. Traditional categories of space on campus will become less meaningful as space becomes less specialized,

boundaries blur, and operating hours extend towards 24/7. Space types will be designed primarily around patterns of human interaction rather than specific needs of particular departments, disciplines or technologies and new space models will focus on enhancing quality of life as much as on supporting the direct learning experience (DEGW 2009).

If these transformations happen, the campus will continue to be relevant and a core part of future generations' learning experiences, albeit supported by a wide range of other physical and virtual spaces and learning experiences – the university of the future will be inclusive of broad swaths of the population, actively engaged in issues that concern them and relatively open to commercial partnership (*Nature* 2007).

BUSINESS AND CULTURAL SPACES

This deepening schools and further and higher education pool of knowledge reveals a proliferating range of spaces accommodating the activity of learning: housing, but also enabling and facilitating. This portfolio extends throughout the period of formal education, from nursery schools/crèches to primary and secondary schools, from spaces for children with special educational needs to sixth form colleges and higher and further education institutions. It also extends both beyond and outside those time and place limitations, to libraries (school, general and academic), research laboratories, public buildings such as museums and galleries, ad hoc public and private spaces such as hotels and conference centres, industrial R&D labs, in-house training centres and work-based, adult activities, delivering apprenticeships and professional qualifications in homes and offices.

Many of these spaces evolved as adjuncts to school and higher education institutions – as overspill, outreach, extra-curricular and extramural spaces. Some did not. One way of systematizing these elements is to see them as part of the vocational training and professional qualification apparatus of business and industry. Another way of framing these unwieldy places is to see them as part of the move – largely driven by central government – to adult lifelong learning: they may stem from the school building and the academy but inevitably outgrow those boundaries.

An understanding of the demands and specific characteristics of this third sector is beginning to emerge as a necessary response to the concept of learning as an inclusive, unbounded landscape. It is certainly our view that in its fluidity, its fluency and its demands this under-reported third stream links many of the themes of provision, procurement, design, change and complexity that define learning environments as a whole. Since it is all these factors acting together that makes the learning environment such a volatile exemplar of all the changes taking place in space and its uses, these learning spaces beyond the institutional bounds of schools and universities are at least as significant a contributor to observable shifts in space use as traditional spaces.

Typologies vary, and are not exclusive. The National Institute of Adult Continuing Education (NIACE) identifies spaces that are initially delineated by chronology (early childhood, schools, family learning, further education, higher education) but become spatially dispersed (private training providers, voluntary and community organizations, local authorities, learning cities, cultural organizations, 'local learning ecologies') (Innocent 2009: 2). A NIACE inquiry into the future for lifelong learning, *Learning Through Life* (Schuller and Watson 2009), takes a chronological approach but focuses on adult learning, and adults returning to learn: 'Learning can occur in education or training institutions, the workplace (on or off the job), the family, or cultural and community setting' (p. 2).

In Europe the Lifelong Learning Programme (LLP), funded by the European Commission, observes the key sectors as schools, higher education, vocational education and training, adult (non-vocational) education and learning professionals. Each has its individual, targeted programme: none has much in the way of an awareness that these slices of the learning universe live somewhere – even virtually – in space.

David Anderson (2011) has identified four kinds of public space that seem to correspond to our third category of business and cultural spaces: cultural institutions (museums, libraries, performing arts venues, community arts centres), cultural spaces (urban parks and protected landscapes), open spaces (streets, rivers, wildernesses, 'the air around us') and media (digital) space. His suggestion is that 'the successful achievement of public policy goals will depend on the systematic and integrated development of all kinds of public space' (p. 160). 'A new model of accountability and governance is needed, that provides a voice for all the key stakeholders and users of these spaces.' He cites the formation of the Exhibition Road Cultural Group (ERCG) in London, UK, as one example of the attempt to provide such accountability – a consortium of national and international cultural and educational institutions and two local authorities working together 'to enhance the physical environment as a public cultural space' (Box 1.4).

Evaluation of these third stream spaces pulls into focus the difficulties associated with determining how physical space – to put it at its most concrete – affects learning. Lorna Unwin (2009) sees a perceptual gap between the – 'now widespread' – recognition that workplaces are learning environments and a full understanding of what workplace learning entails. She sees a similar gap between vocational education and training (VET) and its relationship to workplace learning. The link is freshly enough made in schools and higher and further education (Higgins et al. 2005; Hunley and Schaller 2009) and it should come as no surprise that in the negative capability of space defined as being, essentially, neither of those areas (none of the above), there is little systematic information to be gleaned. Thomas (2010) expresses this at its most wondering: 'our difficulty in understanding the nature of learning is partly brought about by our inability to articulate where learning takes place' (p. 502).

Box 1.4 The Exhibition Road Cultural Group

The Exhibition Road Cultural Group (ERCG) is a London-based consortium of 16 national and international cultural and educational institutions – including the Natural History Museum, the Victoria and Albert Museum and Imperial College – and two local authorities formed in 2004. 'It has two aims: to work together to release the cultural, environmental, creative and intellectual potential of the area through joint cultural and educational programmes; and to work with the two local authorities who manage the streetscape to enhance the public environment as a public cultural space.' Since 2004 the ERCG has run more than 20 major public events, including an annual International Music Day and collaborating in Black History Month.

Source: Anderson (2011)

CHAPTER 2
Driving change

Learning is marked by a complex of drivers all tending to bring about change. As a society we are now committed to the concepts of lifelong learning and learning anywhere at any time – as a result of gross changes in government-driven initiatives as well as shifts in values. Developments within the ideology or philosophy of pedagogy and andragogy, such as the shift from an instruction to a learning paradigm (Barr and Tagg 1995) and from knowledge to thinking, have marked a move from teacher-centred to student-centred education, with an emphasis on peer-to-peer learning, group working and blended learning. Interactions, collaboration and technological developments are now aiding knowledge transfer and communication – or actively driving them – and forming the infrastructure for learning organizations of all types.

Learning space is not alone in experiencing these proliferating changes in its form, function and significance. Across society equivalent pressures are changing the way we use space and the workplace – hybridizing space, dispersing work, annexing non-traditional spaces and blending virtual and physical work arenas (Box 2.1). The corporate workplace has had to respond to a period of unprecedented social, political and economic change, globalization and information overload with its own supportive and adaptive strategies (Figure 2.1). These strategies include simple bottom-line tools of assessment of commercial space that have evolved over the last 25–30 years in response to harsh and implacable corporate realities – and even these tools struggled to deal with sometimes lightning fast shifts in use and values, as the workplace became increasingly associated with the office building (Box 2.2).

When it seems that work can take place anywhere, the question is raised: Why should anyone come to the office? Is it that the office is a means to express the culture and reinforce the values and beliefs of an organization? Or is it that physical work environments, with the opportunities they provide for interaction, collaboration, knowledge transfer and communication, form a vital element of the learning (knowledge) organization's infrastructure? In 2002, SANE (Sustainable Accommodation for the New Economy), an extensive EC-funded research programme, began to provide some answers to leading organizations grappling with the problem of defining – and creating – the appropriate infrastructure for such a dispersed workforce.

These shifts in emphasis did not only make their presence felt in the corporate workplace. In the US, the General Services Administration (GSA), which manages around 380 million square feet of leased and owned government real estate (Finkelstein 2010), has been instrumental in creating a series of methodologies to determine the best ways to design new and rehabilitated GSA-controlled office space. In a long-running project, Kevin Kampschroer, director of research in the GSA's Office of Applied Research, undertook before

Box 2.1 Space change across society

- Technology is hybridizing space, blending space, furniture and information technology.

- Work is becoming dispersed. People are moving outside the physical container of their own buildings into larger organizational networks incorporating both owned and shared spaces that may be located across cities or countries – indeed, anywhere in the world. These may be non-owned spaces such as hotels, airport lounges, clubs and cultural buildings (museums and galleries). They are beginning to form a standard part of many people's working week.

- Space is expressing the culture and reinforcing the values and beliefs of organizations rather than merely being a container in which the work takes place.

- Physical work environments are being integrated into the business process.

- Space is being purchased on demand on an hourly, daily or monthly basis.

Box 2.2 Changing patterns of space use

By the end of the twentieth century, the two concepts of workplace and office building had become almost synonymous, but only in the late nineteenth century, with the increasing bureaucracy associated with the governing of nation states, or the running of large corporations, had office buildings emerged as a specialized type. Previously, office work was accommodated in buildings derived from palaces, industrial buildings or collegiate forms. In its contemporary form, which has outwardly changed little since the early days, the office building emerged largely thanks to American innovation in construction and the need to service a burgeoning economy – a 'new' economy. Chicago provided the archetype, with the high-rise office building now symbolic of the corporate workplace – a building form produced by the emergence of the corporation, with its separation of ownership and management, and the resulting professionalization of the management role.

By the 1960s, the office was seen as a communications system, with the floorplan opening up to facilitate the free flow of information across the open plan (*bürolandschaft* or office

landscaping, pioneered by the German Quickborner Team). In the 1970s, increasing labour power in Europe and the consequent articulation of users' interests saw the development of the office as a place of social engagement. Issues of privacy, acoustic control and the provision of individual rooms and healthy and personally controllable environments became increasingly important.

The 1980s saw a workplace revolution as the computer moved from the computer room to the desktop. At the same time, new network technologies facilitated the increasing globalization of particular industries (especially financial and professional services), with a corresponding demand for consistent worldwide guidelines to regularize patterns of space provision. In the 1990s, a second workplace revolution saw the introduction of 'new ways of working' – a response to the realization that information technology was transforming cultural, social, technological and construction processes.

Source: SANE (2002)

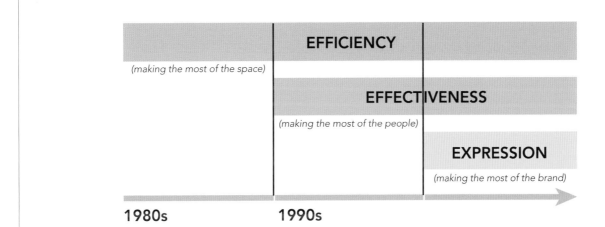

Organizational pressure has in recent decades resulted in a widely acknowledged imperative to move from cost-cutting, space-reducing efficiency to a more holistic effectiveness and then in the best and most adaptive organizations to expression: the mature embodiment of all the values associated with the organization, expressed as a brand by the physical workplace.

Increased efficiency stems from a reduction in the overall space occupied by a single organization, and follows the uncoupling of the sort of one person/one desk mathematics that dominated space budgeting through the 1980s and 1990s. Instead, organizations must build on an increasing reliance on shared facilities, due to the high levels of staff mobility.

Figure 2.1 Pressures and responses of corporate space

Increased effectiveness will come about as the result of more creative, better designed places that meet both individual and collective aspirations. These places will promote the generation of knowledge, enable both the overt and the tacit sharing of ideas across networks (real and virtual) and stimulate a more creative, empowered workforce to exploit the full potential of information technology and intelligent environments.

Stronger expression is a further move forward: a more vibrant representation of the company's core values and beliefs. This expression will communicate a consistent, coherent message both internally and externally. Supporting an increasingly transient workforce, it will need to adapt in order to update and refresh and respond to legitimate national, cultural and individual identities.

Source: DEGW (2005)

and after studies to look at the impact of layout, adjacencies, space allocation and environmental control – creating what he called an 'integrated workplace' (Cassidy 2006). Renamed Workplace 2020, and using multiclient pilot projects undertaken by DEGW, Gensler, HOK Advance Strategies and Studios Architecture, the project made two key discoveries: that user information can be gathered in a 'rapid engagement process' that makes little disruption to the work of the organization and – critically – the client must be guided to a 'clear understanding of the true nature of his or her business' (p. 2). Whether the workplace was in the Coast Guard service, Veterans Administration or the US Department of Energy, the participating teams found that, in Kampschroer's words, it was 'a tool to get things done' (p. 6).

In the UK, a 2004 comprehensive review of case studies drawn from the government's huge and disaggregated building stock showed space in transition from often rather poor sub-private sector quality accommodation to projects that held out the prospect of a work environment that could occupy its place in the modern world of work – integrating business, organizational and cultural change in efficient, effective and expressive physical locations (Allen et al. 2004).

A follow-up publication (Hardy et al. 2008) observed that the years between the two documents had seen a proliferation of work and place factors to be resolved by the successful workplace – that what was difficult but manageable in 2004 had become uncontrollable in the interim. The difference, it argued, lay not in scale – though the central government estate was vast, managed and used by over 300 separate central government organizations and with an asset base of £220 billion (ibid.: 12).

The accelerating factor was complexity – the increasing interaction between such agents of change as space quality and flexibility, environmental sustainability as an aspect of value for money rather than an uncostable overhead and, above all, the unlinking of work and place as office work evolved from the physical constraints of cellular space to an almost complete liberation from space in a non-territorial environment (Figure 2.2). The transformative role of technology, distributed working, the pressure to perform, the increased importance of design and management predicated on a modern business output model rather than a traditional culture more closely focused on inputs – these were powerful agents in isolation and extremely volatile in concert.

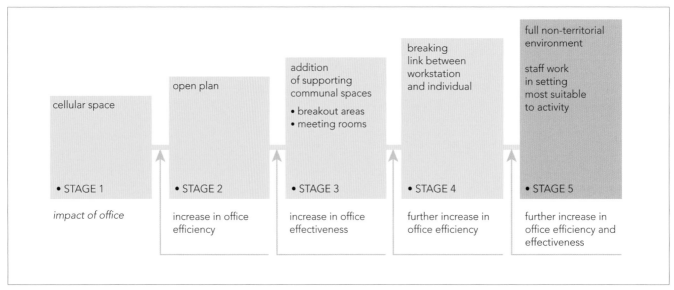

Figure 2.2 Evolution of office work. Source: Gibson and Luck (2004)

As the titles of the two publications make clear – *Working Without Walls* and *Working Beyond Walls* (Allen et al. 2004; Hardy et al. 2008) – the defining characteristic of this phase of the government workplace was a physical and virtual diaspora caused by this complex of change agents acting on a vast portfolio of business premises, standards agencies and government departments.

In learning, many of the same observable trends are being compounded by existential shifts calling into question the very purpose of the activity. But the learning environment is correspondingly more susceptible to change than the corporate and commercial world because the notion of learning itself is developing at a much faster rate, the field is extending its working hours much further, reaching wider into the community from its educational silos, blending the physical and the virtual, the commercial and the social, public and private, free and owned. Even the most fundamental aspects of learning – the function and significance of education itself – are periodically called into question by policy directives or the political pendulum.

More volatile in its space demands for all these reasons, the learning environment is at the forefront of many of the changes wrought by the impact of technology, developing theories of learning and teaching, pressing real world events and government intervention that leads or follows those events. Where there are differences between learning and the workplace – due, for example, to the nature of directed and self-directed works patterns or the greater proportion of freethinkers in education – learning environments are generally more at risk. An understanding of all these drivers must precede any assessment of performance.

TECHNOLOGY

The first and most pressing of the drivers acting on learning space is technology, and in particular information technology (IT). Technology used to connect places: now it connects people. All the moves to distributed work we now see in the corporate world are driven by this ability of IT to connect people. Sometimes this creates new ways of using space, sometimes new ways of connecting traditional spaces – and sometimes entirely new places are brought into the equation, such as parts of the public and semi-public realm. The impact on the world of work (including the work of learning) is immense.

IT liberates people within space, mobile telephony liberates people from space, virtual life is revolutionizing communication, and collaboration and telepresence are creating a diverse net of relationships that form new space types and break down some of the old.

Just as in the workplace (Harrison and Dugdale 2004; SANE 2002), we have to ask, 'If learning can take place anywhere, why should someone come to school, university or college?' The physical environment is increasingly being seen more as an opportunity to express the culture and reinforce the values and beliefs of an organization or institution than as a container in which the concentrated work or learning takes place. The physical environment and the opportunities it provides for interaction and collaboration will aid knowledge transfer and communication and form the infrastructure for learning organizations of all types.

IT has fundamentally changed how we learn. Collecting, analysing, displaying and disseminating knowledge typically involve IT: retrieving information has become an IT function; students often consider the internet, not the library, their information universe. Rather than trying to know everything, students and faculty increasingly rely on networks of peers and databases of information (Figure 2.3).

Enabling schools

A 2010 report by the New Media Consortium's (NMC) Horizon Project (Johnson et al. 2010) identified five key trends in technology to be dealt with by schools as a matter of urgency.

- Technology is increasingly a means for empowering students, a method for communication and socializing, and a ubiquitous, transparent part of their lives. Once seen as an isolating influence, technology is now recognized as a primary way to stay in touch and take control of one's own learning.

- It continues to profoundly affect the way we work, collaborate, communicate and succeed. The digital divide, once seen as a factor of wealth, is now seen as a factor of education: those who have the opportunity to learn technology skills are in a better position to obtain and make use of technology than those who do not.

- The perceived value of innovation and creativity is increasing. Innovation is valued at the highest levels of business and must be embraced in schools if students are to succeed beyond their formal education.

- There is increasing interest in just-in-time, alternate, or non-formal avenues of education, such as online learning, mentoring and independent study. The notion of the school as the seat of educational practice is changing as learners avail themselves of learning opportunities from other sources.

- The way we think of learning environments is changing. Traditionally, a learning environment has been a physical space, but the idea of what constitutes a learning environment is changing. The 'spaces' where students learn are becoming

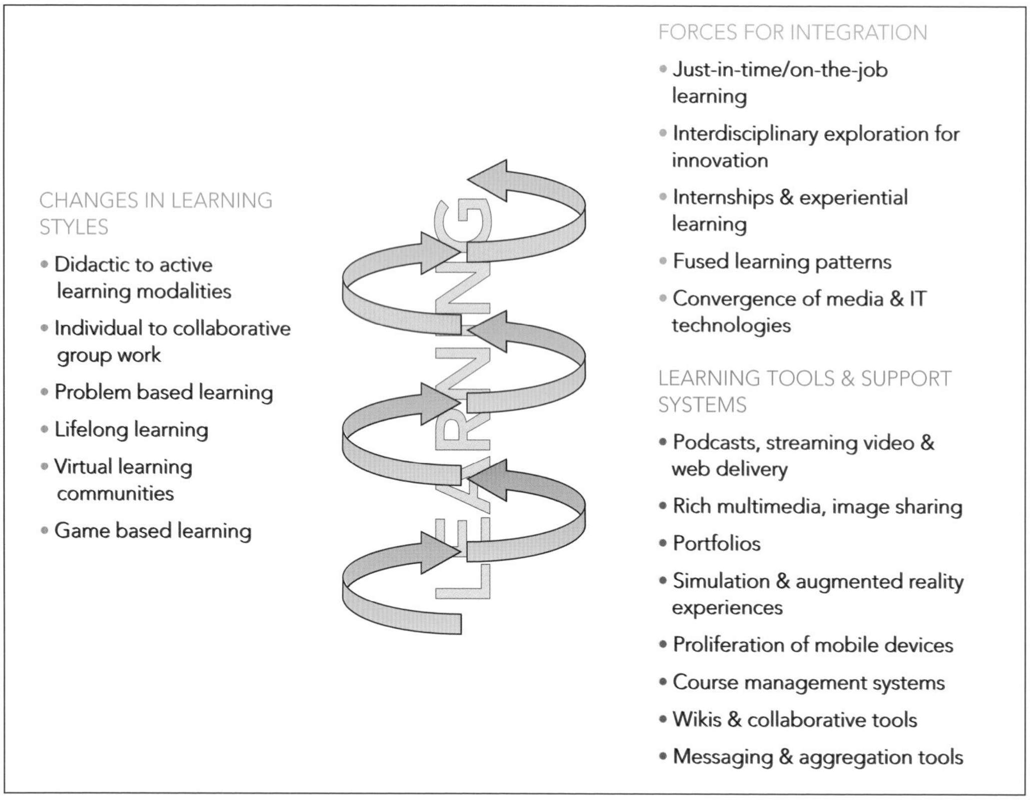

Figure 2.3 Forces influencing learning. Source: DEGW (2006)

more community-driven, interdisciplinary and supported by technologies that engage virtual communication and collaboration. This changing concept of the learning environment has clear implications for schools (Johnson et al. 2010: 4).

The report takes a warning from history stance, offering a countdown to full impact of such phenomena as cloud computing and collaborative environments (one year or less), game-based learning and mobiles (two to three years), augmented reality and flexible displays (four to five years), but taking no account of the spaces to be liberated or constrained by this impending revolution.

In the UK, Green and Hannon (2007) conducted a series of interviews to test the hypothesis that schools need to respond to the way young people are learning outside the classroom – identifying digital pioneers 'who were blogging before the phrase had been coined', creative producers building websites, posting movies, photos and music to share with friends, family and beyond, everyday communicators and information gatherers.

These young people had a mature understanding of a range of technologies and skills that they were using in their daily lives, but were unable to use – or were dissuaded from using – in school:

Responding to concerns about the safety of social networking sites, most schools block MySpace, YouTube and Bebo. Mobiles, iPods and other pieces of equipment are similarly unwelcome in the classroom. Meanwhile, teachers often do not feel confident using hardware or software – many know less than their students. Unless they follow their own enthusiasm, they are unlikely to have the skills – teacher training requires only basic competency in email, Word and Excel.

(p. 24)

The researchers found that secondary schools in the UK spent £91 per pupil per year on information and communication technology (ICT), but noted that 'without an ambitious understanding of how these tools can aid sophisticated learners much of this equipment has gone unused. ICT in schools is predicated on the "top-down" understanding that we know how children should be learning from technology rather than seeking to learn from their existing practices' (p. 25). 'While this type of investment is important', they went on, 'particularly when it comes to children and teachers feeling valued, it has not had the impact on teaching and learning that we might expect. The standard model of teaching with 30 children in a classroom with a teacher at the front remains the same. This is because fundamental behaviours have not changed'

(p. 54). The potential of new technologies will be realized only if the relationships and behaviours that underpin the school structure also change. The change needed in schools is twofold. 'First they need to find ways to recognize and value the learning that goes on outside the classroom. Second they need to support this learning by providing a space to reflect on it, galvanize and develop it so students can recognize and transfer those skills in new situations and contexts' (p. 25). 'In order to see change across the system, there needs to be a shift in thinking about investment. Rather than investing in hardware, schools need to think about investing in relationships and networks' (p. 54).

The report did find exemplar schools in which the four key elements of informal learning – self-motivated, self-owned, goal-based and peer-to-peer, not organized round an authority figure or pedagogue – had been transferred to the classroom without being subsumed into formal learning. At Stiperstones Primary School in Shropshire every child had their own laptop, and was allowed to take it home. This stemmed from a realization by the head of the potential of technology for his pupils and the importance of making the school a community resource, and emerged from a long process of meetings, discussions and deliberations with parents, teachers and governors. This buy-in was crucial; once the laptops were purchased, parents came into the school for a course on the basics so that they would feel comfortable supporting their children at home. The school exploits the participatory potential of technology, with whole class 'silent' debates conducted MSN style. Stiperstones is just one of a growing number of schools that have seen the potential of digital technology and that work to align themselves with the way in which children approach informal learning without seeking to replicate it wholesale.

The Computer Clubhouse (Computer Clubhouse 2012) provides a creative and safe out-of-school learning environment where young people from 'under-served' communities work with adult mentors to explore their own ideas, develop skills and build confidence in themselves through the use of technology. The network supports community-based clubhouses around the world, providing over 25,000 youth per year with access to resources, skills and experiences to help them succeed in their careers and contribute to their communities. The network – set up by Intel – is designed to empower youth from all backgrounds to become more capable, creative and confident learners: providing an unmediated space that acknowledges the different generational experience of digital learning. This approach is grounded in research from the fields of education, developmental and social psychology, cognitive science, and youth development. It builds on research on the role of affect and motivation in the learning process, the importance of social context, and the interplay between individual and community development. It leverages new technologies to support new types

of learning experiences and engage young people who have been alienated by traditional educational approaches. Like the Green and Hannon review for Demos (Green and Hannon 2007), it promotes the values of relationships, community and the use of digital media, art, and technology tools.

The technological impact of transliteracy – facilitating 'the ability to read, write and interact across a range of platforms, tools and media from signing and orality through handwriting, print, TV, radio and film, to digital social networks' (Molaro 2012) – clearly reaches a peak in the public library of the future, but the school library too has a key role to play in its promotion. As Gail Bush from the private US National-Louis University states: 'In the twentieth century we taught that we needed to answer the question and in the twenty-first century we teach that we need to question the answer' (Caserotti 2012).

Digital innovation in further and higher education

An NMC report on the impact of digital innovation on higher education in the US (Johnson et al. 2012) takes a time-to-adoption approach similar to its companion schools report on 'technology to watch' – a year or less to the use of mobile apps and tablet computing, two to three years to game-based learning and learning analytics and four to five for gesture-based computing and what it calls an 'internet of things': smart objects with a unique identifier that can communicate their status on demand, allow real-time access and connect to networks. Physical space again fails to make an appearance in this view of the future: the organization runs a programme, NMC Virtual Worlds, that aims to 'explore the potential of virtual spaces in a manner that builds on community, is cost-effective and ensures high quality' (ibid.). Its service companies include Triple A Learning, providing online workshops for the International Baccalaureate in a cybercampus on NMC's Teaching 2 'sim' (Pfeifer and Abattoir 2012).

A 2008 report commissioned by JISC and the British Library issued a corrective to the usual assumptions about young people of the 'Google generation' – that people born and brought up in the internet age would be most adept at using the web and able to make a critical and analytical assessment of the information they find there (JISC 2008). Young people, it found, demonstrate an ease and familiarity with computers but rely on the most basic research tools, are impatient in search and navigation and show zero tolerance for any delay in satisfying their information needs – and it also found that these are now the traits associated with all age-groups, from younger pupils and undergraduates through to professors. The report – which contained no information whatever on the use of space – emphasized how detrimental this absence of information skills would be to a knowledge economy (ibid.).

While several hundred universities have some form of presence on Second Life, or other virtual world, the number of universities offering entire courses in virtual space is still relatively small. Aalto University in Helsinki has found several uses for Second Life in teaching Swedish to university students, and has also investigated its use in role play to introduce a new worker into a new workplace and in laboratory exercises (Swanström and Rontu 2012). Harvard University, one of the pioneers in this area, offered a course on Media Law being taught in Second Life: discussions and lectures all took place on 'Berkman Island', enabling students from anywhere in the world to interact with one another, in real time.

The use of virtual learning environments is likely to increase in the future as the quality of the visual environment improves and users increase their ability to create content. Multiverse, for example, has created a technology platform and set of software tools that allows the relatively easy development of Massively Multiplayer Online Games (MMOGs) and 3D virtual worlds. Based on computer games technology and graphic development capabilities, Multiverse provides developers with a ready-made infrastructure and a wide range of free content, including a complete game for modification. Players will be able to play all the MMOGs and visit all the non-game virtual worlds built on the Multiverse platform, creating a 'universe' of virtual environments and experiences for learning and leisure (Multiverse 2012).

The distinction between physical and learning spaces is becoming increasingly blurred. Whitespace at the University of Abertay in Dundee (Figures 2.4 and 2.5) 'blends creative academic activities with technical support and commercial outreach to create a knowledge driven environment that directly benefits Abertay's students and staff plus the local business community and a wide range of external organizations' (Whitespace 2012). This melding of learning and leisure is also seen in the growth of machinima in recent years (Machinima 2012). Machinima – a portmanteau of 'machine cinema' – involves the use of real-time interactive 3D engines, typically role-playing simulation or first person 'shooter' games, to generate computer-generated imagery rather than conventional complex computer graphics platforms used in film production. The real-time nature of machinima means that established techniques from traditional film-making can be reapplied in a virtual environment and machinima productions are produced using the tools (demo recording, camera angle, level editor, script editor) and resources (backgrounds, levels, characters, skins) available in a game.

The educational possibilities of machinima are being explored widely. In her 2007 paper 'Machinima and education', Diana Carr (2007) from the Institute of Education, London reviewed a number of educational applications around the world including work by

Novonics Corporation in Florida who produce machinima using the game 'Half-Life 2' to augment training simulations for the US defence sector. The game has been used to create avatars, behaviours and high-fidelity Navy environments at a fraction of the cost of traditional audio/video production costs.

Shortfuze in the UK have used machinima applications to support film-making courses in schools. As Matt Kelland (2012), director of Shortfuze states, machinima offers educators:

> sets, costumes, stunts and special effects that would be impractical or impossible on a student budget. You can very quickly film a scene many times over, reusing the dialogue and choreography, and see the effect of different styles and techniques. A student can be simultaneously actor, director, writer, cameraman, set designer, lighting engineer, sound engineer, and editor, allowing them to appreciate the totality of the film-making process.

Linking business, cultural, extended and virtual space domains

This profound technological ability to enable the activity without the setting – virtuality – perhaps reaches its peak in distance learning. Massively open online courses (MOOCs) deliver learning content online to virtually anyone who wants to take a course. In 2008, George Siemens and Stephen Downes co-taught a class, thought to be the first to use the term MOOC, called 'Connectivism and Connective Knowledge', presented to 25 tuition-paying students at the University of Manitoba and offered at the same time to around 2,300 students from the general public who took the online class at no cost (Thompson 2012):

> Participants can be students enrolled at the institution hosting the MOOC or anyone with internet access. The 'open' students can join in some or all of the course activities, which might include watching videos, posting on discussion boards and blogs, and commenting via social media platforms, though anything hosted by the institution's LMS [learning management system] would likely be off-limits. Although 'open' participants receive no credit for the course and may get little or no direct feedback from the instructor, their involvement can add a dynamic to the course that benefits all students. While a MOOC might accommodate enrolment in the thousands, some of these courses enrol far fewer – the 'massive' part of the name speaks more to the potential to include vast numbers of students than to the actual size of the class.
>
> (Thompson 2011:1)

The curriculum might be identical to that of a standard course, with activities modified to match the scale and range of participation

Whitespace is a multi-purpose space with TV studio, film and digital image realization capabilities – a HIVE (Human [highly] Interactive Virtual Environment) that offers a total immersion video environment for interaction with virtual environments. It includes 3D stereo vision, surround sound, walk and grab capabilities, one person recordable head tracker and the potential to project a live object into a virtual background. The advanced technology in Whitespace is combined with informal meeting spaces and access to refreshments to create an inspired environment that stimulates interaction between students, staff, visitors and businesses.

Source: http://www.abertay.ac.uk/About/WhitespaceFacilites.cfm

Figure 2.4 Whitespace at Abertay, Scotland

Figure 2.5 Whitespace at Abertay, Scotland

– scheduled or asynchronous. To date, those MOOCs that have drawn the largest crowds have been taught by high-profile instructors on popular topics. A recent MOOC at Stanford University, 'Introduction to Artificial Intelligence', taught by AI experts Sebastian Thrun and Peter Norvig, drew a worldwide open enrolment of more than 100,000 students.

It is a significant development both for institutions, which can extend their voice and presence throughout the community, and for participants, who can benefit from an extremely diverse set of ideas. Although MOOCs will not suit everyone – particularly people keen on high levels of instructor contact – and require familiarity with distributed and networked technologies, they allow students to sample courses and offer the opportunity to be part of a learning community with access to some of the major voices in education. Their existence proves the reality of lifelong learning and alters the relationship between learner and instructor, academe and the wider community (ibid.).

MIT extends the inherently wider access implicit in the virtual world to the traditionally hands-on sphere of the laboratory with its iLab project, dedicated to the proposition that online laboratories – real laboratories accessed through the internet – can enrich science and engineering education by greatly expanding the range of experiments that students are exposed to in the course of their education. Unlike conventional labs, iLabs can be shared across the university or across the world. In order to gain an understanding into the complex requirements of operating remote lab experiments and scaling their use, the iLab teams have created remote labs at MIT in microelectronics, chemical engineering, polymer crystallization, structural engineering and signal processing. As a result of this research, the project is developing a suite of software tools to create both easy access and effective infrastructure (MIT 2012).

Third stream space perhaps more than space tied to institutional use has been disproportionately liberated by technological innovation. YouMedia is a 550 square metre space on the ground floor of the Harold Washington Library Center in downtown Chicago. Supported by the MacArthur Foundation, this space opened in 2009 and 'connects youth, books, media, and institutions around Chicago to encourage collaboration and creativity' (YouMedia 2012). Teenagers with a city library card have in-house access to more than 100 laptops, as well as video games and a Wii console. There are flat screen monitors on every wall, a small recording studio, performance space and a 'geek-out area' where they can learn about new media from adult mentors.

YouMedia was designed as the first node of a Chicago-based learning network for youth that will link formal and informal learning institutions, providing young people with seamless learning. The programme is a partnership between the Chicago Public Library and the Digital Youth Network who use digital media to bridge the gap between in-school and out-of-school learning to help youth achieve academically and develop media literacy. The space is 'explicitly designed to facilitate the movement of young people into deeper and more complex engagement in learning with digital media and books', creating 'a continuum of learning based on ever-changing themes and literature-based curriculum developed by the Chicago Public Library and its partners. Young people become engaged in making and producing digital artifacts such as documentary videos, hip-hop songs, fan fiction, games, and virtual worlds grounded in the content of books' (ibid.)

Teenagers can move from an area where they snack and chat with friends to one where they tinker with games, music and other new media to one where they learn the latest digital media skills and pursue specific areas of interest. Library staff said teenagers are checking out more than 1,200 books a month and other resources, such as vinyl records, to support their learning activities through YouMedia. The goal, in time, is to increase substantially the number of youths in Chicago who use online resources and new media as tools to engage in inquiry about their neighbourhoods, the city and the world.

In Thailand an IT-enabled, youth-facing library – TK Park, set on the eighth floor of the Central World Shopping Center in Bangkok (Figures 2.6 and 2.7) – has emerged as the prototype of a space designed to attract the young and to depart from the old concept of a library as a 'book warehouse' (TK Park 2012). As the idea begins to shift away from the view that libraries are just places where books live, public libraries in particular have a key role to play in transliteracy education, promoting a range of platforms, tools and media (Molaro 2012). Fayetteville Free Library (FFL) in upstate New York, towards the end of 2011 announced its intention to expand its library service to create a 'Fab Lab' to support its community in learning new technologies and building new projects – the first library in the US to implement this idea. ('Fab' was used originally

at MIT to refer to digital fabrication laboratories but in this case is short for 'Fabulous'.) 'Libraries exist to provide access to opportunities for people to come together to learn, discuss, discover, test, create. Transformation happens when people have free access to powerful information, and new and advanced technology' (Reeder 2011). FFL's director of transliteracy development Lauren Britton Smedley went further. 'Libraries are a place for social transformation. They're a place that you can go to get computer access, or access to technology that you can't get anywhere else, and access to people. I think one of our greatest resources in a library are the librarians. They're able to help people track things down and make connections, and really bring the skills of a community together in one place' (Reeder 2011).

Further developments along this line include tool libraries and hackerspaces. In the US, the Rebuilding Together Central Ohio (RTCO) Tool Library, for example, makes available over 4,500 tools free of charge to both individuals and non-profit organizations. Hackerspaces are community-operated physical places, where people can meet and work on their projects (Hackerspaces 2012). They are generally membership based and spaces include workshops, tools, and people who generally like to make things. According to a 2009 BBC article, there are more than 200 active or planned hack spaces in basements and warehouses around the world. One of the largest of the UK's nine groups is London Hack Space, which has attracted more than 200 members since it launched in January 2009. In the article, co-founder Jonty Wareing stated that 'endless curiosity is what links us all together. We hack because the thing we want doesn't already exist and we have the skills to make it' (BBC 2009).

Fab Labs – more formalized versions of hackerspaces – are associated with MIT who developed the original concept. They are defined on the openp2pdesign.org website as 'a small-scale workshop with an array of computer controlled tools that cover several different length scales and various materials, democratizing manufacturing technologies previously available only for expensive mass production' (Menichinelli 2012). As of July 2010, there were 45 labs in 16 countries, all similar in terms of the equipment and spaces provided.

A TechShop is a commercial venture that combines the notion of a hackerspace and a Fab Lab – a membership-based workshop that provides members, regardless of skill level, with access to tools and equipment, instruction, and a community of creative and supportive people so they can build the things they have always wanted to make (Torrone 2011). There are currently five TechShop locations in the US and three more under development and TechShop hopes to have 100 locations in five years (Techshop 2012).

Figures 2.6–7 TK Park, Bangkok, Thailand

TK Park was established in 2005 to address what the Thai government observed as an alarming trend of children becoming less and less interested in books. The space itself was inspired by the Bpi Public Information Library at the Pompidou Centre in Paris, the UK's Idea Store in Tower Hamlets, London, Japan's Sendai Mediatheque (severely damaged in the 11 March 2011 earthquake) and Singapore's Jurong Regional Library and Library@Orchard and shows clear evidence of literacy being a priority concern of the government (Romana Cruz 2012).

The country's reading campaign has been boosted in the past two years by the government's move to make reading a 'national agenda' and its designation of the years 2009 to 2118 as the decade for the promotion of reading. There is also felt to be 'a heightened sense of urgency for replicating the TK Park experience in other communities because UNESCO has designated Bangkok as the World Book Capital for 2013'. The mix of elements is the most striking aspect of the space: Stephen Heppell on a visit just after it opened contrasted its 'sound booths, touch screen … furniture [that] encourage you to climb and perch with your books' favourably with the more passive 'rows of screens' (Heppell 2005) in a nearby shopping mall that also aimed to cater to the young but – 'understandably' – attracted few teenagers.

Sources: Romana Cruz (2012); Heppell (2005)

Phillip Torrone, senior editor of *MAKE* magazine and creative director of a New York City-based open source hardware and electronic kit company, has raised the question of whether public libraries could include this type of active learning and workspace within their future development model – 're-tooling' a number of public libraries into TechShop type spaces to provide community access 3D printers, laser cutters and learning electronics (Torrone 2011).

LEARNING THEORY

The second driver is the influence of changing styles in learning theory – pedagogy, andragogy, heutagogy (Box 2.3). Learning theory has in the past offered up behaviourist, cognitive, humanistic and social/situational interpretations of learning orientation (Table 2.1). Emerging new methods of teaching and learning based on an improved understanding of cognition are continually calling into question received wisdom on learning and – less overt – the spaces in which it prospers or languishes. Holton and Swanson, in their updating of the 1973 Knowles classic, *The Adult Learner* (Knowles et al. 2011) reduce 11 categories to three families (conditioning, modelling, cognitive) characterized as association or stimulus response and field theories and arrive at two primary theories – behaviourist/connectionist theories and cognitive/ gestalt theories (ibid.: 21). Reese and Overton (1970) likewise reach a binary – but different – conclusion (elemental and holistic) and andragogists, too, identify two major streams of inquiry: scientific and artistic.

Within this broad scope of changes in theories of learning, there have been great shifts in approaches to learning settings. The 2006 review of learning spaces in further and higher education carried out for the Scottish Funding Council, *Spaces for Learning,* notes – in the section of trends in learning and teaching – that 'Traditional teacher-centred models of education – in which good teaching is conceptualized as the passing on of sound academic, practical or vocational knowledge – are being replaced by more student-centred approaches that emphasize the construction of knowledge through shared situations' (SFC 2006: 4). Together with the increasing diversity of student populations, the report observes, this 'has prompted a new, more tailored, approach to learning. The shift towards student-centred teaching modes has been supported by a growing body of research and theory, pointing to the benefits of a range of learning styles and individual preferences.'

> Barr and Tagg (1995) suggest that this shift from an 'instruction paradigm' to a 'learning paradigm' has changed the role of the higher and further education institution from 'a place of instruction' to 'a place to produce learning'. This is partly driven by changing educational requirements. The shift to a knowledge driven economy is driving demand for a more qualified, highly skilled, creative and flexible workforce. There is less emphasis on factual knowledge, and more on the ability to think critically and solve complex problems. Knowles (1984) argues that, in the modern world, the most socially useful thing to learn is the process of learning.
>
> (ibid.: 4)

Fundamental pedagogical changes within schools have included a debate on the very purpose of the institution – and therefore the space and how it should function. At a 2008 world ministerial conference in London (Cayman Islands Government 2008), the education minister of the Cayman Islands, Alden McLaughlin, rather dramatically put into perspective the problems of accommodating something as fluid and dynamic as learning in something as intractable as planned, designed and procured tranches of the built

Box 2.3 Pedagogy, andragogy and heutagogy

Pedagogy – the art and science of teaching children

According to Knowles many traditional teachers see pedagogy as 'an ideology based on assumptions about teaching and learning that evolved between the seventh and twelfth centuries in the monastic and cathedral schools of Europe out of their experience in teaching basic skills to young boys. As secular schools organized in later centuries, and public schools in the nineteenth century, the pedagogical model was the only existing educational model' (Knowles et al. 2011: 60). In his view, the entire educational enterprise of US schools, including higher education, was frozen into this model and even after 'adult education programs in this country, initiated after World War 1, also used this model because it was the only model teachers had. As a result, until fairly recently, adults have by and large been taught as if they were children' (ibid.: 60).

Andragogy – the teaching of adults

For Knowles, andragogy differs in certain key particulars:

● Adults need to know why they're learning something before undertaking it.

● Adults regard themselves as being responsible for their own actions and decisions.

● They arrive at the educational activity with a greater value and a different quality of experience from that of young people.

● They bring greater readiness to learn to their activities.

● Instead of being subject-centred, they tend to be life-centred (or task- or problem-centred).

● Adults, too, are responsive to external motivators but the most potent motivators are internal drivers – increased job-satisfaction, self-esteem, quality of life.

Andragogy has its detractors as a model. Atherton (2011) sees Knowles' formulation of the principles of andragogy as no more than the integration or summation of other learning theorists, based on the assumptions and values underlying much modern adult educational theory.

Heutagogy – self-determined learning

The term heutagogy, coined by Stewart Hase and Chris Kenyon in 2000 (http://works.bepress.com/stewart_hase/), refers to learning chosen and controlled by the learner and not the teacher:

> It suggests that learning is an extremely complex process that occurs within the learner, is unobserved and is not tied in some magical way to the curriculum. Learning is associated with making new linkages in the brain involving ideas, emotions, and experience that leads to new understanding about self or the world. Thus, learning occurs in random and chaotic ways and is a response to personal need and, often, occurs to resolve some ambiguity.
>
> Hase (2011: 2)

According to Hase, who has used the approach in learner-centric short- and medium-term training programmes in organizations, this 'relatively new concept' is informed by:

> a large body of knowledge and some clever ideas such as: constructivism (e.g. Friere, 1972; 1995); reflexivity and double loop learning (Argyris & Schon, 1996); systems thinking (Emery & Trist, 1965); capability (Stephenson, 1996; Stephenson & Weil, 1992); and complexity theory (e.g. Doolittle, 2000; Waldrop,1992). There have also been a number of educationalists who draw on complexity theory, have challenged some prevailing views about learning (Davis et al, 2000; Doll, 1989; Phelps, Hase & Ellis, 2005; Sumara & Davis, 1997).
>
> (ibid.)

In a review of heutagogical practice and self-determined learning in the *International Review of Research in Open and Distance Learning* (IRRODL), Lisa Marie Blaschke (Blaschke 2012) suggests that heutagogy – which sees learners as 'highly autonomous and self-determined' and where the 'emphasis is placed on development of learner capacity and capability with the goal of producing learners who are well-prepared for the complexities of today's workplace' has recently resurfaced as a learning approach 'after a decade of limited attention' because of the rise of Web 2.0 and the opportunities afforded by technology.

Table 2.1 Learning orientations

Aspect	Behaviourist	Cognitivist	Humanist	Social and situational
Learning theorists	Thorndike, Pavlov, Watson, Guthrie, Hull, Tolman, Skinner	Koffka, Kohler, Lewin, Piaget, Ausubel, Bruner, Gagne	Maslow, Rogers	Bandura, Lave and Wenger, Salomon
View of the learning process	Change in behaviour	Internal mental process (including insight, information processing, memory, perception	A personal act to fulfil potential.	Interaction /observation in social contexts. Movement from the periphery to the centre of a community of practice
Locus of learning	Stimuli in external environment	Internal cognitive structuring	Affective and cognitive needs	Learning is in relationship between people and environment
Purpose in education	Produce behavioural change in desired direction	Develop capacity and skills to learn better	Become self-actualized, autonomous	Full participation in communities of practice and utilization of resources
Educator's role	Arranges environment to elicit desired response	Structures content of learning activity	Facilitates development of the whole person	Works to establish communities of practice in which conversation and participation can occur
Manifestations in adult learning	Behavioural objectives Competency-based education Skill development and training	Cognitive development Intelligence, learning and memory as function of age Learning how to learn	Andragogy Self-directed learning	Socialization Social participation Associationalism Conversation

Source: Four orientations to learning (after Merriam and Caffarella 1991: 138)

environment: 'The goal of our transformation process is to prepare students for jobs that don't yet exist, using technologies that have not yet been invented, in order to solve problems that have not yet arisen' (p. 6).

But is it to prepare a workforce? If it is, the design has a great role to play. Preparation of the workforce is often an unsaid but important driver of the curriculum. The British monitorial schools of the 1800s had a core curriculum based around the employment needs of the poorest class, preparing them to work in the largely agrarian economy (despite, perhaps, the rapid societal transformations being seen due to the Industrial Revolution) by focusing on the 'three Rs' plus vocational activities such as cobbling, tailoring, gardening and agricultural operations for boys, and spinning, sewing, knitting, lace-making and baking for girls (Gillard 2011).

Today, the curriculum of many Western civilizations likewise focuses on educating for the jobs of our time, whether through an academic route (for the future doctors, lawyers and scientists) or a vocational one (for the future plumbers, builders and hairdressers). Indeed, the Qualifications and Curriculum Authority, an English non-departmental public body that operated from 1997 until March 2012, had as an aim that the National Curriculum 'should prepare pupils for the next steps in their education, training and employment and equip them to make informed choices at school and throughout their lives, enabling them to appreciate the relevance of their achievements to life and society outside school, including leisure, community engagement and employment' (DfE 1999: 12).

The difficulty lies in predicting and educating for the jobs of tomorrow. In the US, the run-up to a report by the National Center on Education and the Economy on the content of a curriculum based on educating for creativity asked 'whether an entire generation of kids will fail to make the grade in the global economy because they can't think their way through abstract problems, work in teams, distinguish good information from bad or speak a language other than English'. The areas picked out as creative were research, development, design, marketing and sales, and global supply chain management – all areas that avoided routine work that could be done by people (in 'less developed countries') or machines (National Center on Education and the Economy 2007).

According to the RSA (The Royal Society for the Encouragement of Arts, Manufactures and Commerce), the skills of the twenty-first-century worker within these creative industries are still not always framed within the curriculum (RSA 2012) – despite increasing definition, such as Claxton's 4–6–1 model emphasizing 'habits' to develop (investigating, experimenting, reasoning, imagining) (Claxton et al. 2010) and the RSA's own Opening Minds curriculum emphasizing competencies (citizenship, learning, managing information, relating to people and managing situations).

> All over the world … policy makers typically narrow the curriculum to emphasize a small group of subjects, tie schools up in a culture of standardized testing and limit the discretion of educators to make professional judgments about how and what to teach. These reforms are typically stifling the very skills and qualities that are essential to meet the challenges we face: creativity, cultural understanding, communication, collaboration and problem solving.
>
> (Robinson 2011)

Space can be a powerful catalyst for change – or stagnation. US architect Bruce A. Jilk argues that the overdesigning of schools can lock learning and teaching activities into predetermined spaces: educators and architects can do more for learners if they design less and allow the final shape and space of the school to evolve by its use in the process of teaching and learning (Burke et al. 2008: 166). But this is secondary: is the school to be organized in a curriculum-centric or a people-centric way? Is it to deliver a personalized or a mass-production process?

A curriculum-centric form of school organization, mirroring the higher education split into departments or faculties, matches the physical organization and has been so popular because it supports an efficiency-focused educational philosophy in which learners get small bite-sized exposure to many subjects in a round robin fashion. It also pre-supposes a subject-based curriculum, or a moderate inter-disciplinary curriculum that integrates certain subjects.

This has begun to be challenged. Researchers such as Dr Jane Gilbert (2005) have focused on the shift in educational philosophy away from what is often seen as a 'production line' method which achieves a bell curve of achievement that is often superficial and lacking in deep understanding. A second major shift has been to challenge the notion that children progress academically according to the year of their birth (often favouring significantly those born just after the dividing line over those born before it).

A more indirect approach focuses on the emotional benefits of smaller-sized schools – on the belief that 'human scale' clusters of students and teachers would build a more solid learning community where greater support can take place, in terms of both learning and social (pastoral) care. In this approach, monolithic, mass secondary schools should be broken up – if not physically, then at least organizationally – into units of no more than 450, so that even large schools feel small. That would allow a wider variety of learning environments – vocational, specialist, academic, catch-up – to co-exist within a single school (Leadbetter nd).

This is not new thinking, either in the education sector or in the commercial workplace. For many years, people have discussed how scaling down factories (such as Gore-Tex), workplaces (Virgin and Microsoft) and schools could increase productivity by increasing the feeling of familiarity and comfort. Any more than 150 (known as Dunbar's number) to 250 people, and the chance of having meaningful relationships decreases.

Yet the political arguments for large schools have been going on since Taylor proposed the idea of efficiency of scale. In the UK, figures that showed the number of pupil exclusions rise when the school size is above 1,500, and fall when below 1,000, were dismissed by the former Labour government on the basis that large schools offer 'a wider range of services'. Over half a million learners in the UK now attend a school larger than 1,500, a more than 200 per cent increase between 1996 and 2005 (BBC 2007a). US research, following significant national debate that a large school of 1,900 pupils was responsible for causing the alienation and isolation that led to the 1999 Columbine High School massacre, suggests that schools above 2,000 pupils are 22 per cent more likely to experience serious violence (Leung and Ferris 2008).

In a people-centric approach, the entire student body is essentially divided up, with each section allocated its own zone. The curriculum then becomes a virtual, not physical, organization. This may be a 'vertical' split, one of the most common school-within-school models, whereby students join a mini-school at the beginning of their schooling at that institution, and progress within that mini-school until they leave a number of years later.

This offers the opportunity for significant 'stage not age' learning and at the same time allows schools to apply elements of virtual organization, such as year groups, and the maintenance of some subject-based approaches. It may also be horizontally split, binding students to their year group or cluster of year groups until they progress to a new school the next year. This allows the school to tailor the space to an age range.

Neither model is mutually exclusive. One key issue in the UK education system is the rough transition between the project-based curriculum of the small primary school, where the classroom acts as a home base and one teacher works very closely with one class of pupils throughout the entire academic year, and the secondary model where learners join a significantly larger school where they move around every learning session to the next learning space or department, seeing a wide range of teachers in a very subject-based curriculum model. There is clearly a transition to be made, and many learners struggle in the first year or two.

Between 2008 and 2010, a government-funded research project in the UK, Space for Personalised Learning (S4PL), looked in depth at new approaches to the creation of learning and teaching environment – proceeding from the conviction that certain shifts in society, including the very fundamental move from an industrial to a knowledge-based economy, have pressing pedagogical and spatial implications that must be understood and met. The project (Figure 2.8) used the term 'personalized learning' to characterize the new ways of thinking and acting around these little understood implications. The core research question was 'How do we go about creating a physical environment that delivers education on a universal scale demanded and yet allows schools to implement systems and structures that provide a more customized experience for young people' (S4PL 2010).

Personalization is shaping much of the design of services that are trying to provide less mass-produced approaches to their consumers and it was inevitable that it should be applied to education, a field often accused of having a production-line mentality. Customization in business, says UK educationalist David Hargreaves, means providing tailor-made goods or services at the prices of mass production. Personalized learning is an educational version of this (Richards 2004). 'Whenever a company starts using words like whatever, wherever and whenever, or anything, anywhere and anytime, it is a sure sign that it has begun the shift to mass customization' (Pine 1993). Mass customization, or personalization, means giving the customer the choice and flexibility to take services and fit them around their own needs, or, as Charles Leadbeater (2004) says, 'putting users at the heart of services ... enabling them to become participants in the design and delivery ... Services will be more effective by mobilizing millions of people as

co-producers of the public goods they value.' This is a challenging concept when applied to learning (Box 2.4).

A study of the relationship between building programmes and educational needs, carried out to underpin the Space for Personalised Learning project (S4PL 2008) found that shifts in pedagogical practice informed policy but remained secondary. Though progressive practices have continually been introduced, yielding innovation in the learning environment, a failure to manage these changes has meant that overall changes in the design of schools have been minor, and there has not been widespread divergence from the components of the original public schools constructed in the mid- to late 1800s, other than the scaling up and consequent embedding of efficiency practices during the early 1900s. Most alterations were therefore confined to the settings within the classroom, the scale of the school, its relationship with exterior space, and architectural aesthetic rather than transformation of the base elements of classrooms and large, central gathering space. A powerful lesson from past attempts to initiate widespread change in teaching methods is that space should not be the only driver for transformation. The organizational structure of the school, the buy-in from teaching staff, and support for the teaching staff, including training and CPD, are the essential components for transformation; space is a supporting element.

POLICY

Education is undoubtedly an important plank in social policy making, making an impact on the very structure of society, whether aimed at maximizing the individual's intellectual and social potential, transmitting society's norms and values, training the workforce or overtly bringing about social change. (Spicker 2012 has identified four key educational models that have been influential in Europe: humanism – moral and individualistic; encyclopaedism – based on a shared body of knowledge; vocationalism – linked to the needs of the economy; naturalism – development of the whole person, child-centred and with the school as a community.)

It might be imagined that a need would arise and a policy be formulated to meet the need. Or in another view of society, that an ideological intention would drive an education agenda that would in turn demand an appropriate building programme. But in fact the relationship is complex:

> it is tempting to see school building projects as singular, carefully planned and controlled events, with a certain style of school, reflecting contemporary values, reproduced across a country. However, the building bursts that have occurred do

Figure 2.8 Westhill Primary School, London

The Spaces for Personalised Learning (S4PL) research project was a government-funded project set up to study and to some extent promote new approaches to the creation of learning and teaching environment (S4PL 2010). The research team worked with ten schools across England in 2008–10 on pilot projects that ranged from small-scale refurbishment of existing spaces to whole school briefing linked to the Building Schools for the Future programme. Researchers worked with learners in each school to explore how they learned best and what stopped them learning well. They were asked to identify learning activities that were of high importance and frequent occurrence and describe the characteristics of those activities in terms of group sizes and atmosphere that would support those activities. The researchers then worked with the schools to map these learning activities onto a menu of learning settings which formed the basis of the subsequent design concepts for the pilot spaces.

The S4PL project clearly demonstrated that the process of engagement and co-design that was developed during the research was an effective way of achieving change for a relatively small investment. The change of government that took place before the project was completed led to significant change of government education policy in the UK and educational transformation and personalized learning were no longer priorities.

Source: S4PL (2010: 55)

not stand alone in time, but are instead influenced by previous building; while the production of a different style is generally a complex process of competing factors.

(Woolner et al. 2005: 6)

It is those 'competing factors' that refuse to leave policy cleanly discrete – and in fact make up one of the underlying themes of this book: the accelerant power of complexity. In the UK, the post-war policy to raise the school-leaving age made the housing of children in huts inevitable (HORSA: hutting operation for raising the school-leaving age) and produced an inadequate building stock that eventually drove the Building Schools for the Future (BSF) programme (2004–10), which was itself clearly policy driven: it was intended to carry out one of Labour's 1997 election pledges

Box 2.4 Mass customization in education

Bolstad and Gilbert (2008) offer three models for how mass customization can work in practice, contrasted against a traditional school curriculum. All three of these options ask big questions about the very nature of schooling. What should a school look like, be designed like, operate like? Is it still a building where students go every day?

Mass customization

Creates more flexible pathways through the system, allowing multi-level study, more choice and modular approaches. A certain amount of choice for students as they assemble customized packages of modules to build portfolios of learning. The system provides a more personalized service to its 'customers', but the system and suppliers still define the options, which are mostly standardized with limited information. Teachers are no longer the conduits for all knowledge, but act as 'learning brokers', supporting and advising students as they develop their plans and goals.

Bolstad and Gilbert view this as a modified version of the status quo, not transformative because it uses existing curriculum, pedagogy and assessment, and relies on the old understanding of knowledge, knowledge management and methods of production and consumption.

Diverse suppliers and the market model

This is a similar model to option 1, but offers the opportunity for a range of different suppliers – not necessarily schools – to compete to deliver educational services. Learners – as customers – build their learning programme from a range of options, depending on their needs. However, this still basically involves mixing and matching standardized components, and is still supplier driven, with public education like a shopping mall. Learners are consumers, passive recipients of services designed by others for a mass market. This does, however, provide the opportunity to break out of a hierarchical approach and may threaten the equitable nature of education.

The prosumer – joining supply and demand

In this model, students co-construct their own 'catalogue' or 'menu' of products, and design the products. With informed help from professionals, students organize, direct and generate learning. This is achieved by the joining up of suppliers and consumers in a symbiotic relationship.

Source: Bolstad and Gilbert (2008)

– 'education, education, education' – and its motto was 'beyond bricks and mortar'. But it was also driven by deteriorating building stock (and curtailed by events).

In the UK, the Academies Programme was announced in 2000 by the Labour government's education secretary, David Blunkett, as a measure to replace existing failing schools or create new schools in areas of educational under-achievement. Initially called 'city academies' in the Learning and Skills Act 2000, in the Education Act 2002 they had become 'academies'. Usually set in deprived parts of the country, these schools were seen as the beneficiaries of a policy that would give them a new start in trying circumstances – under-performing schools with high-profile business backers who would give them up to £2 million towards the cost of new or refurbished school buildings.

The 2010 coalition government, in contrast, allowed even the highest-performing schools – including those that make selections on academic grounds – to become academies: nor did they any longer require a sponsor (Academies Act 2010). The result of this value shift was a huge increase in the numbers of academies opening. By May 2010 around 200 academies had opened under the Labour government, with a target of 400 in the longer term; by November 2012 there were 2,456 (Gillie 2012: 3). In some parts of the country (Darlington, Rutland), all state secondary schools had become academies. In others (Bromley, Bexley, Kingston upon Thames, Swindon), all state secondaries were in the process of becoming academies (*Guardian* 6 April 2012). In April 2012, the DfE (*Guardian* 2012a) confirmed that 50.3 per cent of England's 3,261 state secondary schools were academies or had applied to become academies.

Academies shifted from being 'a tool to turn around failing schools' (to raise standards by giving schools independence) to a means to take control for education from politicians and bureaucrats (the state) and give it to teachers and governors: 'The great thing about the academies movement is that it relies not on central direction by politicians, or by bureaucrats second-guessing those in the classroom. The academies movement is all about liberation and emancipating teachers and teaching leaders to do the best for young people' (Gove 2011). By 2013, this 'movement' had resulted in the need to build 261 replacement primary and secondary schools and a commitment to a reduction of 15 per cent in school size compared with the BSF programme guidelines (achieved through a squeeze on circulation space, corridors, assembly halls and canteens) (Barrett et al. 2013).

Was this, as critics claimed, a form of privatization of education – freeing academies from nationally agreed pay and conditions and accountability to (elected) town halls? Michael Gove, the education secretary, was widely accused of having forced schools to become academies against their will – for ideological reasons: a charge that would also be made against many of his subsequent initiatives and (famously) reversals of policy. And all these policy decisions – negative as well as positive – had their spatial implications.

The same legislation that allowed all schools to apply for conversion without sponsors also authorized the creation of free schools – state-funded primaries and secondaries started by parents, teachers, charities and private firms, accountable to central government rather than their local authority and with a great deal of freedom in the timing of the school day, rates of teacher pay and the range of subjects taught. Inspired by similar initiatives in Sweden and the US, the free school movement was designed to raise standards in the state sector.

Here, too, spatial implications were quick to surface. By April 2012, the first 24 free schools had opened – but around 35 of the free schools due to open in autumn 2012 had no premises confirmed.

Findings of the 2013 Barrett et al. report that found a 25 per cent improvement in pupil progress as a result of well-designed classrooms (Barrett et al. 2013: 1) were quickly dismissed by Gove: 'There is no convincing evidence that spending enormous amounts of money on school buildings leads to increased attainment' (*Guardian* 2012b). Lord Rogers, architect of Mossbourne Community Academy in Hackney, east London, affirmed his belief in the findings of the study – 'good design has the potential to have a striking effect on the way children learn' – and the Royal Institute of British Architects (RIBA) criticized the government's 'flat-pack' approach, that would 'place a straitjacket on future genera-tions of teaching professionals and quickly render these schools redundant'. The RIBA statement singled out the narrow corridors and concealed stairs of the new design for secondary schools: 'In many schools, this is likely to result in the need for additional staff supervision to maintain good behaviour and avoid bullying' (ibid.) Schools designed to the new rules were scheduled to open in September 2014 – 15 per cent smaller than those designed under

BSF guidelines, roof terraces and glazed walls banned, corridor, assembly and canteen space squeezed.

The Mossbourne Community Academy, however, cost £3,000 per square metre to build. The budget for a sister school, Mossbourne Victoria Park Academy, was halved and the Rogers Stirk Harbour & Partners designs shelved in favour of those provided by another practice, Jestico & Whiles, with the Rogers partnership sidelined to the role of design adviser. Staff acknowledged that RSHP was first choice but that 'the processes didn't allow it' (*Building Design* 2013). A local design review panel rejected the new designs: 'We are appalled. It took a roasting' (*Building Design* 2013).

Another far-reaching policy initiative, the 2003 White Paper that proposed expansion 'towards 50 per cent participation [in higher education] for young people 18–30 years from all social backgrounds' (DfES 2003), seems to have been drafted with no thought for the space (or, indeed, many of the other) implications for such optimism: but numbers will eventually fight their own corner. (Numbers such as the – potentially disenfranchising – hike in university tuition fees.) Stefan Collini sees the whole document as incoherent and the 50 per cent figure as 'an opportunist soundbite, a figure chosen for its electoral appeal, not as the expression of some deep analysis of the population's intellectual potential, still less of the nature of university education' (2012: 158). It was also, as he points out, an exercise in crystal ball gazing:

> Its premise ... is that higher education needs 'to enable all suitably qualified individuals to develop their potential'. But how many people is this, and how can we know? You may well think that it is impossible to answer that question, and you'd be right. But the government knows. Or at least it knows, apparently, that by 2010 50% of the age cohort in this country will have the potential to develop themselves intellectually and personally in higher education.
>
> (ibid.: 158)

The UK policy initiatives that culminated in the BSF programme (2004–10) had their moral compass set by the Children Act 2004, passed after intense consultation on the 2003 Green Paper, *Every Child Matters* (itself published alongside the Laming report on the Victoria Climbié Inquiry) (Box 2.5). The Green Paper had a fivefold list of recommendations: that children should be healthy; safe; should enjoy and achieve; make a positive contribution; and achieve economic well-being. The Act made these goals a statutory obligation for local authorities and schools. In detail, local author-ities were charged with:

● reforming the education of 14–19 year olds, offering a choice of general diploma qualifications and employer-designed

Box 2.5 The Climbié Inquiry

Victoria Climbié died in the intensive care unit of St Mary's Hospital Paddington on 25 February 2000, aged 8 years and 3 months. Her death was caused by multiple injuries arising from months of ill-treatment and abuse by her great aunt, Marie-Therese Kouao, and her great aunt's partner, Carl John Manning. Following their conviction for her murder, Lord Laming was appointed in April 2001 to chair an independent statutory inquiry into the circumstances leading to and surrounding the death of Victoria Climbié, and to make recommendations 'as to how such an event may, as far as possible, be avoided in the future'.

Source: The Victoria Climbié Inquiry Report, 5 June 2003: 3, House of Commons

specialist (vocational) diploma. This dated back to Learning and Skills Act 2000 and took in the Tomlinson Report.

- implementing the government's e-strategy – specialist ICT-driven classrooms, digitally enabled sports and training facilities, interactive whiteboards, i-desks. Set out in *Harnessing Technology: Transforming learning and children's services* (DfES 2005). The Department made the commitment to allocating almost 10 per cent of BSF's funding to ICT.

- delivering the government's ten-year policy on science, technology, engineering and maths (STEM).

- including special educational needs (SEN) children, to meet the recommendations of two papers – *Excellence for all Children: Meeting Special Education Needs* (1997) and *SEN: a Programme for Action* (1998) – and the 2001 Special Educational Needs and Disability Act, which required that a child should have its needs met, normally in a mainstream setting, and be offered full access to 'a broad, balanced and relevant education'.

- delivering the integrated services for young people and their families laid down in *Every Child Matters* and the Children Act 2004 and that eventually became an extended schools policy (Youth Matters 2005) covering the transition made by young people into adulthood. The 2007 report *Children's Plan – Building Brighter Futures* saw a new role for schools at the centre of their communities, linking schools, the National Health Service and other children's services, with investment priority given certain at-risk groups.

- promoting personalized learning – 'a learner and knowledge-centred approach' which connected to the existing knowledge of pupils, with a greater focus on independent learning, inquiry and thought (*2020 Vision: Report of the Teaching and Learning Review* 2006).

In formulating policy on the links between universities and industry, the Lambert Review (Lambert 2003) made a number of strongly expressed recommendations – that the most effective forms of knowledge transfer involve human interaction, that people from business and universities should be brought together systematically, that the government must support university departments that are doing work that industry values and that the development agencies could play a greater role in developing links between business and universities. It proposed ways to simplify negotiations over intellectual property and to improve the market signals between employers and students and suggested that the university sector should develop a code of governance – and that the government should introduce a risk-based approach to the regulation of universities.

The report makes much of the need to liberalize barriers to access, but much less of the spaces in which such access would take place. It observes only that the clustering seen to be such a key element in the relationship between high-tech industries and US universities shows the benefits of proximity. 'Personal contact is the best form of communication, and distance affects the capacity of firms to collaborate with universities. This applies to large firms in strategic university relationships as well as to SMEs with a more regional outlook. Research by Arthur D. Little on behalf of the Regional Development Authorities (RDAs) confirms this point: "Physical proximity is important in scientific collaboration. The era of the Internet does not remove the need to build relationships by personal contact, even if they can then be sustained through electronic means. Indeed ... the importance of proximity is growing, because of an increasing need for companies to look outside for technology, ideas and co-operation" (Little 2001)' (ibid.: 70).

The two Roberts reports (Roberts 2002, 2006) urged the government to produce exemplars of science lab designs that would excite children's curiosity and engagement and help address a strong underlying concern that Britain was running out of scientists (Gil 2009: 13).

Project Faraday (2007) aimed to improve the design of school science facilities, as part of a wide programme to support the UK government's goal 'to make science a priority in schools at all levels; to improve science learning and teaching and to inspire more young people, from all backgrounds, to study and work in science' (Partnership for Schools 2012). Future science spaces, it argued, should support more interactive and exciting ways of teaching and learning, reflect the requirements of the new science curriculum and exploit the whole school building and its grounds, not just the laboratories themselves (Figures 2.9 and 2.10).

An analysis of school science activities by the Project Faraday research teams found that they ranged from 90 people watching a presentation, to one person sitting quietly to consider how to solve a scientific problem. While 'some practical activities may call for a fully serviced enclosed space (such as a laboratory), there are many science learning activities that can benefit from very different kinds of spaces. By liberating space that may have been used to provide more fully serviced laboratories, other configurations are possible.'

Source: DSCF (2007: 20)

'The Faraday exemplar designs proposed reconfigurable areas (capable of having two groups of 30 students being taught at the same time, or being used for 100-pupils lessons), large open spaces, creativity pods, technology-enabled carrels, stackable seats, laptop-enabled group snugs, mobile demonstration benches, self-contained mini-labs, and a strong emphasis on IT (interactive white boards, ceiling-mounted projectors, high-spec PCs). They also combined ... fully-serviced labs ("super-labs") with a few science theory studios and practical work spaces (to support practical work that didn't require a fully serviced lab) ... This design approach assumed that science teaching would move between the different types of spaces according to the exact content of the lessons.'

Source: Gil (2009: 14)

Figure 2.9 Project Faraday: exemplar designs

Figure 2.10 Project Faraday: exemplar designs

Like S4PL, Project Faraday was funded by the Department for Children, Schools and the Family (DCSF). Under the new Department for Education (DfE), personalization – which characterized so many of the new ways of thinking about child-centred education, the knowledge society and creating a customized environment – ceased to be government policy.

EVENTS

Each fresh set of initiatives has implications for the housing of these aspirations. As Stephen Heppell points out, however, such initiatives and their associated building programmes are 'welcome news if we are building the right schools, but an accelerating crisis if we are not' (Heppell et al. 2004: 2).

The decisive factor in the provision of the right sort of learning space might be an event, not a policy – as in New Orleans after

Katrina (Bingler 2010) or Christchurch after the 2011 earthquake (Figure 2.11). The extent and physical state of the building stock (Woolner et al. 2005: 12) are obviously elements – in Britain and Germany after the Second World War, in the US in the 1830s and 1840s, in the USSR after the 1917 Revolution. Yet even here, with schools actually being destroyed or condemned as inadequate, the catalyst for school building might be societal vision or nationalist fervour: the UK and West Germany responded differently to the same urgent need; eighteenth-century Prussian nationalism responded to the end of Napoleonic occupation with the beginnings of an educational system – a compulsory state system – which was 'for its time, a unique achievement' (Green 1992: 120, cited in Woolner et al. 2005).

Demographic change seems a clear-cut case of a shift in the emphasis of educational provision in response to perceived need – the US population explosion at the end of the nineteenth and beginning of the twentieth century, the climbing birth rate in immediately post-war (and 1960s) Britain. But in the US, the

Figure 2.11 Christchurch, NZ: after the earthquake. Christchurch High Street – by the city mall: before the 2011 earthquake this was the site of an innovative primary school, Discovery 1, located in underused space above a department store and its sister secondary school, Unlimited Paenga Tawhiti, also located above a nearby block of shops

clearly perceived need for expansion was undercut by economic realities which led to a concentration on efficiency rather than universal provision. Platoon schools moved even very young children – the 'human material' (Donovan 1921) – between class-rooms and playgrounds to maintain occupation levels. And in 1950s and 1960s Britain, the correlation between birthrate and building programmes does appear neat (Figure 2.12) – but there had been little building in the tough economic times after the First World War:

> It might be thought that central government involvement is a vital variable, since after WW2 the demands of the 1944 Act to raise the school leaving age to 15 and provide proper secondary education seem to have been very influ-ential. However, the 1926 Hadow Report, which recommended the abolition of all-age elementary schools, with schooling organised into primary and secondary phases, provoked only isolated change and, in general, allowed elementary schools to continue for another twenty years.
>
> (Woolner et al. 2005: 10)

Clearly decisions about the worth of space renewal and innovation cannot be separated from economic considerations: in times of prosperity, there will inevitably be a focus on quality and concerns for the well-being of the whole child, the whole learner in society and on the prospect of building new buildings. Innovation can be expensive. When the economy takes a downturn, new school buildings are deprioritized and efforts are focused on maintaining what is there already, often hand-in-hand with a more standards-focused agenda.

This argument would cite in its favour the open-plan schools of the UK that flourished from the 1950s to the 1970s, now considered to have been driven by a desire for a more child-centred pedagogy, exemplified by teaching methodology reforms, renewing the focus on the individualized learning needs of children and a concern for their emotional and social development. In this golden age, the case would go, schools were viewed not just as sites for the transmission of knowledge but communities with important peer groups that fostered social development. Curricular activities and programmes were designed to raise student self-esteem and promote team teaching, collaborative learning and interdisci-plinary studies. The architectural approach that stemmed from this set of values manifested itself in space with minimal internal divisions and an absence of circulation – in circular structures with moveable dividers, interchangeable storage components and easily re-locatable furniture (Hutchison 2004: 96–9).

Classes were arranged around the perimeter of the circle with a common resource area at the centre where all learners could

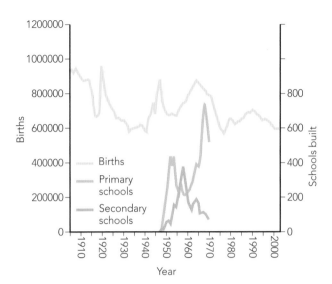

Figure 2.12 The relationship between births (1905–2003) and school building (1945–70) in the UK. Source: Woolner et al. (2005: 10)

come together. Multiple classes were conducted simultaneously in the single large space. The intention was that the open, flexible layout would foster student collaboration, team teaching and inter-disciplinary learning.

But this commitment to child-centred learning has not always been unanimously accepted as the drive behind open plan: teachers were suspicious and many (Bennett et al. 1980) perceived the changes to be predominantly about cost-cutting. One Canadian school principal called the introduction of open-plan elementary schools one of Ontario's 'costliest and silliest mistakes' (McDonald 1997: 7).

> For classroom teachers, the open plan classroom was akin to positioning a newly-designed open cockpit of a 747 jet in the passenger compartment surrounded by 250 exuberant, noisy customers and ordering the pilot to fly the plane with patience, empathy and skill. For many children, it was a loud, chaotic, confusing nightmare. Teacher stress levels rose dramatically, mainly because of the noise, the interruptions, and the confusion of housing so many children in one space. Diverse teaching styles, effective in self-contained classrooms, often proved inappropriate in this throng of lively youngsters. Some special programs had to be radically altered or moved into storerooms in order to contain the noise level. Talk about stacking the cards to ensure teacher and student failure!
>
> (ibid.: 7)

In any case, any overview of the frequent mismatch between high expectations and long-term outcomes over more than a century of building programmes provides a useful corrective to any tendency to such rosy interventionism:

While there are elements of the school environment that are important to learning, there is no evidence of simple causal links between the environment and the behaviour within it. The experience of open-plan schools, in both the UK and the US, shows that setting does not determine behaviour (Proshansky and Wolfe 1975; Canter and Donald 1987), while attempts to link student achievement with physical environments are often equivocal (Weinstein 1979; Pricewaterhouse Coopers 2000).

(Woolner et al. 2005: 6)

There is no doubt that – in good times or bad, economically – one of the main arguments for the betterment of school building stock tends to be that the buildings are ageing. The idea of inadequate schools is generally linked to age, and so can be expected to be a perennial problem as each wave of schools gets old (ibid.).

This may be a simple degradation of the actual building. Even modern schools being built in the twenty-first century tend to have a projected use of 30 years in initial engineering models to look at lifecycle costing of specific materials. It is little surprise that the buildings of the 1970s, with their significant use of prefabricated and standardized parts, should feel dated and in need of refreshment if they have not been well maintained and invested in since their creation (although many historical buildings, such as the UK's Victorian school building stock, are still some of the soundest buildings around). The materials used, and dimensions (such as ceiling height) will have an impact on longevity.

The other age factor, however, may be one of fashion, with certain features becoming indispensable to education. In recent times, the vast rise in the amount of technology provided to schools in the developed world has meant schools have had to consider not only the spatial requirements of housing PC terminals, but also the engineering requirements giving the additional heat gain of clustering 30 PCs within 60 square metres, as well as much greater demands on the school plant. In time, as technology becomes more pervasive, smaller and personal, these demands may fade away again, yet in the meantime schools have had to accommodate them, or build to expand.

In his first budget statement as chancellor on 2 July 1997, Gordon Brown made the announcement: 'Economic success tomorrow will depend on investing in our schools today. But at the present rate of progress, many of our children will be educated for the twenty-first century in classrooms built in the nineteenth' (House of Commons Debate 1997: col 316). After launching a multibillion capital programme in 2001 for repairs and modernization of existing schools, the government shifted thinking in October 2002. DfES noted that only 14 per cent of the schools in England operated

from buildings constructed after 1976, and that school buildings built between the 1950s and the 1970s had a design life of around 30 to 35 years. This meant that most of the school stock was already into its replacement period, and was becoming increasingly expensive to maintain and operate and unsuitable for modern school use (Gil 2009) (Figure 2.13).

In February 2003, DfES published the consultation document on the BSF programme, aimed at the transformation of education: 'School buildings should inspire learning. They should nurture every pupil and member of staff. They should be a source of pride and a practical resource for the community.' The following year the department made its first report on progress:

At the heart of BSF is a desire not only to rebuild and renew individual secondary schools, but also to help LAs to reform and redesign the pattern of education, for example working with local Learning and Skills Councils to best serve each community for decades. It is an opportunity to think differently about all aspects of the process of developing and delivering new schools.

(DfES 2004c: 30)

And this desire was linked to outcomes – linking design and productivity. Priority would be given to the areas with greatest educational and social need, with the prioritization formula weighted by the average of the percentage of pupils not achieving five A*–C grades, including English and maths in the GSCEs (attainment indicator) and by an indicator based on the percentages of pupils from families entitled to receiving tax credits and eligible to receiving free meals (deprivation indicator).

The funding allocated to each project assumed up to 50 per cent of the gross floor area of a local authority's school estate to be new build, 35 per cent major refurbishment and 15 per cent minor refurbishment. While projects for Voluntary Aided (VA) schools normally required a 10 per cent contribution from the school governors, the DfES funded the VA school governors' contribution for the BSF programme. Additional allowances existed for regional variations in building costs and inflation to the projected start of construction date. Furniture and equipment were funded separately on a per pupil basis, adjusted according to the 50:35:15 split. Funding for ICT was also allocated on a per pupil basis, and covered equipment, service establishment, change management and infrastructure costs. The floor area required for classrooms, staffrooms, storage, circulation, toilets and plant was calculated using the non-statutory area guidelines for secondary schools set out in BB98 (DCSF 2004a BB98). Pupil numbers were used in the calculation based on ten-year projections. The calculation for special educational needs (SEN) schools was similar, but used the guidance in the revised BB77 to reflect the requirements for different types of special needs (DCSF 2004b BB77).

(Gil 2009: 4)

The academies were going to revitalize the life chances of young people across society, BSF was set to renew the school building stock and by 2010 everyone who wanted access to the best higher education could have it by statute, regardless of both logical and logistical contradictions. It was going to be a busy decade on the disillusionment front.

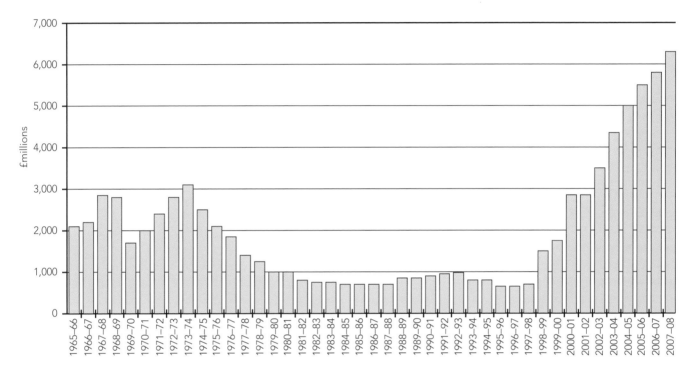

Figure 2.13 Capital investment in Britain's schools 1965–2008. Source: DfES (2006)

CHAPTER 3
Design imperatives for a changing landscape

What, then, should the various types of learning space be providing in response to these often promiscuous policy initiatives, shifting patterns of value and use and the adventitious blows of fate and fashion? A widening universe and proliferating range of drivers are together imposing real constraints on learning space and raising pressing questions about the extent to which outcomes have kept pace. Learning space has an established tendency to react to changing demands rather than set an agenda that permits of long-term resilience, but the design imperatives are now clear.

LINKING PEDAGOGY AND SPACE

Every building programme is predicated on certain assumptions about the link between learning space and learning. When the Design Council commissioned a 2005 literature review of the impact of school environments on learning, it ran an expert seminar to support the need for such a review. The foreword to the report cites Stephen Heppell's presentation to the seminar: 'whereas traditionally, we have designed for productivity, processing large numbers of children through the effective use of buildings, designing a room for learning is very complex. No one knows how to prevent "learning-loss" when you design a room "pedagogically", whereas we know lots about designing for minimum heat loss' (Higgins et al. 2005: 3).

In the UK, the *Classrooms of the Future* report published in 2003 was one of the first initiatives of the Department for Education and Science to help create innovative and imaginative environments that can stimulate learning and inspire children (DfES 2003a). Gil (2009) states that the drivers for innovation in design were developments in ICT, the inclusion of SEN pupils in mainstream schools, the need to stimulate children to achieve more, changes in the organization of classroom environment (teaching variable sizes of groups of children, virtual classrooms, communities of learners, tailored education), and schools open to community use.

The DfES followed up the project with a set of exemplar designs covering a range of types and locations of schools (DfES 2003b). The aim of the project was to help the UK:

move forward and develop new ideas for school design that are exciting and really work. To deliver the best and most effective education, exploiting all the possibilities of Information and Communications Technology (ICT), school buildings need to be designed so that they stimulate children's imaginations and reflect advances in technology. They need to provide high quality environments that are conducive to learning and functional, without being boring. They must be both flexible and adaptable, to cope with changes in a future that we cannot predict.

(ibid. 3–4)

And in the same year as the launch of the BSF programme, the DfES also published 'Transforming Schools: an inspirational guide to remodelling secondary schools', designed to support the schools in the Building Schools for the Future programme that would not be moving to new schools on new sites and would remain on their existing site in a mixture of new and replacement buildings, adaptations and refurbishment (DfES 2004). The aim was to show that educational transformation could still take place in existing buildings. Case-study examples of real schools that have had recent transformational projects were used to highlight the benefits of refurbishing some buildings and replacing others, show how the basic budget for each school will be set and give some guidance on how schools 'can make the best use of their budget and identify the option that best suits their vision and ethos' (ibid.: 5).

In 2004, the Commission for Architecture and the Built Environment (CABE) and Building Futures published '21st Century Schools: learning environments of the future' (CABE and Building Futures 2004). The report illustrated four provocative scenarios for learning environments in 2024, ranging from: 'the "network of learners" where learning would be entirely on-line (school buildings would be limited to an administrative suite) to the "fortress school" where teachers would monitor, teach, assess, and lead, whilst the students would learn, perform, attain, and follow (a single campus school with rigid security protocols)' (Gil 2009: 12).

The report stated that education was evolving and new pedagogies were driving a move towards:

- increasing use of ICT (a catalyst for change, as well as a key tool to deliver change)

- virtual classrooms and communities of learners

- tailoring education towards the individual child's needs

- different means of grouping within schools

- opening up schools to the wider community

- dispersing learning environments within the community and off-site schools

- greater integration of special needs within mainstream school (CABE and Building Futures 2004: 8).

The study concluded that there was the beginning of a move away from the traditional design of schools and specialized teaching spaces and classrooms, a set school day and curriculum, accommodated at a school site. The future was likely to comprise more multipurpose spaces, with flexible timetables and individual learning plans accommodated at multiple locations across the neighbourhood. Future learning environments will need to be flexible at different scales and timescales, allowing for variation in use, occupancy and layout, inspiring to those working, learning and visiting them, supportive of effective teaching and learning, accommodating a wide range of experiences and activities. They will also need to involve the users and the wider community, linking with learning spaces elsewhere (ibid.: 6).

In 2005, the Design Council launched designmyschool.com, an online service offering teachers and pupils an interactive approach to identifying the key issues in their environment, with practical examples, research summaries and advice on how to make improvements. It drew on 24 specially commissioned case studies and an international literature review as well as the experience of the campaign project schools and links to other relevant sites. (This site ceased existence after the conclusion of the Design Council's Schools campaign and the change in the school development landscape with the cancellation of the Building Schools for the Future programme in 2010.)

The Design Council's report *Learning Environments Campaign Prospectus: From the inside looking out,* published in 2005, stated that school designs needed to be linked to learning aims, and that the standard classroom design needed to be reformed as it undermined the value placed on learning. Standard classroom designs also hindered creativity, reduced the range of teaching and learning styles possible, and failed to adapt to individual needs (Gil 2009: 13).

These conclusions were based on earlier work that the Design Council had undertaken that looked at how classrooms perform. The

'Kit for Purpose' project (2002) involved multidisciplinary teams of designers and other experts working with teachers, pupils and other users in 12 schools over 18 months to understand the design and procurement issues underlying the state of school learning environments.

The 2005 research showed that low quality, standardized and institutional classroom environments and resources are not just uninspiring, they actually:

- reduce the range of teaching and learning styles possible and affect interaction between teacher and student

- undermine the value placed on learning

- fail to adapt to individual needs

- hinder creativity

- are inefficient

- waste time and effort

- cost more in the long term (Design Council 2005: 18).

The Commission for Architecture and the Built Environment (CABE) published a report in 2006 assessing the quality of the designs of the secondary schools built over the previous five years. The report stated that the design quality wasn't good enough to secure the government's ambition to transform children's education and it also stated that 'too many of the mistakes of the past look like being repeated in the first waves' of schools being built in the Building Schools for the Future programme (Gil 2009: 13).

CABE described half of the completed schools as 'poor' or 'mediocre' and concluded that despite exemplar design guidance, standardized contractual documentation, and the use of design quality indicators, there were not enough schools being designed that 'are exemplary, innovative, inspiring or flexibly designed to allow for a diversity of approaches to education in the future' (CABE 2006: 2).

The authors of the report state that high-quality design is essential to achieving the goals of the Building Schools for the Future programme: 'This is not just because the quality of the buildings matters but also because the buildings are seen as essential to achieving a transformation in education and learning. Research shows clear links between well-designed schools and academic standards but good design can also impact on the attendance, morale and behaviour of our children. Bad design can have the reverse effect' (p. 9).

The weakest area of performance found in the review was in innovation and developing new understanding about both construction and education. Contributing to development of new knowledge was the weakest criterion, and only those schools in the top band – the excellently designed schools – achieved a positive rating for this. They also found that there is 'less evidence of schools being used as tools to aid transformational learning, with the criteria [*sic*] "the building makes you think" ranked fifth from the bottom' (p. 27).

Reacting to the CABE finding that 50 per cent of new schools in the UK were mediocre or poor, Futurelab asked the question: 'If the design quality is insufficient – what is the quality of the educational strategy underpinning that design?' (Rudd et al. 2006: 1). The Building Schools for the Future programme at that time was setting out to rebuild or renew every secondary school in England over the next 10 to 15 years and Rudd et al. believed that the design of these schools would shape the ways in which education is thought about, experienced and conducted for the next 50 to 100 years:

> We need to start, then, by asking not 'what buildings do we want?' but instead 'what sort of education do we want to see in future?' We need to ask not 'how many classrooms do we need?' but 'what sorts of learning relationships do we want to foster? What competencies do we want learners to develop? What tools and resources are available to us to support learning?'
>
> (pp. 3–4)

What if learning spaces were designed around a particular function, process or learning goal – would this affect the design? For example, would it be possible to have learning spaces that were designed specifically to develop 21st century skills, such as creativity, innovation, risk taking, collaboration, presentation and performance skills, or to promote health, helpfulness, discovery, concentration, honesty and so on? Steiner schools, for instance, offer an alternative educational approach and many of the spatial designs focus on nurturing young people through a holistic approach to early development by promoting environments that feel 'safe' and comforting. Given the numerous recent fears raised in relation to children's health and wellbeing, might the design of new learning spaces consider embedding tactile, sensory and playful learning tools firmly within the design process, thereby creating both very different and non-threatening environments?

> (p. 8)

Rudd et al. noted that the brief for the Building Schools of the Future programme and its exemplars of school design emphasize the need for flexibility to enable different room layouts, adaptable enough to suit longer term 'both evolutionary and revolutionary change', such as 'developments in ICT' and 'innovations in curriculum delivery'. However, they believed there was still the inherent assumption that schools would remain largely unchanged, with the average school size and average class size (of around 30) remaining fairly constant.

The brief also points out that, apart from specialist areas, teaching will take place in 'standard classrooms' with an allocation of one computer per eight primary pupils, and one per every five in secondary. Teaching rooms should provide a space that is sufficiently flexible to accommodate a broad range of activities and a variety of furniture and equipment which can generally be achieved by keeping any fixed furniture and equipment to the perimeter and leaving the centre clear for loose furniture (p. 11).

Rudd et al. state that while, theoretically, learning can – and does – take place in any location, most school designs imply learning can take place only in designated places at designated times within particular constraints. They quote Prakash Nair: 'The truth of the matter is that school buildings have been and continue to be places to warehouse children. New schools just do it in more comfortable settings' (p. 12).

In *The Language of School Design* (Nair et al. 2009), the authors develop the thesis that just as Christopher Alexander's ground-breaking *A Pattern Language* (1976) had made a direct connection between the built environment and the human psyche with a series of 'spatial patterns that nourish the human communities they support' (Nair et al. 2009: 12), a common vocabulary of 28 patterns for school design could '*begin* to define the graphic language for the design of healthy and functional learning environments' (p. 14) and make the link between the 'actual design of a majority of school facilities' and 'widely acknowledged best practice principles' (p. 13).

The patterns aim to be universal in principle if not in application: they are 'not to be used as a template or prototype of how any given element in a particular school should be designed' (p. 14) but should provide a starting point to answer two key questions.

- Do the facilities created as a result of external educational forces such as state standards and required curricula help or hurt learning goals?

- How does the physical design of a school affect the social dynamics of the school community?

Most school architecture, Nair et al. say, tends to look at spaces in a linear way – which means that we first decide what a space will be used for and 'then we design the space for that activity' (p. 18). This kind of thinking ignores 'complexity and research about the human brain and human experience, resulting in the design of static spaces that inhibit learning'. Their pattern language method, by contrast, 'deals with four major and simultaneous realms of human experience' – spatial, psychological, physiological and behavioural, each characterized by multiple attributes – and celebrates such interconnectedness. Nair et al. are in no doubt that if designers and school stakeholders share a common language of school design informed by this multidimensional approach, their method 'can help build consensus quickly, and create superior design' with 'far less investment of money and effort than the traditional system' (p. 17).

Kenn Fisher has also been exercised by the link between pedagogy, space and learning environments (Scottish Government 2007: 16). He cites Piaget's classification of children into developmental phases: 'pre-operational' (2–7 years), 'concrete-operational' (7–12 years) and 'formal-operational' (12 years to adult). His view is that there should be a progressive approach to flexibility in the learning space where the level of flexibility and the amount of 'open' space increases as the child develops:

> Pre-operational students require structure and a sense of security that must be spatially represented, whereas concrete-operational and formal-operational students require spaces that will facilitate and promote their pursuit of exploration and shared knowledge. In response to this initial under- standing of space allocation, a type of zoning occurs involving a ratio of spaces where students can 'belong', 'share', 'retreat' and 'explore.'
>
> (p. 20)

Spatially this translates into a need to provide spaces that promote feelings of safety and security. Most often, this comes in the form of 'home rooms' that may be called pods and club rooms, where a regular routine is established in a familiar environment. Fisher notes that at this stage:

> learning space most closely resembles the traditional classroom spaces of old, but new designs offer increased flexibility, for example using movable walls to facilitate collaboration and team teaching as well as connections to larger shared spaces, often designed to welcome families as well as students. ...

> The need for a sense of belonging gradually decreases in the formal operational stages, along with the amount of space shared with parents. In the later stages of schooling, 'exploring' and 'retreating' are more heavily weighted. Having gradually experienced exposure to larger shared spaces, students become more comfortable in their interactions with others and also require spaces for more independent thinking and reflection. The flexibility of the space increases as the students develop,

until in the final stages of learning the environment provides a range of spaces and facilities that respond to the individual needs of students pursuing future pathways.

> (p. 22)

Stephen Harris, director/founder of Sydney Centre for Innovation in Learning (SCIL), noted in an article in 2010 (Harris 2010) that the last decade has seen an increasing focus on the nature of evolving 'twenty-first century' pedagogy – learning suited to a post-indus- trial era context and a growing interest in designing spaces with 'twenty-first century learning' specifically in mind. While different education jurisdictions around the world have responded to these challenges with varying degrees of vision and in some cases policy he believes that for most countries, the core work in both areas is largely still to be undertaken: 'Pedagogy will not change with significant groundswell, enough to provide a "twenty-first century" learning experience for the majority of students, until this key essential work is undertaken.'

That work needs to focus on:

- providing cost effective and targeted professional development so that all teachers shift from a default practice grounded in their own learning experiences within an industrial-era framework, to a pedagogy able to support learning in a twenty first century age of constant change

- supporting existing schools to adapt inherited learning spaces, so that the default industrial-era model is no longer the predominant resourced model

- creating new spaces for learning, designed around new paradigms (ibid.).

Harris noted that in the last decade, there has been some advancement in spatial thinking related to school designs for the future – creating new spaces by altering existing environments or creating new environments for learning. He cited individual innovators such as Fielding Nair International, the work of organi- zations such as JISC in the UK and school redesign programmes such as Building Schools for the Future as examples of where this innovation is occurring (ibid.: 5).

TRANSFORMING THE FURTHER AND HIGHER EDUCATION CAMPUS

The shift in learning paradigm – from instruction to learning – has also had direct implications for the university estate. Traditional categories of space are becoming less meaningful as space becomes less specialized, boundaries blur and operating hours extend toward 24/7. In many institutions, space types are increasingly being designed primarily around patterns of human interaction rather than specific needs of particular departments, disciplines or technologies.

New space models for universities may focus as much on enhancing quality of life as they do on directly supporting the learning experience. The 'learning landscape' concept has been used to develop spatial models for universities that recognize that learning is not just confined to formal teaching spaces and that the quality of the student experience is impacted by all aspects of their physical environment. Learning spaces within this model can be categorized as 'specialist', 'general' or 'informal' (Figure 3.1).

Many institutions are seeking to minimize the amount of specialized learning space and to instead create highly adaptable teaching and learning spaces that can be shared across faculties and subject areas.

In the US, Diana Oblinger (2006) notes that today's students – whether 18, 22 or 55 – have attitudes, expectations, and constraints that differ from those of students even ten years ago. She suggests that learning spaces reflect the people and learning approach of the times, so spaces designed in 1956 are not likely to fit perfectly with students today:

> Learning is the central activity of colleges and universities. Sometimes that learning occurs in classrooms (formal

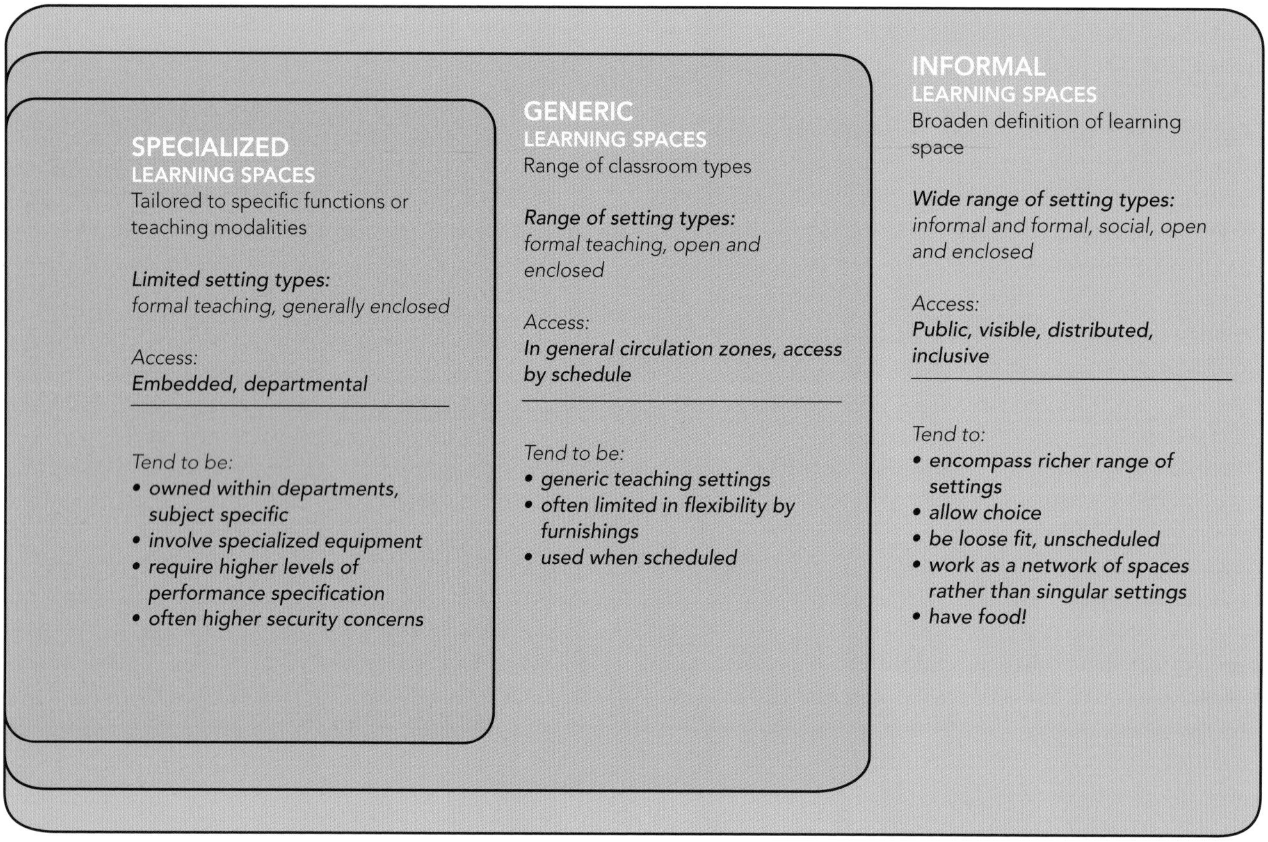

SPECIALIZED
LEARNING SPACES
Tailored to specific functions or teaching modalities

Limited setting types:
formal teaching, generally enclosed

Access:
Embedded, departmental

Tend to be:
- *owned within departments, subject specific*
- *involve specialized equipment*
- *require higher levels of performance specification*
- *often higher security concerns*

GENERIC
LEARNING SPACES
Range of classroom types

Range of setting types:
formal teaching, open and enclosed

Access:
In general circulation zones, access by schedule

Tend to be:
- *generic teaching settings*
- *often limited in flexibility by furnishings*
- *used when scheduled*

INFORMAL
LEARNING SPACES
Broaden definition of learning space

Wide range of setting types:
informal and formal, social, open and enclosed

Access:
Public, visible, distributed, inclusive

Tend to:
- *encompass richer range of settings*
- *allow choice*
- *be loose fit, unscheduled*
- *work as a network of spaces rather than singular settings*
- *have food!*

● Specialized learning space, tailored to specific functions or teaching approaches.

● Generic learning spaces adaptable for multiple uses and teaching approaches.

● Informal learning spaces that support ad hoc, individual and small group activities.

Source: DEGW (2009)

Figure 3.1 Specialist, generic and informal learning space

learning); other times it results from serendipitous interactions among individuals (informal learning). Space – whether physical or virtual – can have an impact on learning. It can bring people together; it can encourage exploration, collaboration, and discussion. Or, space can carry an unspoken message of silence and disconnectedness. More and more we see the power of built pedagogy (the ability of space to define how one teaches).

(ibid.)

Many of today's learners favour active, participatory, experiential learning – the learning style they exhibit in their personal lives. But their behaviour may not match their self-expressed learning preferences when sitting in a large lecture hall with chairs bolted to the floor. The single focal point at the front of the room sends a strong signal about how learning will occur.

As we have come to understand more about learners, how people learn, and technology, our notions of effective learning spaces have changed. Increasingly, those spaces are flexible and networked; bringing together formal and informal activities in a seamless environment that acknowledges that learning can occur anyplace, at any time, in either physical or virtual spaces.

(ibid.)

In 2006, the Institute of Education in the UK was commissioned by the Space Management Group (SMG) to investigate the impact on space of future changes in higher education (SMG 2006a). A literature review and a series of interviews with a range of higher education institutions (HEIs) across the UK led to certain key observations – a mix of status quo, prescriptions and predictions.

It is observable, says the report, that learning space is merging with aspects of general amenity space, including common room areas and cafeterias. Lectures are still seen as a good way of inducting students into a discipline and will continue to occur for the foreseeable future – but more creative lecture theatre designs will allow these spaces to be used in more diverse ways. IT developments are enabling more intensive use of space for teaching and learning but will not permit significant reductions in overall space use. The design of generic teaching space in new buildings is also taking account of the need for more flexible provision, to allow for different-sized groups working in different ways over extended working hours. Most modern higher education buildings now provide much more of their space in units which can be reconfigured and in small rooms designed for group learning.

Predictions included the suggestion that there is likely to be a modest increase in space use across the sector over the next decade, reflecting the expansion in administrative functions in many institutions and the provision of more flexible teaching spaces, with the quality of an institution's physical facilities increasingly seen as an important marketing asset and accordingly attracting more resources and management attention. In HEIs, the existing space will increasingly be remodelled to meet new learning and teaching requirements or to meet new standards. Future changes in pedagogic approaches will affect the size of student groups, the frequency with which they meet and the type of space they need, with more provision needed for student-led and 'blended' learning, which will demand more relatively small and adaptable spaces. HEIs will provide more space for unstructured/ ad-hoc self-directed learning and peer-teaching among students and there will be increased blurring of the boundary between academic and social areas.

At postgraduate level in the humanities and social sciences, there is a move towards providing the equivalent to a laboratory environment where students could work privately and on joint tasks, with access to advanced computing and facilities such as virtual reality environments. It is likely that such facilities will attract research partners from outside the HEI to work on joint projects. There is likely to be little net change in space requirements per unit of research activity: equipment in many disciplines is becoming smaller and more portable, allowing more people to access the same equipment and rethinking laboratory design to create shared write-up space is also leading to space efficiencies. Campus-based e-learning (virtual learning environments) will continue to develop and should improve the efficiency of space use by allowing students to work more flexibly, on and off the campus.

The provision of academic office space is still a sensitive subject in most HEIs. As tutorial group sizes increase, the office becomes too small to house these sessions and the demand for seminar rooms is likely to increase. Shared offices for three to six become more common in new/refurbished buildings, which then brings with it a requirement for conveniently located small and medium-sized rooms for teaching and meetings. The demand for administrative space in HEIs is increasing because of the creation of new functions such as quality assurance, marketing and external fund raising. It is likely that there will be further growth in demand for administrative space.

More open workplace models may result in some space savings, although if adequate teaching, meeting and support service space is also provided, the savings will normally be modest. Greater flexibility and adaptability may reduce distinctions between space type and allow more intensive use but any reductions in space needs are likely to be small. New buildings provide opportunities to collocate administrative services to improve efficiency and offer an enhanced service in one-stop-shop-type facilities.

For teaching-led institutions, the authors predicted that large lecture theatres and large seminar-style rooms (for 30–40 people) will continue to be used. These spaces will increasingly be multi-functional, with a range of digital technologies allowing teachers and learners to produce and manipulate images and data of all kinds. Laboratory and workshop space will have reduced substantially in area, with greater reliance on computer modelling and digital representation and more multidisciplinary use of the spaces (SMG 2006a: 17).

They also suggest that the role and function of the university library will change substantially, with most learning materials being available digitally with the library having few traditional books or journals. The social spaces across the university will have merged with informal working areas and the library or learning centre as students carry with them most of the learning materials they need in light, easy-to-read digital form. They will access additional material from the HEI's own virtual learning environments (VLEs) and from the web wherever they are.

As well as external societal changes impacting higher education, the Institute of Education also stressed the importance of endogenous changes within institutions that will impact the demand for space during the next decade or so. These are likely to include changes in the nature of academic disciplines, causing them to need either more or less space to undertake the same quantity of teaching and research as now. Another will be changed pedagogic approaches, affecting the size of student groups, the frequency with which they meet, and the type of space they need. The third set of factors is managerial, covering issues of institutional organization, structure and methods such as changes to the length of the teaching day or year, space allocation methods, and technological changes (in IT, particularly) (p. 10).

For JISC in the same year (JISC 2006), research indicated that an educational building is an expensive long-term resource and as a consequence the design of its individual spaces needs to be:

- flexible – to accommodate both current and evolving pedagogies
- future-proofed – to enable space to be re-allocated and reconfigured
- bold – to look beyond tried and tested technologies and pedagogies
- creative – to energize and inspire learners and tutors
- supportive – to develop the potential of all learners
- enterprising – to make each space capable of supporting different purposes.

'A learning space should be able to motivate learners and promote learning as an activity, support collaborative as well as formal practice, provide a personalized and inclusive environment, and be flexible in the face of changing needs' (ibid.: 3).

The Scottish Funding Council's study of learning spaces, carried out by AMA architects and the haa design consultancy (SFC 2006), argued that we are now in

> the fourth phase in the evolution of buildings for tertiary education. The earliest was the inception of universities, communities of scholars integrated into the urban fabric in centres such as Oxford, Cambridge, St. Andrews, Glasgow, Aberdeen and Edinburgh. Redbrick universities of the nineteenth century were the second phase. The third was the post-war creation of campus environments. Now is the period of expanded access to education, lifelong learning and pedagogical changes from a teaching-based culture to a student-centred learning environment for student 'consumers' who take a more pro-active role in shaping their education than earlier generations.
>
> (p. 6)

The report identifies seven types of learning space that have evolved, been reshaped or designed specifically to respond to this widespread change:

- Group teaching and learning. Lecture rooms and classrooms form a large component of the HE and FE estate and will continue to dominate – but the traditional format of these spaces is being transformed to incorporate multiple learning modes. Flexible furniture arrangements will be needed to accommodate groups of varying sizes, using varying layouts, preferably in square rather than rectangular rooms (the former being more adaptable).

- Simulated environments. Active modes – learning by doing. Practical learning can take place in technological subjects requiring space for observation as well as for performing the task in hand.

- Immersive environments. Virtual representations play an important role in drawing learners into contact with complex information – in real time from another location or from prepared sources. These can be HIVEs (highly interactive virtual environments), with advanced ICT – possible in many subjects but more likely to be found aligned within scientific or technological studies.

- Peer-to-peer environments and social learning spaces. Spaces to facilitate the positive effects of being in a learning group that is part of a learning community. Settings where informal learning can take place (in cyber cafes, for example).

- Learning clusters. Groups of learning spaces designed for a range of learning modes, building on acknowledged benefits of using multiple learning modes to reinforce understanding. Traditional clusters include large group learning spaces and small seminar rooms. Newer clusters incorporate interactive and group learning spaces and social learning spaces as well as more traditional lecture halls and classrooms (though with enhanced technology).

- Individual learning spaces. Effective learning usually involves time in active, solo study and writing or creation mode – typically in library areas, computer rooms and study bedrooms.

- External spaces. Outside space, and particularly space between buildings, plays an important role in aiding learning. Wireless broadband provision and microclimate design can extend the use of these areas.

Three of these spatial types – group learning, peer-to-peer and social learning, learning clusters – were examined in detail in four case studies drawn from John Wheatley College (FE), the University of Strathclyde, Edinburgh's Telford College (FE) and the Saltire Centre, Glasgow Caledonian University. In each case the success of the building or campus in rising to the challenges of a specific spatial type was assessed, with the results feeding into a summary of recommendations for creating good learning environments and funding mechanisms to achieve this outcome, along with certain more general predictions by space type (SFC 2006: 33–42, 44–45).

The threats and challenges to higher education were highlighted by Alexandra den Heijer in 2011, Dutch in context but applying internationally (Den Heijer 2011a). In particular she cited problems emerging from an ageing and poorly maintained educational estate, the impact of rapidly increasing global student numbers – an increase from about 100 million to 200 million students by 2025 (OECD 2009). She states that the future university campus will have to be flexible enough to accommodate a population that is less predictable in size and more diverse in character and notes the 'importance of the campus for the university's performance – positively or negatively influencing production, attractiveness and competiveness in an international market for knowledge workers – is confirmed by networks of campus managers all over the world, by rapidly growing universities as well as universities that struggle with decline or quality issues (Wiewel and Perry 2008; Perry 2009)' (Den Heijer 2011a: 34).

Den Heijer suggested that the major trends are:

- increased sharing of space and less space allocated to individual territory

- provision of less mono-functional and more multifunctional space (to intensify space use)

- shift from quantity of space to quality of space – move towards occupying less floor area but more intensively used, with increased quality of fit-out

- increased place independency with ICT developments allowing students and employees to study and work wherever they want – the best and most meaningful places for them

- increased re-use of existing buildings rather than the construction of new facilities – linked to sustainability goals and the trade of quantity for quality of space

- reducing the footprint on campus – setting the example for a new generation. The increased use of the campus and individual buildings as core elements of the university's branding strategy and identity

- increased partnering with other institutions in higher education and related businesses as well as leisure, retail and cultural institutions who are willing to share space use, management tasks and ownership.

Performance of higher education facilities in the UK is monitored in an annual report for the Higher Education Funding Council for England (HFCE) by Estate Management Statistics (EMS), which shares estates information among UK higher education institutions with the declared aim of empowering them to improve the management of the physical infrastructure (HEFCE 2011). The most up-to-date data set was collated during the period 2009–10 and covers the 2008–9 financial year, incorporating data from 160 higher education institutions in the UK. It highlights five different aspects of estates performance: institutional sustainability, space efficiency, condition and functional suitability, environmental performance, and residential ratios. Case studies look at key performance indicators (KPIs) which vary year on year: the 2010 report selected:

- building condition as a percentage of gross internal area (GIA) condition A and B

- functional suitability as a percentage of GIA grade 1 and 2

- GIA per student and staff FTE

- energy consumption per student and staff FTE.

The report's analysis makes it clear that 'overall, the UK's higher education estate is now far better able to withstand the effects of significant change than it was 10 years ago' (HEFCE 2011: 3). Institutions are becoming more profitable despite above-inflation cost increases in 'some elements of property cost, such as utilities',

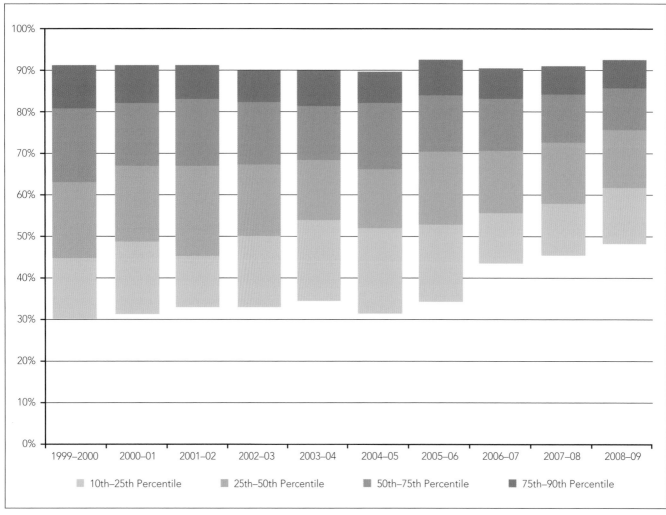

Figure 3.2 Percentage of UK HE space (gross internal area) in 'good condition'. Source: EMS (2010:19)

unprecedented levels of capital investment have resulted in 'major improvements in the quality of the estate, and space is being used more efficiently' (p. 3). The report acknowledges the importance of quality in attracting and retaining students 'particularly from overseas', and also – which is more to our thrust here – 'in meeting the needs of teaching, learning and research' (p. 18). Figure 3.2 shows the percentage of space (gross internal area) in 'good condition' for all UK HE institutions over the past ten years. The overall condition has improved significantly, with the median percentage of space in good condition rising from 63 per cent in 1999–2000 to 76 per cent in 2008–9. The overall functional suitability has also improved significantly over the same period (Figure 3.3), with the average institution reporting over 83 per cent functionally suitable compared with 66 per cent in 1999–2000 (pp. 18–20). The report points out that this is particularly

impressive because 'functional suitability is not fixed; space needs to align with the evolving requirements of students and changing styles of teaching, particularly the transition from traditional "chalk and talk" to more flexible and interactive styles' (p. 20).

BEYOND THE INSTITUTION

Perhaps it is inevitable that school and higher education buildings – spaces formally dedicated to full-time learning – should have received far more attention than the spaces (and places) not designed or procured for learning in any systematic way, but increasingly used for that purpose: meeting rooms in the workplace, specialized conference and meeting venues, entire training facilities

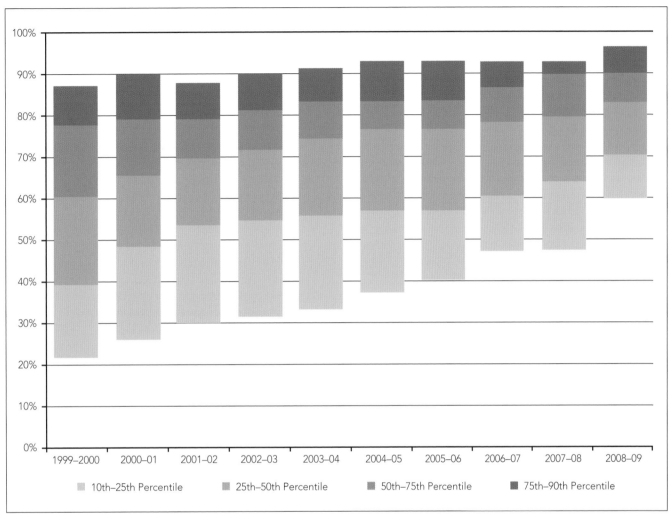

Figure 3.3 Overall functional suitability of HE space. Source: EMS (2010:20)

for industry, private colleges for professional and vocational quali-fications, public libraries, museums and galleries. These are what the OECD would characterize as 'non-formal' learning spaces (OECD 2010).

Where formal learning, OECD argues, is 'always organized and struc-tured and has learning objectives' and informal learning is 'never organized, has no set objectives in terms of learning outcomes and is never intentional from the learner's standpoint', non-formal learning is:

> by general consensus ... rather organized and can have learning objectives. This is an intermediate concept, which takes account of the fact that such learning can occur at the initiative of the learner but can also happen as the by-product of more organized activities, whether or not those activities

have learning objectives. In some countries, the entire sector of adult learning falls into this category. In others, most adult learning remains formal.

(p. 2)

A number of countries, observes the OECD, are putting recognition of these activities and places at the top of their policy agenda – 'and the time has come for a thorough evaluation of what it entails' (p. 2). What 'it' – the recognition – entails can largely be accounted for in terms of the professional workplace, the widening academic community and the extension of adult lifelong learning through the exploitation of ad hoc public and private spaces and a better understanding of the new role of existing cultural spaces such as libraries, museums and galleries in the whole landscape of learning.

Lorna Unwin (2009) insists that since workplace learning 'arises from, and is embedded within, everyday workplace activity and social relations of production' and is therefore extremely difficult to define and measure, all three phenomena must be examined together. Her conclusion is that to improve learning 'we need to improve the conditions of work': one way is to reconfigure the way work is organized and

> the design of workspaces to enable much greater team working, collective learning and sharing of expertise. The importance of how workspace is designed has been shown to have a considerable impact on the quality of learning environments [though she does not indicate where], yet in further education colleges in England, staffrooms are being removed as buildings are configured to provide as much space as possible for learners, whilst teachers are required to use 'hot desks' and to regard classrooms and workshops as their sole workspace.
>
> (p. 4)

The academic community has come to play a larger part in professional education, increasingly relying on it as an important source of revenue, with conference and short course university experience maximizing the efficient use of university residences outside term time. But academic institutions partnering with other organizations have to be mindful of the possible effect of the partnerships on their academic reputation. In 2008 in the UK, Buckinghamshire New University agreed to provide work-based, degree-level education for bed retailer Dreams (THE 2008) and triggered articles in the press with headlines such as 'Bucks New University to offer degree in selling beds' (Bucks Free Press 2012) and 'Selling beds is now degree course' (BBC 2008). And the London School of Economics and Political Science (LSE) found its reputation seriously at risk over its multilevel relationship with the former government of Libya that included a £2.2 million partnership to provide training to senior Libya civil servants (BBC 2011a).

Adult lifelong learning can be seen as part of the great tradition of people coming together in new forms of organization to find new subjects for learning and in the process refreshing the relationship between learning and democratic action. In the UK, the Levellers in the seventeenth century, coffee house debates in the eighteenth century, the temperance movement in the nineteenth, all led to new forms of association, developing and enriching people's learning and their quality of life. This has continued through the mutual improvement societies and independent lending libraries of the nineteenth century, the women's movement and the green alliances of more recent times – all the way to Tent City University set up by the Occupy London protesters in London in October 2011 (Figures 3.4 and 3.5) (Schuller and Watson 2009; THE 2012).

A 2009 government White Paper (DIUS 2009a), *The Learning Revolution*, emphasized the historical importance of this tradition, which in many cases eventually led to structured organizations such as:

> Trades Unions, cooperative societies, women's institutes and non-conformist religious groups [that] were formed first for people to address challenges their members shared in common, and grew to offer a wide range of opportunities for learning and development for the communities they served. The National Trust and the Ramblers' Association were formed to offer people living in confined city streets access to country air. The Workers' Educational Association and University of the Third Age emerged to provide stimulus and challenge for people with time and curiosity aplenty. The breadth and vibrancy of voluntary and community organizations are testament to the resilience of that tradition. All play a role in offering practical learning in democracy, as well as opportunities for people to develop skills, knowledge understanding and capacity, and to contribute to the wider welfare of society.
>
> (p. 48)

In 2009, the report of a National Institute of Adult Continuing Education (NIACE) inquiry into the future for lifelong learning (Schuller and Watson 2009) made ten recommendations for a lifelong learning strategy and identified several systemic blocks to achieving this – only one of which – 'inadequate infrastructure: buildings, technologies and services are not well integrated' (p. 4) – addresses space issues, though 'spaces for local groups to engage in learning' (p. 9) form part of their suggested local learning exchanges (LLEs).

The introduction of formal education programmes in museums, galleries and other cultural institutions is relatively recent, although education, in its broadest sense, has always been central to the role of the museum, as George Hein points out: 'Museum education, the deliberate interpretation of museum objects for pedagogic purposes, is as old as museums' (Hein 2006: 161). An inquiry into the future for lifelong learning by the Museums, Libraries and Archives Council (MLA) detailed ways in which museums, libraries and archives contribute to learning and called for their 'collections, spaces and learning programmes to be integrated into a new joined-up framework that connects formal and informal learning providers' (Schuller and Watson 2009: 4).

The report looked at four ways in which these resources could contribute to a new lifelong framework: opening up spaces to create more opportunities, acting as the backbone of a lifelong learning sector, ensuring they are truly universal by filling gaps in

Tent City University – a pop-up seat of learning outside St Paul's Cathedral, London: 'questioning of knowledge, discussion, intellectual freedom' free of 'market forces'. But how much does it have in common with a structured course of learning at a traditional university?

Source: THE (2012: 35)

Figure 3.4–5 Occupy Tent University

audiences and reaching out, and developing the core role of public libraries as local information hubs in their communities. The report sees these developments as part of the learning revolution called for by the 2009 White Paper of that name (DIUS 2009), connecting spaces and making them widely available: 'Museums, libraries and archives are (largely) publicly funded, based in local communities and open to everyone. They are ideally placed to support people to pursue learning throughout their lives. ... New approaches are emerging through the co-location of libraries with health services, children's centres and one-stop shops, but The Learning Revolution requires a change in thinking' (p. 7).

Suggested innovations include:

- a learning continuum stretching beyond blockbuster exhibitions and reading groups to include third sector, health and self-organized learning partners

- a shift in thinking from being gatekeepers to being facilitators, opening up our publicly funded spaces and resources to people and communities

- integrating the lifelong learning offer available in museums, libraries and archives with that available from other local learning providers, including further education, higher education and community learning providers – ensuring digitized museum, library and archive resources, funded through public investment, are used to their maximum

- taking a harder look at who is using their services and who is not – particularly young and, in an aging society, older people – the Department for Culture, Media and Sport (DCMS) Taking Part survey indicates that participation in culture drops sharply at 75 years of age

- building on the skill of librarians in handling information and establishing them in the role of local information hubs

- signposting learners to opportunities, whether these are offered by HE, FE, local authorities, third sector, private providers or self-organized learning groups (p. 7).

The challenge for the future is to find new and financially sustainable ways for museums and galleries to continue to develop their involvement in all levels of education – to move away from the notion of the annual school museum visit towards one where museums and galleries are part of an integrated network of learning spaces used by schools, colleges and universities as a fundamental part of their learning and teaching approach.

PART 2
Innovating space

CHAPTER 4
Schools

INTRODUCTION

In 1966, Karl Otto (1966) observed that schools 'are not only institutions for instruction, but at the same time visible symbols of educational conceptions of their time'. This becomes graphically manifest if we look now at the design of the UK schools that finally brought mass education to the population: E.R. Robson's Victorian take on Queen Anne architecture. Such buildings are evidently not designed in isolation: they are the more or less finely tuned response, as we saw in Chapter 2, to global trends and forces, national policies and local funding decisions, and the personal beliefs of a headteacher or staff of a school. Designers of physical learning environments must 'look to societal expectations and emerging learning theories to determine the possible use of school facilities in the future. Designing with those trends in mind will help create facilities that accommodate change more easily' (Akinsanmi 2008: 4).

Innovation in response to those developing trends can be inflected in a number of ways. In the first instance, it can be as a direct response to government-driven design codes, regulations and building bulletins that aim to enforce or recommend key design principles such as the size of a classroom. In addition, there is a huge variety of organizations providing support and advice – these include but are not limited to the Organization for Economic Cooperation and Development (OECD), the National Clearing House for Educational Facilities (NCHEH), the British Council for School Environments (BCSE), the Design Council and the Commission for Architecture and the Built Environment (CABE). Innovation can also be traced to the output of the designers themselves – organizations and individuals who have worked closely with school design. It can spring from the professional experience of teachers, designers, architects and researchers. And it has undoubtedly emerged from a period of fundamental questioning about the nature of schools, of learning, of teaching.

Sometimes this questioning has faced head-on the issue of what a school is, and how it should function. Participants in the debate about the nature of future schools have during the last two decades variously approached the subject in terms of metaphor (David Thornburg), learning modalities or patterns that represent the foundation for building creative and innovative citizens (Prakash

Nair, Randy Fielding and Jeffery Lackney) and as a bridge from curriculum to pedagogy to spatial concepts (Kenn Fisher).

Metaphor
The educationalist David Thornburg differentiated the ways students learn by using the metaphor of mankind's earliest learning environments: the campfire, the watering hole and the cave. The campfire was where stories were passed on from elders to younger generations, who in turn would become elders and pass on the same stories: stories have always been a powerful way of learning, delivering messages and aiding comprehension of difficult concepts by wrapping them up in entertainment. The watering hole was where mankind gathered and exchanged information with peers from other tribes and places. Caves were places of reflection where mankind would be isolated to gain special insights.

Thornburg found traditional school spaces wanting in their supply of these settings:

> Students have experienced the campfire of the traditional classroom setting and relied on the playground for their watering hole. Quiet time for reflection, when made available, takes place in libraries or study halls, or is deferred until the student goes home at the end of the day. The watering hole is being brought into classrooms today through the medium of cooperative learning ... tragically, the hands-on application of what has been taught is rarely found. This application goes beyond 'homework' to the construction of new projects or learning based on the things the student (presumably) now knows how to do.
>
> (2007)

One problem with these metaphors is that the use of place names can give the impression that discrete spaces need to be created for each; in fact, a small table in a nook can be a cave for individual reflection, a watering hole discussion space for two students or even campfire space for a small group.

Modalities
American education consultants and architects Prakash Nair, Randy Fielding and Jeffery Lackney expanded this concept to take in teaching (campfire), collaboration (watering hole) and reflection

(cave), emphasizing that some settings are specific to these, and others support multiple aspects (Nair et al. 2005, 2009). In their book *The Language of School Design,* inspired by earlier work by Christopher Alexander on pattern language and design, they developed a series of patterns and what they called a 'common design vocabulary' which they believed would allow all stakeholders in school design to communicate more effectively. Rather than designing to meet the requirements of the curriculum, their goal was to create an architectural and design framework that would 'honor as constant the ergonomic principles that relate to our development as human beings' (Nair et al. 2005, 2009: 15).

Included within this is the principle that learning communities should not exceed 150 since beyond this size the nature of the community will change substantially and feelings of anonymity will increase exponentially (Nair et al. 2005, 2009: 15).

They aimed to produce a spatial model for twenty-first century schools that would support 'different students (of varying ages) learn different things from different people in different places in different ways and at different times' (Nair et al. 2005: 27) and outlined 18 'learning modalities' (Figure 4.1) which they claim represent crucial foundations for building creative and innovative citizens who can compete in the twenty-first-century knowledge economy (Fielding and Nair 2005: 19–20).

They believe only two or three of these are supported in a traditional classroom model. 'A traditional cells-and-bells design will come up short against the above list because it is primarily set up for the lecture format,' note the authors (ibid.: 20), before highlighting other designs and design patterns that support additional modalities: flexible, multifunctional spaces.

Nair and Fielding's work has influenced the work of schools architects around the world and helped create a common language for school staff and designers, resulting in a shift away from pure classroom-based school design.

One criticism that could be levelled, however, is that the list of modalities is a large and complex one that covers and mixes both pedagogical choices and curriculum approaches. One-on-one learning, for example, and team collaborative work are highly pedagogical: they refer to the specific activity of learning. Project-based learning, naturalist learning, social learning and art-based learning are more concerned with the curriculum structure and approach.

Making the link between pedagogy and space

In early 2005, Australian educational planner Kenn Fisher produced a document for the Department of Education and Training in Victoria, Australia, 'Linking pedagogy and space' (Fisher 2005) in

1	Independent study
2	Peer tutoring
3	Team collaborative work (2–6 students)
4	One-on-one learning with a teacher
5	Lecture format – teacher or expert on the stage
6	Project-based learning
7	Technology with mobile computers
8	Distance learning
9	Internet-based research
10	Student presentation
11	Performance or music based learning
12	Seminar-style instruction
13	Community service learning
14	Naturalist learning
15	Social/emotional learning
16	Art-based learning
17	Storytelling
18	Learning by building

Source: Nair et al. (2005: 19–20)

Figure 4.1 Eighteen modalities of learning

which he attempts to make the link from curriculum to pedagogy to spatial concepts. Published online, this document became a highly successful reference for many educational planners around the world, creating a simpler model that again attempted to focus designers first and foremost on the activity of learning.

The document draws on the work of Lennie Scott-Webber, who had previously linked environmental behaviour research to the design of learning space in higher education:

> In order to develop a working model [for explaining person/place needs] we must first determine the intended behaviors (e.g. knowledge sharing activity) in order to plan environments supporting those behavioral requirements ... The archetype list that follows includes five intended behavioral considerations with primary functions defined for planning purposes.
>
> (Scott-Webber 2004: 41)

Scott-Webber describes a list of five 'environments' that, in similar fashion to David Thornburg, aim to support learners in the knowledge age, in particular in developing skills suited to learning 'on the job' to support the long-term employability and flexibility of workers. These environments are areas where knowledge can be:

- delivered: information is imparted in a formal method so that others may learn

- applied: an organization puts knowledge into practice

- created: organizations create, innovate and implement new ideas

- communicated: people exchange information, formally and informally, verbally and non-verbally

- used for decision making: information is distilled and judgments are made and acted upon.

Scott-Webber develops a series of icons, behavioural premises and process steps, outlining the key attributes of each archetype. There are parallels with Thornburg's metaphors, in particular in specifying different settings for transmission of knowledge (the campfire), and communicating it informally (the watering hole). We can also make a criticism similar to that levelled at Thornburg's work: that the types, being so focused on the environment, may preclude the combination of different archetypes in one setting. In *Linking Pedagogy and Space*, Fisher sidesteps this by recasting the environments as 'pedagogical activities': delivering, applying, creating, communicating and decision making.

He then develops a series of 'settings' and spaces, such as a student home base, that have a particular purpose (such as space for an individual to personalize, work and study), and is linked to one or multiple pedagogies (such as applying, creating and communicating).

These form a useful basis for planning the types of spaces that a school could include, and they are notably specialized towards specific purposes, with no 'one size fits all' spaces such as a classroom. Instead, Fisher recommends presentation spaces for the transmission of knowledge, combined with group and individual workspaces. These spaces are then 'clustered' together in a range of combinations to provide a variety of patterns of learning space.

This framework is a highly accessible one, and many of Fisher's later applications of these ideas in his own school designs are innovative and provide interesting learning environments. The question, however, is whether these archetypes represent a robust enough approach to cover the full range of pedagogical possibilities.

The need for flexibility

More than a decade ago the Scottish government set in train the process to determine what was working well and what needed to change in school education – the 2002 National Debate on Education leading to the 2003 establishment of the Curriculum

Review Group and the publication in 2004 of *A Curriculum for Excellence* (Education Scotland 2004).

In 2007, a Scottish government publication, 'Building excellence: exploring the implications of the Curriculum for Excellence for school building', explored how new and refurbished schools in Scotland can best 'meet the needs of students and teachers working within Curriculum for Excellence, and find opportunities within the curriculum for learning from the surrounding spaces' (Scottish Government 2007: 2).

In this publication, John Worthington from DEGW makes the point that a sustainable building shell is 'generic' in its configuration – it adapts to different teaching approaches, while providing a sequence of spaces that inspire the user to reconfigure the layout to meet their needs (Worthington 2007: 14). He cites the work of the Dutch architect Herman Hertzberger – including his Montessori school at Delft (1960) – that created standard repeatable classroom units that when combined made a unique and memorable place.

A 2008 publication from the British Council for School Environments (BCSE) – *Family Guide to School Environments* – aimed to help schools, governors and parents find out about schools 'and to prompt thinking about which aspects of the school environment are most important to you and/or your child' (BCSE 2008: 1). Teaching methods, it noted, have become much more flexible and ways of learning more varied and this requires classrooms and other learning spaces to be used in much more varied and flexible ways. The authors recommend that all classrooms and learning spaces should be a good size, light, bright, warm, airy and have acoustics appropriate to the task in hand. Learning spaces should be age-appropriate and allow students the space to work in groups as well as individually. Every student should be able to see and hear their teacher – and their co-students – when they speak to the class as a whole (p. 6). They also stressed the importance of good quality furniture in the classroom:

> Over the time that they attend school, children spend, in total, around 15,000 hours (that's just under two years) sitting down. Despite this, a lot of school furniture that's considered fine for school children is of such a low standard that it could actually be illegal for adults to use at work. 13 per cent of children aged 10–16 experience significant, recurrent back pain. Good school furniture is important, and where it's available, reduces the incidences of this.

> A recent study showed that switching to adjustable school desks and chairs improves students' sitting posture instantly and also, over time, the way they stand. Children who work on

sloping surfaces and sit on well-designed chairs, behave and achieve better as well as enjoying their work more.

(p. 6)

The Senses of Place: Building Excellence project aimed to develop aspirations for the design of school buildings and their grounds in the context of Scotland's Curriculum for Excellence. The goal was to demonstrate how well-designed learning environments could support the delivery of the new curriculum and changes in teaching methodologies. The project explored how school spaces could be developed to better support learning, and focused on the design process and the value of involving children and young people in school design from an early stage.

The project 'was not working within a time scale that involved real build projects' (Lighthouse 2008: 6). In other words, none of the schemes developed during the project was actually built. The authors of the report state that the process used for the project should be employed during the initial visioning stages of either a new build or refurbishment project and they stressed the fact that the co-design process and the involvement of children in itself contributed to the Curriculum for Excellence's goals of creating responsible citizens, effective contributors, confident individuals and successful learners (Lighthouse 2008: 40–1).

One of the themes being explored in the project was the creation of teaching spaces in nursery and primary education to support active learning and purposeful, well-planned play. The designers working with the school felt a rectangular classroom could not accommodate all the functions asked for by teachers. Instead they developed a hexagonal space that created additional indoor and outdoor areas that fulfilled the additional functions required. The learning spaces they created blurred the division between inside and outside and introduced display areas, technology and a mobile storage unit to subdivide a room (ibid.: 54).

Another team created a design exemplar for recently built secondary schools that would enhance science education in the context of the new Scottish Curriculum for Excellence. The brief included the desire to create unconventional spaces 'that can change with the times, with the flexibility to move things and use them in new ways – tables, cupboards, display walls, even mezzanines'. Users would want to experience science in the classroom using virtual reality, planetarium projections, 3D glasses, or laptop computers, and they would also want hands-on experiences 'with exciting, unusual experiments involving animals, plants, different materials, and "big explosions"'. They also wanted to create a healthy space to reflect in comfort – a creative, confident, bright, and colourful space where the temperature and ventilation can be controlled. 'It should be an uncluttered roomy place, laid out so that people can

talk and relate to each other – with space for beanbags for talking about science, as well as all the "hidden spaces" for preparation and storage' (ibid.: 69).

This initiative was followed in Scotland by the Changing Classrooms project which explored how redesigned classroom spaces could support the delivery of the Curriculum for Excellence that focuses on the total educational experience for every child and young person including increased emphasis on interdisciplinary projects and learning. The project worked with eight schools to create exemplar learning environments that combined good functionality and flexibility in learning and teaching spaces to maximize learning opportunities including the provision of ICT spaces and reflecting seasonal changes in the use of indoor and outdoor learning environments. Immediate and longer-term opportunities for the transformation of learning spaces were identified for each of the eight case study schools (Sims nd).

In 2009, a publication by Salford Centre for Research and Innovation in the Built and Human Environment (SCRI), *Optimal Primary School Environments* (Barrett and Zhang 2009), emphasized the link between learning and space:

> Considerable evidence shows that there is an explicit relationship between the physical characteristics of school buildings, and the spaces within them, and educational outcomes. Poor school conditions make it more difficult for teachers to teach and pupils to learn. Every effort should therefore be made in the design stage to create the ideal conditions for learning to take place. However, a variety of teachers with specific and very different groups of pupils will subsequently inhabit and inherit these spaces. Each teacher and each group of pupils is different, and teachers must develop the generalized environment for specific purposes and groups.

(p. iv)

In this publication, Peter Barrett and Yufan Zhang seek to frame the multitude of opportunities during the design phase for new school projects within 'a few major design principles derived from the basics of how people experience spaces in response to the environmental data they gain through their senses and synthesise in their brains. This leads to a focus on naturalness, individuali-sation and level of stimulation' (p. iv).

Their view is that schools face a major challenge in balancing the need for individualization and the desire to create inspiring buildings with functional spaces that are appropriate for new educational developments and new technologies but adaptable enough to cater for the pupils' changing needs in the future. They suggest that 'individualization' as a key design principle can play out in two ways: particularization and personalization. 'Particularisation concerns accommodating the functional needs of very specific types of users, for example learning and way-finding in the context of age and physical requirements. Personalisation concerns an individual's preferences owing to their personal life experiences of spaces' (p. 14).

Barrett and Zhang do not believe it is possible to create a plan that will work forever: they make the observation, however, that three key issues seem to link school design with considerations of individualization, and provide a framework within which change can take place. The issues are:

- choice – concerned with the fit between individual personality and the physical environment, which consists of the mental process of judging the size, shape, height of alternative spaces and how appropriate they are for the task

- flexibility – which refers to designs that can adapt when changes occur, sustaining or increasing the possibilities for personalizing space and delivering value in a timely and cost-effective manner

- connection – referring in the main to the relationship between spaces within the building, but also between the school and the neighbourhood within the community. In either case issues arise of distinctive personality, easily identifiable destinations and the opportunity for inclusion (p. 14).

Design and performance

A 2010 report by the Commission for Architecture and the Built Environment (CABE), 'Creating excellent primary schools: guide for clients' (CABE 2010a), also stressed the importance of good design: 'Good school design matters. It is about the education and life chances of young people. Evidence shows a clear link between well-designed schools and pupil performance and behaviour. Good design alone doesn't raise standards, but bad design impacts on the quality of teaching, the aspirations and self-perception of pupils, and the sustainability of a school' (p. 5). A key study (Figures 4.2 and 4.3) describes the successful refurbishment of Canning Street Primary, an inner-city Newcastle, UK primary school, as part of the BSF programme – creating a calm and distinctive open-plan environment.

The report looks at the implications raised by the Department for Children, Schools and Families' goal of educational transformation that included the delivery of creative, flexible designs that support the best thinking on teaching and learning, and effective use of new technologies and that produce places for learning that are exciting, flexible, healthy, safe, secure and environmentally sustainable:

School buildings will have to become more accessible and adaptable for community use, the change in learning patterns and the implications of increased ICT use. At the same time the buildings still need to be durable, and secure but welcoming.

(p. 20)

To support the personalized learning agenda at that time, CABE states that the size, shape and furnishing of classrooms should be sufficiently flexible to meet a variety of teaching needs, additional spaces should be provided for smaller groups and individual learning, both with and without adults, and outdoor spaces in the school grounds can also provide space for small group and individual learning.

The design of future primary schools was also the subject of a research project by the Economic and Social Research Institute in Dublin. 'Designing primary schools for the future' was published in 2010 (Darmody et al. 2010) and explored the perceptions of students, teachers and key stakeholders of the interaction between school design and teaching and learning in the Irish context, specifically focusing on primary schools.

The research found that class size and classroom density were seen as of even greater importance than school size. Smaller classes were seen as allowing for the use of more active learning methods and for more individual attention to pupils. In contrast, larger class sizes were seen as contributing to more directive, teacher-focused methods.

In some of the older schools in the study, restricted space was seen as constraining the range of teaching methodologies, particularly group work, while in the newer school, staff and pupils were more satisfied with the space available for teaching and for storage. The participants in the study felt the ideal classroom layout comprises seating in small groups with various activity areas within the room for different learning activities and with the flexibility to move furniture if required. Space constraints in older schools meant that many pupils were seated in rows facing the teacher, thus hindering the possibility of group work (p. 40).

Participants in the study generally did not feel that ICT was well integrated into day-to-day teaching and learning in the primary classroom (p. 45). As well as providing more computers in the classroom, the 'stakeholders mentioned that the use of interactive whiteboards is becoming more common in schools and suggested that these (along with projectors) should be automatically built into new classrooms' (p. 45). The report stresses the importance of looking at how the technology is actually used and cites Smith et al. (2006) who found that in the UK the use of interactive whiteboards has been accompanied by an increased use of whole-class teaching, which suggests a continued reliance on traditional didactic pedagogy.

Canning Street Primary School is a 1970s building that had been used very successfully, but was starting to create limitations for teaching as the class bays were too small and there were overheating problems in some areas caused by large roof lights. The school was extensively refurbished by architects Parsons Brinckerhoff as part of the Newcastle Building Schools for the Future (BSF) programme, and re-opened in September 2008.

The teaching space now consists of a single, very large curved area with no fixed partitions in the centre. A central circulation route runs the full length of the space, separated from the teaching areas by low storage cupboards. Behind this is a shared area used by all the classes in a variety of ways. Beyond this are the classroom bays, divided only by fixed screens that do not reach fully to the ceiling. Toilets are in small extensions beyond the classroom bays. On the other side of the circulation route, there are various group teaching rooms and a library area.

The staff adapt the layout to suit individual lessons. For subjects such as maths and literacy, the teachers tend to teach their own class within their own bay, and the teaching assistants will support small groups within the class where necessary. For other subjects, there may be a more thematic approach, and the year group is split up into smaller groups involved in two or three different activities, making use of the shared space as well as the classroom area.

The authors of the CABE report state that this method of teaching works well at Canning Street, and is popular with staff. They find the open plan arrangement supportive, and it is particularly appropriate for newly qualified teachers who can work in a co-operative environment and learn from more experienced colleagues. While 'the design of the school and the way it is used can look anarchic, and some express concern about the potential for disturbance from noise. However, the reality is a calm environment where learning is enjoyed and where older children provide support for younger ones, and welcome new pupils. It is also apparent that the unique design makes a significant contribution to the inclusive character of the school.'

Source: CABE (2010: 17)

Figure 4.2 Canning Street Primary School, Newcastle upon Tyne

Figure 4.3 Canning Street Primary School, Newcastle upon Tyne

The overall conclusion was that spaces within schools should be flexible (different rooms/areas can be used for a number of activities) to allow for a variety of methodologies as well as changes in teaching practices in the future and that there should be sufficient room to allow for a range of methods in day-to-day teaching and learning, including group work, pair work, individual work, play-based learning and use of ICT. Within the classroom there should also be sufficient space for different 'zones' and there should be space for display areas within the classroom and in communal areas of the school. Smaller rooms should be provided for learning support and English language teaching, which are well-designed and stimulating environments for children. They also stated that classroom furniture should be ergonomically designed to cater for the different age groups of pupils and for the fact that children are much larger now in primary schools than they would have been in the past (Darmody et al. 2010: 47–8). How much of this would have been news to the compilers of nineteenth-century school pattern books?

CORE TEACHING SPACES

The classroom for 25–30 pupils remains one of the most commonly provided learning spaces in the world. Filled predominantly with re-arrangeable desks and chairs, with a board – interactive or otherwise – at the front and a desk for the teacher, the origins of the classroom can be traced back to the church with pews facing the pastor at the pulpit. This design allows the teacher to make eye-contact with all the students and the students to see a screen or board at the front of the room, and it facilitates traditional teacher–student delivery and questioning, or 'teacher-centred' teaching, but in order to talk to each other the students need to either turn in their seats or address the back of a fellow-student's neck (Atherton 2011).

What is the future of these currently ubiquitous spaces? Mäkitalo-Siegl et al. (2010) ask 'Will classrooms still exist 20 years from now?' They note that a quick glance at the history of pedagogic practices reveals that the classroom has scarcely evolved over a period of many years and ask whether the traditional classroom is intrinsically outdated or has it rather survived the test of time because it is already self-reconfigurable and has been adapted for many contexts of use:

> Do we even need a classroom any more? Do we need a teacher in the classroom? What do we teach and what do we want the pupils to learn? What kinds of knowledge and skills will be required in the future? These are some of the questions we should bear in mind when thinking about the classroom of the future.

Over the last few decades, our understanding of learning and the conditions under which it is facilitated has substantially improved. In most contemporary theories, learning is conceived as a constructive and social activity, as a result of which the roles of the teacher and the learner within the classroom have been redefined.

(p. 1)

Classroom evolution

It is clear that there has been a technological revolution in the classroom for both learners and teachers, initially marked by the inclusion of a small number of fixed terminals, giving way in more recent years to laptops as the price of a laptop dipped below that of a fixed PC, and more recently still to mobile and tablet technology; for example, to replace textbooks and preserve digital archives of studio progress (Hu 2011). Technology has begun to be seen as the twenty-first-century pencil case (Galloway 2007), extending the range of pedagogies available in a classroom setting – though not necessarily making an impact on the design of the classroom itself.

Stephen Harris (2010) believes that evolving notions of space can have a critical role in incorporating ICT-enabled pedagogical change into the core of classroom practice and that the area that presents the greatest challenge – and has arguably lagged behind in institutional planning across the world – is creating or transforming the physical spaces so that they provide better support for learning in a twenty-first-century environment of constant change.

While acknowledging the rapid developments in technologies that can be used to enhance and support learning, Mäkitalo-Siegl et al. (2010: 1) state that it appears that the majority of the classrooms in today's schools and universities remain untouched by these developments and that multidisciplinary efforts to design the classroom of the future are scarce.

They point out that as long ago as 1987 Resnick indicated that school environments differed from most everyday environments in continuing to highlight individual work (p. 2). More than twenty years later – according to Mäkitalo-Siegl et al. – educational spaces continue to provide little support for more student-centred processes of teaching and learning such as collaborative learning (p. 2).

> Meaningful and efficient collaboration requires a specific place which formally or informally enhances collaborative learning. In opening up new channels for collaboration, technology is also stretching the limits of physical space. With the help of new technology, collaboration and community thinking is no longer limited to the inside of the classroom but can also occur in a number of other places.

(p. 3)

Andreas Schratzenstaller (2010) states the need for a fundamental rethink of the classroom even more forcefully:

> The pressure of change is on the classroom; it is utterly unthinkable that it can continue to be built, structured and equipped as it has been for all these decades. It is rather grotesque that societies which essentially depend on and intently strive for innovation and progress should try to source the power and energy for their innovative and progressive future from the physical and conceptual conditions of the educational mills of the 19th century.
>
> (p. 19)

He acknowledges that this is not to say there is been no innovation in classroom design over the last 200 years – he cites Gotthilf Salzmann's 1784 philanthropic school in Schnepfentel, Germany, which aimed to foster self-directed learning and to base tuition on sensual experience gained via contemplation and vivid experience (p. 28). And the open-air schools at the turn of the twentieth century included well-lit classrooms with plenty of fresh air, designed according to the new paradigm of learner-centred tuition.

But reviewing the relative failure of progressive school and classroom design in the twentieth century, Schratzenstaller concluded that 'the lessons to be learned from 20th century educational history are unpleasantly unequivocal: school reforms are all too rapidly held up by a profit-oriented rationale – in the 20th century, educational rhetoric and an actual willingness to invest in our children's future prove to be seriously at odds' (p. 33).

There has recently been a marked advance in spatial thinking related to school designs for the future (Harris 2010: 5): in the UK, the 2003 'Classrooms for the future' report argued that schools needed to be delightful and relaxing places to learn; to have spaces with flexibility to facilitate various patterns of group work; to have walls that opened up to the outside and roofs that opened up to the sky; to feel fresh, safe, and new; to provide a lot of natural light and fresh air (Gil 2009: 12).

This project included the construction of a series of innovative classrooms in schools across England. The pilots included sustainable centres of e-learning and environmental discovery; state-of-the-art ICT classrooms; and self-contained high-tech re-locatable buildings. As the 2003 report states in its opening pages, 'in the classroom of the future the learning environment will look and feel very different' (DfES 2003a).

Each of the pilot projects responded to the needs of the host school but the educational concepts of the Bedfordshire pilot are, to some extent, representative of the overall aspirations of the project.

The DfES followed up the Classrooms for the Future project with a set of exemplar designs: 'flexible spaces that could be used in traditional format or as a large open plan; social spaces; class-bases without doors; re-locatable "learning pods" for individual study; movable partition walls; play decks; mobile classrooms; technology-rich laboratories; and themed learning centres' (Gil 2009: 12).

The authors of the report note that some of the innovative spaces and furniture layouts shown in the exemplar designs would need to be tested thoroughly at the design stage. Flexible spaces created with moveable walls and sliding doors may cause acoustic insulation problems although they do state that the option of merging spaces can be useful for examinations at some times of the year.

Other exemplars in the report included the use of relocatable 'pods' for small group rooms, stores or similar. Here the authors felt that the pods helped to address the need for small group rooms to have an acoustic separation for use by assistants or as 'break-out' spaces for pupils with behavioural difficulties (DfES 2004: 14).

Many of the design teams believed that more open-plan arrangements would be more common in the future, and had developed learning areas that could provide a traditional arrangement, or could be used as larger rooms with smaller seminar rooms adjacent, following the higher education model, or even totally open plan. The authors again suggested caution and said that this is 'perhaps most likely to be in parts of the school rather than everywhere (for instance for GNVQ courses with a heavy use of ICT)' (p. 15).

Classrooms were clustered in groups of rooms rather than in more traditional linear arrangements along corridors. While user focus groups saw the advantages of the cluster layout – which clearly enhances a feeling of belonging for each class, whether as part of a year group, house group or department – the authors maintain their cautious stance by stating that classroom clusters 'may not address a common need for adaptability in a secondary school: the varying sizes of departments and even year groups. Even in clusters of six, a seventh classroom is inevitably "left out in the cold", with less links to the rest of the group than in a more traditional linear arrangement' (p. 17).

In an interview with Fast Company Design in 2010, Stephen Heppell observed that:

> regions and communities throughout the world are embracing and developing new 'ingredients' of learning: superclasses of 90 to 120 students; vertical learning groups; stage not age; schools within schools or 'Home Bases;' ... project-based

work; exhibition-based assessments; collaborative learning teams; mixed-age mentoring; children as teachers; teachers as learners; and so much more. Obviously, in a world where every culture, context and community is unique there will be no one-size-fits-all solution, however enlightened that solution might be.

(Le 2010)

Heppell has been working with the headteachers of several schools in Portland, Dorset, in the UK, who wanted to enhance the performance of their island community (Portland is a 6 km x 2.4 km island near Weymouth connected by a tombolo to the mainland). He is acting as lead sponsor for a new 'all through school from birth to university graduation' with students remaining in home bases of about 300 students throughout their time there.

Heppell states that he has a 'simple rule of three' for third millennium learning spaces: they must have:

- no more than three walls so that there is never full enclosure and the space is multifaceted rather than just open

- no fewer than three points of focus so that the 'stand-and-deliver' model gives way to increasingly varied groups learning and presenting together (which by the way requires a radical rethinking of furniture)

- the ability to accommodate three teachers/adults with their children. The old standard size of about 30 students in a box robbed children of so many effective practices; these larger spaces allow for better alternatives (Le 2010).

This sounds very innovative when compared with the traditional classroom that still predominates, but Stephen Downes (2012) from the National Research Council of Canada points out on his own blog that concepts such as open-plan learning, small groups and team teaching have all been around since the 1970s: 'Not that it's all bad, but it seems like quite a stretch to represent this as 21st century learning.'

Linking learning and classroom design

The Design Council's 2005 report, 'Learning environments campaign prospectus', insisted that school designs had to be linked to learning aims and that the standard classroom design needed to be reformed because it undermined the value placed on learning – these conclusions were based on the Kit for Purpose Project (2002). The report included a description of a pilot project undertaken with a Liverpool school to create a 360° Flexible Classroom prototype. The concept centres on the 'heart', a secure and mobile multimedia projection module at the centre of the room. The combined table/chair reduces the footprint of a traditional desk and chair, leaving

space for the teacher to circulate around the 'racetrack' and so access each student individually. The flexibility of the table/chair means it can also be moved by the students to support individual, paired and group work, while the whiteboards around the walls can be removed (to reveal additional display space) and placed onto the tables to facilitate group work.

The authors of the report acknowledged that the 360° Flexible Classroom was not a universal solution for the classroom of the future but they hoped that the project would lead to the design of new products and provoke a debate and offer a proven methodology for schools to adopt as they develop their own future learning environments and practice (CABE and Building Futures 2004: 32).

The traditional classroom is completely absent from Kenn Fisher's (2005) proposed planning principles for the State of Victoria (Australia). The closest space that fulfils a similar role is the 'project space', a 40–50 square metre space, generally dividable, that provides a variety of work surfaces, storage spaces and access to tools and technology. This provides space to produce information, services or products and encourages critical thinking, problem solving and teamwork. Learning activities that require specialized equipment and furnishings (such as science, technology, art, music, dance, fabrication, 'troubleshooting') or larger groups of students take place in 80–100 square metre 'specialised focus laboratories' (ibid.).

In *The Language of School Design,* Nair et al. (2005, 2009) proposed that classrooms should evolve into L-shaped learning studios where the irregular plan creates breakout spaces and flexible learning zones that can support a wide range of learning modalities for both individuals and small groups. These studios can be grouped together in pairs to create 'learning suites' that can also incorporate adjacent indoor circulation areas or external space to create additional informal learning settings.

While Nair et al. believe that learning studios and suites offer significant advantages over traditional classrooms, they state that the next 'level of development' is an Advisory Model of school design where the school is broken down into groups of 10–15 students which are grouped around shared areas such as cafes or project areas. Students have their own workstations, advisory workstations are provided for teachers/advisors and Nair et al. suggest that additional spaces may include a closed seminar room for lectures and possible distance learning which is separate from the project labs and 'messy areas.' They believe that the advisory model 'makes learning the centrepiece of the design intent and builds the plan around learning activities, rather than a theoretically appropriate building block like the classroom' (Nair et al. 2009: 38).

In an article that originally appeared in *Edutopia* magazine in June 2006, they argue:

> In schools across America, the factory model is still alive, and nowhere is it more readily apparent than in the classroom. In these little factories, every day we can find teachers encouraged (and often compelled) to mass produce learning and marginalize the differences in aptitudes, interests, and abilities. The industrial-age classroom was not all bad in its time; after all, America did all right in its heyday. But this model is no place to prepare students for the fast-changing global society they will inherit.
>
> (Fielding et al. 2006)

They imagined three learning spaces – named for 'great thinkers' Leonardo da Vinci, Albert Einstein and Jamie Oliver – that would make a better job of supporting twenty-first-century learning and teaching.

Da Vinci studio: a place with lots of daylight and directed artificial light, connection to an outdoor deck through wide or rolling doors (for messy projects), access to water, power supplied from a floor or ceiling grid, a wireless computer network, lots of storage, a floor finish that is hard to damage, high ceilings, places to display finished projects, reasonable acoustic separation, and transparency to the inside and outside with the potential for good views and vistas. To take full advantage of the studio, teachers would need to collaborate more, offer students the opportunity to work on real projects, and encourage cross-disciplinary thinking in a way rarely seen within the four walls of traditional, unrevised schools.

Einstein studio: might include a place that encourages creative reflection, an inspiring setting not sealed off from the world outside or from those real problems and issues that must always have some place in abstract theorizing. To imagine an Einsteinian classroom, conjure the various ways the main lobby of a five-star hotel is furnished: it welcomes people alone or in small groups, it offers comfortable furnishings, it may nurture aspiration and inspiration with high ceilings, lots of glass, and easy connection to natural elements and water features, and it creates zones of privacy that remain firmly connected to the activity throughout the larger space.

Oliver Studio: a teaching kitchen connected to a cafe. With student participation as the centerpiece of its operations, it would contain a mirrored cooking station visible to the whole 'class' and small, round cafe tables with comfortable chairs. Like the Einstein studio (but unlike the da Vinci studio), the Oliver studio could occupy a space with soft edges. That means

it doesn't need to be defined by four walls, but might spill over into circulation areas and also onto outdoor patios.

(ibid.)

The Spaces for Learning project in Australia (2007), undertaken by the Sydney Centre for Innovation in Learning (SCIL) and the Northern Beaches Christian School, also created a new space for 'twenty first century learning' (the SCIL building: Figures 4.4, 4.5 and 4.6), exploring the nature of change in educational space to see how the gap between pedagogy, space, technology and architecture might be narrowed.

More recently SCIL has extended the boundaries of available space for learners and learning into virtual space, establishing two separate virtual environments within Second Life. One of these, Booralie, is a secure island on Teen Second Life available only to approved students and teachers. Using this virtual environment, Harris has found that 'with some guidance, students are very capable of developing the spatial infrastructure on the island and teachers have been able to focus on using that spatial [infrastructure] for pedagogic diversity' (Harris 2010: 9).

The revised edition of *The Language of School Design* (Nair et al. 2009) made the observation that since the publication of the first edition in 2005 there had been a pronounced move away from the classroom as the standard building block of a school towards a new standard: the Small Learning Community (SLC). This is a 'home base' for between 80 to 150 students that allows for everyone in the SLC to know each other.

The members of the SLC are likely to use it for more than 60 per cent of their curriculum needs and the teaching team assigned to the SLC are likely to work there for more than 60 per cent of their time. According to Nair et al., an SLC is likely to consist of learning studios paired to create learning suites, small group rooms, a multipurpose lab, a common space that can also function as a cafe, space for student storage, a staff work area, a resource area, a kitchenette, shared storage and staff and student toilets – and it should also have a dedicated entry point and ample outdoor connections (p. 33). The design of the Djidi Djidi Aboriginal School in Australia (Figures 4.7 and 4.8) demonstrates how learning studios can be combined with other common spaces to create self-contained SLCs.

Within the SLC, students have a variety of settings in which they can set up a temporary personal or group workspace and Nair et al. believe that these settings are ideal to support the development of self-directed learning skills.

Initial phases of the project created 'distinct virtual spaces that could be brought into the everyday pedagogy of all teachers across the school. Every physical class or course has a virtual space, complementing the work occurring within the physical realm' (Harris 2010: 7). This was followed by the creation of specific integrated collaborative teaching and learning programmes at the junior secondary level (Australian Stage 4) which required the modification of existing learning spaces to suit a self-directed inquiry-based paradigm. To deliver these programmes, five conventional classrooms were opened up into one less formal space to create the Global Learning Village, with ready access to sufficient PCs to create a one-to-one

student-to-computer ratio. Refurbished open plan collaborative spaces were subsequently created for other year groups.

The SCIL building was 'designed so that the physical space intentionally engages the observer upon entering, through a combination of technology, informal space, strong use of light and a stimulus rich environment. Spaces have been created to provide zones that can be used as connected spaces or independently. The distinct zones have been given playful names such as the Brainforest, Parklands, Glasshouse, Sandpit, Loft and Mini-park, connecting all aspects of the building. The traditional rectangular classroom space is largely absent' (p. 10).

Source: Harris (2010)

Figure 4.4 SCIL building, Sydney

Figure 4.5 SCIL building, Sydney

Figure 4.6 SCIL building, Sydney

Djidi Djidi Aboriginal School, Western Australia – based on one of Nair et al.'s Design Patterns, this is a learning studio design

combined with common spaces to create a self-contained Small Learning Community (SLC).

Source: Nair et al. (2009: 34–5)

Figures 4.7–8 Djidi Djidi Aboriginal School, Perth

After a short period in a well-organised Advisory-based or Community Centre Model SLC, students typically change their expectations of the school setting so that after entering the space they immediately get on with their planned work.

Teacher-directed workshops and seminars punctuate the student's day, with the students at upper elementary and beyond able to schedule their own days. This is in significant contrast to the message of most classroom spaces being the teacher's domain: 'Wait until the teacher enters the room and tells you what to do before you do anything. You are not capable of directing your own learning.'

(p. 41)

While Nair et al. would prefer the creation of small schools, they note that most school districts implementing this model of school design are doing so by breaking up larger schools into smaller communities on the same campus. They suggested that this leads to opportunities to create a new type of space on campus – the learning street – that links the SLCs together and fulfils similar functions to Main Street in most small towns, being the unifying element that ties the town's various neighbourhoods together and gives the town its identity (p. 37).

For Barrett and Zhang (2009), classrooms are the core space of a school. Maximum flexibility should be built in to anticipate changes in pedagogical goals and educational programmes which may be reflected in organizational strategies (such as grade-level groupings to multi-age groupings of learners) or instructional strategies (such as team teaching and interdisciplinary instruction). In contrast to traditional classrooms, being used for lessons for groups of between 14 and 30 pupils, open-plan classrooms are intended to provide more opportunity for pupils to explore the learning environment and allow the school to respond more easily to changes in delivering teaching and learning:

For example, the open-plan classroom allows for as wide a variety of group learning sizes as possible and ... learner groupings from an entire 'family' of 30 or 40 learners, to groups of 12, 4–6 and 1–2 learners. At the same time, each large-group, small-group, and/or individual learning space should be an architecturally well-defined 'activity pocket' with all the furniture, equipment, storage, and resources necessary for that learning activity contained within.

(p. 18)

They conclude that there is no perfect classroom design but they cite Lippman's research (2002, 2003) that found that providing a variety of spaces within a classroom supports student–teacher/child–adult relationships. They also cite Franklin's (2003) criteria for an effective modern classroom:

- It has to accommodate the formation and functioning of small learning groups while providing a sense of separation, because groups working together will experience distractions and non-productive interaction.

- It has to be flexible enough to allow the continual reorganization of the whole class into various sizes and number of small learning groups. This means the space must be as free as possible of permanent obstructions.

- It has to be manageable by a single teacher who has command of the entire space. This means the space must be compact and open (Dyck 1994).
  (Franklin 2003, quoted in Barrett and Zhang 2009: 20).

Building on Dyck's earlier work (1994), Franklin proposed the 'Fat L' classroom layout as a design pattern that offers teachers options in how they might organize their classrooms to facilitate the development of their students in various learning activities.

This large L-shape allows the formation of several learning zones within the class to support various activities, from individual or paired one-to-one work, to small group learning or whole class instruction, activities that could occur simultaneously without disrupting other activities.

Barrett and Zhang also reported the findings of extensive research into the impact of a wide range of environmental conditions in the classroom on learning outcomes. This even included reference to the three-year study carried out by Henner Ertel at the Institute for Rational Psychology in Munich. This research painted rooms in different colours and they found that: 'the more popular colours were light blue, yellow, yellow green and orange. The use of these colours could raise IQ by as much as 12 points over environments where colours considered ugly – white, black and brown – were used. The popular colours also stimulated alertness and creativity, whereas white, black and brown playrooms made children less attentive. Orange, in particular, improves social behaviour, cheers the spirit and lessens hostility and irritability' (ibid: 26). One suspects that there are major methodological issues that would need to be looked at closely before generalizing from research of this kind.

Accommodating technology

Sutherland and Sutherland (2010) analysed the provision of two secondary schools that had been built in 2006. They noted that while both schools provided 'traditional' classrooms, the location of these classrooms was different in each school. In one, the classrooms were clustered around an open triangular space that contained computers and was used for self-directed learning, and in the other, the classrooms were located off dead-end corridors. The authors suggest that this difference was significant in supporting different ways of learning and described the open spaces in the first school as 'semi-formal learning spaces' where the space has clearly been designed for a learning purpose but the teacher does not play a central role in such a space (p. 53).

They believe that Information and Communications Technologies (ICT), now an integral part of all new schools in the UK, could profoundly alter learning in schools, the knowledge communities that are accessible to teachers and students, and the two-way knowledge exchange between inside and outside of school. However, they do not think that, despite the potentially transformative potential of ICT, most schools and teachers are harnessing this potential (p. 57).

Holleis et al. (2010) also stress the potential impact of ICT on learning: 'Mobile multimedia technologies, support for ubiquitous capture and sharing, physicality of user interfaces, easy means for communication, and access to a multitude of original information are prime examples that may significantly impact learning and teaching' (p. 63). They believe that learning will be enhanced by embedding technology into known, every-day devices that 'offers the possibility to increase the motivation of both, pupils and teachers, to help in mere memorizing as well as in understanding and reflecting about information. Tangible representation of data and tangible devices to manipulate data can increase the illustrative understanding, influence social abilities and massively stimulate cooperative and communicative behaviour' (p. 63). Novel technologies can create a new quality of learning and teaching with minimal effort for its introduction on the side of the pupils and students who have grown up with new technologies and for whom these technologies already highly influence their lifestyle outside educational settings.

Pervasive technologies for the classroom they explored in their research included the implanting of sensors and a processor into a cushion that allowed it to be used as an input device that 'provides fun, full body experience and interaction' (p. 68). Test applications were developed that used the active cushions to steer a virtual car through a race track where, at specific points, the student had to answer multichoice questions to be able to proceed.

Holleis et al. concluded:

> there is a great deal of potential to create new learning experiences with new technologies. We can move classical learning more into exploration and discovery and change the classroom more into a concept than a physical room. Mobile technology is a key to move the classroom to the object of study. Thus learning can become more engaging and motivation can be increased.
>
> (p. 83)

Baraldi (2010) suggests that if we consider the future classroom as a community – that is, going beyond the walls of a room – there is already growing interest towards current social networking technologies such as blogs and wiki-based knowledge building communities as the best candidates to become the new learning contexts: 'Mobile computing and the possibility for students to physically move across different places and receive location-aware information on personal devices, is certainly a way to augment the experience of learning, extending the concept of the laboratory to the physical world' (p. 89).

Baraldi also explored the opportunities created by embedding digital artefacts and interactive furniture into the classroom. These included interactive whiteboards which, Baraldi noted, were envisaged as 'the big step' in contemporary education tools and the way to bring interactivity to the front lesson. Baraldi states that despite some successes they have still not replaced normal hard or whiteboards. He cites Rudd (2007) who highlighted how the concept of the whiteboard is related to the educational model that still puts the teacher at the heart of the lesson and notes that usually the class is in a passive state and just the teacher, or a student, is performing some action on the whiteboard. He also notes that there are some very basic human factor issues associated with whiteboards. A whiteboard that is big enough for everyone to see is often very extended and reaching every zone with the hands could be difficult or impossible for some categories of users such as pupils in primary schools.

He also discussed the opportunities created by interactive tables, smart objects with embedded sensors and interactive walls. These walls could provide 'ambient information' for a classroom – a tangible knowledge space that could include interactive displays, context information for lessons and contain knowledge elements and media that could be explored by the class using natural interaction methods:

> According to a pre-selection of materials, the classroom could be turned into a knowledge itinerary and the teacher could stimulate students to walk around and visit a sort of 'temporary exhibition' related to some topic. The interactive function of a wall in this case would be to allow the users to explore a map, or browse through media elements which manifest as audio, video or textual data, using their own hands.
>
> (Baraldi 2010: 101)

Baraldi concluded that:

> the social and co-located context of the classroom needs novel ways to let students and teachers interact with knowledge-related digital contents, introducing new paradigms and

procedures at different levels. To effectively support the learning process, the whole concept of digital and physical interaction with objects and spaces must be rethought with that objective in mind, creating a flexible environment where knowledge elements can be spontaneously accessed and authored.

(ibid.: 111–12)

Reinventing the classroom

In a US study published in 2011, De Gregori looked at three innovative school classroom types (De Gregori 2011) – a Dewey-influenced modular classroom, the 'Harkness Table' and a new take on the 'one-room schoolhouse':

- The Crow Island School (1940) is an elementary public school in a suburb of Chicago designed by Eliel Saarinen (Figure 4.9). The school is based on John Dewey's progressive educational philosophy that stresses children's need for self-expression, the development of their attitudes, and their emotional and social adjustment. The school's modular classroom is described as an L-shaped, multifunctional and adaptable physical component of a fully integrated learning environment.

- The 'Harkness Table' is a large conference table (Figure 4.10), usually oval in shape, that was originally devised for high school classes at the Phillips Exeter Academy in Exeter, New Hampshire in 1943.

- The Discovery Charter School in Newark, New Jersey is a middle urban school for mostly underprivileged children that has an enrolment of about 75 students in the fourth to eighth grades. The founders and co-leaders, Dr Irene Hall and Barbara Weiland, advocate the importance of the physical environment of the school in support of teaching and learning and they conceive of the classroom as a kind of 'one-room schoolhouse'. The school consists of one extended classroom made up of a central open space, a great room that gives access to small workrooms for arts and crafts, a couple of offices and a food-serving kitchen.

De Gregori states that despite their clear social, cultural and pedagogical differences these three schools have in common a physical environment that has been intentionally designed to support each school's model for teaching and learning. The classroom is not treated simply as a background setting within which teaching and learning occur, but as an active variable that supports and enhances both.

De Gregori asks how this type of process can be effectively applied to the typical classrooms found in many schools and what needs to be done in order to facilitate a broad 're-imagining' of how

classroom spaces can be optimized to meet pedagogical goals. He believes that a critical first step will be to create basic benchmarks on how to analyse and manipulate a classroom space to optimize teaching and learning. Formal guidance on how to systematically create and implement such adaptations is lacking and research has not been done in this area because it falls somewhere between the core competencies of several disciplines.

Architects and interior designers have considered these issues, but primarily from a design perspective, with a particular focus on new schools and not on how teachers in existing 'typical' classrooms can adapt and optimize their own learning environments. Formal research on the topic has not been undertaken by either profession, so neither has a strong, evidence-based research tradition in this area. Educators, on the other hand, who have a long and venerable tradition of evidence-based research, have largely ignored the physical environment as a topic of investigation.

(2011: 10)

De Gregori suggests that there may be lessons to be learned from the commercial office sector, where there has been significant advancement in the functional optimization of space:

Advances in commercial office space optimization resulted from rigorous analysis, sustained over long periods of time, on what knowledge workers actually do and how their physical environment – the office – can help them do it. Such an analysis for K–12 schools – one that looks at what different pedagogical models are trying to do and then investigates how the physical environment can help them do it – is long overdue. The results could include significant interventions like making better use of movable partitions, tables and desks – elements so common in today's office environments – to create multiple learning 'scenarios' within one space ... Or, the results could be much more basic and essentially no-cost: simple instructions on how to use color, lighting and furniture to delineate different learning zones – for example, 'quiet zones' – within a classroom space. But almost certainly, many of the results will be discoveries we cannot foresee with our current knowledge. What will drive such solutions will be new knowledge based on a coherent body of research.

(ibid.: 11)

The urgent need to reinvent the classroom has also been stressed by Prakash Nair, in a July 2011 article in *Education Week*, 'The classroom is obsolete: it's time for something new' (Nair 2011). Nair regards the classroom as the most visible sign of a failed educational system:

The design concept for the classroom originated from an early understanding of the nature of learning, following to the end a coherent logic. Because studies and observation showed that people learn in different modes, the physical environment of the classroom had to be adaptable and organized to promote the various ways in which a person primarily acquires knowledge: visually, by listening, by reading or by solving problems and experimenting 'hands-on', individually or in cooperative projects.

Source: De Gregori (2011: 3)

Figure 4.9 Crow Island School, Chicago

Students sit around the table and discuss the assignment of the day. They must be prepared to enrich the dialogue or lose the trust of their peers. The teacher's role is primarily to observe, listen, ask questions, explain and give assignments. The table becomes the core of the classroom, supporting teaching and learning. The use of tables of this type has expanded among private high schools, and, more recently, has started to be used in some public schools. In several private schools, the table is adopted for all types of classes, including science labs where it is placed in a corner of the classroom, or in the instructor's adjacent office, separated by a glass wall.

Source: De Gregori (2011: 6)

Figure 4.10 The Harkness Table, College Preparatory School, Oakland, California

Almost without exception, the reform efforts under way will preserve the classroom as our children's primary place of learning deep into the 21st century. This is profoundly disturbing because staying with classroom-based schools could permanently sink our chances of rebuilding our economy and restoring our shrinking middle class to its glory days. The classroom is a relic, left over from the Industrial Revolution, which required a large workforce with very basic skills. Classroom-based education lags far behind when measured against its ability to deliver the creative and agile workforce that the 21st century demands.

This is already evidenced by our nation's shortage of high-tech and other skilled workers – a trend that is projected to grow in coming years. As the primary place for student learning, the classroom does not withstand the scrutiny of scientific research. Each student 'constructs' knowledge based on his or her own past experiences. Because of this, the research demands a personalized education model to maximize individual student achievement. Classrooms, on the other hand, are based on the erroneous assumption that efficient delivery of content is the same as effective learning.

(p. 1)

Nair believes that the research clearly demonstrates that students and teachers do better when they have variety, flexibility and comfort in their environment – the very qualities that classrooms lack. He is not advocating a blanket return to the classroom experiments of the 1970s but stresses the importance of designing schools to follow instructional needs:

> This new model does not dispense with direct or large-group instruction. Instead, it provides opportunities for traditional teaching to seamlessly connect with many other modes of learning. Simply put, it is form following function, not function (unsuccessfully) following form.
>
> (p. 2)

Enclosed spaces will be needed for direct instruction, but Nair suggests that these could be adjacent to a visible and supervisable common space for teamwork, independent study, and internet-based research: 'Arts, science and technology, and performance could be integrated in ways that would be impossible in a traditional, classroom-dominated school layout. Before we know it, we would have created a true 21st-century school' (pp. 2–3).

Nair advocates that the existing 'dysfunctional education infrastructure' should be converted into effective places for teaching and learning through redesign and refurbishment projects, that would not 'necessarily get rid of classrooms, but instead redesign and refurbish them to operate as 'learning studios' and 'learning suites' alongside common areas reclaimed from hallways that vastly expand available space and allow better teaching and learning. In many parts of the country, limited classroom space can be significantly expanded by utilizing adjacent open areas while simultaneously improving daylight, access to fresh air, and connections to nature' (p. 3).

A major pan-European four-year research project – iTEC (Innovative Technologies for an Engaging Classroom) – is exploring the future classroom with a particular focus on the use of technology and blended learning (Ellis 2010). This is the largest and most strategic project yet undertaken by European Schoolnet and its supporting ministries, with €9.45m funding from the European Commission, the involvement of 15 ministries of education and school pilots in up to 1,000 classrooms in 12 countries.

The key aim of the project is to develop engaging scenarios for learning in the future classroom that can be validated in a large-scale pilot and be subsequently taken to scale. This will be achieved through an increased understanding of the ways in which new and emerging technologies can support more effective forms of learner engagement. The project will create ambitious scenarios for the future classroom but it will also recognize the realities and pace of the educational reform process.

> By the end of the project, schools will most certainly still exist but the organization of learning will be changing as

social interaction and personalization becomes much more prevalent. iTEC, therefore, will explore a vision of the future where schools will remain the key location for learning and assessment as part of a wider network of physical and virtual learning locations ... and that the starting point for change is current teaching practice and that educational policy making in the real world must be understood as the context for this change.

> (p. 4)

The project will also examine how innovative technologies can be deployed and determine the underlying change processes needed for innovative teaching and learning practices to be mainstreamed and taken to scale. Underpinning principles of the project's approach are that an appreciation that the power of technology to significantly enhance learning and teaching is not always transparent to practitioners and that technology in itself cannot bring about schools that are competent in the use of ICT without other factors such as vision and competency, and technology that is designed with usability in mind (p. 5).

The iTEC project is conceived as a 'Living Lab' for pedagogical and technical innovation, involving ICT in schools and allowing both public and private sector stakeholders to rethink and test designs for the future classroom. It continues more than a decade of research and design exploration into the nature of the core learning spaces in schools. Dozens of studies, exemplar designs, guidance documents and pilot projects do not seem to have made a substantive difference to the development of a shared understanding of what exactly a twenty-first-century classroom is, how technology will be used in these spaces and what learning activities will be supported.

INFORMAL LEARNING SPACES

Just as practitioners and academics have challenged the role of the classroom as the primary 'container' for learning, so there has been an increased interest in where else learning can take place within the school. Classrooms in innovative school designs have morphed into larger learning studios or suites of connected spaces. The boundary between inside, outside and between learning space has blurred, often increasing the emphasis on informal spaces – either creating new atrium spaces, reimagining corridors and other circulation spaces or finding ways to layer learning activities on to spaces used for other activities such as dining or playing.

In his preface to a 2009 publication reviewing 50 years of his school designs, Herman Hertzberger made the point that the 'designs and concrete school buildings' show that the development of spatial conditions is 'wholly bound by the dictates of the world of education. What doors are closed by educationalists and government with their implacable regulations, and what doors are opened?' (Hertzberger and de Swaan 2009: 2).

He noted that educational units have become steadily larger as kindergartens are absorbed into primary schools and those primary schools in turn join to become extended schools. This organizational scale expansion has brought about a transformation of school buildings which has disadvantages but also presents enormous spatial opportunities which must be exploited (p. 2). 'The building should provide a general framework for education and learning, while being flexible enough to respond to changing demands and even, in a spatial sense, hold out a suggestion of pursuing avenues other than those laid down in the brief' (p. 9).

Hertzberger's school designs treated classrooms less as enclosed units and the corridors more as learning spaces. He is passionately opposed to the ubiquitous school corridor:

> Corridors do not belong in schools. Those corridors that are dominated everywhere and always by rucksacks and odd bits of clothing, and by endless pulling and shoving, badgering and carping that means they need to be made extra wide using up a large proportion of what might otherwise be inspirational space, while they could instead be ideal places for meeting others, as well as helping to solve the everlasting problem of cramped corridors. Completely eliminating corridors and adding corner areas, making the space suitable for communal use by diverse groups of pupils, created greater social cohesion and more places for smaller groups, while whole-class instruction could continue to take place in classrooms.
>
> (p. 11)

Hertzberger stresses the importance of cohesion and community building in school design and sees the provision of a single school entrance and some kind of central shared space as key architectural elements that will help achieve these things. He is not, however, in favour of the abolition of the classroom, believing that this would create a fluid world with blurred boundaries where everything flows into everything else, there is nothing left to exchange and nothing has its own place anymore. In this situation, people will be left without a place they can call their own 'and will have to navigate a confusing world in the manner of nomads. It is not just buildings that need structure; people too need a structured environment, in which each person can feel at home. You need to have a home base to which you can always return, and from which you can venture out and explore the world' (p. 15).

Hertzberger's ideas and the schools he has designed over the last 50 years have contributed very significantly to the 're-appropriation' and reinvention of circulation space and the increasing importance placed on informal learning spaces in schools. In many ways his work can be thought of as an architectural response to the pedagogic shifts occurring during this period.

Open-plan schools

'Profiles of significant schools: schools without walls', a 1966 report by Educational Facilities Laboratories (EFL) in the US, stated that the continued effort to create 'educational containers' that mould themselves to the fluid activities within, rather than the other way round, has led to the creation of 'open-plan schools' – schools without interior partitions comprising unbroken spaces containing from three to five class-sized groups of children and their teachers (EFL 1966: 3). This creates:

> an educational process unbound by the barriers built into the conventional schoolhouse with its rows of standard classrooms. The major aim in these open-space schools is to provide an environment which encourages greater interaction between teacher and pupil, and between teacher and teacher. There are no partitions to fragment learning by dividing teachers, children, and subject matter into tight standardized compartments. And there are no halls to funnel children from compartment to compartment at the arbitrary dictate of a bell. Each child finds his own place, creates his own path.
>
> (p. 3)

The creation of large, open learning spaces that contained a wide range of formal and informal learning activities had the potential to create significant management and noise problems which the authors of the report were aware of:

> It is not so easy to see how such an open space avoids extending an invitation to chaos as well, given upwards of 100 children pursuing half a dozen activities, from poetry writing to public speaking, in the same place at the same time. Yet the typical elementary schoolroom – full of sound, movement, and varied activity – harbors much the same potential problems that lurk in open spaces four times the size. Teachers have been dealing with these problems for years.
>
> (p. 11)

The open spaces can be made to work more effectively by scheduling classes to avoid clashes between 'noisy' and 'quiet' activities, the use of curtains and carpets to reduce noise levels and create separation between learning activities and teachers learning to modify and focus their delivery: 'By contrast, the teacher in a self-contained classroom, confusing visual privacy with acoustic privacy, may pitch her voice to a level that readily carries Latin declensions through a concrete block wall to the Spanish class next door' (p. 13).

The report discussed the acoustics and audio-visual issues associated with the creation of large learning spaces as well as the scheduling of classes, the requirement for partitioned and adjunct space for specialized activities and the selection of furniture to support large room use. The linking of the new spaces to pedagogic reform was also seen as very important in many of the case studies discussed in the report.

The authors concluded that the benefits of open-plan teaching outweighed the negative aspects but they admit that open space is not for everyone. They quote one of the teachers in an open-plan school who felt strongly that in an open room you 'should have only teachers who want to be there, who welcome new experience, are not afraid to make mistakes, have a capacity for excitement, are somewhat nonconformist and are child-centered. You cannot have people whose security rests on four walls; they must have security inside themselves' (p. 55).

History has not been kind to open-plan schools and there are numerous publications detailing why, precisely, they did not work. James F. McDonald, from the Organization for Quality Education, in an article entitled 'Lurching from fad to fad' blamed the province of Ontario's publicly funded school system for major, costly mistakes during the past 30 years, 'due in part to a lack of common sense', including the construction of hundreds of open-plan elementary schools throughout the province (McDonald 1997: 7 and Chapter 2 in this volume).

Much of the criticism reflects the fact that spatial innovation by itself is not enough – it must be combined with pedagogic innovation and teachers must be taught how to use the new spaces effectively. At Hellerup in Denmark (Figures 4.11, 4.12 and 4.13), for example, all teachers received more than 100 hours of instruction on how to use the new learning spaces before being allowed to start teaching the students. A continuous professional development programme also ensures that the spaces continue to be used effectively.

In recent years, the notion of creating learning spaces that are more open and blend formal and informal learning activities has been rehabilitated to support the delivery of more learner-centred curriculum and a much wider range of learning activities. ICT is now also supporting the use of these spaces in very different ways from 'first generation' open spaces – such as Vittra, in Stockholm (Figures 4.14 and 4.15).

Inside and outside space

The schemes developed as part of the DfES Schools for the Future: Exemplar Designs project (DfES 2004) all contained a range of 'non-classroom' learning settings and these ranged from small break-out spaces to large central resources areas used for timetabled IT spaces for a group of up to 30, or to house practical spaces to support design and technology or art activities. Many of the schemes also blurred the boundary between outside and inside space, creating covered external 'agora' spaces, courtyards, streets and atria that can provide a useful heart to a school and additional learning and social areas: the most radical (from de Rijke Marsh Morgan Architects (S3)) enclosed the entire school in a weather-proof bubble (Figure 4.16).

The 2004 CABE and Building Futures report, '21st century schools' (CABE and Building Futures 2004), predicted that there would be a shift from dedicated, specialized and centralized teaching spaces to more shared, non-dedicated, multipurpose and dispersed spaces that will extend beyond the school itself, enabled by the increased use of a flexible ICT infrastructure. In the same publication, Richard Feilden, Senior Partner at Feilden Clegg Bradley Architects, noted that increasingly the cellular classroom will need to be supported by other kinds of space whether these are for larger or smaller groups and class sizes in the future are likely to vary more than they have in the past (ibid.: 16–17).

Kenn Fisher also advocated the creation of groups of learning settings and the provision of shared facilities in a 'learning hub' – somewhere 'multiple learning settings are clustered so that individuals and groups have easy access to a range of pedagogical settings' such as libraries, resource centres, learning commons, multimedia centres, learning studios and learning laboratories. Groups of learners can be clustered in different ways, based on syndicate or home group, or 'family' sized groups of students (2005: 3.01).

Nair et al. used the expanded four-part version of David Thornburg's 'primordial learning metaphors' – the campfire, the watering hole, the cave and life – as the basis for the development of several of their core design patterns: 'Campfires are a way to learn from experts or storytellers; Watering Holes help you learn from peers; Caves are places to learn from yourself; and Life is where you bring it all together by applying what you learn to projects in the real world' (2005, 2009: 128).

Campfire space is similar to traditional lecture space and may consist of more formal teaching spaces or simple arrangements of beanbags or cushions with a raised chair or platform for the speaker or storyteller. Watering hole space is designed to support informal

Hellerup Skole (2002) is a Danish school for 6–16 year olds that has come to be highly regarded as an example of innovative European school design. Of the 80 staff who support the learning of the 750 pupils, 55 are defined as teachers, most of the remainder are 'pedagogues', who look after the very young children.

The school consists of a nursery and three main home areas. Each of the three home areas has three smaller home bases within it, which supports 75 learners. These then break down further into small groups of 25. One teacher team is responsible for the nursery, and another for each of the three home areas. Each team contains a variety of expertise, and smaller teams of four to five teachers facilitate each group of 75 within the home base on a daily basis. Age is mixed within the home area, but the different areas support different ages of children – 6 to 9 in home area I, 9 to 12 in home area II, and 12 to 15 in home area III.

Learning within Hellerup is highly focused on personalization, with much of the school designed around the needs of learners, including the spaces and the management model.

Source: http://www.arkitema.com/Laering+Learning/Projekter/
Hellerup+Skole.aspx

Figure 4.11 Hellerup Skole, Copenhagen

Figure 4.12 Hellerup Skole, Copenhagen

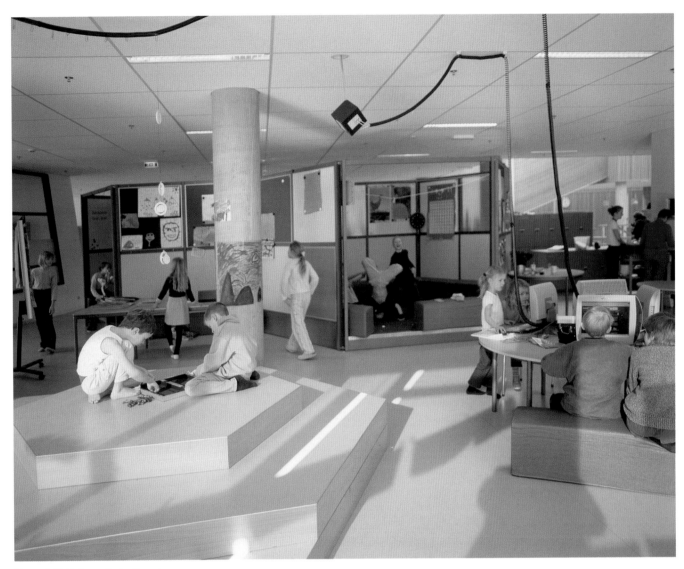

Figure 4.13 Hellerup Skole, Copenhagen

interaction and collaborative learning and it may be located in centralized commons type spaces or they may be inserted into circulation or linking spaces within the school. Cave space supports individual study, reflection and quiet reading. These spaces may be located within the school library but can also be part of many other parts of the school including garden or cafe space or niches within corridors or other shared spaces.

When CABE (2006) reviewed the schools that had been built in the previous five years, they found that, in the better schools, circulation spaces were consistently generous, easy to navigate and clearly defined into primary and secondary zones with breakout, and teaching bases and supervision were well considered. The assessors noted that multipurpose use of spaces, such as the canteen combined with the 'street' were extremely successful if they were designed well.

They also found that frequently schools included unheated circulation spaces such as 'covered streets' which saved on service installation and running costs and provides circulation space while maintaining a low gross internal area (GIA) since such spaces do not necessarily have to be counted within area. They found that, while the provision of a covered, unheated internal street is more advantageous than a covered or uncovered external circulation route, it is not without potential problems. In one school they inspected 'it failed to be anything but extensive, and expensive, circulation space because it was too cold for a large part of the year to form sociable breakout space' (CABE 2005: 30).

Rudd et al. (2006) asked whether new technologies could allow learners to choose to learn elsewhere other than at the school:

Could new technologies enable learners to access learning opportunities from a range of locations, such as the home, a

Figures 4.14–15 Vittra Telefonplan, Stockholm

Vittra is a private Swedish education organization set up in the wake of Sweden's 1992 education reforms. It runs 27 schools across Scandinavia and the Baltic states, designing schools that are intended to provide children with individual curriculum choices to meet their needs. The organization is overtly pioneering pedagogical space without walls. 'Gone are the classrooms and their rigid alignment of desks, and in their place emerges a colorful, seamless landscape of abstractly themed learning environments. The principles of the Vittra School System revolve around the breakdown of physical and metaphorical class divisions as a fundamental step to promoting intellectual curiosity, self-confidence, and communally responsible behavior. Therefore, in Vittra's custom-built Stockholm location, spaces are only loosely defined by permeable borders and large, abstract landmarks. As the architects explained, "instead of classical divisions with chairs and tables, a giant iceberg for example serves as cinema, platform, and room for relaxation, and sets the frame for many different types of learning," while "flexible laboratories make it possible to work hands-on with themes and projects".'

Source: http://www.architizer.com/en_us/blog/dyn/37250/vittra/#.UVvysI63IAQ

community learning centre, a youth club, a university, college, hospital, another school, or indeed in the street? Will learners also be able to access learning from any location within school buildings, including foyers, lounges, common spaces, corridors? Could they also learn in outdoor or remote spaces?'

(p. 5)

Increasingly digital technologies offer opportunities for flexible, distributed learning, which could provide learners with more varied opportunities to engage with learning in diverse environments. The mixing of a range of online or virtual experiences with face-to-face learning opportunities potentially changes the physical space that is required. The potential for this type of blended learning forces us to reconsider what education might look like in the future and how learning might become more distributed and diverse through the use of new digital technologies.

(p. 14)

One of the possible school futures that Futurelab imagined was one that is designed and 'zoned' around particular types of broad activities, or, more specifically, workflows, rather than around existing or traditional notions of schools or how they are organized. In this scenario, learners are free to enter each 'zone' and can spend as much time there as needed and do not necessarily have to progress through each one in a linear fashion.

Each zone reflects and utilizes the sorts of tools, competencies and problem-solving skills that would be used to turn an idea into a reality. The space is completely wireless and furnished with a range of other specialist technologies. Technology experts move around the whole environment, whilst educators are on hand to offer support, ask questions regarding the focus and purpose of the activities being undertaken, and engage learners in reflective dialogue about the quality of their learning. It is a community-'owned', intergenerational learning space and working relationships are also fostered with local businesses and other educational institutions. The principles behind the design of this space are to encourage collaborative work and create new knowledge and outputs from the educational pursuit.

(p. 31)

Multipurpose spaces

The importance of informal learning spaces was recognized by the exemplar projects in the DCSF-funded Project Faraday, set up in the UK in 2007 to improve the design of school science facilities: 'All the Faraday exemplar designs comprise a varied range of spaces that complement each other. They work best when they are seen not as individually owned spaces but as a whole, as "our space", where staff have shared access and shared responsibility for it' (DCSF 2007: 22).

A core part of the brief to the Project Faraday design teams was to use the whole school as part of the science 'experience', putting their classroom and lab-based learning into context and helping to inspire students and underscore the importance of science.

Many of the designs also used the school's structure and fabric as learning resources, making abstract topics concrete:

Some schools integrated energy monitoring into their facilities – useful in teaching about the environment, levels of CO_2 and climate change – while others incorporated rainwater harvesting with displays showing how much water is collected.

Many of the Faraday designs support 'kinaesthetic' learning, where students can move around and use their bodies to improve their understanding. For example, one school is using a neoprene mat that students can walk on, linked to a PC so that students can mimic the movement of molecules in gases, liquids and solids. Others are using 'drop zones', where

The most radical of the DfES 2004 schools for the future exemplar scheme came from de Rijke Marsh Morgan Architects and included a 'dura' which enclosed the entire school in a weatherproof bubble. The architects described their scheme as a 'hyper-modern school' and the dura as a 'place that is spatially grand but which has intimate sub-places that people can make their own; where they can meet, talk and work' (DfES 2004a: 79). Under the dome they positioned a variety of modular classroom types with adjacent spaces that could be colonized when necessary: 'This spectacular inside/outside open space creates a generous social collective, and gives every school the right to plan and change their own departmental layouts according to pedagogy, phasing or ambition' (p. 79).

CABE reviewers were unconvinced about the acoustics of the large spaces created in the scheme and the co-location of sports and learning spaces and concluded that the dura 'will be an enclosed environment users will either love or hate' (p. 85).

Source: DfES (2004a)

Figure 4.16 Dura: DfES exemplar designs 2004 – de Rijke Marsh Morgan

students allow objects to fall several storeys under experimental conditions, using sensors and cameras. The designers in Project Faraday also used other areas of the school for science learning, building in chance encounters with science artefacts, for example – a fossilized dinosaur, a stairwell designed to look like a rainforest canopy, or slow-run experiments like a drop of tar falling.

(ibid.: 27)

In a similar vein, one of the Space for Personalised Learning pilots, Chantry School, aimed to create an environment that allowed the school to test ideas about supporting personalized learning from both the learner perspective and the teacher perspective – even for those students who are disengaged with education. In response to this brief, the design team created an area known as 'the Hive' – a flexible space that would best support these themes for personalized learning (Figure 4.17).

The versatile space created by the Hive creates a positive environment for improving team building though group work, but its flexible nature also provides closed seating areas within the larger space for informal, smaller sets of groups. It is divided into five main zones: a large space for briefing, a group-based project space, small intimate group work in snugs, informal breakout, and individual or paired work at high-end computers.

By encouraging learning in smaller groups, the Hive presents an opportunity for teachers to spend more time with fewer pupils at one time and provides a fresh way of learning for both. The space encourages experimentation for pupils and teachers; it has given teachers the prospect to work with colleagues from other departments, awarding each staff member the freedom to move through Hive and provide a one-to-one pupil-centred learning experience.

The space is being used in a variety of ways, in particularly testing approaches such as inter-disciplinary, large group, week-long, team-teaching approaches. This has provided significant opportunities for change management, and the school is finding a high degree of engagement from learners.

Source: S4PL (2010)

Figure 4.17 Space for Personalised Learning: Chantry School

The Scottish Government's (2007) review of the implications of the Curriculum for Excellence for school building concluded that the new curriculum does not require radically different designs for classrooms or schools but it does provide an opportunity to think about how spaces are perceived and whether they are being used effectively. The review also noted that the teacher-centred classroom, originally intended to house rows of desks facing the front, can no longer satisfy a differentiated pedagogic model that recognizes that people learn in different ways at different times. It cites the assertion of the Department of Education in Victoria (Australia) that the key frameworks for learning in the twenty-first century include enquiry and project-based learning and, most importantly, personalized learning, drawing attention to studies (Dudek 2007) that show that there needs to be an increase of some 30 per cent in the space allocation for learning environments to allow specialized personalized activities such as remedial reading to be carried out (Scottish Government 2007: 21).

> By recognising that learning takes place throughout the school and beyond, the boundaries between the traditional teaching environment – the classroom – and the rest of the school building and grounds become blurred. Spaces can have multiple uses which might vary depending on the time of day – social spaces can be learning spaces, and vice versa. There is an opportunity for schools to rethink the spaces they have and use them more creatively. Existing spaces might be reconfigured at relatively little cost ... Similarly, there is an opportunity for designers to reconsider learning environments, facilitating education in a much wider setting than was previously considered.
>
> (ibid.: 46–7)

Gordon (2010a) notes that the concept of multipurpose spaces in schools is not a new one. Multipurpose spaces have been part of US schools for more than 150 years and by the turn of the century it was common for New York City elementary schools to include an assembly room that could be subdivided with track-mounted wood partitions. These early attempts at flexibility in configuration and use did not, however, work well: instead of 'several different areas, each designed to perform a specific function well, schools had one enclosure that handled multiple uses poorly. As individual class-rooms, the spaces were noisy because wooden partitions weren't soundproof. And as assembly space, the flat floor kept children in the back from seeing or hearing well what was going on at the front (Morisseau, 1966)' (p. 1).

Gordon does state, however, that refinements in technology and design configurations have improved the performance of these facil-ities and the combination of cafeteria and auditorium (and sometimes indoor physical activity space as well) is now a well-established approach to maximizing the use of school space and a school district's

budget. A May 2010 article in the UK *Daily Telegraph* drew attention to the great success of a 2005 refurbishment of a failing 1959 school based on a large central atrium (Figure 4.18).

The creation of a blend of formal and informal learning spaces, rather than traditional arrangements of classrooms and corridors, was stressed by Nair and Gehling (2010) in a paper they wrote to support the schools transformation programme at the London Borough of Croydon. Corridors, they insist, do not support the creation of good quality 'public' space in schools.

The spaces between formal learning areas are designed specifically for the purpose of informal learning: learning from peers, learning by application, and learning a range of highly sought-after 'soft' skills that are increasingly demanded by the business community as well as anyone with a desire for safer neighbourhoods.

> In these indoor public spaces, often referred to as 'Learning Commons' ... students are not forced into a particular way of behaving, as they are in a classroom, 'Sit down and wait for some spoon feeding,' or a corridor, 'Get out of here and into a nicer, lighter place with a spot to sit.' Instead, there are subtle cues offering an invitation to learn, each of them contributing to its marketplace/ thoroughfare/ meeting place qualities.
>
> (Nair and Gehling 2010)

In these spaces there are interesting things happening, invita-tions to participate, places to meet and places for solitude and reflection. They cite Jan Gehl (1973) who stated in *Life Between Buildings* that successful public spaces – the space between buildings (self-contained destinations) in a city – have three main features: marketplaces, thoroughfares and meeting places.

Marketplaces can refer to shops and stalls but also to any place at which a transaction of ideas or performance might occur. In schools this might include learning studios, lecture theatres, libraries, cafes and specialist facilities. Thoroughfares encourage people to move through public space by foot or on bike, so it needs to have desti-nations at either end as well as along the route. In a school setting this means that the space is used to access a number of different semi-private rooms or facilities. Meeting places use furnishings that encourage people to stop and chat with each other. In urban settings this means benches and tables to sit at, pillars to gather around and lean things against, and trees to provide shade. In indoor school settings this might mean small, round tables to gather at, 'edge' seats in windowsills or booths, and floor cushions.

Nair and Gehling concluded that school campuses need to consider their own public space – indoor and outdoor – and work to ensure it is productive, safe and inviting:

A 2010 article in the *Daily Telegraph* –'The future of schools' by Paul Kendall – had the strapline 'Riotously colourful atriums? Dining halls "cool enough to chill in"? There's a revolution afoot in school design, and it's not just the buildings that are being transformed' (Kendall 2010). The focus of the article was the 2005 de Rijke Marsh Morgan redevelopment of the 1959 Kingsdale School in London – described in 1998 by the chief inspector as 'failing' and one of the worst schools he had ever seen. Bullying was rife, there were 280 student exclusions a year, including 30 permanent exclusions, and only 15 per cent of students were leaving the school with five decent GCSE grades. The school now, the article pointed out, 'includes a central atrium the size of half a football pitch … the roof is the largest of its kind in the world … Here, the 1,200 pupils eat their lunch cafe-style in an atmosphere you could almost call continental. Then, after lunch, many take in a film in the school's cinema, a futuristic egg-shaped auditorium that looks like something from the set of *Doctor Who*. Others attend clubs in the new state-of-the-art music centre. A few simply sit with friends and hang out.' The former 'sink' school, the article notes, had been transformed. 'Now, with the new atrium, the cinema and the music centre, that figure of 15 per cent has increased to 70 per cent, bullying is firmly under control and expulsions are down to almost zero. Kingsdale is one of the fastest improving schools in the country.'

Source: Kendall (2010)

Figure 4.18 Kingsdale, London

The checks of 'thoroughfare, meeting place and marketplace' are useful indicators of a space's effectiveness at supporting a wide range of formal and informal learning activities for teachers and students, and indeed supporting life between classrooms.

(ibid.: 32)

The integration of formal and informal learning spaces is now a standard feature of school design in many parts of the world. An alignment of space and pedagogy, supported by a wide range of information and communication technologies, is enabling the informal space in the schools to become the buzzing heart of the school – somewhere to learn but also to play, socialize and interact with other students and staff and provide the focus for a wide range of out-of-hours and community activities.

STAFF WORKSPACE

There has now been a considerable amount of discussion about school spaces and a great deal of sporadic innovation, even if much of this innovation has failed to 'scale up' and enter the mainstream of school design. One spatial element that has received very little attention, however – because of the concentration on learning spaces and the student experience – is the staff workspace, including administrative and academic office space, laboratory prep rooms and the school staffroom.

In the UK, the Education (School Premises) Regulations 1999 require that, apart from pupil referral units, every school must have a staffroom, separate from teaching accommodation, for teachers to use for work and for social purposes. The size of the staffroom is not specified; it is implied that it should be reasonable. The Workplace (Health, Safety and Welfare) Regulations 1992 also apply to all types of educational establishments in the UK and these require employers to provide facilities for rest and to eat meals and to obtain or prepare hot drinks. The room used for eating facilities may double up as a rest area, but the space should be large enough for the number of workers likely to use it at any one time (ATL nd).

A study published in 2000 by Jane McGregor at the Open University showed that if the staffroom is not of a reasonable standard and well equipped, most teachers will find a more pleasant alternative. The research also found that a clean kitchen area came top of teachers' wish lists, followed by a quiet workspace with good computers, telephone links and a photocopier. Many of the schools interviewed for the study had substandard staff facilities that were scruffy, untidy and cluttered (Hastings 2004).

The 2004 Exemplar Designs report produced in the UK by the Departments for Education and Skills states that quality of the working environment is essential for the whole of the workforce – support staff as well as teachers and headteachers. While there are issues of self-esteem and motivation, linked with recruitment and retention, the authors of the report stress that school designs need to reflect the implications of the workforce reform agenda and the contractual elements of the National Agreement 'Raising Standards and Tackling Workload', which will have an impact on all schools (DfES 2004: 24).

The purpose of these agreements between the government, employers and school workforce unions was to create capacity for teachers to focus on teaching and to help schools to deliver the personalized teaching and learning that pupils and parents are entitled to expect. With more support staff undertaking activities to free teachers to concentrate on their core professional responsibilities, there would inevitably be more adults working in schools needing accommodation.

Many of the exemplar designs included spaces that would enable teachers to make the most of their time for planning, preparation and assessment – a key feature of the government's school workforce reform agenda. In one scheme, for example, a staffroom and terrace for relaxing and socializing were provided on the first floor above a 'quiet' workspace (ibid.: 24).

Paechter (2004) notes that school staffrooms are spatially very interesting places: where people choose to sit can reflect on wider power relations within a school and provide clues to other ways in which people and groups will interact. Staffrooms are not static, but change over time, and can, Paechter suggests, be manipulated by the judicious use of space either by senior managers or by individual teachers. The way in which the staffroom is set out can make it into a workspace, a place of relaxation, or a waiting room where no one stays for very long (ibid.: 34).

Fisher (2005) only includes two staff settings in his learning settings. The first is a 'teacher meeting space', 20–25 square metres in size, that contains individual or team spaces for staff with adjacent material preparation area and meeting space that will encourage team teaching, mentoring of other faculty members, integrated planning and informal discussions. The second is a 'resources, supply + store space', 20–30 square metres in size, that is within or adjacent to the learning activities spaces and is used to store learning resources, supplies for classroom projects, tools and learning products (p. 2.09).

He notes that these spaces should not be isolated from students – but at the same time acknowledges that an adult learning approach supports staff taking 'time out'.

The provision of science prep rooms and accommodation for science staff was part of the brief for the exemplar projects in Project Faraday. One of the design teams created shared prep room and science staff space to increase interaction and coordination between technicians and science teachers. The staff working area was designed to provide hot desks and soft meeting facilities or breakout space and, in one of the designs, the main meeting space for science staff was moved outside into the circulation area/ science zone to provide more visibility and passive supervision, as well as extra space for student project groups when not being used for meetings (DCSF 2008: 38, 63).

Hastings (2004) notes that refurbishing the staffroom often comes a long way down the list of budget priorities but suggests that this is a mistake: a cramped and dirty space sends out bad messages about the way staff are valued. Time pressures and the creation of local tea points within departments has meant that school staffrooms are often underused. Indeed, some new schools were being built without staffrooms but with departmental bases or 'open learning' spaces that will be shared by staff and students. While this has the advantage on a large site that staff do not have to waste time walking to a central location it does mean that staff may not get to meet colleagues in other parts of the school.

Hastings also reported that some of the best-used staffrooms are in primary schools:

> Primary staffrooms are usually smaller and often female-dominated, and, of course, there are no departmental cliques. They are often popular social spaces: primary teachers are more likely to start their day with a drink in the staffroom, whereas many secondary teachers boil a kettle in the classroom. And because staff don't have free lessons, the staffroom can be used for small group teaching during the day.
>
> (ibid.)

Day (2009) stressed the need to radically rethink school office accommodation:

> When planning a new or renovated education facility, schools tend to count the number of people and plan from there – because that's the way they always have done it. The technology tools that are available have had little, if any, effect on office planning or design. Research tells us that 70 per cent of office work is collaborative, and 30 per cent done individually. The modern office was conceived when that ratio was reversed – yet the layout and design have remained virtually the same.
>
> (pp. 28–31)

Day believes that the office environment ten years from now will be very different with more office staff organized around processes rather than functions and a shift to more team-based working with teams and the nature of the projects they work on changing over time. Space will also need to be provided to support private working and confidential conversations with students, parents or law-enforcement officials. Day suggests that modern thinking and technology may impact how school office space is laid out and managed. Office spaces in the future will need to be very flexible to allow for continual reconfiguration.

Moving to digital records systems may allow for the removal of filing cabinets and other document storage from administrative areas. This may provide the space that could be renovated to provide areas for waiting, reception and clerical staff, with smaller private offices and meeting spaces nearby. Further changes to school workforce will be triggered by the introduction of integrated school administration systems, mobile technology and pervasive wireless networks and increased use of video conferencing. Day concludes that 'the main goal of tomorrow's office will be to help workers capture and organize information more easily and efficiently. These changes in technology for the office space are exciting because it makes institutions look at the office and at "work" from a new vantage point' (ibid.: 28–31).

As part of its drive to improve the quality of staffrooms, the Queensland Teachers Credit Union in Australia (now a bank) runs the 'staffroom for improvement' competition among the schools in its area to 'win the ultimate staffroom': staffroom improvement was also one of the elements of the British Council for School Environments' Big School Makeover programme undertaken in the autumn of 2009.

In the US, a blog entry by Sophie Spyrou (2010) provides advice for substitute teachers: 'How to relax in the staffroom as a substitute teacher'. She notes that the 'staffroom can be an intimidating place for substitute teachers who are not yet familiar with other members of staff, the school's staffroom etiquette and so forth. As a result, some substitute teachers go off school grounds to eat their lunch or wait to get home to eat with their family' (ibid.). She suggests ways to find the staffroom in an unfamiliar school and to establish staffroom etiquette, and recommends familiarizing oneself with the layout of the room while it is unoccupied.

It does not appear that much has changed since Paechter's (2004) observation that:

> even further down the pecking order, but very much present in the staffroom, are the supply teachers. They sit where they can, usually the darkest and least hospitable corner of the

room, where colleagues have to make a conscious effort to visit them. They have their own friendships and camaraderie (theirs is the worst job in the school, after all) but they are not usually fully accepted into staffroom life, even after years of service in the same school.

(p. 33)

It seems that the school staffroom is not a place for the faint-hearted. Power politics are rife in the staffroom, and the furniture and settings in the space can be used to contribute to this. In many cases the rooms are neglected and underused. Where improvements are made they tend to address the physiological end of Maslow's Hierarchy of Needs with running water, a hygienic kitchen, comfortable seating and matching crockery being priorities.

Gordon (2010b) discussed the link between staff workspace and student achievement: 'Well-designed and equipped teacher workspaces provide the opportunity to improve student achievement at every step of their K–12 education. Shared workspace enhances communication among teachers as they evaluate student performance individually and collectively, and share insights with one another' (p. 1).

In elementary school, the classroom tends to be used as the teacher's home base with supplemental discussions with other faculty and administrators occurring elsewhere in the school. In a classroom-based workspace, teachers often use their desks to demarcate a corner as their de facto office, which some teachers may even decorate with personal items.

Gordon (2010b: 1) notes that the boundaries of these imaginary offices are respected as private by other teachers who will not step into that space and he cites Bissell's (2004) finding that other teachers using the classroom temporarily will only tenuously encroach on the home-base office space and take pains to return it to the original condition when finished with the room.

More discussion among teachers is necessary in middle and high schools to track the progress of any one student or group of students. Gordon (ibid.: 2) states that the teacher's primary workspace moves from the classroom to areas shared with another faculty or a separate office which is also used for curriculum planning, preparing for classes, and grading. He cites research that shows that shared workspace fosters professional communities and promotes networking and collaboration among teachers (Lieberman 1996) which has been shown to affect students' academic achievement positively and builds cohesion both within and across disciplinary boundaries (Duke et al. 1998).

Office-based teachers' workspaces may include private offices; a teacher workroom with workstations, a breakout room, and a conference room; a lounge area; and restrooms. Gordon (2010b) states that teacher workrooms should serve as a focal point for teams, clusters, departmental or interdepartmental units. They can be placed at the hub of a cluster of classrooms, adjacent to class-rooms sharing a common space, or overlooking high-use interior and exterior areas – such as restrooms, student commons, and courtyards where they can also provide additional supervision of these areas. Individual or shared workspaces can be provided for staff to use, with shared spaces for four to six teachers providing flexibility and increasing spatial efficiency.

The teacher workroom should be adjacent to a conference room or breakout rooms to support activities such as one-on-one consulta-tions and faculty meetings. The teachers' lounge may be part of the teacher workspace, adjacent to the teacher workspace, or deliber-ately placed in a less trafficked area to promote a more relaxed atmosphere. Gordon is very specific about what should be in the lounge. It should 'have a kitchenette with a microwave and two refrigerators, comfortable furniture, a phone in a quiet spot, and a television with cable access. A dishwasher and vending machine are also useful. Windows or outdoor access to the outside fosters a restful environment.' (p. 3).

He concluded that teacher workspaces should be seen as a critical element in the success of the academic programme of the school. Without adequate space, teacher preparation and innovation may be negatively affected:

> The teachers' lounge that serves as a place in which to relax with coffee and exchange gossip is being transformed into an office-type setting. Spaces for reflection, research, and collaboration have become necessary as teaching professionals increasingly share their classrooms with colleagues. Teacher workspaces encourage sustained planning and preparation time, facilitate interaction and collaboration among teams and departments, and foster a professional community across and within grade levels.

(p. 3)

While staff workspace is being re-valued and improved in some schools, it is still well down the list of priorities for many schools and school administrative regions. This continued neglect may contribute to the disappearance of the staffroom all together. In the UK in November 2011, the Education (School Premises) Regulations 1996 went out to consultation on planned amend-ments to the Act. These covered a number of key areas including acoustics, toilets, lighting, playing fields and school meals. The provision in the current Act that schools are obliged to provide 'accommodation for use by the teachers at the school, for the purpose of work and for social purposes' has been removed.

As Mike Matthews wrote in the *Guardian Professional* blog in February 2012: 'These revised regulations, if agreed to, could spell the end of the staffroom. Not just the physical space set aside for staff but the very spirit of a collective calling.' Matthews, a teacher, recognizes the importance of the staffroom to many teachers: 'your staffroom chair means so much more than a place to rest your tired teacher bones. It's your place in the room, the place where ideas are born, complaints are regularly aired or simply a place to chat to your friends. If the head's office is the brain of the school, the staff and staffroom are its heart.'

OUTDOOR LEARNING SPACES

In 2008, Hertzberger pointed out that since schools are often sited in the middle of green spaces, or in the – non-existent – centres of new residential areas, one might expect their midspace siting to be exploited for its 'great educational potential but the surface area is invariably kept to an absolute minimum and most of the green space around it is largely inaccessible "visual greenery"' (2008: 199).

> Generally, though, the school area beyond the actual building falls outside the sphere of education. Odd, when so many activities are ideally located outside, such as ones involving lots of water which gets spilt and sloshed around. Indeed you can learn just as much outside as inside. For that, the customary artificial environment should be purposefully conditioned and cultivated into a testing ground for projects relating to biology, ecology, meteorology, geology and all the other ologies best enjoyed outside.
>
> (p. 199)

Hertzberger does not go far enough. There is an increasing awareness that the school grounds can provide a valuable learning environment and set of learning experiences that can support all areas of the curriculum as well as contributing to the social development and health of children.

In the UK, *Building Bulletin 71: The Outdoor Classroom* was published by the Department for Education and Employment (DEE) (1990, 1999). This document aimed to highlight the potential of school grounds as a valuable resource that could support and enrich the whole curriculum and the education of all pupils and demonstrate how the necessary resources can be created and managed effectively.

It drew directly on the Learning through Landscapes research project, 'which established that much learning, common to a range

of curriculum areas, can be promoted strongly and naturally outside. In order to maximise such opportunities the scale and character of spaces should relate far more closely to the needs of pupils and more variety should be created in the outdoor environment' (ibid.).

The bulletin also noted that in schools where the grounds have been developed and used as an educational resource this has usually been achieved by enthusiastic teachers, often in cooperation with pupils, parents and the local education authority, and sometimes with the help of members of the community and other outside agencies.

These initiatives may have started with ideas about extending the learning from the classroom to outdoors, as a consequence of which the need for changes in the landscape were identified and work on the school grounds undertaken. The available budget may mean that the amount of change will vary from school to school – from a small part of the grounds to a project in which the whole site has been enriched with new features and improved qualities by seeding, planting and other landscape works. The authors of the bulletin note that generally it has proved more successful to provide for recognized curricular needs than to create resources and then contemplate their uses (ibid.).

The creation of outdoor classrooms was also one of the themes that emerged from the 2004 DfES project that led to the publication of *Schools for the Future – Exemplar Design Concepts and Ideas* (DfES 2004). The authors noted that landscaping is often vulnerable when funding has to be reduced, but many of the design teams considered it to be a key part of the overall design of the school.

Many of the design teams involved with this project considered how the grounds could enhance learning and links with the community, through allotments, gardens and social areas as well as sports facilities. The design teams working with confined urban sites included 'sky gardens', 'play decks' and terraces at upper levels to make up for the lack of external informal and social areas on the ground (ibid.: 19).

Futurelab's Savannah project, carried out in partnership with the BBC and Mobile Bristol in 2003–4, created a strategy-based adventure game in which a virtual space is mapped directly onto a real space in the school grounds:

> Children 'play' at being lions in a savannah, navigating the augmented environments with a mobile hand held device. Children are given GPS-linked PDAs through which they 'see', 'hear' and 'smell' the world of the savannah as they navigate the real space outdoors as a pride of lions. The second domain, the 'den', is an indoor space where children can plan, research

and reflect on their outdoor game-play through accessing resources such as the internet, books, adult experts and an interface that has tracked their outdoor activities.

(2006: 1)

In 2006, the DfES published its *Learning Outside the Classroom Manifesto* (2006c), focusing on the 'use of places other than the classroom for teaching and learning' and stressing the need to provide more meaningful learning through direct experience with the world outside the classroom. It also recognizes this can and should happen at all times of the school day, during holidays, and in a range of different contexts and situations. As Tim Rudd has pointed out (Futurelab 2008), the manifesto also stressed the importance of developing engaging and stimulating play and learning spaces to support the emotional, physical and social well-being of young people within their schools and communities.

In the same year the DfES also published *Schools for the Future: Designing School Grounds* (2006a) which aimed to provide information, guidance and ideas to inspire the best possible designs for school grounds. The authors of the report believe that school grounds can enrich teaching and learning across the whole curriculum:

> Children's learning can be enhanced outside – they find lessons outdoors more relaxed, interesting and easier to understand, and they think their teachers are 'friendlier outdoors'. Teachers report that the grounds provide access to resources not available in a classroom and opportunities to use different teaching styles. Making more use of school grounds can also foster stronger relationships between staff and pupils, and between pupils themselves, leading to significant improvements in behaviour, attitudes to learning and attainment levels.
>
> (DfES 2006a: 8)

As well as playing an important role in delivering the formal curriculum, including much of PE, school grounds should also be designed to address both the informal curriculum (the social use of the grounds at break time and during the extended day) and the hidden curriculum (the messages and meanings children receive indirectly). The grounds also provide opportunities to engage in projects supporting the management of their school environment and through these projects they can develop 'new skills, understand the value of team-working, assess needs, make decisions on priorities and manage projects' (p. 8).

The report recommends that the participation of all stakeholders using the outside space – pupils, teachers, other school staff and the local community – should be fundamental to its design. School

pupils can be involved through the taught curriculum or through extracurricular structures such as school councils, and this process also supports the development of participatory skills among staff and pupils and links closely to citizenship initiatives (p. 17).

These recommendations are consistent with the conclusions of a paper presented at a conference in Scotland in 2006 by Anne Meade from Victoria University in New Zealand, emphasizing the importance of outdoor space and the different learning behaviours associated with it (Figure 4.19). She cited earlier research from Victoria University Wellington by Stephenson (1998) that found that the majority of children actively chose to be outdoors for more than half the time once the doors were open. This was true for all ages, but more so for boys and older children. Stephenson also found some notable differences between outdoor and indoor behaviour:

> Outdoors, children take more risks and call, 'Look at me'; indoors, children request, 'Look at what I've made'. Outdoors, children and adults are constantly changing equipment and materials; indoors the layout is fairly permanent. Outdoors, freedom is prevalent; indoors there is more control of behaviour. Outdoors, teachers move in and out of interactions and give skill instructions; indoors, teachers can be ambivalent about joining in. Outdoors is seen as an open environment that has more potential for children's theorising.
>
> (Stephenson 1998, quoted in Meade 2006: 2)

The Scottish government's *Building Excellence* report in 2007 stressed the importance of the school grounds as a learning environment, citing a 2005 House of Commons Education and Skills Committee report which concluded that 'school grounds are a vital resource for learning. Capital projects should devote as much attention to the "outdoor classroom" as to the innovative design of buildings and indoor space' (Scottish Government 2007).

Futurelab's (2008) *Guide to Reimagining Outdoor Learning Spaces* states that it may be worth considering how outdoor space might be designed and utilized as a way of modelling new or different behaviours and approaches to learning and teaching inside the school: 'Designing a new learning and/or play space can offer opportunities to make significant advances around pedagogical aims, practices and relationships, or to integrate elements within school or wider community spaces that support other agendas...It could also represent an opportunity to embed learning approaches or indeed extended services and other provision into day-to-day aspects of school life' (p. 33).

The guide noted that new technologies can, and do, enhance outdoor spaces in school settings; with the exception of a number

Meade related the use of outdoor space to the early years curriculum, Te Whāriki, produced by the Ministry of Education in New Zealand. This reflects Maori tradition and is 'designed to be empowering, holistic, community-based, and fundamentally about reciprocal relationships with people, places and things' (Meade 2006).

Children are seen as active learners, and learning and teaching are seen to be reciprocal processes where often the teacher learns and the child teaches and space is seen as important for providing contexts for the processes of learning. She notes that New Zealand's early education settings were seen as bounded settings where the teachers put out, then supervised, a rich array of equipment and materials. As sociocultural learning theory became more widely adopted the environment was viewed and managed differently, including the use of more cultural symbols, particularly Maori ones, and greater use of natural materials. Space use is less bounded by 'areas' – or the fence – as excursions into the community increase and a rich array of equipment and materials is organised in order to help children interact with people, places and things so they become confident and competent explorers and communicators. 'Outdoor spaces in particular change in response to children's interests. Parents mingle with children. Engagement prevails' (Meade 2006: 3).

Teachers Claire Maley-Shaw, Jude Sandilands and Tracey Bevan from the Fiordland Kindergarten in New Zealand have strong feelings about the children's relationship with the land.

We use the unique features of our environment throughout the programme and in our teaching strategies to support and develop children's learning. The passion for living in this environment and the knowledge we have of the area is passed to the tamariki (children) through our interactions, programme planning and implementation. By tamariki having knowledge and appreciation of 'To Matou Wahi Ahi Kaa/Our Special Place', its people, its history, the environment they then develop a pride and a sense of belonging. We use the wider community to help implement this learning through inviting members of the community to visit Fiordland Kindergarten and taking the children out into the environment to interact with and get to know their unique place in the world. Twice a week a group of older children experience the outdoors in a nature discovery programme, to make them 'nature literate'. If we want the best possible future for our children and our environment we need to give them the opportunity and time to connect with nature in its wildest forms, a place where they can build emotional and physical resilience – they need to love the Earth before we ask them to want to care and protect it. Then they will become true nga kaitiaki (guardians) of our whenua (land).

(Maley-Shaw 2012)

Figure 4.19 Natural discovery programme, Fiordland Kindergarten, Fiordland, New Zealand

of special schools, however, the incorporation of new technologies had been relatively limited. Futurelab itself had undertaken various research projects exploring the use of mobile devices, such as mobile or handheld computers, mobile phones, games consoles, personal navigation devices, video cameras and media players to enhance learning activities:

> Using mobile devices for technology-enhanced outdoor learning and play, for example, can be seen through the use of portable computers to collect data sets, using images, sounds and video to help children create and support them in interpreting their outdoor experiences and comprehending abstract information. They can also be used to enable children to have a 'voice' by helping them to express their interests, concerns and opinions in alternative ways, or when used as a tool for young children to initiate enquiry.
>
> (ibid.: 41)

The Commission for Architecture and the Built Environment (CABE) guide *Creating Excellent Primary Schools* (CABE 2010a) expresses the opinion that investing in the design of school grounds can create stimulating and creative places, which support curriculum learning and give children rich and varied experiences that may not be available to them at home. Of particular importance to primary-age education, the imaginative design of outdoor spaces can encourage creative play and help children develop social skills.

The guide also suggests the creation of outdoor classroom spaces that can be used for many teaching activities in good weather. These spaces may be big enough for whole class activities or they may be quiet areas with seating for small groups and individuals for independent study and socializing.

The school grounds should be used for environmental education, providing opportunities for studying nature, growing food and observing climate even if the school is located on a tight urban site.

Grass sports pitches and hard games courts are needed to satisfy the curriculum requirements for physical education classes and to comply with the PE, as well as the Education (School Premises) Regulations.

A number of organizations in the UK actively advocate the importance of play and the use of the school grounds to support learning and teaching. Several of these operate under the umbrella of the National Children's Bureau. Play England campaigns for all children and young people to have freedom and space to play throughout childhood, Play Matters is the national body for toy and leisure

libraries and the Children's Play Information Service (CPIS) is a national information service on children's play.

Learning through landscapes (England), Learning through landscapes (Wales) and *Grounds for learning (Scotland)* focus specifically on enhancing outdoor learning and play for children. They advocate the benefits of outdoor learning and play at school and pre-school and the design of inspirational outdoor environments to support children's development and they provide support to teachers and early years practitioners to help them develop the confidence, ideas and skills they need to make better use of outdoor spaces (LTL 2012).

In the years that have passed since the publication of *Building Bulletin 71: The Outdoor Classroom* (DEE 1990, 1999), the opportunities provided by school grounds to create a wide variety of external learning environments have continued to be developed and many schools now use these spaces as an important part of curriculum delivery for all subjects. It is important to realize, however, that the external learning experiences do not stop at the school gates. To return to Hertzberger: 'A city is a Learning City when it arouses our curiosity, draws us in, a place where discoveries are to be made, that invites associations, stimulates thinking' (2008: 235).

SCHOOL LIBRARIES

The library has been a key part of the school environment for a very long time: Laurel Anne Clyde, in her PhD thesis on the history of school libraries (Clyde 1981), traces the origin of libraries in English schools to the eighth century, notably at Canterbury, York, Winchester and Hexham, where they were closely associated with religious foundations. Over the intervening years these school libraries have developed and changed in response to developments in education and in the field of librarianship (p. 65).

> Since the Middle Ages, school libraries have been recognised as an important feature of many schools; even the idea of the school library as the 'pivot' or 'centre' of the school is several hundred years old. The physical form of the school library has changed over the centuries, with libraries increasing in size and in sophistication of organisation and administration. However it needs to be stressed that, while the physical expression of the idea of a school library has undergone great change, the idea itself is far from new.
>
> (p. xvii)

Clyde distinguishes five main types of school library – those established:

- to support the teaching and learning activities of the school

- to provide recreational reading

- to serve both the school and the community

- as a scholars' library to serve the needs of a particular group within the school

- as a memorial.

Curriculum-related school libraries have altered in character as both the school curriculum and the methods of instruction employed have changed in response to new theories and developments in education: 'While the centralised school library resource centres of the twentieth century have little physical resemblance to the chained libraries of the sixteenth century English grammar schools, they still share essentially the same purpose: to support the teaching and learning activities of the school' (p. 693).

UNESCO guidelines

The important role of school libraries was recognized in the UNESCO manifesto for school libraries, adopted in 2001: school libraries provide 'information and ideas that are fundamental to functioning successfully in today's information and knowledge-based society. The school library equips students with life-long learning skills and develops the imagination, enabling them to live as responsible citizens' (UNESCO 2001).

The implementation guidelines that followed the publication of the manifesto were designed to inform decision makers at national and local levels around the world, to give support and guidance to the library community and to help schools to implement the principles expressed in the manifesto (IFLA/UNESCO 2002: 2).

The guidelines stated that the strong educational role of the school library must be reflected in the facilities, furniture and equipment and that it is vitally important the function and use of the school library are incorporated when planning new school buildings and reorganizing existing ones (p. 7).

While the guidelines recognized that libraries varied considerably from school to school they stated that, if possible, libraries should be centrally located within the school, on the ground floor, if possible, and close to all teaching areas. The library should be largely free from external noise with appropriate and sufficient light, both through windows and artificial light and appropriate room temperature (created by air-conditioning or heating) to ensure good working conditions all year round as well as the preservation of the collections.

The library should be designed to meet the special needs of disabled library users and be of an adequate size to give space for the collection of books (fiction, non-fiction, hardback and paperback), newspapers and magazines, non-print resources and storage, study spaces, reading areas, computer workstations, display areas, staff work areas and a library desk. Spaces should be flexible to allow for a multiplicity of activities and future changes in curriculum and technology.

The guidelines suggested that certain specific areas should be considered when planning a new library (p. 7). These would include:

- a study and research area for information desk, catalogues, online stations, study and research tables, reference materials and basic collections

- an informal reading area for books and periodicals that encourage literacy, lifelong learning, and reading for pleasure

- an instructional area with seats catering for small groups, large groups and whole classroom formal instruction, 'teaching wall' with appropriate instructional technology and display space

- a production and group project area for functional work and meetings of individuals, teams and classes, as well as facilities for media production

- an administrative area for circulation desk, office area, space for processing of library media materials, audio-visual equipment storage, and storage space for supplies and materials.

The guidelines also noted that 'the school library serves an important function as a gateway to our information-based present day society. For this reason, it must provide access to all necessary electronic, computer and audio-visual equipment' (p. 8). School libraries should also be considered as vital means for fulfilling ambitious goals regarding information literacy for all, the availability and the open dissemination of information and knowledge for all student groups to exercise democratic and human rights (p. 14).

School library systems under threat

Despite the international recognition of the importance of the school library in the UNESCO manifesto, the school library systems of many countries have been under threat and the relevance of the school library in the twenty-first century challenged.

Haycock (2003) reviewed the situation for school libraries in Canada in his report *The Crisis in Canada's School Libraries*. He found that across Canada

> teacher-librarians are losing their jobs or being reassigned. Collections are becoming depleted owing to budget cuts. Some

principals believe that in the age of the Internet and the classroom workstation, the school library is an artifact. In a growing number of Canadian schools, in fact, the libraries are shuttered all or part of the time, with well-meaning parents scrambling to fill the void. Through neglect, too many school libraries are now little more than storage rooms.

(p. 9)

Haycock felt that Canadian school libraries were being neglected just at the time when many other countries were investing in these facilities – 'increasing support for school libraries and teacher-librarians to promote economic development, while philanthropic foundations are funding school libraries and teacher-librarians to further cultural development'. He cited the US Congress allocation of $250 million for the purchase of school library materials to get its school libraries back on track (p. 9). He believed that these investments were being made because there was clear evidence of a strong and compelling link between student achievement and the presence of well-stocked, properly funded and professionally developed school library programmes and services. He also felt that the decline in Canada's school libraries was 'almost certainly linked to the erosion of research skills among students at the post-secondary level' (p. 11).

In Australia, Georgia Phillips, co-founder of The Hub blog, notes that 1969–80 was a period of considerable growth for school libraries, with around $200 million of federal government funds spent on school libraries and about 1,200 new secondary school libraries built by 1977. By 1978 there were 3,500 qualified teacher librarians in Australia.

Since that time the situation has changed, with Commonwealth school library grants ceasing, changing staffing structures in schools, a decline of central library services, the cutting of many library courses across Australia and the impact of an aging teacher librarian population. Phillips believes that school libraries are currently facing a crisis as principals, faced with global budgeting shortfalls, are 'forced to make cutbacks, and unfortunately, the library has often been the easiest place to do this. Evidence tells us that library budgets have plummeted across the country. Staffing levels have also been greatly reduced in an effort to save money' (Hubinfo 2012).

Budget cuts are also threatening school library services in the US. An article in the *Boston Globe* in 2010 stated that 'as the school budget crisis deepens, administrators across the nation have started to view school libraries as luxuries that can be axed rather than places where kids learn to love reading and do research' (Blankinship 2010). The article also highlighted the reduction in the number of school librarians across the US, with the Association

of School Administrators projecting that 19 per cent of the nation's school districts will have fewer librarians next year.

In 2011, an article in the *New York Times* stated that 'Budget belt-tightening threatens to send school librarians the way of the card catalog', reporting on school library staff cuts in many parts of the US: 'In New York, as in districts across the country, many school officials said they had little choice but to eliminate librarians, having already reduced administrative staff, frozen wages, shed extracurricular activities and trimmed spending on supplies' (Santos 2011).

The article also discussed the impact of technology on school libraries, quoting a Mr Polakow-Suransky, chief academic officer for the city of New York, as stating that as more classrooms are equipped with laptops, tablets or e-readers, students can often do research from their desks that previously might have required a library visit: 'It's the way of the future.'

This view was contradicted in the article by Nancy Everhart, president of the American Association of School Librarians, who said that, on the contrary, the internet age made trained librarians more important, to guide students through the basics of searching and analysing information they find online. The library, Ms Everhart said, is 'the one place that every kid in the school can go to learn the types of skills that will be expected of them when it's time to work with an iPad in class' (ibid.).

As a consequence of the cuts occurring across the US, the American Association of School Librarians has published an 'AASL Crisis Toolkit' on its website to help members whose library programmes are about to be reduced or eliminated.

In the UK, Ward (2010) noted that there is no statutory requirement for local authorities to provide school library services to the schools in their area: 'Since 2000, local authorities' library funding has had to be passed on to schools. In some cases, it is still earmarked to be spent on library services, but elsewhere this is not the case'. With increasing pressures on school budgets, some heads are cutting library services to maintain staffing levels.

An article in the *Telegraph* (2010), 'Future of school libraries in doubt', discussed the implications of the country's largest local authority cancelling the school library service for tens of thousands of pupils. Schools in Kent were told by the county council that they will have to borrow books from their local libraries from now on. To make matters worse, schools are also being restricted in the number of books they can borrow from their local libraries – Kent schools have been told they will only be able to borrow 100 books for eight weeks at a time free of charge. The changes were justified by the council in a notice sent to schools: 'Existing take-up has been very slow in recent years and the service was failing to cover costs.'

The article stated that with public spending cuts set to hit local authorities hard over the next few years it is thought that school libraries could soon become a thing of the past. Alan Gibbons, a children's author and libraries campaigner, responded by saying that 'the progressive closure of school library services is a catastrophe. There is no sign from Government of setting the basic principle of retaining a reading culture. We have the axe swinging in every direction' (ibid.).

Quantifying the learning and teaching contribution of school libraries

The role of school libraries has been challenged repeatedly during the last decade on the grounds of both economic value and relevance in the twenty-first century where information is increasingly available 'anywhere, any time' on the internet.

To counter these arguments, a large amount of research has been undertaken in many parts of the world to try to quantify the contribution of school libraries to the learning and teaching activities of the schools they support.

The International Association of School Librarianship (IASL) website includes links to major US and international studies that make a link between the provision of school libraries and increased academic performance (IASL online). One of these studies, School Libraries Work (SLP 2008) reviewed more than 60 studies in the US and found that there was clear evidence of a connection between student achievement and the presence of school libraries with qualified school library media specialists. Students in schools with good school libraries learn more, get better grades and score higher on standardized test scores than their peers in schools without libraries.

The authors note that school libraries are no longer just for books: they have become 'school library media centers' with computer resources that enable children to engage meaningfully with a wide variety of information. These centres with trained staff support the use of electronic information resources not just in the centre, but help to integrate these resources in classrooms and throughout the curriculum (ibid.: 4).

The important contribution of libraries to achievement in schools was also stressed by Stephen Krashen, Professor Emeritus at the University of Southern California in 'The case for libraries and librarians', a paper submitted to the Obama-Biden Education Policy Working Group, December 2008:

Study after study has shown that library quality (number of books available or books per student) is related to reading achievement at the state level (Lance, 1994), national level (McQuillan, 1998), and international level (Elley, 1992; Krashen, Lee and McQuillan, 2008), even when researchers control for the effects of poverty.

The library is especially important for children of poverty, because they have very little access to books at home (Feitelson and Goldstein, 1986), at school, and in their communities. The library is often their only source of books. Unfortunately, children of poverty are the least likely to have access to quality libraries (Smith, Constantino, and Krashen, 1996; De Loreto and Tse, 1999; Duke, 2000; Neuman and Celano, 2001).

(Krashen 2008b)

Krashen's submission was based, at least in part, on the findings of his earlier 2008 multivariate analysis of the impact of libraries on learning. In this research he found that all the multivariate analyses undertaken, even when controlled for the effects of poverty, confirmed the importance of the library:

In all of the multivariate studies considered here the library emerges as a consistent predictor of reading scores. This is remarkable, especially when we consider that the measures used are crude: library holdings, and even general circulation, in the case of public libraries ... what is clear is that libraries definitely matter and they matter a lot.

(Krashen 2008a)

Similar links between the provision and staffing of school libraries and academic performance have been found by other researchers and librarians (Williams et al. 2001; Ofsted 2006; Kachel 2011; Bonanno 2011; ASLA nd; Todd et al. 2011).

The contribution of school libraries to education in the UK was explored in 2010 in the School Library Commission, chaired by Baroness Estelle Morris and jointly established by the Museums, Libraries and Archives Council and independent charity the National Literacy Trust.

The commission's report, School Libraries: A Plan for Improvement, stated that a high-performing school library and school library service has a powerful role in raising pupils' literacy levels and improving their access to knowledge. Young people who read above the expected level for their age are twice as likely as young people who read below their age to be school library users (77.7 per cent as opposed to 35.9 per cent). The report acknowledges that this link is not necessarily causal but 'it does suggest that if school libraries do not perform to the highest level there will be significant implications for pupil achievement. Cuts to schools library services will exacerbate this problem' (Douglas and Wilkinson 2010: 4).

The authors of the report also noted that while school libraries have a unique role in raising pupils' literacy levels, promoting reading for pleasure and improving their access to knowledge, in many schools the library is a wasted resource because it is poorly embedded in the infrastructure of the school and absent from school development plans. School libraries, they state, are failing to play a full and active part in raising literacy levels and creating an innate love of reading. As information skills and digital literacy increase in importance, the school library, as the hub of information flows within the school, needs to be a central player in making pupils information literate (p. 5).

The commission found examples of excellent practice in planning libraries which responded to the needs of young people – libraries that were 'comfortable and welcoming environments, offering: more social reading opportunities (book clubs, peer recommendations, drama and games based on reading); excellent book stocks which stimulated the reading of young people; more access to up-to-date technology; more targeted services aimed at meeting the particular needs of particular groups' (p. 6).

The commission recommended that the Department for Education in the UK should endorse the role of school libraries and schools library services in supporting the government's renewed commitment to literacy. More detailed recommendations related to the provision of tailored resources in all media, effective staffing of school libraries by qualified librarians and the provision of additional library training for teachers and library assistants, partnership with planning and teaching in the school and with external organizations and the personalization of library services to meet the very differentiated needs of children and young people.

The commission concluded that partnerships to improve and deliver school libraries are particularly important for schools where resources were scarce: 'At a time when the public sector is facing tighter economic management the potential of schools working in partnership to purchase and deliver improved provision will become increasingly important. Schools will be encouraged to develop partnerships with other schools, schools library services, businesses, charities and public libraries as the primary mechanism of improving their provision' (p. 17).

Key partnerships should be established with public libraries and between clusters of schools: public libraries would offer joint working and co-located provision, primary schools should work with secondary schools in cross-phase libraries and primary schools

should also work together in primary cluster collaborative libraries (pp. 17–18).

Library design

The School Library Commission's report says little about the physical design of school libraries other than to recommend that pupils should be involved in library design, management and delivery (Douglas and Wilkinson 2010: 17–18).

In the UK, the provision of libraries in primary and secondary schools was included under 'learning resources' of the relevant building bulletins (BB98, BB99). Recommendations on the amount of resources spaces based on the number of pupils are provided in both cases but little is said about the nature of the library, other than noting that a school may choose to provide one library, or to disperse several areas around the school (DfES nda, ndb).

In 2007, the Museums Libraries and Archives Council (MLA) and the Chartered Institute of Library and Information Professionals (CILIP) published *Designed for Learning: School libraries* – a set of guidelines and case studies and an accompanying DVD. The layout guidelines advised that designers:

- identify how, when and by whom the library space will be used
- consider the size of footprint that will be needed to enable these functions
- consider break out spaces
- consider the needs of individuals, small and large groups
- consider the needs of disabled users
- consider the need for circulation space and access routes
- consider making use of the perimeter for fixtures, to create a central space that can be reconfigured
- consider how best the space can enable learning
- incorporate 2D and 3D exhibition/display space
- ensure visible sight lines
- consider the advantages of single/multiple entry/exit points
- consider the needs of students and staff for storage and lockers
- consider how resources will be loaned; self-issue stations
- consider a focus for student enquiries
- consider zoning with colour
- consider the need for staff workspace (MLA/CILIP 2007).

The area guidelines page of the School Library Association's website states that the location, size and quality of the environment of the Learning Resource Centre (LRC) are crucial in ensuring its effective use by students and staff and recommend:

> that the use of the LRC to support learning and teaching should be planned within a framework of whole-school, cross-curricular delivery of the curriculum. The learning resources provided within the LRC will be in many formats to ensure that the curriculum is fully supported and that multiple learning styles are accommodated. Careful planning of the layout of the LRC and the arrangement of the resources will help staff and students to make the best use of all types of stock and information, but it is vitally important that the LRC has enough space to take this into account.
>
> (www.SLA.org)

The guidelines make the point that the LRC will require a flexible layout to support the range of activities carried out in the library and this may include the provision of low chairs, soft seating and coffee tables to allow for comfortable browsing. They also suggest the inclusion of small tables and appropriate height chairs for group work and a separate study and appropriate furniture and storage to support the use of technology (www.SLA.org).

In the US, the School Libraries Project (SLP) in Washington DC transformed eight existing school libraries during 2005–7 (Figures 4.20–22), building on earlier work by the Robin Hood Foundation's Library Initiative in New York: this worked with schools in high poverty neighbourhoods with low academic achievement to transform school libraries into vital resources for the whole school community – students, teachers and parents – and contribute to improved student performance. Since 2002, 62 libraries have been 'reinvented' in this $40 million programme (Robin Hood Foundation 2012).

Designing for the library of the future

Key trends in the use of space in new or refurbished libraries have been the introduction of flexible, movable furniture to support the easy reconfiguration of spaces in the library, the provision of a wide range of individual and group study settings that support self-directed and team-based learning and the support of technology through the provision of both fixed PCs, laptops, e-book readers, interactive whiteboards and multimedia stations (Sullivan 2011b).

In an online discussion, the School Libraries 21C Project, commissioned by the NSW Department of Education and Training, asked librarians in Australia about the future of the school library. A number of respondents described the school library as an intellectual space for the development of a wide range of information handling, using competencies that lead to the creation of deep knowledge and understanding:

> Everyone within the school community helps build both a physical and a virtual place we could term an information commons, a learning commons, a knowledge commons where ownership is held in common and construction/collaboration are constants ... According to one respondent: One major advantage of this 'commons' approach is the marrying (and in many cases, reconciling!) of library/information and technology departments, people, resources and services within an educational institution to better reflect this convergence of information and technology within a digital society.
>
> (Hay and Todd 2010)

The school library:

> provides a common place across the school for investigating and experimenting with information, examining multiple perspectives in an environment where students are guided by professionals and given appropriate instruction to effectively utilize information and the most appropriate technology tools to support student achievement. As such, it is conceived as a unique learning environment – common, central, flexible, open, providing the opportunity for teams engaging in pedagogical experimentation to access and use information and web tools to empower learning through creativity, discovery, inquiry, cooperation, and collaboration.
>
> (p. 6)

The discussion produced a template for the school library of the future. It will be:

- a facility that features fluid library design and allows for the customization and personalization of learning, where space is iterative, agile, transitional, transformational, evolving, and shifting based on the needs of individuals, small groups and whole classes

- a place where students and teachers have the ability to create and own their own individual and collaborative learning space(s)

- a blended learning environment which harnesses the potential of physical learning spaces and digital learning spaces to meet the needs of students, teachers and parents, in school, at home or by mobile connectivity

- a learning centre whose primary focus is on building capacity for critical engagement – giving emphasis to thinking creatively, critically and reflectively with information in the process of building knowledge and understanding

- a centre of learning innovation where teachers and teacher librarians are involved in creatively designing learning experiences by way of testing, trialling and experimenting with information and tools to bring about the best knowledge outcomes for students: the teacher librarian was identified as a key person in leveraging emerging technologies – trialling, taking risks, modelling and mentoring teachers and students in the use of a range of technologies to support effective information access and knowledge creation

- a learning environment that demonstrates the power of pedagogical fusion, where pedagogy underpins the decision making behind a school's information architecture – where technology infrastructure and support services, networked information services and provision of access do not restrict innovative and flexible use of space, resources or expertise: the information services, technology and learning support provided by a school library of the future will transcend physical space and fuse not only classrooms, but homes and mobile learners

The public elementary and middle school libraries in Washington DC were considered by the school communities to be inadequate, antiquated, and to lack the basic resources to support learning and achievement. The School Libraries Project (SLP) in the city transformed eight existing school libraries in 2005–7 to fit them for a modern role – as learning spaces that would inspire students to learn and achieve. The goal was to create state-of-the-art libraries with new book collections and technology and certified library media specialists, and to strengthen these modern library media centres so that they would support each school's curriculum. In this way they would serve as the educational heart of the school, and provide a practical and replicable model of transformation and renewal for other public schools locally and nationally.

The emphasis was on recasting the library as a 'public classroom', with performance spaces and amphitheatre seating. Each of the libraries was also equipped with fully stocked book and media collections as well as state-of-the art technology.

Source: www.schoollibrariesproject.org/designs.html

Figure 4.20 Robert Brent Elementary School Library, Washington DC: Studio 27 and Lawler Architects

Figure 4.21 Payne Elementary School Library, Washington DC. Architect: Studio 27

Figure 4.22 Peabody Elementary School Library, Washington DC. Architect: Jennifer Cahn at Studio 27

- a facility consisting of seamless search interfaces, with federated searching embracing user tagging (folksonomies) as well as standardized controlled vocabularies to enable intuitive access and support conversation with the user as an interactive tool for enquiry and discovery

- a facility which seeks a balance between print and digital collections and which does not privilege one format over another, consistent with the multiformat nature of our information world. At the same time, it is increasingly conscious of the need to redesign and reshape physical spaces to better support teachers and students as digital researchers. With shrinking hard copy collections, we need to explore ways to best utilize these spaces for collaborative digital production

- a centre that supports literary learning, where students become immersed in imaginary worlds, explore personal reading interests, develop sustained voluntary reading practices, and develop reading for meaning and independence as critically capable readers (pp. 15–16).

It is clear that, just as the role of the school library evolves, so will the spaces to support that role. As one respondent to the Schools 21C online discussion put it: 'Imagine an activity and we will make a space for it' (p. 15).

CHAPTER 5

The further and higher education campus

INTRODUCTION

Universities are institutions with long lifespans. Since the creation of the first university at Bologna in 1088, universities have created campuses and buildings to enable them to deliver their academic vision and instruct successive generations of students (Gaston 2010: 18). While some buildings may last hundreds of years, others become rapidly obsolete and are torn down and replaced with new buildings to meet new academic or research imperatives. Campus real estate is often expensive and in short supply and there are many drivers to make sure that the institution gains the most from the space it has.

These gains extend far beyond effectiveness: it could be said that the built estate functions in much the same way as the nest of the bower bird, attracting in this case not a mate but the best students and faculty and the largest research grants. Alumni and other benefactors fund the creation of new buildings and facilities not only to support the institution but also to signal their own success and achievement and connection to the institution, as instanced by the naming of everything from buildings down to individual classrooms.

While campuses overall may evolve slowly, as new land is acquired and buildings are replaced or renovated, the cycle of change is accelerating rapidly at the level of the spaces within the campus. Virtually every space type on campus is being radically rethought to see how the student and staff experience can be improved and the efficiency and effectiveness of every square metre of space on campus enhanced.

General teaching spaces are having to support a wider range of pedagogies, techniques and technologies and are becoming increasingly interactive. Specialist areas – laboratories, studios, research facilities – are increasingly becoming shared spaces with centralized support facilities, interdisciplinary, and committed to the stimulation of knowledge transfer and innovation. Academic and administrative staff are sharing the workplace, libraries are shifting from a passive role as book depositories to an active role in learning as part of the total student experience, and social learning spaces are integrating formal and informal learning and social activities on – and off – the campus.

In each area of the campus there is a pronounced drive to greater inclusivity, a more open approach to breaking down barriers between space types and space uses, and an awareness – not always formulated – that future resilience depends on present porosity of design. This observation holds true for each of the ten physical aspects of the higher education campus discussed in this chapter (Table 5.1).

GENERAL TEACHING SPACES

General teaching spaces have been dominated throughout the last century by one type of design: tutor-focused, one-way facing and presentational, with seating arranged in either a U-shape or in straight rows (JISC 2006: 10). Modes of learning in the future are likely to be different (Figure 5.1) – more collaborative and active, integrated and multidisciplinary, blending technology and social activity, immersive and hybridizing online and face-to-face activities – and call for changed learning settings (Figure 5.2).

As learning spaces become more flexible and offer more options for accommodating different styles of teaching and learning and increased use of individual and collaborative technology, more

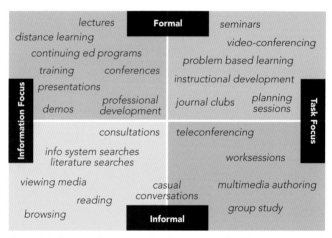

Figure 5.1 Changing learning modes. Source: Dugdale (1997, in Duggan and Dugdale 2003)

Table 5.1 Key space trends across the higher education campus by type and usage

Space type	Trends
General teaching spaces	● Support for wide range of pedagogies resulting in increased diversity in learning settings ● Increased use of group working and collaborative learning ● More space per student required to increase flexibility ● Increased use of technology to support learning – blending of physical and digital space ● Lecture theatres becoming more interactive through different space configurations or use of technology
Laboratories and research facilities	● Creation of multipurpose/ flexi-labs to support undergraduate teaching ● Grouping of labs into science clusters with centralized support facilities ● Creation of science landscape with different degrees of servicing and equipment provision ● Separation of write-up and teaching space from laboratory experimentation spaces ● Increased requirements for alternative research spaces to support interdisciplinary research ● Increased importance placed on social spaces to stimulate knowledge transfer and innovation
Specialized learning spaces	● Increased sharing of workshops, studios and other technical spaces with centralized support infrastructure ● Rethinking of architecture and design studios to become more events-based rather than space-based ● Creation of multidisciplinary studio spaces to more closely mirror professional practice ● Partnering with external organizations to create shared facilities
Social learning spaces	● Creation of wide range of social learning spaces on campus to support informal learning and social activities ● 'Reclaiming' of circulation and other spaces such as cafes to create additional informal learning settings ● Creating spaces that can be appropriated and 'owned' by students for periods of time ● Campuses conceived as 'networks' of places for learning, discovery, and discourse between students, faculty, staff and the wider community ● Recognizing that the city is the campus – learning goes beyond the campus boundaries and must be supported ● Library has evolved to become a key hub of social learning through the creation of learning or information commons type spaces
Academic libraries	● Shift from role as repository of books to being centre of active learning on campus ● Concentration of book collection with low-use material placed in high-density storage or moved off site ● Creation of a wide range of study settings that integrate physical and digital learning activities ● Increased group project spaces while continuing to support individual scholarship ● Increased support of total student experience – cafes, social areas, games spaces ● Library used to house shared advanced technology including video conferencing, data visualization, broadcast and recording studios
Academic and administrative workspace	● Application of space guidelines to reduce the amount of space dedicated to academic and administrative workspace ● Move towards more open and shared workplaces for both academic and administrative staff ● Creation of wider range of workplace support settings including spaces for tutorials, pastoral care with students, staff meetings and informal interactions

Space type	Trends
Student centres	• Incorporating a wider range of student amenities including recreational and sports facilities, retail and catering outlets, student meeting and events spaces as well as social learning and work areas • Creation of 'one stop shops' to deliver student services • Seen as important recruitment aid for students
Academic innovation centres and business incubators	• Level of provision varied widely from university run start-up space for academic spin-off companies to creation of integrated university–commercial research facilities • Connection to campus, academic research activities and shared facilities important • Important and visible part of knowledge transfer and engagement with surrounding business community
Student housing	• Demand for higher-quality housing options with more shared facilities such as cafes, fitness facilities, study lounges • Inclusion of teaching spaces and other academic functions in the housing complexes to create mixed-use facilities • Increased use of external partners for provision of student housing
Sports facilities	• Diversity of sports offer based on institutional priorities, availability of land and funding. • Important recruitment tool for many institutions making it a priority for investment • Integration of sports facilities with academic spaces to support sport-related programmes

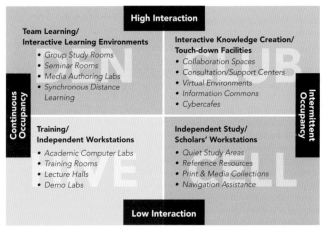

Figure 5.2 Changing learning settings. Source: Dugdale/DEGW (1998, in Duggan and Dugdale 2003)

space is required per student (Box 5.1). Figure 5.3 makes the point that the degree of flexibility required is likely to have direct implications on teaching space capacity and space planning. Where flexible teaching spaces have been introduced, the extra space requirement is often compensated for by trying to increase the utilization of the flexible rooms. In the UK, for example, utilization of teaching rooms during the core week in higher education is often only 20–30 per cent: there is considerable opportunity for the intensification of use of these spaces.

Increased diversity of learning settings

As the learning experience becomes increasingly multilayered – with learning spaces providing a number of flexible activity zones to support learning, living and working – users will be able to choose appropriate settings and technology for the tasks they want to achieve. The spaces and experiences will change over the course of the day: changing to reflect different types of users at different times of the day. More space will be devoted to collaborative activities and informal meeting and work areas will need to be provided to support mobile learners.

There will be a requirement for ergonomic, easily reconfigurable furniture and power everywhere (in the short to mid-term at least). In the longer term, the performance of laptop batteries is likely to improve to the point where a full day's use will be possible with a single charge or through the use of hydrogen fuel cells (*Taipei Times* 2012). Learning spaces will need to be able to incorporate a wide range of technology-enabled work settings capable of supporting larger or multiple screens, webcams, telepresence systems, voice input and increased use of audio/video materials.

JISC (2009a) developed a categorization for technologies to support blended learning, grouped under four key headings – mobile learning, visual and interactive learning, connected learning and supported learning (Table 5.2). These technologies will have implications on design for the learning spaces in terms of acoustics,

Box 5.1 Space to achieve multipurpose learning

Research by DEGW North America in 2007 (DEGW 2008) found that a typical classroom with tablet arm chairs requires 1.4–1.67 square metres per person and really only supports a lecture format well. The ability to undertake group work is constrained and little space is provided for student laptops.

At 1.9–2.8 square metres per person, moveable furniture and shared tables for students can be utilized, offering more flexibility and spontaneous group work can be better accommodated.

At 2.3–3.25 square metres per person a true multipurpose learning space can be achieved, allowing instructors to teach the way they want rather than 'teach to the room' and enabling different learning modalities to be accommodated.

Source: DEGW (2008a)

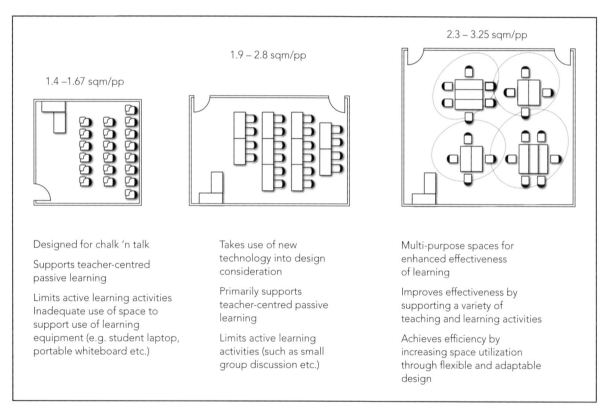

Figure 5.3 Impact of active learning on space requirements. Source: DEGW (2008a)

light and enclosure to support hybrid physical/virtual learning and research settings. Figure 5.4 illustrates the range of settings required to support the diverse learning and teaching approaches used at contemporary universities.

Access to daylight has always been seen as a key component of a healthy building but digital learning settings will require a controlled light/sound environment. The zoning of university buildings to include these settings in the deeper, less well-lit areas of each floor and the use of internal mobility to allow individuals to select appropriate learning settings will help to ensure that future learning environments are still a healthy place to be.

The status of lectures is also changing: their role and effectiveness have long been a source of debate and the size and configuration of a traditional lecture theatre or classroom are frequently seen as constraining the introduction of innovative learning and teaching approaches. Immobile furniture or a lack of storage space in which unwanted furniture can be placed, a defined 'front' to the room, insufficient technology infrastructure and poor lighting and

Table 5.2 Technologies to support blended learning

Mobile learning	Visual and interactive learning
• Tablet PCs	• Video conferencing
• Laptops	• Video streaming
• Mobile phones	• Image projection
• Wireless keyboards/mice PDAs	• Interactive whiteboards
• Digital cameras	• Voting devices
Connected learning	**Supported learning**
• Wired computing	• Assistive technologies
• Wireless networks	• Accessible USB ports
• Wireless-enabled laptops/ tablet PCs	• Audio-visual prompts
• Internet-enabled PDAs and mobile phones	• Video recording facilities
	• Plasma screen information information points

Source: JISC (2009a: 6–7)

acoustics can make the transition from didactic to small group learning daunting in a 50-minute class period.

Acker and Miller (2005), for example, noted that new learning space design paradigms must adapt to student learning styles while still taking account of the institution's need for fiscal efficiencies:

> Previously, the cost savings associated with large lecture halls, fixed seating, and minimal investments in technology drove decision making. Today, the emphasis is more balanced, and the roles that attractive learning spaces play in bringing the most accomplished students and faculty to campus and in increasing student engagement with learning are better recognized.
>
> (p. 2)

They cited a 2001 project at the Ohio State University that was undertaken with the institution's Center for Academic Transformation. The Statistics 135 course was taken by approximately 3,250 students and consisted of three lectures a week in

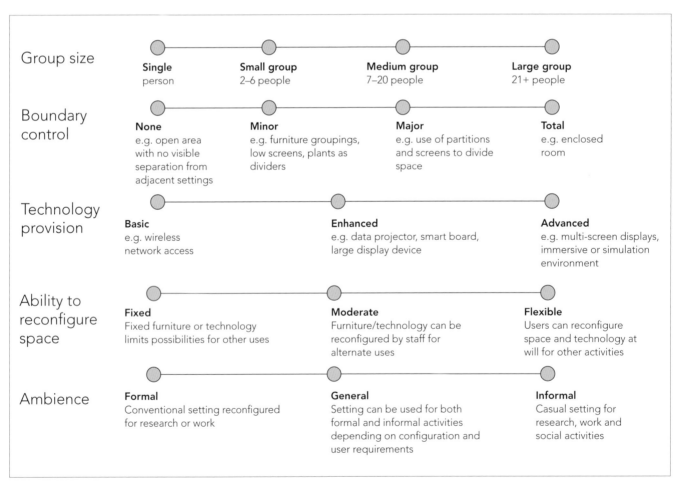

Figure 5.4 Taxomony of future learning settings. Source: DEGW(2008a)

a large lecture hall plus bi-weekly lab sessions led by a graduate student. The course was redesigned based on a survey of student learning styles using the Felder-Soloman Learning Styles Inventory (Felder and Soloman 2002) in which the student population was divided into those who preferred lectures, those who preferred small group discussion and those who preferred independent online learning: 'By adapting teaching method to learning style, and delivering it in three different space configurations, student grades increased by .5 standard deviations. Dropouts decreased from 20 per cent to 12 per cent, reported course satisfaction went up, and the cost per student fell from $190 to $142' (ibid.: 2).

The limitations of the traditional lecture theatre have also been discussed by Jamieson (2007). In a publication resulting from a design workshop with the University of Melbourne and partici-pants from a number of international universities, he noted that 'the lecture theatre is directly oriented towards a "presentational" approach [and] it also indirectly works against the adoption of collaborative or discursive approaches. In order to implement a new approach, the teacher must find the time for related adjustments in teaching methods and possibly in course material while often relying on furniture and/or facilities designed for other approaches' (ibid.). In 2006, a project at the University of Melbourne led Jamieson to remove a 100-seat chemistry lecture theatre and replace it with a 40-seat learning lab to support collaborative, small group learning (Universitas 21 2012).

There has also been innovation in lecture theatre design in an attempt to integrate elements of interactive and small group learning with more traditional didactic instruction. In what has become known as a 'Harvard style' classroom (Figure 5.5), the lecture theatre – more properly, a case study room – becomes a more intimate space, with a limited number of rows, where the instructor or facilitator can see and interact with all the students. These rooms may also be technology-enabled, with built-in micro-phones at the desk, audiovisual and presentation and recording systems, multiple screens to display digital information from a variety of sources, either built-in desktop computers and/or LAN/WAN/internet connections for laptops and videoconferencing to allow links to speakers and participants in other locations.

Figure 5.5 The Harvard-style classroom – involving and interactive

At the University of Strathclyde in Glasgow, Scotland the refurbishment of the James Weir Building gave the Department of Engineering the opportunity to rethink its learning and teaching strategy and to re-design existing lecture theatres. In one configuration, swivel chairs were provided so that students could turn round to access computer workstations on a work surface behind them for either individual or group study tasks.

In another auditorium, seats were divided into four-person 'banana-shaped' tables for group working. At the start of their course, students are assessed on their subject, computing ability, personality, where they are living or where they are from, and placed in 'cohorts' for the year. Students in each cohort then get to know and help one another, and work together.

The 'banana' seating configuration was developed to accommodate these cohorts of four persons and to encourage students to learn from and interact with each other. The format enables the students to switch easily between group work and formal teaching, and uses technology to facilitate the presentation of information. This approach to lectures is considered to be very successful with '90% continuing attendance, compared with 50% for the old-style classes' (SFC 2006: 36).

An electronic voting system was also introduced in these lecture spaces to help students test their understanding of concepts in response to multiple-choice questions, and collaborative discussion before and after voting became established as an integral pedagogic approach within the department (JISC 2006: 12).

Space for small group work can also be created in a lecture theatre by having two rows of seats per tier with swivel chairs in the front row allowing students to turn around from their writing surface to face the students in the row behind who are at the same level. This layout creates work surfaces for laptops and more extended breakout work opportunities.

Innovative learning spaces

Many institutions have been experimenting with larger, more flexible 'flat floor' teaching spaces that can support both didactic instruction and small group working. These spaces may be referred to as technology-enabled active learning classrooms, learning labs, learning studios or even hyperstruction studios. In essence, the concept originated in work at North Carolina State University with SCALE-UP (student-centred active learning environment for undergraduate programmes) (Figure 5.6), and was further developed at Virginia Tech (Figure 5.7), Strathclyde and MIT (Figure 5.8), which created the TEAL programme to support physics teaching.

The concept has been taken up in institutions from the University of Melbourne to Aga Khan University (Figures 5.9–5.15), encouraging active learning rather than passive listening and dependent on technology-rich learning spaces.

Figure 5.6 SCALE-UP, North Carolina State University

In an effort to deal with increasing student numbers – but fixed staffing levels – a 60,000 square foot space in a former department store was converted to create a math emporium that contains 550 computers in groups of six. The space is used for a wide range of parallel learning activities including 'lectureless' online learning, with staff on hand 15 hours daily. In addition to the open area, where computers are arranged in six-station circular pods, the math emporium has space for large orientation sessions, small conferences and tutoring, a maths education lab, quiet study areas and student lounges. The facility is open 24/7 and staffed days and evenings by members of the faculty, graduate students, and advanced undergraduate students who offer personal assistance when students request it. Peer group projects, collaboration, and tutoring are also encouraged (Oblinger 2006: 42.2).

Robinson and Moore state that the development of the math emporium has led to 'demonstrable improvements in student learning and significantly reduced costs for staffing and space' (Robinson and Moore 2006, in Oblinger 2006: 42.2).

Source: Oblinger (2006)

Figure 5.7 Math Emporium, Virginia Tech

MIT developed the TEAL (technology-enabled active learning) programme to support physics teaching. The drivers for the programme included the desire to increase lecture attendance (previously around 50 per cent) and student engagement at introductory courses, encouraging students to 'come away from these introductory courses with more of an appreciation for the beauty of physics, both conceptually and analytically' and to encourage students to continue to take more advanced physics courses.

The TEAL classrooms are based on the SCALE-UP concepts developed at North Carolina State University. Learning takes placed in teams of three, grouped around large tables of nine people in a room for 120 learners. Each team has a networked laptop connected to surrounding projection screens. Desktop experiments and visualizations developed by the team can be shown to the whole class. Thirteen cameras record the activity at each table's shared work surface, allowing projection for sharing to all the others (SFC 2006: 7).

Source: http://icampus.mit.edu/teal/content/?whatisteal

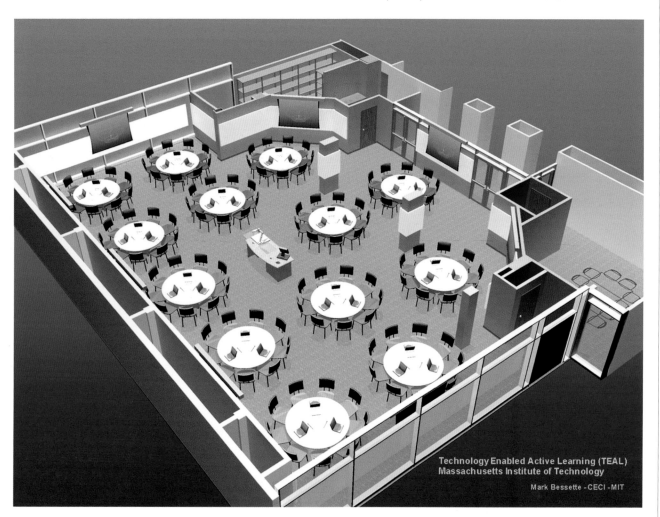

Technology Enabled Active Learning (TEAL)
Massachusetts Institute of Technology

Mark Bessette - CECI - MIT

Figure 5.8 MIT TEAL classrooms

Innovative learning spaces can, however, equally be 'low tech', using existing spaces as well as 'appropriating' spaces to use for formal learning, whether this is sitting under a tree on campus or trips to cultural institutions, field study or trips to other cities or countries.

The Institute for Educational Development (IED) at the Aga Khan University (AKU) in Karachi, Pakistan, for example, has created a learning space called 'the kiva' based on the kivas of the Puebloans of the American South West (Figure 5.16). This bookable space consists of a sunken circular pit with two levels of seating in

Figure 5.9 The Learning Lab, University of Melbourne, Australia – prior to refurbishment

The Learning Lab at the University of Melbourne is a 100-seat chemistry lecture theatre converted into a 40-seat collaborative classroom to improve student experience – the didactic lecture and tutorial elements of the courses had been identified as the weakest element of the course by both staff and students. The lab is not discipline specific and accommodates a class of up to 40, arranged in five groups of eight or ten groups of four. The lab has been designed to promote collaborative group learning, interaction and a more student-centred approach.

it that can hold 20–30 students for group discussions. While technology is present at the perimeter of the room, the primary pedagogy for the space is face-to-face discussion with only paper-based support.

And at AKU's regional Faculty of Arts and Sciences campus in east Africa currently under development in Arusha, Tanzania, the intention is to take advantage of the mild climate and create a wide range of semi-enclosed 'hybrid' learning spaces that have shelter from direct sunlight and rain but are open and connected to the environment. Some spaces will be explicitly derived from east African traditional learning spaces such as the baraza, the veranda or stone bench outside the house where village discussions would take place and information would be exchanged.

It is also possible to appropriate space temporarily to create innovative learning spaces. Aalto University in Helsinki in 2010 rented a train ('Aalto on Tracks') to take a group of around 100 students and faculty to the Shanghai Expo (Figures 5.17 and 5.18) (Aalto on tracks 2012) – and in 2011 took another group of students by cruise ship from Lisbon to Sao Paulo in Brazil ('Aalto on Waves') (Aalto on waves 2012).

The space has been designed over four levels to deal with the significant change in level between the inside and outside of the building and also to assist with the creation of individual and separate smaller group settings. Each zone has IT access that includes group use of PCs, laptop points, external input sources, a document camera in each zone and a large LCD display that can be driven 'centrally' or be under the control of the zone group to share their work within the group or to others in the class. Tasks can be set for groups in the class that require online access to electronic databases, e-journals and resources: gathering the information as it is required and the problem solution that is enabled become part of the class reporting and presentation task.

The lab is also equipped for remote video observation and recording which is used for reflective analysis by staff, as records and examples of good practice and innovation, and as the basis of research analysis and evaluation in the use of the lab for teaching and learning.

Sources: http://www.universitas212.bham.ac.uk/TandL/Presentations/LSB.pdf; http://www.caudit.edu.au/educauseaustralasia07/authors_papers/Tregloan.pdf

Figure 5.10 The Learning Lab, University of Melbourne, Australia

The University of Minnesota Active Learning Classrooms (ALCs) were designed to foster interactive, flexible, student-centred learning experiences, and operate using central teaching stations and student-provided laptops. They are a modification of the 'SCALE-UP' (student-centred active learning environment for undergraduate programmes) concept that originated at North Carolina State University and the TEAL (technology-enabled active learning) concept at MIT, and uses an adaptation of the Projection Capable Classrooms (PCC) technology system.

The rooms also include a 360-degree glass surface marker board, multiple flat-panel display projection systems, round tables that accommodate nine students each and a central teaching station that allows selection and display of table-specific information.

Both classrooms feature reconfigurable low-profile flooring with internal power and cable management and demountable wall systems. Demountable wall systems in the larger room allow the room to be reconfigured, or flexed, on an annual basis to meet changing room size or pedagogical requirements. The 117-capacity room has the ability to flex smaller into two Active Learning Classrooms (72 and 36 capacity), two traditional seating table/chair classrooms, or one Active Learning Classroom and one traditional classroom.

Source: http://www.classroom.umn.edu/projects/ALCOverview.html; http://www.classroom.umn.edu/projects/alc_report_final.pdf

Figure 5.11 Active Learning Classrooms (ALCs), University of Minnesota

A grant from AT&T allowed Abilene Christian University, Texas, to explore the impact of mobile learning through the creation of a mobile research fellows programme, a digital learning institute programme and the further development of the AT&T Learning Studio. Facilities in the studio include a resource desk, a media lab including editing workstations, and a 'speaking centre' where students can develop, rehearse and record presentations. The studio also includes a range of smaller spaces where students can work on projects:

Idea rooms (2–4 people)

- Outline a group presentation on a whiteboard wall.

- Take photo of brainstorming on whiteboard wall.

- Create a document on a networked computer.

Studio rooms (1–4 people)

- Record a podcast on high-quality studio microphones.

- Capture an audio screencast with slides and voice-over.

- Record a practice speech to your mobile device.

Collaboration rooms (5–16 people)

- Share laptop and iPad screens to contribute to a project.

- Practice a group presentation in a conference room.

- Watch a film with a study group in the screening room.

Digital diners (2–6 people)

- Meet a group for an informal study session.

- Access to power makes booths ideal for laptop users.

Source: http://blogs.acu.edu/learningstudio/
exploring-mobile-media-at-acu/

Figure 5.12 AT&T Learning Studio, Abilene Christian University, Texas

Figure 5.13 AT&T Learning Studio, Abilene Christian University, Texas

Figure 5.14 University of Virginia School of Medicine Learning Studio

The University of Virginia School of Medicine decided to implement a radical change to its undergraduate medical curriculum – moving away from the traditional approach of making students spend two years sitting through long lectures and regurgitating facts on tests, followed by the shock treatment in their third year of suddenly dealing with patients in a hospital ward. Rather than just learning and regurgitating facts (50 per cent of which will be obsolete within five years), the goal is to create a learning experience that will develop the habits of mind – curiosity, scepticism, compassion, wonder – that will prepare them to be better physicians. The new curriculum focuses on the critical nature of understanding and using integrated content relevant to working with patients.

The Learning Studio is a large space (4,500 square feet) in which the entire first year class of about 155 students work together in team-based learning. Rather than being anchored by a dominant teaching wall, the UVa Learning Studio utilizes multiple presentation spaces that allow faculty to cycle from small group case study to large group learning as needed. The room is filled with round tables wired into the presentation system, all surrounding a high-tech lectern in the middle of the room. In teams of eight, the students debate patient cases and work together in sessions that last a number of hours rather than the traditional 50-minute lecture period. The room's interactive technology links student laptops, big screens and a document camera that works like an overhead projector. Absentees can view a podcast of the session.

The faculty members working with the first-year medical students in the Learning Studio had more than 160 hours of development and training in pedagogy to teach the newly designed curriculum using new technologies in the new learning spaces.

Sources: http://uvamagazine.org/features/article/adjusting_the_ prescription/; http://k12albemarle.wordpress.com/tag/ uva-learning-studio/

The Aga Khan University Faculty of Health Sciences in Karachi, Pakistan, plans to significantly increase the number of students and range of courses it offers on the Stadium Road campus. In parallel with a campus redevelopment and expansion programme, the Faculty is reviewing its learning and teaching strategy including the use of blended learning to link the medical campuses, hospitals and medical clinics in Pakistan and East Africa.

The Learning Studio project is one of a series of pilot projects under consideration across the university exploring new learning approaches and spaces. The goal is to create a flexible learning space that is easy to reconfigure in different ways to support a wide range of learning activities.

The Learning Studio will be located in the 220 square metre space currently used as the Dissection Hall. This space is currently under-utilized and does not support activities in an optimal way.

The Anatomy Studio will support learning activities associated with the study of Anatomy alongside the practice of dissection but will also be used to support a wide range of other activities, supported by reconfigurable furniture, flexible walls and appropriate technology. The learning activities to be accommodated in the Anatomy Studio will include:

- full body dissection – up to six tables with six to eight students per table

- pre/post dissection briefings for up to 50 students and instructors

- OSCEs (Objective Structured Clinical Examinations) – six OSCE stations including trolley/bed space

- problem-based learning for groups of four to six

- seminars for 10 to 20 participants

- individual learning using anatomical resources and/or PCs

- paper based examinations for up to 50 students

- video conferencing/distance learning with other campuses.

Flexible furniture, in-room storage for furniture and other items and easy access to adjacent cadaver stores, reconfigurable lighting, good acoustics and a high-speed fibre optic infrastructure for recording and broadcast will be crucial for the success of the Anatomy Studio.

Source: Spaces That Work project documents

Figure 5.15 Anatomy Studio, Faculty of Health Sciences, Aga Khan University, Karachi

Figure 5.16 Institute for Educational Development, Karachi in Pakistan – 'the kiva'. Innovative learning spaces need not be high tech, as the Aga Khan University's kiva indicates

Evaluation of learning spaces

While there has been considerable interest in the development of innovative learning spaces in recent years, less attention has been paid to evaluating the impact of these spaces on learning outcomes (Temple 2007: 5–7). The performance of the first learning studio created at the University of Missouri–St Louis (UMSL) was, however, the subject of a detailed evaluation by Tom et al. in 2008 (Figure 5.19) (Tom et al. 2008: 43), emerging as an important harbinger of change on the UMSL campus, in terms of both the university's conceptions of teaching and learning and its approach to development of physical space. Researchers were struck by the way in which the completed space challenged faculty and students to rethink their possibilities at UMSL.

In 2009, Whiteside et al. carried out an evaluation of the impact of the University of Minnesota's two pilot Active Learning Classrooms (ALCs) shown in Figure 5.11 (Whiteside et al. 2009). They found

(based on questionnaires and interviews with faculty and students) that the ALCs changed the learning experience through deepening instructor–student relationships, supported the transition of the teachers to the role of 'learning coach' or facilitator and created environments where learning could easily occur. Students stated that they found the ALCs to be effective for teamwork and collaborative projects, the spaces helped them feel more connected to their instructor and, especially, to their classmates and encouraged discussion and helped them feel active and talkative.

The researchers subsequently explored the impact of the ALCs on learning outcomes. When comparing the same biology course taught in a traditional classroom and one of the ALCs the researchers found that:

> despite the professor's explicit attempts to conduct the same learning activities in both sections, he behaved quite

During the Aalto on Tracks 10-day trip, a wide range of learning and social events took place in the train's conference cars – including workshops on innovation and entrepreneurship and the future of internet banking, lectures on Russian and Chinese culture, a course on Chinese project management practices and a mobile TedX event as well as a range of cultural, social and sports activities.

Source: http://aaltoontracks.com/

Figures 5.17–18 Aalto on Tracks

In 2008 Tom et al. noted how well the University of Missouri–St Louis (UMSL) Learning Studio expressed the nascent cultural change that the university was experiencing (p. 43). One student is quoted at length:

> This is my 2nd semester in this classroom, and every day, I like it more than the first. I feel that this classroom promotes a positive learning environment the second you walk in the door. No longer do we sit in a stark classroom, walls white, with windows that make a classroom feel like a prison. No longer are we confined to one, hard-seated desk ... The warm walls and pictures, colorful carpet, and welcoming couches beg to be noticed. Students sit where they choose, at group tables or individual tables ...When you walk in the room, you want to learn.

Evaluation methodologies for the learning studio consisted of faculty observation, analysis of student blog entries, video observation, surveys and faculty debriefing sessions. The authors felt that the Learning Studio seemed to encourage a more positive attitude in students and a readiness to become engaged and the student assessments showed that the students clearly found the environment conducive to learning, judging from their own assessments. One group of users were undergoing major course review and pedagogic change while they were using the studio and Faculty in that department unanimously agreed that changes in pedagogy were enabled, facilitated, and informed by use of the studio classroom.

The authors conclude that 'the Learning Studio has succeeded in stimulating change, especially pedagogical change, at UMSL. The term "studio" continues to be appropriate; it's a place to try new expressions of the principles of teaching and learning and to change the "institutional context"'.

They did, however, acknowledge the possibility that some of the benefits of the learning studio may be a result of the 'Hawthorne effect':

> The institution has built this new space, the instructors are excited, the space and equipment are beautiful, and people are paying attention, but what happens when the novelty wears off? What happens when all classrooms are built this way? Although that would be a pleasant problem to have, will the effects persist?
>
> (Tom et al. 2008: 51)

Figure 5.19 UMSL Learning Studio

differently in the two classrooms, lecturing significantly more in the traditional room and conducting discussion significantly more in the ALC ... Additionally, given the physical constraints of the traditional classroom, the professor remained at or near the instructor's podium significantly more than he did in the ALC, which afforded considerably greater freedom of movement throughout the space. The instructor also consulted (discreetly) with individual or small groups of students significantly more in the ALC than in the traditional classroom. Finally, students in the ALC participated in group activities about 9 per cent more than students in the traditional classroom.

(ibid.)

There were significant differences in student perceptions of the impact of the ALC on learning (in terms of engagement, enrichment, effectiveness, flexibility, fit and instructor use) with the classrooms receiving higher ratings from students from a metropolitan rather than a rural background and from freshman and sophomore students rather than more senior students.

Whiteside was also part of a 2008 study to explore relationships among formal and informal learning spaces, teaching and learning practices, and student learning outcomes. The goal was to develop evidence-based criteria for student-centred, integrated, active learning spaces using flexible design and an innovative use of technology tools (ibid.). The study found that furniture and the layout of the space were important: round tables inherently supported the creation of 'a collaborative environment for learning and, in most cases, allowed students to quickly and easily create a community of learners. Round tables forced students to look at each other, thus changing the relationship' (ibid.: 4).

Staff and students differed in their opinions of the larger learning studio type spaces. In one case, students in the focus group reported that they enjoyed the open space and that the space made them feel closer to their instructor than they would have in a more traditional classroom. The instructor, however, felt overwhelmed by the openness and size of the space and preferred the control that a smaller classroom would provide.

Students and instructors also differed in their views regarding the availability and access to technology. When laptop computers with wireless connectivity were available in the classroom, many students came to class earlier and stayed later. Student focus group participants reported that availability of technology in their learning space elevated their learning experience and helped them to become more efficient, effective citizens. The instructor, however, saw students' use of technology during class as disrespectful and disruptive to learning. This instructor also reported

that students were noticeably less comfortable when technology tools were removed from the learning space (ibid: 4).

An article by Craig Lambert in the March–April 2012 *Harvard Magazine*, 'Twilight of the lecture', discussed the benefits of interactive learning over traditional lecture teaching. In his view, interactive learning triples students' gains in knowledge as measured by conceptual tests and a range of other assessment methods. He quotes Eric Mazur, Balkanski professor of physics and applied physics at Harvard University, who believes that interactive learning reduces the gender gap between male and female performance in Harvard physics courses:

'If you look at incoming scores for our male and female physics students at Harvard, there's a gap,' Mazur explains. 'If you teach a traditional course, the gap just translates up: men gain, women gain, but the gap remains the same. If you teach interactively, *both* gain more, but the women gain disproportionately more and close the gap' (Mazur, in Lambert 2012: 3). Mazur admits there is no definitive research on what causes this but speculates that the verbal and collaborative/collegial nature of peer interactions may enhance the learning environment for women students.

Lambert also quotes Mazur as believing that there is better retention of knowledge following interactive learning, as peer-instructed students who have actively argued for and explained their understanding of scientific concepts hold onto their knowledge longer. Another benefit of interactive learning is in cultivating more scientists: 'A comparison of intended and actual concentrators in STEM (science, technology, engineering, mathematics) fields indicates that those taught interactively are only half as likely to change to a non-STEM discipline as students in traditional courses' (ibid: 3).

The spatial implications, Mazur feels, are profound:

Most classrooms – more like 99.9 per cent – on campus are auditoriums ... They are built with just one purpose: focusing the attention of many on the professor. The professor is active, and the audience is just sitting there, taking in information. Instead, you could get away from the auditorium seating and set up classrooms like you see in elementary schools, where four children sit around a square table facing each other, and you give them some kind of group activity to work on: that's active learning. It's no accident that most elementary schools are organized that way. The reason is, that's how we learn. For some reason we unlearn how to learn as we progress from elementary school through middle school and high school. And in a sense, maybe I'm bringing kindergarten back to college by having people talk to each other!

(2012: 6)

LABORATORIES AND RESEARCH FACILITIES

The relationship between science spaces and the willingness of students to engage in science at both school level and in higher education has been long discussed. Research in 2006 by the Royal Society of Chemists and the laboratory advisory service CLEAPSS (now a name, not an acronym: Consortium of Local Authorities for the Provision of Science Services) found that 65 per cent of school laboratories were sub-standard or uninspiring (CLEAPSS 2006). Concern about the impact of poor-quality school laboratories on future science take-up at university also led to Project Faraday (2008), an initiative by the UK government of the time to make 'science a priority in schools at all levels; to improve science learning and teaching and to inspire more young people, from all backgrounds, to study and work in science'.

Many universities are also becoming more concerned about the utilization of the existing teaching laboratories on campus.

In 2003, Ira Fink noted that for many colleges and universities, the amount of space dedicated to class laboratories exceeds the amount of space used for classrooms:

> As campuses work to increase their efficiency, improving space utilization has gained importance as a key facility planning activity. Increasing classroom use and utilization has long been under the microscope as a target for improving the use of campus space. Improving class laboratory use is another matter altogether. These important instructional spaces remain under the radar, because they are not well understood and because they are so varied.
>
> (Fink 2003: 17)

Fink suggested that while class laboratories are essential to the teaching mission, allowing hands-on instruction to be carried out in rooms tailored to a specific academic programme need, underused or unused class laboratory space provide an opportunity to reclaim and reuse excess space for other high priority needs, such as research.

Fink differentiates between science and non-science laboratories, each with identified spatial needs to meet the teaching patterns of the sponsoring discipline and to optimize the station count for span of control and safety. Science class laboratories require unique furniture and specialized equipment, both fixed and movable, while non-science class laboratories have less or no equipment generated needs.

With few exceptions, class laboratories are used only for undergraduate instruction. Graduate students generally conduct their experimental work in their own laboratory stations, usually in research laboratories, which have separate room use classification, use, and utilization patterns (Fink 2003: 17).

Fink notes:

> it is difficult to gauge the significance of information on class laboratory utilization, because the data is usually an average taken across all class laboratories on a campus and because the requirements concerning the class week vary so widely. For campuses that conduct such studies, the utilization results should not be an end in themselves. Rather, the data can be used as part of an analysis to help identify the circumstances that control the amount and level of class laboratory use. If it is possible to consolidate or better schedule the class laboratories, a campus may gain better efficiencies or reclaim unused class laboratories for other uses.
>
> (Fink 2003: 24)

It is not only the utilization of space that is of concern to many institutions but how well the spaces support the learning and teaching strategy for science: this may use technology and simulation as a core part of the instruction, may be multidisciplinary, thematic or problem based, or utilize a wide range of non-laboratory spaces on and off campus.

Project Kaleidoscope (PKAL) was established in the US in 1989 to advocate the building and sustaining of strong undergraduate programmes in the fields of science, technology, engineering and mathematics (STEM). It has more recently partnered with the American Association of Colleges and Universities to create a national dialogue about creating, scaling up, and sustaining more engaging, learner-centred STEM environments to enable students at all types of institutions to learn and succeed (PKALAACU).

The nature of future STEM learning environments is being explored by the PKAL Learning Spaces Collaboratory (LSC), which will explore 'whether, how, and why 21st century learning spaces make a difference to 21st century learners' (PKALLSC).

> Faculty and administrators must determine if and how their physical facilities can support the research-rich, technology-intensive environments that lead to robust learning by undergraduate students; in like manner, they must explore if and how their spaces can foster the kind of natural science community that attracts all students into the study of STEM fields and motivates them to pursue careers in these fields.
>
> (PKALLSC 2010)

Improved spaces make a difference, the report states, in that they:

- create the opportunity for strengthening learning, with greater student access to opportunities to 'do science' from introductory courses through upper-level courses for majors

- introduce an increasing number of students to the art and excitement of doing research, thereby fostering critical thinking, problem-solving and communication skills

- enable flexible scheduling and use, accommodating students with different learning styles and different career aspirations

- play a role in recruiting strong faculty, as candidates see the value the institution places on these disciplines and its commitment for the future

- accommodate emerging interdisciplinary thrusts in teaching, research and learning

- provide expanded technology infrastructures that support programmatic reforms based on an increased use of instructional technologies, and give students a command of the tools of information exchange essential for work and lifelong learning

- leverage the search for external support, making the institution more competitive in obtaining grants for research, curriculum faculty development and instrumentation

- are occasions for revisiting institutional priorities, and for considering the allocation or reallocation of resources so that those priorities can be funded over the long term (ibid.).

The need for flexibility in science learning spaces and teaching laboratories is stressed in *The Whole Building Design Guide* (2010): 'Today's teaching laboratory acts as a flexible framework, holding dynamic student work groups, research zones, and support equipment in unlimited arrangements' (Watch et al. 2010).

To enable this flexibility the guide recommended the installation of additional extra power, data, cooling and space over and above the minimum current requirements to serve the future. Laboratories will need to become more dynamic, holding a range of short and long-term 'special events' and the laboratories will need to be supplemented by visualization and virtual reality labs that will have a significant impact on the way space will be used.

> Interaction of learners and teachers occupying the same room has become more intentional, flexible and transparent to eliminate barriers and energize immediate and seamless collaboration. Classrooms must provide a greater level of visual and auditory contact between those sharing the room, and

those beyond, to meet a higher standard of service to collaboration. Virtual reality and computer simulation technologies require more flexible space to serve these rapidly growing fields. Spaces must respond by becoming more flexible, changeable, and attuned to the senses.

(ibid.)

Pressure on space and faculty resource is resulting in the creation of larger, general purpose 'flexi-labs' that can be used for delivering a wide range of undergraduate science courses. These are often grouped together to form science clusters with centralized science support areas including the prep rooms/technical resource centres, stores, open access computing areas for students to do their write-ups and science classrooms or studios where blended learning activities can occur.

In larger teaching laboratories the main instructor may be supplemented with a number of teaching assistants or demonstrators or screens can be used to relay what is happening at the demonstration station to other parts of the room. In the science 'superlab' of London Metropolitan University, this is taken to extremes, with 280 individual laboratory workstations and 12 teaching stations. The laboratory is a CL2 (Containment Level 2) facility, with 1,000 data points and a computer at every workstation. Twelve different teaching sessions, from undergraduate to PhD level, can take place simultaneously. Cameras at each teaching station relay live and pre-recorded sessions to screens and headphones at each workstation, which is equipped with its own interactive computer, a flat screen and audio-visual equipment. This technology enables students to be taught at the same time and also to progress at their own pace and revisit teaching sessions if they need to. In addition, students can access the internet to undertake research rather than having to move to a computer room located elsewhere.

Instructors can digitally record science experiments undertaken by their classes and store them on a central database, which can then be made available to absent students and to future students via online streaming. Alternatively, they can transmit lectures anywhere in the world making the laboratory a global hub for science (Labnews 2012).

The recognition that 'science does not just take place in the laboratory – science is everywhere and it affects everyone' is fundamental to the concept of an integrated landscape of spaces being developed at the Aga Khan University's Arusha campus. The science spaces will 'need to support a wide variety of learning, working and research experiences, and it will be essential that these spaces will be able to change over time to reflect changing pedagogies, fields of enquiry and use of technology' (FASAKU 2010a).

Broad principles include the imperative to:

- create a seamless science experience from core curriculum to post graduate research

- design science spaces to foster integration, communication and team working

- build in flexibility to accommodate change (short term to long term)

- design science spaces for changing technology use

- create multipurpose shared facilities wherever possible

- create sustainable science spaces

- make science visible and ensure the whole campus is a science learning experience (ibid.).

Research laboratories

Fink (2004) has found that the amount of space devoted to research at research-intensive universities generally exceeds that of classrooms and class laboratories. Research space includes both wet laboratory bench space and dry laboratories used for computation, imaging, engineering and electronics. It also includes core services available to faculty and investigators across a campus, as well as common laboratories where shared instrumentation is available. In health science centres, it includes clinical research space designated for patient studies. Offices and office support space, while part of the research environment, is generally separately classified in university space databases (ibid.: 5).

Just as undergraduate research laboratories are changing to meet changing institutional demands, research laboratories are also becoming more agile, able to respond to the changing short-, medium- and long-term needs. Bonge (2002), for example, noted that advances in nanotechnology, ongoing rapid advances in computerized research modelling and imaging, and new national political and economic priorities on university research programmes are all forcing change in biosciences laboratories.

Stanford University School of Medicine undertook a review of research facilities within Stanford and a number of other institutions to inform the development of more than one million square feet of biomedical research facilities they are planning during the next 15–20 years.

The review (Stanford School of Medicine 2007) suggested that future laboratories should be smaller in scale with investigators having a home base that they can customize while still sharing space and equipment with others. Locating the faculty offices within or adjacent to the laboratories was preferred. While the

majority of research in the future will continue to require benches, write-up desks, shared equipment space and access to fume hoods, the report believes that there will be an increasing need for alternative 'typologies' of primary research space such as electro-physiology, imaging, computation, bio-engineering and chemistry.

The creation of research buildings that facilitate interaction between faculty, the members of their research group, and investigators from other groups or departments was seen as very important. Informal encounters with other scientists were felt to be critical to fostering collaborations and creativity. Such interaction often occurs along circulation routes but more formal spaces such as break and conference rooms on each floor were also regarded as important.

It was also felt that the amount of support space required to promote the range of future research will increase. Support space should be adaptable in terms of room size, infrastructure systems, casework, biohazard containment level, and control of light, sound, vibration and access.

A key planning principle for future facilities is the anticipation of change. The review stated that future research facilities should plan for a diverse mix of research types, install redundant utilities, including ability to add fume hoods, use modular, flexible casework systems (with ability to raise, lower, reconfigure and remove), provide ubiquitous access to information including fibre optic cabling to servers and enable control of access, light, vibration, climate, sound, cleanliness, biological and chemical hazards, HVAC and so on (Task Force Report: 5). The Blizard Building at Queen Mary, London (Blizard nd) is a good example of a flexible research facility (Figures 5.20–5.22).

Many private research companies make physical changes to an average of 25 per cent of their labs each year – compared with academic institutions, which habitually change the layout of only 5–10 per cent of their labs (WBDG 2010). To deal with these changes GlaxoSmithKline (GSK), for example, has developed a FlexiLab concept which combines large, open floor plans with modular services and moveable furniture to create 'loose fit' flexible research space that is highly configurable by the end user. Key features include few, if any, walls, re-locatable fume hoods and simple plug 'n' play services that drop down from the ceiling. Researchers can customize FlexiLab space for a variety of uses, at no additional cost, simply by moving furniture around.

By merging traditional 12-person laboratories, plus their associated office/write-up space, into larger open multi-use research spaces, GSK increased researcher occupancy in the same space by 50 per cent and initial post-occupancy studies show an estimated 15 per cent higher level of scientific productivity.

The Blizard Building at Queen Mary, London, houses the Blizard Institute: around 500 staff and students based in eight academic centres each with focused programmes of research that examine the cellular mechanisms of the maintenance of health, the response to injury and repair and the pathogenesis of disease. The building provides open-plan laboratory and office accommodation, a 400-seat lecture theatre, meeting rooms and core facilities in flow cytometry, imaging, global siRNA screening and transgenics.

The laboratories are all on a single-floor plate five metres below ground level but with natural light coming in at high level. An air curtain separates the open laboratory space (CL1) from the write-up space on a mezzanine, facilitating communication between researchers. Closed labs (CL2 and CL3) are in adjacent fully glazed spaces. The large open-plan laboratories and juxtaposition of research centres from different backgrounds provides a perfect environment for the development of interdisciplinary collaborative research.

Hanging above the laboratory floor are several pods containing meeting rooms and a Bioscience Education Centre, which aims to engage young people in the principles of scientific and biomedical research and provide the background to many of the major scientific and ethical issues facing them, educationally and socially. This centre opened in September 2009 and 10,000 children visited during its first year of opening.

Source: http://www.icms.qmul.ac.uk/

Figure 5.20 The Blizard Building, Queen Mary, London. Architect: Alsop Architects

Figure 5.21 The Blizard Building, Queen Mary, London: flexible laboratory space

Figure 5.22 The Blizard Building, Queen Mary, London: collaboration space above the laboratory level

As the director of Strategic Facilities Planning for GlaxoSmithKline's European R&D division noted: 'Most good innovators, whether teams or individuals, are those who spend a lot of time interacting with others. In a traditional lab, people are focused on the group around them. When you move them into an open laboratory space they will inevitably interact more with other teams and exchange ideas' (Allen 2005).

Making science and research more visible within the institution and engaging the surrounding community is a feature of a number of recent research centres. The Clark Center at Stanford, for example, is an interdisciplinary research centre for the Biological Sciences (Bio-X) for 600–700 researchers and faculty, affiliated to 25 departments (Biox 2012).

Key goals for the building were to stimulate ad hoc interdisciplinary knowledge transfer and to provide a highly flexible environment that changes over time, supporting varying team sizes and relationships. The laboratories are large, open spaces with mobile laboratory furniture and a flexible services infrastructure that are shared by a number of research teams. Within the laboratory areas there are 65 bright yellow three-foot lab benches in clusters that

are available to researchers for temporary occupancy. The benches provide an opportunity for any of the researchers affiliated with the Bio-X programme to work in close proximity during the early stages of projects.

All core facilities are shared by all the research teams in the buildings and include an auditorium and seminar rooms, a teaching laboratory, a Biofilm Center, the Stanford Center for Innovation in In-vivo Imaging, low vibration laser labs, special projects space and two super computers (ibid.).

There are no interior corridors within the building and all circulation between labs and support spaces is along exterior courtyard balconies to maximize opportunities for interaction. The external walls onto the balcony are all fully glazed: everyone walking up the central circulation towards the cafe at the top of the building gets the opportunity to see into the research laboratories and watch the research in progress. It should be noted that this is not universally popular among the research community in the Clark Center and a number of research teams have used furniture to block views into the laboratory and work areas.

The 6,400 square metre Centre for Research on Adaptive Nanostructures and Nanodevices (CRANN) at Trinity College Dublin, completed in 2006, is an example of a research facility that engages directly with the wider public. The CRANN Nano Centre is located in an inner-city campus on a major thoroughfare. The building consists of a series of academic laboratories, associated clean rooms, offices, stores and accommodation for visiting staff. The Research Centre has a very public street frontage that includes a public science gallery and display area, a cafe and a student gym at ground level and a 200-seat lecture theatre at basement level for university and public events (CRANN 2012).

Overall the science environment on campus is undergoing major change, shifting from the standard provision of traditional teaching and research laboratories towards a much richer landscape of science settings that flex and change over time to meet the needs of the students and staff, the researchers and the institutions. Future science spaces are shared, interdisciplinary, technology rich and people centred – and they are as much about discourse, sharing of ideas and engagement with diverse set of internal and external stakeholders as they are about rows of laboratory benches and fume hoods.

SPECIALIZED LEARNING SPACES

A significant amount of space on most university campuses is taken up with specialist learning spaces such as studios, workshops and laboratories. The proportion of specialist learning spaces is even higher at most vocational colleges and further education colleges.

These spaces can be large and filled with specialized equipment, limiting their flexibility and making them difficult to share within the university with resultant low utilization of the spaces. The cost of the space and the equipment in the space, combined with high levels of teaching and technical support often required to deliver vocational courses and ongoing maintenance costs of the equipment, is making many institutions look closely at the future of their specialist learning spaces.

The amount of specialist space required by subject areas varies enormously, which can have a major impact on departmental or faculty finances if an institutional space charging policy is in place that allocates the total cost of space occupied back to the relevant entities.

In Australasia, the Tertiary Education Facilities Management Association (TEFMA) issued a set of space guidelines in 2009 (TEFMA 2009) that included recommendations about the amount of 'dedicated' faculty space required for each area – space primarily used by one faculty, department or discipline and that does not take into account the central pool of timetabled teaching space (Table 5.3). The guidelines suggest that the guide ratios are useful for an initial assessment of needs for faculty/department/discipline dedicated space.

At a departmental level the requirements for academic space varied even more widely (Table 5.4), ranging from one square metre per FTE student for accounting and business to 18 square metres per FTE student for veterinary sciences.

The review of specialist learning spaces is taking place in a turbulent economic environment that has hit the further and vocational education sectors particularly hard. In the UK, for example, funding has been cut significantly and has altered the way in which further education is delivered and by whom. (The 2010 Comprehensive Spending Review announced a reduction in

Table 5.3 Space requirements by broad category (TEFMA)

Broad Academic Category ASCED Code	m² UFA / EFTSL 2002 Blue Figures 2009
01 – Natural and Physical Sciences	10 8
02 – Information Technology	2 4.5
03 – Engineering and Related Technologies	10 6.7
04 – Architecture & Building	6 8
05 – Agriculture, Environmental & Related Studies	5
06 – Health	14
07 – Education	3 3.7
08 – Management & Commerce	1 1.3
09 – Society and Culture	3.5 2.1
10 – Creative Arts	6 6.1
11 – Food, Hospitality and Personal Services	6.5
12 – Mixed Field Programs	Insufficient data

the Department for Education's capital funding by 60 per cent, from £7.6 billion in 2010 to £3.4 billion in 2014/15. Over the same period capital funding for the Department for Business, Innovation and Skills was to be cut by 52 per cent (GVA Grimley 2010: 2).)

The Rebuilding Programme of Colleges across the UK has been severely curtailed and the Learning Skills Council that was responsible for the further education sector has been disbanded. GVA Grimley, in its 2010 report, *Further complications: Further Education estate management in the age of austerity*, discussed the direct impact these economic and political shifts will have on the estate management and property strategies of schools and colleges across the country. The report stated that the cuts in funding would result in reductions in staff numbers, course closures and reduced space need. It also cited research by KPMG suggesting that up to 50 colleges could close as a result of funding cuts (ibid.: 2).

Table 5.4 Space requirements by department (TEFMA)

Subject	SQM / FTE Student
Accounting and Business	1
Law	1.5
Nursing	2.5
Librarianship	3.5
Computer Science	4.5
Building	6
Graphic design	6
Architecture and Urban Environments	6.1
Performing Arts	7
Electrical Engineering	9.5
Biological sciences	10
Earth Sciences	11
Civil Engineering	11
Environmental Studies	11
Physics and Astronomy	12
Chemical Sciences	13
Visual Arts and Crafts	13–14.5
Mechanical and Industrial Engineering	14
Medical Studies	14
Dental Studies	16
Veterinary Sciences	18

GVA Grimley suggested that colleges in the future would need to increase the utilization of the space that they currently occupy and refurbish these spaces to deliver their academic and vocational programme rather than developing new campuses or buildings. They also felt that there is scope for increasing efficiencies through shared spaces and services and through developing alternative income streams from their estates, including the provision of services to the surrounding community based on their vocational programmes.

Vocational spaces

The 2006 JISC report *Designing Spaces for Effective Learning* noted that vocational spaces had often been missed out in the campus transformations that were taking place:

> Vocational spaces are diverse, and have highly specialised requirements for equipment, room size and supporting infrastructure. As a result, the use of learning technologies within these environments has not always been given priority. Vocational areas have often lagged behind other parts of the institution in providing a technology-rich learning experience, apart from the use of digital equipment in particular activities.
>
> (p. 16)

They argued that priorities are changing and that a higher priority is being given in the twenty-first century to developing learners' creativity, adaptability and wider skills. Rethinking vocational spaces and embedding learning technologies into the design of vocational teaching spaces can make a difference by providing immediate access to learning resources, diversifying routes to understanding, and supporting opportunities for on-the-spot recording and assessment of skills:

> Adding a presentation area with a screen and projector to a workshop environment will also help to enhance learning. Vocational learners need to develop e-portfolios and update learning diaries, and an environment with prompt access to IT will support these essential activities.
>
> (p. 17)

Studios

On a university campus, the specialized learning spaces go beyond the traditional 'wet' laboratory to include a wide range of discipline-specific spaces including art and design studios, theatre and performance spaces, greenhouses, film studios, engineering workshops and simulation spaces.

The amount of specialist space required by subject areas varies enormously. This can have a major impact on departmental or faculty finances if the institution has a space charging policy in place that allocates the total cost of space to the relevant entities.

In art, architecture and design studios there has been a particularly lively debate about the relationship between pedagogy and space and an exploration of how these disciplines could, perhaps, use space differently in order to increase efficiency and improve the quality of the student experience.

The intensity of the studio experience in architecture was discussed by Peter Monaghan in 2001 in 'The "insane little bubble of nonre-ality" that is life for architecture students', an article in the *Chronicle of Higher Education*:

> They work much of almost every night, while fewer and fewer cars and buses whiz by outside on Broadway, and then they stand on the deserted avenue at 3 or 4 a.m., waiting for a cab to get them home. They have more to learn each semester than they can recall learning during all their undergraduate years. Their friends and loved ones keep asking them, Don't you want to just chuck the whole thing? Such is the life of a modern-day architecture student here at Avery Hall at Columbia University, and everywhere else that architecture programs are offered.

The impact of the studio culture in architecture was explored by the American Institute of Architecture Students (AIAS) Taskforce on Studio Culture in 2002, which wanted to understand how well the studio-based approach to architectural education served the students and the profession.

The authors believe that the design studio lies at the core of architectural education, with studio courses commanding the most credit hours, the largest workloads, the most intensive time commitment from educators and students, and supreme importance and studio courses intended as the point of integration for all other coursework and educational experiences (AIAS 2002: 3). The report acknowledges that the 'design studio teaches critical thinking and creates an environment where students are taught to question all things in order to create better designs' (p. 3).

While there are many positive benefits to a studio-based education, the report acknowledges that it also has its problems. Participation in studios may involve 'late nights, exciting projects, extreme dedication, lasting friendships, long hours, punishing critiques, unpredictable events, a sense of community, and personal sacrifice' (p. 3) but it also helps to form the attitudes and values that will unpin the future professional and academic lives of the students. One of the key concerns discussed in the report was that the construction process is now much more complicated than when the studio system first emerged and relies on active collabo-ration between a diverse group of stakeholders – both within the construction team and within the client organization.

The authors believe that much of architectural education focuses on the student's experience as an individual:

> Students work side-by-side, but alone, often guarding their ideas from each other, competing for the attention of the studio critic. Group projects are most often limited to pre-design activities of research, analysis, and site documentation. The synthetic processes of design, in which negotiation and collaborative skills are most critical and difficult, are limited to individual efforts. Through these practices we unintentionally teach that the contributions of other designers, clients, consultants, and users are not valuable in the design process.
> (p. 12)

The authors felt that a challenging studio learning environment should relate knowledge to student experience and vision and involve a multiplicity of pedagogical and learning styles along with a variety of student-faculty and student-student encounters. It will also enable students to take risks, and provide an opportunity to share power to construct new knowledge and transform thinking.

Fiona Duggan looked in more detail at studio spaces and settings, and how they are used or not used in her 2004 paper, 'The Changing Nature of the Studio as an Educational Setting', for CEBE Transactions, the online publication by the Centre for Education in the Built Environment:

> The studio has long been recognised as the key focus for art and design education – the place where work is generated, reviewed, displayed and stored. As institutions become increas-ingly aware of the need for ongoing evaluation of the academic and economic effectiveness of their facilities, the studio is coming under considerable pressure to prove its value as a key resource. The problem is seen to be the resource-hungry nature of both studio teaching methods (namely one-to-one tutorials and group reviews or 'crits') and the quantity of space required.
> (Duggan 2004: 71)

Duggan notes the increasing diversity of the student population and the extent to which increasing numbers of students are managing their education as simply another part of a complex life with many 'full-time' students having jobs, some of which involve a considerable time commitment per week. This has the result that the students no longer have the time to spend extended periods in the studio.

The teaching profile is also changing in art, architecture and related disciplines, with the studio workforce being increasingly made up of part-time tutors and a growing trend towards contracts being awarded on a term rather than annual basis (or longer). This can lead to tensions – full-time staff feeling that they are left with the burden of administrative tasks while part-time staff are able to focus on the more rewarding aspects of teaching, part-time staff feeling that they are excluded from decision-making and the life of the department, despite the key role they play in the delivery of programmes (pp. 70–1). This sense of disconnection may be heightened by the lack of space or facilities available to the part-time faculty when they come to teach, particularly where staff common rooms and other community spaces have already been sacrificed to make way for additional teaching or office space.

Based on her work with a wide range of arts and architectural institutions in the UK, Duggan's view is that the studio space provided by many institutions is often inadequate, occasionally in terms of quantity but more often in terms of quality, with poor storage facilities for both work and personal belongings, inadequate (or non-existent) technology provision, insufficient pin-up space, poor atmosphere and lack of companionship. Reductions in teaching time per student have resulted in most institutions focusing their teaching resources on just one or two 'studio days' per week. The tradition is being eroded of students working in the studio, learning from each other, with teaching help on hand as and when required. The time allocated to individual tutorials has also decreased.

As a consequence of these changes, Duggan noted that, particularly in the upper years, students are only coming in to the studio on the days when teaching staff are available. The studio becomes little more than a temporary meeting place, where students can catch up with their tutors and fellow students. The desertion of the studio is being further accelerated by technology:

> As increasing numbers of students have access to home computing, their requests for technological support are changing from basic provision towards ready access to specialist equipment, software, printing services and technical support. Such resources tend to be located outside the studio … and often act as powerful attractors that pull students away from the technology-deprived studio.
>
> (p. 72)

Duggan suggests that these changes can lead those responsible for providing and managing space to conclude, as they wander around empty studios on non-studio days, that there is too much space whereas the reality may be that in some situations there is not enough space to support heavily attended studio days.

Addressing the issue of studio space ownership may be the biggest challenge that studio practitioners face in their desire to creatively respond to a changing educational environment.

> Staff want to 'own' the space they teach in – to provide students with a sense of identity and belonging, and themselves with the freedom to adjust teaching activities in response to the type of learning their students require at any particular time … Students too want space that they can personalise for working, socialising and, most important of all, belonging.
>
> (p. 74)

Duggan feels it is increasingly hard to justify the value of the studio in art and design education if the studios are without life and, even more often, without soul. She suggests that adopting a less territorial, more flexible attitude to space would expand rather than constrict freedom, as well as offering the possibility of belonging to something greater than one's immediate learning group. This is leading towards a concept of studio identity being primarily defined, not by space, but by events, where students are beginning to identify more with studio days than studio space. Studios will provide 'drop-in' access to space and resources rather than providing individually owned spaces.

The issue of studio culture was revisited by the AIAS Studio Culture task force in 2008. Following the 2002 research, the conditions for accreditation were changed to include studio culture with all schools of architecture being required to have a written policy on the culture of their studio environment. The 2008 research reviewed the studio culture policies of each school and sent a questionnaire to the policy administrator at each school.

While most of the report dealt with the learning practice within architecture, including the studio-based critiques and project work, three of the recommendations of the task force touched on the impact of the physical learning spaces.

- Studio culture narratives should relate student educational experiences to the institution's broader learning cultures and pedagogical identity, as well as recognize larger support networks and resources available to students throughout the larger institution.

- Broader focus should explicitly describe the relationship of the studio environment to the integration of practice settings and cross-disciplinary educational environments.

- Studio culture narratives should reveal the relationship of the studio experience to 'everything else' students can and should engage in as part of their academic and curricular experience.

> (AIAS 2008: 27)

The connection of the studio experience to the wider learning landscape and what happens in the rest of the institution was reinforced in the conclusions of the report:

> Schools have cultures beyond 'studio' culture, and diversity exists within the ecosystem of these cultures. Architecture schools must strive to be an active and conscientious participant in this cultural ecosystem, rather than remaining isolated from the larger culture of the academic institution.
>
> (ibid.: 28)

The participation in the wider academic ecosystem will provide opportunities to create a wide range of learning spaces and events that will overlap, and can be shared by other students and faculty – whether these are workshops for model making, spaces for presentations and crits or studios for extended project working.

Sharing space and resources

Other specialized learning spaces may be more difficult to share between departments and faculties. We have seen the move of some technology settings into the relative neutrality of the learning commons or library in an effort to encourage shared use and increased utilization of expensive spaces and technology.

This is also happening in science and medical research environments, where core facilities may be grouped together into shared technical resource centres that can be managed more efficiently with central technical support. Concentration of the technology into a smaller number of spaces may also increase the efficiency of building services, including air conditioning and filtering, provision of gases and -80 degree freezers that require power supply backups.

A close analysis of the learning and research activities that actually take place in a specialized space reveals the opportunity to institute much more diverse partnerships for sharing space and resources. At Aalto University in Helsinki, for example, the move of the Faculty of Art and Design onto the main Otaniemi campus allows several of the timber research labs and workshops to share space with art and design projects since both schools are making and testing wooden structures.

Aalto has also found ways of using specialized teaching spaces for other functions. The High Voltage Laboratory, for instance, is used to develop and test high voltage components for the power industry. Some of the test equipment is large, very heavy and capable of producing and discharging one million volt charges. The High Voltage Lab, however, is also one of the main party and events venues for the School of Engineering, with the lab equipment pushed to one side (Figures 5.23 and 5.24).

Specialized learning spaces can be expensive to create and expensive to operate over time and may be shared with external organizations – earning revenue from contract research projects or as part of multi-institutional research centres that could involve multiple universities or academic institutions or public–private partnerships.

Many universities are trying to reduce the amount of monofunctional learning and research space and to increase the amount of shared resource areas that group together specialist resources to improve the utilization and central management of the facilities. In addition, partnerships between institutions or with private companies may provide opportunities to create shared use technical buildings for commercial and academic research.

SOCIAL LEARNING SPACES

In a 2004 MIT presentation William Mitchell made the point that as architects discover new ways to take advantage of computer and communications technologies, the forms and functions of learning spaces will change rapidly to accommodate them. His view was that as the new types of learning space were incorporating new technologies, they were also creating new patterns of social and intellectual interaction, altering the demand for space on campus and suggesting new strategies of overall campus design – so that 'the entire campus becomes an interactive learning device' (ibid.). He felt, therefore, that all campus space, including outdoor spaces and mobile spaces, should be considered as potentially wirelessly serviced ad hoc classroom space.

The impact of information technology on learning spaces was further discussed by Diana Oblinger in an *Educause Quarterly* article, 'Leading the Transition from Classrooms to Learning Spaces' (2005a):

> The Internet has changed notions of place, time, and space. Space is no longer just physical; it incorporates the virtual. New methods of teaching and learning, based on an improved understanding of cognition, have emerged, as well. As a result, the notion of a classroom has expanded and evolved; the space need no longer be defined by 'the class' but by 'learning'.
>
> (p. 14)

Future learning spaces should be designed to support multiple modes of learning (discussion, experiential learning, reflection and so on). In addition, Oblinger notes that learning spaces may support informal learning, through using the walls to display current research or artefacts from previous discoveries and spaces

Figure 5.23 High Voltage Lab, Aalto University – extreme divergence of use types

Figure 5.24 High Voltage Lab, Aalto University

adjacent to classrooms, such as hallways, can be used for informal gatherings and social learning.

Oblinger explored the needs of future learners further in a collection of papers, *Educating the Net Generation* (2005b), the purpose of which was to 'help educators make sense of the many patterns and behaviors that we see in the Net Generation but don't quite understand' (p. 2.1). In the introduction, Oblinger posed the question: 'If the Net Generation values experiential learning, working in teams, and social networking, what are the implications for classrooms and the overall learning environment?' (p. 1.4).

This question was answered within the book by Malcolm Brown from Dartmouth College, stressing the almost symbiotic nature of the relationship between IT and Net Generation (Net Gen) students:

> The characteristics of Net Gen students mesh very closely with IT and IT's increasing mobility, its 24 x 7 availability, and its increasing value as a communications tool. Net Gen students are social and team oriented, comfortable with multitasking, and generally positive in their outlook, and have a hands-on, 'let's build it' approach – all encouraged by the IT resources at their disposal. Net Gen students have embraced IT, using it in ways both intended and unforeseen by programmers.
>
> (Brown 2005: 12.2)

These students, using a variety of digital devices, can turn almost any space outside the classroom into an informal learning space. Brown felt that educators had an important opportunity to rethink and redesign these non-classroom spaces to support, encourage, and extend students' learning environment. Classroom, informal, virtual learning spaces should be thought of as a single, integrated environment. What happens in the classroom should be connected with what happens in informal and virtual spaces (p. 12.3).

Informal learning spaces outside of the classroom present, according to Brown, intriguing opportunities for pioneering and cultivating new teaching and learning practices and constitute key areas for student academic work – students spend far more time in these spaces than they do in formal classrooms.

> Research, Web browsing, writing, statistical analysis, and compiling lab reports all take place in the library, study hall, media center, dorm room, and learning commons. Because of their enthusiasm for IT and their experiential, hands-on approach to learning tasks, Net Gen students will easily 'tune into' the virtual aspects of informal spaces. Well-designed and integrated physical layouts and IT 'tool sets' will find a ready audience with Net Gen students.
>
> (p. 12.8)

The impact of technology and Net Gen students on learning spaces was further explored in Oblinger's edited collection of papers, *Learning Spaces*. As she states in her introduction:

> Learning is the central activity of colleges and universities. Sometimes that learning occurs in classrooms (formal learning); other times it results from serendipitous interactions among individuals (informal learning). Space – whether physical or virtual – can have an impact on learning. It can bring people together; it can encourage exploration, collaboration, and discussion. Or, space can carry an unspoken message of silence and disconnectedness. More and more we see the power of built pedagogy (the ability of space to define how one teaches) in colleges and universities.
>
> (2006a: 1.1)

One theme that resounds throughout the book is that learning takes place everywhere on a university campus, as well as in a wide array of other spaces – anywhere, in fact. As Van Note Chism states in her chapter: 'Human beings – wherever they are – have the capacity to learn through their experiences and reflections.' She also, however, acknowledges the powerful impact that space can have on learning, citing the assertion of Strange and Banning (2002) that 'although features of the physical environment lend themselves theoretically to all possibilities, the layout, location, and arrangement of space and facilities render some behaviours much more likely, and thus more probable, than others.' Because we habitually take space arrangements for granted, we often fail to notice the ways in which space constrains or enhances what we intend to accomplish (Van Note Chism 2006: 2.3).

Given the Net Gen preference for small group working and the integrated use of IT, the availability of smaller places for debriefing, project work, discussion and application of information becomes paramount. Outdoor spaces, lobby spaces, cafes and residence halls all need to be considered in terms of how they can support learning.

Oblinger stresses that while learning is continuous and can occur in any place at any time there are different ways of learning, and different types of spaces are conducive to specific types of learning (2006b: 14.5). Within this complex matrix of learning times, styles and spaces, Oblinger notes that many institutions are shifting from classrooms to learning complexes where learning ebbs and flows depending on need and circumstance. In these learning complexes, informal spaces are adjacent to classrooms and eating spaces and atria serve as gathering spots. Group spaces are interspersed with areas for individual reflection and faculty offices and support desks may be nearby. Technology is the enabler that allows the complex to function effectively (p. 14.5).

In 2006 the Institute of Education in the UK investigated the impact on space of future changes in higher education (SMG 2006b). Among its predictions on future space use in higher education in the UK was that more provision would be made for student-led and 'blended' learning which will demand more relatively small and adaptable spaces. More space will be provided to support unstructured/ad hoc self-directed learning and peer-teaching among students and there will be increased blurring of the boundary between academic and social areas such as common rooms and cafeterias.

The value of social learning spaces was also discussed in the 2006 JISC report on learning spaces.

> Learners have been shown to benefit academically from social interaction with their peers. Open-plan informal learning areas provide individualised learning environments which also support collaborative activities, and they can often be created from previously underutilised spaces. An example is the internet café. In many institutions, entrance spaces now include open-access IT areas with refreshments and informal seating. Utilisation data have proved the worth of such areas – their value lies in the way they encourage learning through dialogue, problem solving and information sharing in the most supportive of contexts.
>
> (JISC 2006: 4)

Rather than adding additional space to a campus to create social learning space, JISC suggests that most colleges and universities already have large under-utilized spaces that could be re-purposed to create social learning areas: 'If catering facilities, common rooms, even corridor space, are reconsidered as social meeting and group learning environments, institutions could both save on large-space provision and make a statement about their vision for learning as a pervasive and inclusive activity based on social interaction' (p. 28).

The report also suggests that social learning spaces should be designed for use by both faculty and students to support the notion of pervasive, communal learning.

> Emerging designs place emphasis on one high-quality social space as a central focal point in the building, which caters for the needs of all users of the building – visitors, staff, learners and potential learners of all abilities. The area is both a public facility providing meals and refreshments, and a place where learners and staff can meet for short discussions. Wireless enabled, it is not set apart from learning – student services may also be located adjacent to this space to take advantage of its widespread use.
>
> (p. 28)

In the same year the Scottish Funding Council also noted that formal teaching spaces for large groups – with a 'sage on a stage' – are becoming less common than smaller, less formal settings where students learn from one another as well as from their appointed teachers. New buildings are not essential for the creation of new learning environments. Radical learning approaches can also be carried out in intelligently refurbished academic or other urban buildings (SFC 2006: 6).

Seminar rooms have traditionally contained the 'group conversation' form of learning: they are being overtaken by more informal gathering places for social learning with informal areas for sitting, informal teaching and flexible seminar spaces. These spaces may be within computer commons or internet cafe-type spaces, group study rooms or areas in libraries, studio/workshop areas or in shared access computer rooms in residence halls, to name just a few examples (pp. 8–9).

Learning landscape

Dugdale and Long (2007) noted in their ELI Webinar on 'Planning the Informal Learning Landscape' that the importance of non-designated space for students to work together outside the classroom – the space between – (Figure 5.25) is increasingly being recognized for its educational value and contribution to creating a sense of community.

They use the phrase 'learning landscape' to describe the complete range of physical and virtual spaces where learning takes place. Traditional categories of space are becoming less meaningful as space becomes less specialized, boundaries blur and operating

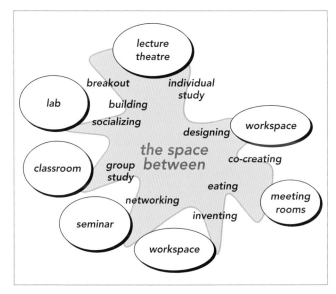

Figure 5.25 Non-designated space – the space between. Source: Dugdale/ DEGW in Dugdale and Long (2007)

hours extend towards 24/7 access. Future space types are likely to be designed primarily around patterns of human interaction rather than specific needs of particular departments, disciplines or technologies with new space models focusing on enhancing quality of life as much as on supporting the learning experience (ibid.).

They discuss a series of principles that should be considered when planning informal learning spaces – it is important, they feel, to:

- support mobility – to create 'touch down' settings on campus where students can choose to work, supported by personally owned technology. These settings should include movable furniture that can be reconfigured by students and fully accessible wireless and power networks.

- exploit transitions – to help students to make the most of time between activities or classes by creating informal learning and social areas in the circulation space on campus, particularly near lecture and seminar rooms, creating 'front porch' spaces. These spaces should be places to settle and linger and they should encourage serendipitous encounters and discussions for both faculty and students.

- create blended spaces to support blended activities – making social learning spaces that support a range of activities such as individual and collaborative study, relaxing, eating and socializing. Multiple activities should be supported with diverse settings that can be reconfigured by the users. Learning discourse should be supported by the technology infrastructure including wireless access, marker boards, display screens and text message displays.

- exploit food as a catalyst – food can act as an attractor, creating a number of destinations on campus that can encourage both students and faculty to visit areas of the campus with which they are not directly connected. The quality of both food and settings is important.

- create 'club' settings – spaces with a strong identity that encourage and support drop-in use as well as intermittent scheduling for group activities. Club spaces should include a choice of settings, both shared and individual to create rich, highly services interactive environments supporting collaboration.

- support media co-creation – provide media-rich drop-in environments that support co-authoring activity by both faculty and students, creating multimedia products together. The identity of these spaces can be created through the display of visual material as well as the range of technology-enabled settings. Acoustics and lighting will need careful attention in these spaces to support video/audio editing, creation of podcasts and playback/viewing of video.

- protect sanctuaries – while encouraging and supporting collaborative activities in informal learning spaces there is a continued need to provide places on campus that allow focus, concentration and reflection, including both internal and external spaces.

- provide external spaces – make opportunities to create both individual and collaborative external learning and social spaces. These spaces may have varying amounts of boundary control (open bench to protected table in a university garden area) but all settings should have access to wireless network and, if possible, power.

- recognize the city as campus. Learning activity extends beyond the edges of the campus, both physically as well as virtually with students and faculty meeting in bookshops, galleries and cafes. Recognition of community-based learning spaces may be limited to off-campus access to virtual learning environments or may extend to semi-programmed use of public space for small group study or discussion (ibid.: 29–50).

Shirley Dugdale was also instrumental in creating a strategy for the future enhancement of the learning landscape as part of the development of the 2020 masterplan for the State University of New York at Buffalo, leading a DEGW strategy group that worked closely with the university and the masterplanning team. In this strategy, the entire UB Campus is conceived as a 'network of places' for learning, discovery, and discourse between students, faculty, staff and the wider community. The principles that underpinned the learning landscape strategy included certain key goals:

- Animate all significant paths and places with visible activities and landmarks.

- Create magnetic hubs or 'anchors' using core shared learning spaces.

- Increase diversity and density of space types, uses and 'ownership models'.

- Include a balance of 'communal' and 'territorial', 'formal' and 'informal' spaces.

- Intersperse 'specialized' spaces with 'multipurpose' and 'in-between' spaces.

- Enable significant places to serve multiple uses and user-groups, and empower students to interpret and use spaces in creative ways.

- Improve flow and connections for people, activities and information.

- Consolidate and integrate service access points.

- Demonstrate results with pilot projects and learn from experimental spaces.

- Organize and clarify space uses. Help users understand locations relative to visible landmarks, indoor and outdoor, and specific program elements (DEGW 2008b: 8).

One of the most significant elements of the learning landscape strategy was the re-use of corridors and other circulation elements across the university estate. The 'learning corridor' proposed by DEGW was 'a system of distributed indoor spaces that provided convenient, comfortable places to study and relax before and after class. Located near formal learning spaces, these niche-like refuges vary in size and are found along primary and secondary circulation corridors, allowing students and faculty to take advantage of a variety of settings and technology for collaborative work, individual work, meeting, and socializing' (ibid.: 32).

Combinations of settings such as lounge seating, work tables, enclosed group study rooms and 'touchdown' study counters were used to create six different informal learning settings that could be retrofitted into existing corridors on campus:

- Study nooks – small, informal study spaces carved out of formal learning spaces along major circulation routes. Nooks are spaced along a corridor to create visual interest and generate activity, and provide a comfortable waiting area. Nooks may be outfitted with lounge seating for relaxation, or may contain plasma screens and work tables for small working groups.

- Study booths – fronted by glass and found along major circulation paths. Study booths are small, enclosed spaces that give users the opportunity to have a space in which they can engage in more concentrative individual work. In addition, the larger study booths can accommodate group study activities that require more acoustic separation than is provided in more open work settings.

- Front porch – a semi-private space adjacent to a major circulation route and associated with a formal learning space. When closed, a 'garage door' separates the front porch from the adjacent classroom/seminar room allowing learning discourse to extend the formal to the informal and visible active space. When open, the 'garage door' creates a new and dynamic space. The front porch is outfitted with a range of individual and collaborative learning furnishings and spaces.

- Linear cafe – a set of work tables, lounge seating, study counters and collaboration tables distributed along the edge of a single-loaded corridor that takes advantage of light and views. The linear cafe is not associated with a specific instructional space, but instead transforms a long and desolate corridor into an active 'street'. Food service is an important factor for attracting and retaining passersby, and creating 'buzz'.

- Cul-de-sac – a hub of informal learning activity immediately adjacent to and visible from a major circulation route. The cul-de-sac occupies the space of a would-be classroom, catches spillover from the surrounding classrooms, and accommodates pre-class and post-class activities. It is outfitted with flexible furnishings and collaborative technology to support group meetings and informal exchanges between students, and students and faculty.

- Open theatre – a demonstration space outfitted with a theatre set for students or faculty to display data, make presentations, or screen movies. The theatre is immediately adjacent to and visible from a major circulation route, creating interest and allowing passersby to 'stop by' and engage in activities at will.
  (ibid.: 32–3)

The authors of the report state that the creation of learning corridors should be considered as part of the broader learning space renovation and construction strategy and should create a continuous network of diverse spaces that varies in density and complements existing hubs of activity to generate more activity. Learning corridor elements should be located adjacent to the appropriate formal learning spaces and should respond to the diverse curricular, space and technology needs of different academic neighbourhoods and units. It is also important to ensure that spaces have a visible, public face by locating them along major circulation routes and, where possible, they should incorporate food service, especially in areas of the campus that are underserved (ibid.: 34).

The learning landscape was also at the heart of a major research project funded by the UK Higher Education Funding Councils (HEFC) in 2007–8. This project looked at the relationship between campus planning and specific exemplary teaching and learning spaces in all the participating universities. Of particular interest was the degree to which pedagogical principles are captured in the design of teaching and learning spaces and express the values and aspirations of the universities within which they are sited as well as how these exemplary spaces were integrated into an overall campus plan.

The report authors discuss the strategies adopted by universities to advance the learning landscapes agenda which include analysing the whole campus as a learning space, developing insights from user engagement, supporting multiple layers of learning, enabling experimentation and increasing space utilization, forming strategic partnerships to develop informal spaces, linking space performance to assessment and developing learning spaces beyond the campus (Neary et al. 2010).

One of the case studies described in the report, and more fully on the project website (learninglandscapes.lincoln.ac), is the Hive at Queen Mary University of London – a social learning space designed to provide an extension to the more traditional services that the university library offers students. The Hive is situated on the first floor of a three-storey catering building, which runs across a linking bridge to the physics department and provides students with a social learning area for collaborative group work.

The idea of the Hive was to encourage cooperation and collaborative working between students and staff, and it achieves this through the creation of a variety of different spaces for students and academics, including technology-enabled social learning areas and student-bookable glass-panelled teaching rooms. Students are allowed to bring food and drink into the new space, which is supervised by the students themselves.

Building on the findings of the case studies, the learning landscapes project team developed a series of tools to be used to map the learning landscapes on campus, evaluate the settings in terms of their efficiency, effectiveness and expression and facilitate innovation and experimentation. The goal was to create a common language by which academics, estates and other key stakeholders can articulate their professional expertise across academic subject areas and occupational proficiencies (ibid.).

Informal learning across the campus

The importance of considering the whole campus as a learning environment was stressed by Jamieson in his article 'The Serious Matter of Informal Learning' (2009). He suggests that the future university will need to consist of a mix of formal classroom types, with traditional-style spaces for more didactic, larger classes and new-generation spaces for more collaborative, active learning approaches – and believes that many universities regard the provision of informal learning spaces as a less serious matter than the requirements for formal teaching spaces, with a consequent reduction in resource allocation.

Jamieson defines informal learning as those 'other' activities students undertake between formal classes, including course reading, class preparation, and assignments and project activity. He notes that learning involves social interaction and it is not easy to separate purely student social activity from that which is learning-related, particularly as both forms of peer-to-peer engagement often take place in the same campus settings: informal learning, he observes, typically takes place in the library, the student refectory, cafes, and other social spaces (p. 19).

While historically the university campus has been shaped by the emphasis on traditional instructional methods and the classrooms this has required, Jamieson believes that the future campus will be determined to a large extent by the university's response to informal learning, with the balance of formal and informal settings changing as students are required to be more self-directed.

Social hubs are appearing as key features of campus life, along with internal 'student streets' within buildings that feature a mix of functions expected to promote both social and learning-related activity. Jamieson states that another institutional response has been the creation of comprehensive student centres that offer key administrative and course support along with information technology access and other services (p. 19).

Jamieson defines the campus learning centres as dedicated, centralized facilities created explicitly by the university to support informal learning, and discusses three distinct types – the library, the information commons, and the learning commons:

> The university library has evolved from its role as the campus 'knowledge center' – the symbolic and functional repository of scholarly knowledge – to its modern incarnation as the campus 'learning center' that serves as the hub for the teaching, learning, and research activity on campus (Jamieson 2005). This evolution has transformed the library from a setting for research-based activity and quiet, individual learning to a more diverse environment. The library has become the primary on-campus facility outside the classroom that students use in order to learn in more social-constructivist ways (which require collaboration and small-group activity), while still being able to draw on the human resources and learning materials available there.
>
> (pp. 19–20)

He also notes that the library has been the spatial laboratory in which many universities have explored the possibility of other formal and informal learning settings (such as IT training rooms and video-conferencing centres) and has been the place for initiating the use of new technologies, developing dedicated training centres for staff and students, and even incorporating cafes into formal working areas.

The second type of learning centre, information commons, is made up of technology-rich environments that are often located within a designated area of the library building. The development of the information commons was an acknowledgement by universities of the need to provide students with greater access to information technology for research, communication and learning-related purposes. It also reflected the changing nature of data located within the library as well as data accessible from other remote sites via IT systems.

Jamieson noted the problems that many university libraries have had in meeting their new role as an IT hub and to quench the apparently insatiable student appetite for computer access. Many of these centres became little more than 'battery hen' computer ghettoes – areas bulging with computers and with students constrained to individual computer use by the physical arrangement of the setting. In such facilities, there is little possibility for peer-to-peer collaboration, the use of print-based materials in conjunction with computer use, or even student movement throughout the space (p. 20).

The provision of wireless networks on campus and increased use of personal laptops by students has facilitated a shift away from mass computer barns located in the library or elsewhere on campus. Jamieson notes, however, that many campus planners have unfortunately done little to exploit the potential of mobile IT systems – most campuses currently have few comfortable, functional and, most importantly, ergonomically sound sites where laptops can be used (pp. 20–1).

Jamieson believes that the third type of space, learning commons, represents the most mature form of centralized facility developed to support the growing importance of informal, on-campus learning and is a conscious attempt to improve on the narrow IT focus and often limited functionality of the information commons.

The key idea behind the development of the learning commons is the notion that learning is a 'situated' process and is likely to be enhanced when it occurs in a dynamic, social context offering a range of opportunities for students to learn according to their shifting needs and preferred learning styles. The learning commons space type is the clearest expression yet that universities acknowledge the growing emphasis on students to assume responsibility for their own learning and that, as a result, they must provide a more socially oriented physical environment in which this can occur.

The learning commons may be part of the campus library or it may be located in an entirely separate, purpose-built facility. Within the learning commons there is an emphasis on providing furniture types and arrangements that encourage collaborative and group-based learning activity to promote a greater sense of user 'ownership' (rather than institutional control) of the physical space. The learning commons may also house a range of other learning-focused services, including learning skills units, multimedia development centres, and student IT support, which further cements their institutional role as the centre of learning (p. 21).

Jamieson uses the Saltire Centre at Glasgow's Caledonian University (Figure 5.26) as an example of a contemporary learning commons that represents a major commitment by the university to support student-led, socially based, informal learning – a five-storey facility incorporating the campus library, a centralized student service point, 450 fixed computers with a further 150 laptop devices for loan, and a large cafe. With an area of 10,500 square metres and seating for 1,800, the Saltire Centre is intended to be the campus focal point both educationally and socially, as well as a major public facility for the wider central urban community:

> Users can choose to move throughout the eclectic mix of settings according to individual preference for quiet spaces or more active, noisy areas. In particular, the use of inflatable and other mobile pods to provide enclosure for individuals and small groups, together with the use of mobile IT/AV systems, overwhelmingly bespeaks 'user-control.' As a consequence, the ground-floor concourse is in a constant state of flux as the occupants change its physical arrangement to meet their own needs.
>
> (p. 21)

While generally supportive of Saltire's achievements, Jamieson notes that the learning centre is not without its problems since the centralization of informal learning spaces within a central facility may actually reduce the use of other parts of the campus for these activities and result in students having fewer choices about where and how they will interact with their peers outside the classroom. The concentration of activities in the one central location may also have an impact on the quality of life in other parts of the campus, particularly in those areas furthest from the central attraction.

The solution, Jamieson suggests, is to provide multiple sites for the range of learning-focused facilities in order to locate services in convenient, user-friendly settings:

> Ideally, this would be done to develop discrete learning 'precincts' across the campus – zones formed through the logical integration of buildings, external spaces, core functions, and common need. In this way, the campus may eventually comprise numerous hubs of activity and learning support and provide genuine opportunities for communities to form in ways that are sustainable in the long term.
>
> (p. 23)

The creation of networks of learning places was also supported by Shirley Dugdale in a 2009 article, 'Space Strategies for the New Learning Landscape' in the *Educause Review*. 'Applying a learner-centered approach, campuses need to be conceived as "networks"

The Saltire Centre is well known for its 2,500 square metre 'services mall' on the ground floor which provides a one-stop access point for all services for students. A main service desk, auxiliary desks, service kiosks, meeting pods, semi-private inflatable meeting corners, six private consulting rooms and access to the consulting suite are all set within a lively mixture of study space, a cafe and access to 40 per cent of the centre's book stock on compact shelving.

The centre offers a wide range of spaces to suit different people, learning methods and styles – from open and interactive to closed, structured study spaces. The large, open ground floor contrasts with the smaller-scale top floor, and there is a gradual shift from noisy front ground floor to quiet back top floor.

The centre recognizes the importance of flexible learning, supported self-learning and similar learning concepts that are made possible by the electronic delivery of information. It goes further, by making itself the starting point of the learning process and by encouraging 'deliberate socializing'. This includes accepting noise, combining learning environments with food and drink with the associated risk of damage to equipment and property. This approach places confidence in the students, trusting them to identify what constitutes acceptable behaviour.

> The Saltire Centre is designed to be the social heart of the campus, a place where students meet and converse as well as study. The design of the centre and the way in which it is administered recognize the social origins of learning and the need for interaction between learners on different levels and in different forms. It is also a self-regulating environment which places discussion on an equal footing with solitary learning – it is the policy of the university to give students responsibility over their learning environment as well as over the way in which they learn.
>
> (JISC 2006: 24)

By 2008 the footfall of students through the door was 1.4m visits a year, a figure more than double the usage of the library it replaced. Tom Finnegan, director of learning support and in charge of the library stated that 'Saltire has reversed a trend that saw library visits falling' (Hoare 2008a).

Sources: JISC (2006); http://education.guardian.co.uk/librariesunleashed/ story/0,,2275365,00.html

Figure 5.26 The Saltire Centre, Glasgow, UK

of places for learning, discovery, and discourse between students, faculty, staff, and the wider community' (Dugdale 2009: 52).

Dugdale believes that a learning landscape approach to campus planning acknowledges the richness of the diverse landscape of learning settings and seeks to maximize encounters among people, places, and ideas, just as a vibrant urban environment does. The planning process also needs to acknowledge the fact that learning activity extends well beyond the edges of the campus, both physically and virtually.

> Now that students are enabled with mobile devices, they seek out those community places offering the late hours and blended settings that may not be available on campus. GPS-enabled portable devices and tools enable groups to coordinate and converge anywhere. More outreach programs providing work experiences in authentic settings will blur the distinction between academic and real-world learner experiences and will likely offer opportunities to gain efficiencies in the use of campus space.
>
> (Dugdale 2009: 62)

Dugdale notes that virtual worlds such as Second Life also promise to offer a complementary place in which learners can gather. This activity may be either independent of physical campus activity or blended with it, as learners in a real space interact with participants in the virtual world.

The links between physical and virtual social learning spaces were discussed in a 2011 Educause Initiative article, '7 things you should know about … the modern learning commons' (ELI 2011).

As a place where students can meet, talk, study and use 'borrowed' equipment, the learning commons brings together the functions of libraries, labs, lounges and seminar areas in a single community gathering place. This face-to-face forum supports the sharing of student ideas outside the classroom, complementing the shift in pedagogy towards collaborative media and team efforts. As a bonus, the learning commons can be an ideal venue to blend face-to-face with virtual meetings, allowing the broad population of students who commute or telecommute to join their teams in project discussions.

The article also suggests that increased mobile use and innovations such as augmented-reality learning scenarios, and more touch-and gesture-based computing mean that the learning commons as a physical space will be obliged to integrate even more of the virtual world into the face-to-face environment it now successfully provides:

> In such an environment, students might use mobile applications like Foursquare, a location-based social networking site, to reserve workspaces or resources. Or perhaps they will utilize interactive 3D displays to work with content in new ways. More assistive technology might become available, including haptic assistance for those with vision difficulties. At the same time, new and expanded partnerships across disciplines will facilitate and promote greater levels of collaboration in the learning commons. New services will emerge, expanding the opportunities for new, highly effective learning activities.
>
> (ELI 2011: 2)

The article does highlight some of the problems associated with the creation of learning commons. One of the key issues is the expense of new equipment and the fact that legacy spaces may be difficult or costly to reconfigure. Difficulties may also arise when selecting the appropriate blend of spaces, services and technology to offer within the learning commons.

> Since there is no single model of the ideal learning commons, it can be anything designers conceive to suit each institution's unique needs and culture. This flexibility is an opportunity, but it also means institutions might have to 'roll the dice' on some features based on their best guesses as to what will work well. Even then, when a commons is well designed and executed, the space can become a victim of its own success, with areas that are overcrowded, especially during peak periods. As a result, some have had to adopt scheduling procedures, making their gathering areas less available for just-in-time projects.
>
> (ELI 2011: 2)

The evolution of the academic library to include learning and information commons is discussed in more detail in the next section of this chapter. It is clear, however, that the shift towards a learner-centred approach to learning has implications far beyond the library. Social learning space is everywhere on campus and extends into the surrounding community as well as into virtual space.

ACADEMIC LIBRARIES

Edwards (2000) makes the bold claim that the university library is arguably the most important building on the campus: 'the library is the signifier of learning … libraries are study centres, buildings where student-centred learning takes priority … (irrespective of changes in media) the library retains its central position in the environment of learning'. On a more pragmatic level, Brophy (2007: 31) suggests that the 'massification' of higher education in recent years has led to much greater prominence being given to the academic library's role in supporting learning and teaching.

There is no doubt, however, that the way in which knowledge is acquired, produced and disseminated is changing due, in the main, to new technologies and research methods. Most information is now 'born digital' (though information is also proliferating at an unprecedented rate as materials created in traditional formats, such as print, are being digitized) and new technologies, such as Web 2.0, facilitate the sharing, re-purposing and creation of more information that has value in its own right. The new generation of learner and researcher – the Net Gen – has high expectations: these individuals need immediate access to content, anytime and from anywhere. They want to store, personalize, manipulate and share information with their peers, increasingly using mobile devices.

These changes have brought about major shifts in the research community. New subjects are being explored in new ways. Many researchers now reject solitary research practices and favour more collaborative working methods, with a growing number of theses, reports and publications being created in multiple formats and by multiple authors, who may well be from different disciplines and involved in multinational collaborations.

Some of this activity is taking place within virtual research environments (VREs); studies show, however, that both academics and practitioners – whether from the arts and humanities, social sciences, creative industries, business, schools or the general public – still want to work in physical spaces that are inspirational, dynamic and conducive to the learning and research process.

A 2007 report by the British Library about the proposed British Library Digital Centre (BLDC) makes clear that library users also value:

- access to a wide range of authoritative material in both traditional and digital formats

- experts in collections and technology who can help them find relevant and reliable information

- sophisticated search engine technology, particularly in view of the growing importance of ephemera

- the latest equipment that will enable them to repurpose materials, copyright permitting, and turn creative theory into creative practice (BL 2007).

Peter Jamieson noted in his 2005 paper, 'Positioning the University Library in the New Learning Environment', that many university libraries are seeking to shift from their traditional role as repositories of information and other resources for individual, passive learning to places where learners meet, collaborate and interact in learning processes that are much more dynamic: 'The primary role that the central campus library plays symbolically, geographically, and functionally in the life of a university ensures that this building is an integral element of the university experience for most students' (pp. 5–11).

This view was supported by the UK Space Management Group's 2006 research project that looked at the impact on space of future changes in higher education, which found that, in the future, institutions will provide more space for unstructured and ad hoc self-directed learning and peer-teaching among students and that there will be increased blurring of the boundary between academic and social areas.

However, the authors of this report also predicted that by 2015 learning materials in teaching intensive universities would be available digitally and the library would contain few traditional books or journals. Students would carry most of the learning materials they need in light, easy-to-read digital form. They would access additional material from the HEI's own VLE and from the web wherever they are (SMG 2006b: 17).

They felt that the library, in its more traditional form, would continue to live on in research intensive universities where it will remain 'at the heart of the institution, with a large stock of traditional books, and with specialist collections which play a part in institutional branding. But it is also the place from where the digital learning environment is managed' (p. 17).

The dynamic places for interaction and collaboration that Jameson discussed were often located in an emerging library 'add-on' variously called a learning or information commons or learning centre. In 2006, JISC noted that the concept of the learning centre is still evolving, usually blending with other previously distinct spaces to absorb more of their functions. Rethinking the learning centre has led to substantial new-build projects in universities especially, where this space is envisaged as the social and academic hub of the campus. However, smaller-scale learning centres are also appearing – connected to teaching accommodation to form curricular clusters, for example, or as a separate high-tech, highly personalized learning environment in addition to the library (JISC 2006: 22).

We now expect that learning will involve many different activities, each having different behaviours associated with it. This can make the learning centre the most multifunctional of spaces. A large central learning centre in a university, for example, provides social spaces, student services and study support, book and laptop loan, access to IT, and different kinds of working environments, from comfortable seating for collaborative group work, to 'board rooms' for practice presentations. Some elements of teaching may also take place within a learning centre environment.

(ibid.: 22)

Lippincott (2006: 7.1) stated that many institutions were renovating their libraries to become information commons or learning commons. These commons often occupied one of the main service floors of the library, alongside or replacing the library's reference area. The introduction of these spaces can have a substantial input on the level of library visits. As an example of this Lippincott cited Indiana University where the main library gate count almost doubled from the year prior to the opening of the information commons to the second full year of its existence.

Information commons blur the boundaries between library space, technology space and social space. The goal in an information commons is to support the students' learning and research activities by providing a blend of spaces, individual and collaborative work settings and technology:

Information commons have drawn students by offering environments that address their needs, bringing together technology, content, and services in a physical space that results in an environment different from that of a typical library.

(ibid.: 7.2)

The Information Services Building at the University of Otago in New Zealand, for example, completed in 2001, provides 2,200 study places in the main library that are broken down into 27 different types of study settings, varying in terms of group size, degree of enclosure, privacy and technology provision (University of Otago 2012b).

Group study areas are prevalent in many learning and information commons:

Much of the space is configured for use by small groups of students, reflecting students' desire for collaborative learning and combining social interaction with work. Information commons frequently have furniture built to accommodate several people sharing a common computer and provide large tables where several students can use their laptops while working together, comfortable seating areas with upholstered furniture to encourage informal meetings, cafés with food and drink, and group study rooms, often with a computer and screen, so students can work together efficiently on projects.

(Lippincott 2006: 7.3)

The extension of service provision beyond traditional library information services – such as evidenced in the UK in Glasgow

Caledonian University's Saltire Centre – is typical of learning commons, meeting users' technology needs, including hardware and software support, particularly in relation to multimedia and graphics support. Other campus services may also be part of the commons, including student services, assistive technologies, careers, writing and literacy services, faculty learning and teaching development.

This integration of the learning commons with other functions is demonstrated in the University of Santa Clara Learning Commons, Technology Center and Library which opened in 2008. The name says it all – the library function is the third on the list. The 19,400 square metre facility provides more than 1,100 reader seats in a variety of formats, including carrels, small tables, movable lounge furniture, and outdoor seating in the cafe and terraces. It also contains two assistive technology stations, a multimedia laboratory, a drop-in computer lab with dual-display computers, a videoconferencing room and two video editing suites.

There are also two training rooms for library and technology instruction and a faculty development lab where staff are encouraged to experiment with new learning approaches and the use of digital resources and three Educational Experimentation Rooms for testing new educational technologies.

There are still physical resources in the library but most of the book stock has been transferred to an adjacent Automatic Retrieval System that houses more than one million volumes (DEGW 2008a).

The use of the library and learning commons as a neutral home for shared technology spaces such as broadcast and edit studios, high-specification graphics computers, telepresence and videoconferencing suites is becoming more common. Rather than embedding these spaces within a faculty of department, risking the development of ownership claims or lower utilization because of relative inaccessibility, the central location (both geographically and politically) makes the library the ideal home for these expensive technology investments.

The changing balance of spaces within the academic library was also discussed by David Lewis (2007b) in his paper, 'A Strategy for Academic Libraries in the First Quarter of the 21st Century', suggesting that the wide application of digital technologies to scholarly communications has disrupted the model of academic library service that has been in place for the past century. Libraries, he says, now need to provide a new mix of different kinds of spaces and work environments that can accommodate different uses and possess different ambiances. Library space will need to be shared with a variety of partners and it is likely that the distinction between the library and other informal campus space will blur.

The provision of information to academic library users has undergone a radical transformation over the last ten years, with increases in the electronic information resources available, particularly as full text journals, but also through a variety of databases and e-books. Much of this information is available not only on the library premises, but also at researchers' desktops and, increasingly, wherever an internet connection can be made.

The Council on Library and Information Resources (CLIR) report, *No Brief Candle: Reconceiving Research Libraries for the 21st Century,* suggested that the twenty-first century library will mirror basic changes in how scholars work and will evolve in step with new scholarly methodologies and the scholarly environment. Working at the nexus of disciplines and across boundaries, libraries will have the flexibility, expertise, and organizational capacity needed to be partners in research involving large heterogeneous datasets. The library will not necessarily be a physical space, and it may not be a collection: it may take the form of a distributed project (2008: 8).

The 2008 UCL report, *Information Behaviour of the Researcher of the Future,* had very little to say about the role of space on future information behaviour of researchers apart from discounting the physical in favour of the virtual:

> The implications of a shift from the library as a physical space to the library as virtual digital environment are immense and truly disruptive. Library users demand 24/7 access, instant gratification at a click, and are increasingly looking for 'the answer' rather than for a particular format: a research monograph or a journal article for instance.
>
> (p. 8)

The record falls in academic library visits by 7 per cent during the last five years in the UK support this reported change in behaviour, although, interestingly, this levelled off in the most recent two years of the analysis, at 72 visits per FTE student per year, or around two per student per week during term time. Users may be making fewer visits to academic libraries, but this does not appear to affect the number of loans. Students are continuing to borrow, with loans per FTE student up by 13 per cent over the last five years, to an average of 60 loans per FTE student in 2007–8. This pattern of loans per FTE student supports the view that remote use of non-loan services is likely to be the main factor in declining visits (SCONUL 2008).

Douglas Suarez, Reference Librarian at Brock University, St Catharines, Ontario, Canada wanted to understand what students actually did when they visited the library. In 2006–7, he carried out an ethnographic study involving both participant observation and semi-structured interviews to determine whether students were

engaged in their studies when using the library and to see if the library nurtured academic engagement in its study areas.

His conclusion was that students in the library were pursuing study behaviours (engaged in activities that one would normally expect to find in an academic library), and that these behaviours were mostly academic activities that support their course work at the university in question. He found the students to be attentive and involved in what they were doing and felt that the library was providing an atmosphere that encourages these behaviours.

Suarez found that, despite his initial impressions about the high level of noise, high pedestrian traffic, social gatherings and general 'hubbub' in the group study area on the main floor of the library, the students seemed to be working on course work most of the time:

> Even when it may appear that small groups of students are 'chatting', or eating/drinking, flirting, or whatever, they are also generally studying as well. Behaviours that students exhibit in the library appear to be practical activities and goal-oriented behaviours. These behaviours can be grouped together as behaviours that involve a range of skills, routines, and habits that are probably learned over time and appear consistent with a wide range of behaviours that support academic engagement.
>
> (2007)

These behaviours can be called 'study behaviours' and examples of these include reading, writing, consulting with fellow students, using computers to do literature searching, communicating with others and writing assignments.

He grouped another set of observed behaviours together as 'leisure or social behaviours' but he stated that these behaviours did not seem to distract from academic work being done in the library:

> Students using cell phone, personal sound devices, or chatting, or napping are generally not the main behavioural activities observed although they do appear. The context of academic learning takes precedence and these other activities seem to promote personal relaxation, and social bonding between students.

Students interviewed for the study acknowledged that, at times, there were distractions that they wanted to avoid. They wanted as much physical comfort as possible to help them study. They wanted convenience and they wanted quiet areas to get away from others so they could concentrate better. The nature of their assignments was a powerful factor in their preferences for group study areas.

Suarez also noted that the behaviour patterns he observed were not static in nature and depended on a range of factors including student preferences and predilections – students will adapt to their surroundings. Students create their own learning spaces by using facilities provided by the library and enhancing them if possible to accommodate their study activities.

He believes that the forthcoming evolution of the library into a learning commons and the library's own vision statement will try to create structures more conducive to the development of a learning community. The community that students participate in while at university can be viewed as an integral part of a sociali-zation process in which it is assumed that students learn in groups throughout their lives. He cites O'Connor's (2005) research study at Sewanee University that includes high praise for the university library and how it fits well with the college's overall mission:

> Any well educated person appreciates the unity, worth and community of knowledge. That's what a good library offers and students need to learn before they leave. After all, wedded to practicality, the workplace does not and cannot readily teach these vital values.
>
> (p. 73)

A subsequent series of studies in 2008–9 by Jordan and Ziebell (2009) explored how libraries in Queensland, Australia were used by students. One study asked 1,500 respondents how they used one of four libraries on a particular occasion. Participants were asked to keep a record during their time in the library, reporting why they had come to the library and what they had hoped to accomplish, what they actually did (where and with whom), and, on exit, what they had achieved during their time in the library. According to Keith Webster, University Librarian and Director of Learning Services at the University of Queensland, Jordan and Ziebell reported 12 key findings:

- Most respondents visited the library to undertake individual study-related activities, and they accomplished this.

- Respondents also visited the library to undertake social or group learning activities.

- In all but a few instances, respondents did less of what they had intended to do.

- In all but a few instances, respondents did more 'other' things than they had intended to do.

- Most respondents chose to work in the library because it is conveniently located and provides good study spaces.

- All respondents put location, atmosphere, study space, and

finding what they need above social reasons (e.g., group meetings) for visiting the library.

- Most respondents visited the library after they had been at home or at a class.

- Most respondents planned to stay in the library for between 30 minutes and two hours.

- Respondents were regular library visitors.

- Students spent most of their time in the library using computers and quiet study spaces.

- Students also used e-mail, the internet, and Facebook, met and chatted with friends, ate, and borrowed books.

- Students wanted the library to provide more computers and more quiet areas (Webster 2010: 10–11).

What was particularly striking to Webster was the extent to which the library was a prominent feature in students' lives: almost 60 per cent visit a library each day, with around half spending between 30 minutes and two hours and almost a quarter spending more than two hours in the library. Webster concluded that despite being heavy consumers of online information resources, electronic journals, databases and e-books, 'they value the library as a place – somewhere that offers an academic ambience for their work, a forum for engagement with others, and a flexible space that meets their shifting needs during the cycle of the semester' (ibid.: 10–11).

The researcher of the future

Changing user behaviour has also been at the centre of work being undertaken by the British Library to understand the needs of the researcher of the future. The British Library is the National Deposit Library for the UK and has a collection well in excess of 150 million items with at least three million items being added each year on a further 12km of shelving. The collection is diverse and includes manuscripts, maps, newspapers, magazines, prints and drawings, sound archives, stamps, music scores and patents (bl.uk).

While some resources are available online through the British Library website, the collection is generally accessed at the main St Pancras library in a series of traditional reading rooms that are divided by subject area. During the last decade, the British Library realized that the needs of the researchers who used the library were changing with the proliferation of digital material (both from large-scale digitization programmes and born digital material), the increase in multi-author, multilocation PhDs, use of multiple data formats and the expectation of researchers that they should be able to access the library at any time from any place and have the ability to store, personalize, manipulate, re-purpose and share information.

As part of the evaluation of their role in the information age of the twenty-first century, the British Library undertook a feasibility study in 2007–8 for the creation of a Digital Research Centre at the St Pancras site that would meet the needs of the new generation of researchers and create a suitable place for both digital research as well as for access to physical resources. The goal of this project was to create a unique information destination, a place containing the world's foremost repository of both physical and digital information, a place of scholarship and a knowledge community that will integrate learning, working and leisure in new and exciting ways.

The spatial concept for the proposed Digital Research Centre that was developed by DEGW in 2008 integrated the core digital research function with a wide range of publicly accessible research and social amenities as well as an extended academic and business hub to support international universities and the UK business community. The spaces within the proposed Digital Research Centre comprised a series of activity hubs that varied in terms of their accessibility to the public:

- Social hub – active area with a wide range of activities including reception, informal gathering and conversation by visitors, eating/drinking, viewing of digitally inspired art and performance pieces.

- Work hub – a range of individual and group work settings possibly including 'on-demand' meeting rooms, video conferencing and reprographic services.

- Research and learning hub – wide range of research and learning settings that will support both individual and group activities.

- Skills hub – home base for BL information and technology specialists.

- Support hub – IT infrastructure and administrative support facilities.

A significant part of the research hub was devoted to collaborative research settings that range from open meeting areas to technology enabled group rooms with video conferencing facilities, editing suites and immersive data environments (Figure 5.27).

The need for a rethinking of the academic library was stressed by Stephen Hoare in the *Education Guardian*'s Libraries Unleashed supplement in April 2008:

> Academic libraries are changing faster than at any time in their history. Information technology, online databases, and catalogues and digitised archives have put the library back

at the heart of teaching, learning and academic research on campus.

(Hoare 2008)

He notes that libraries are leading the way in developing innovative learning spaces in which people can make productive use of powerful combinations of information and technologies on their desktop – including communication and collaborative tools through which they discuss and develop ideas online. He considered the technology and digital resources of libraries, however, to be more important than the spaces: 'The scope for digitisation is endless and libraries are ideally placed to lead the way towards a learning environment without borders' (ibid.).

While the Digital Research Centre has yet to be built, the British Library continues to explore the nature of the future physical and digital research environment. Their 2010–11 exhibition and research programme 'Growing Knowledge: the evolution of research' asked the big questions: How have digital technologies changed research? What are the new challenges they pose? What role should a research library play in the twenty-first century? (British Library 2012).

The future of the academic library was also explored by the Helen Hamlyn Centre at the Royal College of Art in London in 2010. The Living Libraries project, sponsored by DEGW, Haworth and Unwired and carried out by Catherine Greene, took an in-depth look at the way that academic researchers worked, with the aim of informing the design of new settings for the library and, more broadly, the future knowledge workplace (Living Libraries Project 2012).

Greene felt that universities are putting greater emphasis on social learning and teamwork at undergraduate level in an attempt to provide a more relevant education and recent developments in the library have focused on providing spaces for such work. Based on her interviews with researchers, she believes that many academic researchers feel disenfranchised by this and considers that the library should do more to meet their requirements. The Living Libraries project aimed to determine what additional settings are needed to make the library more relevant to research communities:

> An initial literature review showed that despite the vastly different fields of research, the basic journey is very similar. The project developed a generic cycle of research, which moves from getting information during the 'discover' and 'gather' phases to actively using information during the 'analyse', 'create' and 'share' phases. This cycle exists in many variations, it can span a day or a number of years, but is broadly recognised as generic by researchers.

Figure 5.27 Digital Research Centre concept sketches. Source: DEGW/Sketch Studio London (2008)

Traditionally, libraries focused on the 'getting' part of this process. Their service was designed around the assumption that a researcher arrived with a question, and the library was there to provide the resources to find the answer. Today's libraries must instead embrace the entire process, welcoming researchers and providing them with the space and resources needed at every stage.

(ibid.)

Greene goes on to describe the characteristics of successful library settings that would support this research cycle (Box 5.2) and to identify the space characteristics of the research settings that can be overlaid over the research cycle.

A change of emphasis

Despite the evidence of the widespread transformation of the traditional academic library into a vibrant and varied landscape of learning and research settings, there are still those who predict a dark future for the academic library.

In 2009, David Greenstein, vice provost for academic planning and programmes at the University of California system, predicted that the university library of the future will be sparsely staffed, highly decentralized, and have a physical plant consisting of little more than special collections and study areas. He also felt that the future would be about economic pressures forcing the creation of outsourced library systems with shared print and digital repositories where they store books they no longer want to manage. Understandably, this view of the future did not go down well with other US research librarians at the time who felt it did not acknowledge the varied new roles that libraries were taking on, such as working with faculty in introducing technology into teaching.

The Society of College, National and University Librarians (SCONUL) in 2010 published a vision statement for future libraries in the UK and Ireland that stated that: 'Library and information services will move from a "one-size-fits all" approach to the personalisation of the delivery and support of space, services and content provision. For example, library buildings will be designed with very different user needs in mind, providing discrete areas for social learning, research-based learning, group activity, etc' (2010).

Physical and virtual space will be equally important and the main challenge will be in providing a blended service where the virtual and the actual space are complementary, influenced by the number and diversity of new technologies. SCONUL believes that library buildings will continue to play an important role although visitor numbers for traditional use of content will decrease as more material is made available over the web.

It also felt that increased cross-institutional alliances, driven by changes in the market, will lead to more shared space across

Box 5.2 Library settings that support the research cycle

- *Flexible* An academic year puts strains on the library at specific times. The space needs to be able to adapt and change to cope with evolving needs. It must be possible to scale spaces up or down so that they can adjust to accommodate more people and changing functions. Adaptable furniture and a variety of partitioning will help to achieve greater flexibility.

- *Tunable* Spaces should be designed to allow people to adjust them to their personal preference. Users can then tune them to their individual needs, either by increasing privacy, reducing noise, altering the light or moving furniture.

- *Defined* Boundaries are important to define different zones and indicate the function of a space. These can range from light-weight screens to full enclosures but can also be created through changes in colour, lighting, acoustics, texture, floor surface, screens and furniture. These should be used to create an interesting landscape of spaces, creating different atmospheres which help to suggest an appropriate behaviour for that space – for example, cool colours, dark furniture and high partitions suggest a quieter space for concentrated activity.

- *Comfortable* In order to promote the library as a good alternative to the academic office or home it needs to be made to feel comfortable, welcoming and personal. Academics want to be able to dock down immediately and get on with work. Shared desking must therefore be comfortable, easy to configure and with clear protocols of use.

- *Stand-alone* Settings can adapt and change far quicker than a building and are a much cheaper way to effect organizational change. They should, therefore, be thought of as architecturally independent, a set of furnitures and boundaries that are able to be arranged and realized in a variety of different situations.

Source: Living Libraries Project 2012

the sector, impacting on how library services are delivered. The range of services being provided within the library will also expand to incorporate a range of non-traditional activities such as student support services, learning cafes and social learning space. Building design will acknowledge the needs of diversified communities and accommodate and exploit activities associated with available technologies. For example, different space will be provided for social learning, research and group activity. A genuinely flexible IT support infrastructure will be provided, with a blend of wireless, hard-wired and portable devices. Bandwidth for wireless provision will be enhanced but the increased capabilities of hard-wired facilities will mean that the existing discrepancy between the two will continue. More off-site storage will be developed for less used or 'copy of last resort', using collaborative ventures (ibid.).

In 2010 the British Library (BL), the Joint Information Systems Committee (JISC), Research Information Network (RIN), Research Libraries UK (RLUK) and the Society of College, National and University Libraries (SCONUL) sponsored a research project to look at the future of the academic libraries:

> Libraries are at a turning point. As technology rapidly transforms the way we access information, and resources are increasingly available online and in digital formats, the established role of the library as a physical space housing racks of books is looking increasingly out of step with the needs of students and researchers.
>
> Allied with technology, library users' needs and preferences are helping to drive the change in libraries. Students, researchers and teachers now expect to be able to access information around the clock, from almost anywhere in the world and via a growing number of devices, from laptops to phones.
>
> What does this mean for the academic library as we know it? What will it look like in 10 years' time? Will it exist in its current physical form? What role will librarians play in supporting learning and research in the digital age?
>
> (JISC 2010: 3)

In an unattributed quotation in this initial brochure, *Libraries of the Future,* the authors also warn: 'libraries must rethink the way they work and the way that they support learning, teaching and research' (ibid.: 3). This seems to be stating the obvious. Academic libraries are well aware of the changing world within which they operate: the embrace of digital content and the transformation of library space into the learning commons are just two of the many responses to this.

The first full report produced by the project was published in May 2011. The report describes three scenarios for future libraries in the year 2050 – Wild West, Beehive and Walled Garden (Box 5.3) – though it notes in the introduction that 'there can be no universal assumption that a library, librarians or librarianship will exist in 2050' (Curtis et al. 2011: 5). The report provides a set of early indicators that would tend to suggest which of the scenarios is more likely to occur than the others and the authors suggest that the scenarios should be used to assist the strategic planning processes for academic libraries.

The gloomy and pessimistic tone of these scenarios was continued in the US in a rather tongue-in-cheek article published in the *Chronicle of Higher Education* on 2 January 2011, 'Academic Library Autopsy Report, 2050', by Brian T. Sullivan, an instructional librarian at Alfred University:

> The academic library has died. Despite early diagnosis, audacious denial in the face of its increasingly severe symptoms led to its deterioration and demise. The academic library died alone, largely neglected and forgotten by a world that once revered it as the heart of the university.
>
> (Sullivan 2011a)

The causes of death that Sullivan lists include:

- book collections becoming obsolete as fully digitized collections of nearly every book in the world rendered physical book collections unnecessary.

- library instruction no longer being necessary as database vendors were forced to create tools that were more user-friendly, or else risk fading into obscurity. As databases became more intuitive and simpler to use, library instruction in the use of archaic tools was no longer needed.

- information literacy being fully integrated into the curriculum.

- libraries and librarians being subsumed by information-technology departments. Library buildings were converted into computer labs, study spaces, and headquarters for information-technology departments.

- reference services disappearing and being replaced by ever-improving search engines and social-networking tools, along with information-technology help desks that were relatively inexpensive to run.

- economics trumping quality. So few students were taking full advantage of the available resources that the services were no longer economically justifiable. Ever since it became so easy and inexpensive to find adequate resources, paying

Box 5.3 Three scenarios for the academic library of the future

Wild West scenario

The world is dominated by capitalism and corporate power, including the HE sector. Private providers compete with each other and the state to offer students educational services, including information services and learning material. The power lies in the hands of the consumer ('student' being a rather old-fashioned term) who is able to pick and choose from courses and learning materials to create a personal educational experience.

In this scenario, changes occur at every level both for users of academic library services and academic librarians. In 2011, a librarian is someone who works in a library. In 2050, it is difficult to define a common group of librarians who share a common set of skills and values and libraries that in 2011 were in FE, HE or local authority control are merged into local cooperatives which have contractual relationships with bodies in education. New models of 'library' have emerged at a local level and as chains.

Beehive scenario

The Beehive scenario is a world in which society and HE have open values and the state is the primary funder and controller of HE. Its overriding aim is the production of a skilled workforce, and to this end it has created a largely homogenous HE system for the masses while allowing the elite to attend the few traditional institutions. A limited market is used to provide competition within the HE system to drive up quality.

While much of the study can be done from home or the workplace, the provision of high-quality physical space for teaching, learning and social purposes has grown in importance to the elite universities as a differentiator. Library knowledge, information and learning support services are packaged within the learning modules with standard support offers and additional chargeable elements. For example, Oxford provides the UK-wide hub for classical studies and mathematics, and University College London provides that for biochemistry. Integration of such services across Europe is also well developed.

Higher Education Institutions (HEIs) offering arts and humanities courses tend to be closely integrated with museums, galleries and archives to create a richness of material to support the learner. The arts and humanities library is typically part of a local cluster of HEIs rather than necessarily a part of the HEI itself. Special collections,

particularly those related to arts and humanities subjects, are now largely the preserve of the elite HEIs and a few remaining specialist local museums and archives around the country.

Walled Garden scenario

HEIs in this scenario are 'Walled Gardens'. The closed nature of society makes HEIs insular and inward-looking, isolated from other institutions by competing value systems. Provision of information services in this world is as much concerned with protecting their own materials from others as it is in enabling access.

The number of different groups has led to a diverse closed-value system and the sense of universal knowledge has been lost. Sharing of knowledge between groups is possible but requires significant contractual and financial negotiation. 'Libraries' are aligned to individual institutions, or networks of value systems and library services are available at a sector level only for the publicly funded minority of institutions. Institutions choose to work only with those that share their values and they also rigorously enforce who has access to their academic output.

Libraries also find themselves becoming increasingly specialized around specific disciplines and services (such as specialist STEM libraries serving students, researchers, NHS and business). Some institutions that have become highly specialized have sold or otherwise divested themselves of their 'non-relevant' holdings and physical special collections, or now house them off site. Libraries serve the goals of their sponsor institution, and are fiercely protective of their IP. This holds both for research outputs, for which they often act as publisher, and for teaching materials. Procurement, dissemination and restriction of knowledge all present special challenges in this future. The rise of libraries for specific value/geographical groups has meant that the importance of the British Library has declined; it is now called the National Library of England.

In this scenario, the physical space traditionally associated with information services and the old-fashioned 'library' continues to be valued in 2050 and in some cases has increased in importance as a social learning space. However, in 2050 these learning spaces are not always provided by the library. In particular, the more vocational and business-oriented institutions are more creative in their attitude to the provision of physical working environments.

Source: Curtis et al. (2011)

significantly more for the absolute best was no longer an option for perpetually cash-strapped colleges.

The article was clearly a call to action for today's librarians.

> It is entirely possible that the life of the academic library could have been spared if the last generation of librarians had spent more time plotting a realistic path to the future and less time chasing outdated trends while mindlessly spouting mantras like 'There will always be books and libraries' and 'People will always need librarians to show them how to use information.' We'll never know now what kind of treatments might have worked. Librarians planted the seeds of their own destruction and are responsible for their own downfall.
>
> (ibid.)

A 2011 report by the American Library Association on the state of America's libraries took a more optimistic view of the current and future state of academic libraries (ALA 2011). The report noted the increasing financial pressures faced by academic libraries across the US and stated that almost 47 per cent of US academic libraries are introducing or increasing user charges, while 40 per cent are looking externally for new funding sources and 19 per cent are advocating internally for a greater share of the institutional budget. Additionally, almost two-thirds of academic libraries are accelerating the shift from print to electronic resources, and many (29 per cent) are increasingly directing users to free electronic resources (p. 29).

Students and faculty, according to the report, seem to be using academic libraries more than ever. During a typical week, academic libraries had more than 31 million searches in electronic databases, answered more than 469,000 reference questions and made more than 12,000 group presentations attended by more than 219,000 students and faculty. Library websites received more than 722 million virtual visits from outside the physical library building, and visits to online library catalogues totalled more than 479 million (p. 30).

Academic libraries continue to evolve from being storage spaces, becoming vital places to collaborate, connect and learn. The new and improved library spaces integrate information management, technology, and student-centred settings.

More than 20 major library construction or refurbishment projects were completed in the first 11 months of 2010 and the report noted the importance of the library on student experience and student recruitment. In some cases the drive to improve student experience has led to increased financial support for academic libraries.

Electronic books currently represent 27 per cent of academic library holdings, and content in electronic formats accounts for 57 per cent of library resource budgets. The most important benefits of digital content were rated by faculty and students as cost savings to students as the top benefit of digital content, followed by instant access to content, access to current content and ease of note taking (p. 31).

Approximately 94 per cent of academic libraries now offer e-books and 12 per cent circulate preloaded e-reading devices, while 26 per cent are considering it. E-books were most likely to be offered in the social sciences (83 per cent), followed by science at 82 per cent, technology (80 per cent), humanities (77 per cent), medicine (69 per cent) and law (51 per cent) (p. 36).

The authors of the report, however, also cite research that shows that college students are clearly floundering in information overload, and helping them develop research fluency remains one of the most important roles for academic librarians (p. 30). The conclusion of the report was that both American academic libraries and the institutions of higher education they serve are under increasing pressure to adapt so that they will be able to continue to thrive in the future (p. 31).

This is also the view put forward by Steve Kolowich in 'What students don't know', an article that appeared in *Inside Higher Ed* in August 2011, reviewing the findings of a two-year, five-campus ethnographic study examining how students view and use their campus libraries (Asher et al. 2010). The study, ERIAL (Ethnographic Research in Illinois Academic Libraries), found that students rarely ask librarians for help, even when they need it:

> One thing the librarians now know is that their students' research habits are worse than they thought. At one of the universities, for example, researchers found that 'the majority of students – of all levels – exhibited significant difficulties that ranged across nearly every aspect of the search process,' according to researchers there. They tended to overuse Google and misuse scholarly databases. They preferred simple database searches to other methods of discovery, but generally exhibited 'a lack of understanding of search logic' that often foiled their attempts to find good sources.
>
> (Kolowich 2011)

The authors of the study noted 'Many students described experiences of anxiety and confusion when looking for resources – an observation that seems to be widespread among students at the five institutions involved in this study.'

Kolowich feels that the results can be taken in a positive light: as the library building has receded as a campus mecca, librarians have often had to combat the notion that online tools are making them irrelevant. The evidence from the study lends weight to their counterargument: librarians are more relevant than they have ever been, since students need guides to shepherd them through the wilderness of the web (ibid.).

The Taylor Family Digital Library at the University of Calgary that opened in 2011 may provide a vision for the future academic library. The library was conceived as a state-of-the-art learning and research centre that is both a model for the twenty-first-century library and an important new gathering place for students, faculty, staff, alumni and the broader Calgary community (TFDL 2012).

The six-storey building is a total of 24,000 square metres and contains 600,000 of the latest and most requested books and journals. Sixty per cent of the library's total book and journal stock and much of the library's archival holdings are housed in the new off-campus High Density Library. The library building also includes an art gallery, archives and rare collections, a student success centre and a wide range of digital learning and research tools: 'technology that encourages experiential learning, exploration and innovative ways of creating new knowledge' (ibid.).

The resources of the library are available for the entire community. A community reader card enables users to borrow up to 50 books at one time and renew books online: visitors have 24-hour access, five days a week, to more than 200 computer workstations with 100 per cent wireless and cellular coverage in the Library's Learning Commons. Users can automatically check out and return items and students can get help from roving students providing peer-to-peer help.

Collaborative workspaces are equipped with large wall-mounted flat screens and ergonomic furniture. Students can book rooms via touch-screens located on every floor. Presentation rooms with ceiling-mounted cameras allow students to playback their presentations to review their performance. Touch-tables in the cafe allow visitors to browse through a digital copy of the *New York Times,* play with a digital sketchbook, or leaf through images of the rare collections in the library's holdings.

Visions of the future

Either the academic library is under threat because of the increasingly digital nature of scholarship – e-journals and e-books will make it irrelevant to most students and researchers – or diversification of library spaces, resources and services position the library at the point of intersection between the physical and the digital world and as a place where information skills and expertise will continue to reside and be valued by the academic community and by society as a whole.

Whichever future lies in wait for it, it is clear that the twenty-first-century academic library will be a different type of place from the traditional library. It will need to be multilayered, providing a number of flexible activity zones to support learning, living, working and leisure. It will be up to the users to choose appropriate settings and technology for the tasks they want to achieve. The library space and experience will change over the course of the day: changing to reflect different types of users at different times of the day, week, month or academic year.

More space is likely to be devoted to collaborative activities and informal meeting and work areas will be provided to support mobile learners. There will be ergonomic furniture and power everywhere in the short- to mid-term at least. The library will also need to incorporate a wide range of technology-enabled research and work settings including larger or multiple screens, webcams and telepresence systems, voice input and increased use of audio/video materials along side traditional print materials.

A vision for the future library that brings many of these ideas together was put forward by Massimo Riva, Professor of Italian Studies and Director of the Virtual Humanities Lab at Brown University as part of the British Library's Growing Knowledge project. In an interview that is posted on the project website he said he saw:

> the library of the future a little bit like an airport for books or a convention centre for the meeting of minds ... so a place like an old fashioned Italian piazza where one can sit and sip your coffee and stroll leisurely or act as in a marketplace, exchanging and trading information and knowledge. This is happening at the same time in a physical space as well as in a virtual space and the interface between the physical and the virtual space is going to be crucial for our envisioning of the library of the future.
>
> (Riva 2012)

ACADEMIC AND ADMINISTRATIVE WORKSPACE

A significant part of most universities' estates consists of academic and administrative offices. In the US, Fink puts the estimate at between 22 per cent and 30 per cent of non-residential space (2005: 2): these figures are supported by Stanford University's *Space Planning Guidelines*, which state that 22 per cent of their 12 million square feet, 670 building estate consists of office space, compared with 14 per cent for laboratories, 9 per cent for libraries and 3 per cent for classrooms (Stanford University 2009).

Comparable UK figures are likely to be in the same range but may vary depending on the age and type of institution. DEGW projects with UK universities have found the percentage of net usable space used for offices varying from 11.5 per cent to over 28 per cent (DEGW 2006–8).

The academic office has not changed in any fundamental way for well over a hundred years. It is a space for reflection, for concentrated working and for meeting with students and colleagues. It has also traditionally been a physical symbol of a person's seniority within the academic community: the more senior one is within the department or faculty, the larger and better equipped the office is likely to be.

While the provision of academic and administrative workplaces varies from university to university, there are some common elements that will be recognizable within most universities.

Academic departments often consist of rows of offices, teaching rooms and other support spaces arranged on either side of a central corridor or surrounding a central core. Social or interaction space for staff is often limited to a small tea point or kitchen area and many academics or administrative groups choose to have their own 'unofficial' coffee and tea facilities within their own space, despite the consequent health and safety issues. The size of offices provided is generally based on an assessment of the work undertaken by the occupants and the rank or position of the person within the university hierarchy (Fink 2005). Large academic offices for deans and professors may contain a meeting table or soft seating area as well as the standard desk, filing cabinets and bookshelves. More junior staff members may have small individual offices or may share two- or three-person offices. Postgraduate research students may be allocated a desk in a shared research centre or in a postgraduate area within the department.

Academic 'office hours' typically involve students queuing up in the corridor waiting to see their lecturers. The frequency of meetings varies considerably during the year, as at certain times the lecturer has to sign off course options or review progress. The unpredictability of whether students will turn up for their meetings means that it is considered more practicable to hold the meetings in the academic's office rather than elsewhere because the lecturer can get on with other tasks while waiting for students. Visits outside these hours may or may not be welcomed, depending on the preferences of each staff member.

Administrative and clerical staff frequently share offices or may be in open-plan areas. Administrative staff generally do not provide a reception or filtering function within departments and access to academic staff is typically uncontrolled apart from at the level of the dean or head of department. Interaction between staff and individual students primarily occurs in the academic's office.

Because the departmental space is open to everyone, all offices are kept locked when the occupants are absent. Staff occupying academic offices generally keep the doors closed while they are working to minimize disruption from passersby and if there are glass vision panels in the doors, they are often covered over with paper or fabric to prevent anyone looking into the office. It should be noted that this practice is in breach of good practice relating to fire and safety regulations but it is almost universal in many higher education institutions.

Fink (2005) notes that despite the significance and importance of offices as a campus space use, the literature of higher education provides skimpy evidence about offices. Offices as a place of work are important for individuals to be productive and for institutions to be successful. They are 'where university employees work, hang their pictures, make their calls, hold meetings, advise students, use their computers, conduct research and, in many cases, store the operational histories of their institution. It is where many, if not most, university employees spend their entire working day as well as their entire university career' (p. 1).

The Space Management Group's *Review of Practice* (2005c: 22) found that 79 per cent of Higher Education Institutions (HEIs) undertook space utilization surveys and 53 per cent carried them out at least once or twice a year. Utilization data, however, are usually only collected for teaching spaces and sometimes only for pooled teaching spaces, followed by at least some of the specialist teaching spaces. Information on research space, libraries, catering facilities and technical, research and support offices is less often included in the surveys.

Seventy-eight per cent of respondents to the SMG's review of practice used space norms for allocating space, remodelling space and/or planning new or replacement space. More used them for planning new space than allocating or remodelling existing buildings (ibid.: 29). Forty-seven per cent of respondents used space standards and generally these related to office space.

The SMG's report *The Impact on Space of Future Changes in Higher Education* (2006b) notes that the provision of academic office accommodation is a sensitive topic in most HEIs. In many pre-1992 UK universities (before former polytechnics were reclassified as universities), offices were provided on the assumption that they would be used for tutorial teaching of perhaps two to four students at a time. The academic office was therefore a complex work environment: a private study space, a semi-public teaching space, a room for small staff meetings, and a space for the reception of professional visitors (ibid.: 11).

The size of tutorial groups has increased in many institutions to eight to ten students and academic offices are often now too small to house them. The consequence is an increased demand for small and medium-sized seminar rooms. This new teaching space may be obtained by taking space from non-teaching functions, or by reconfiguring laboratories or workshops. However, the likelihood is that there will be some net expansion in overall space requirements in excess of that strictly called for by student numbers. Building configuration may prevent remodelling of office space to reduce the academic office size to take account of the changing use pattern and accommodate the additional requirement for seminar rooms (ibid.: 11).

An analysis of work activity in academic offices at the Department of Civil and Building Engineering at Loughborough University published in 2005 found that on average staff spend 30 per cent of their work time in their office, much of which (Figure 5.28) is spent working on individual tasks (Parkin et al. 2006: 7).

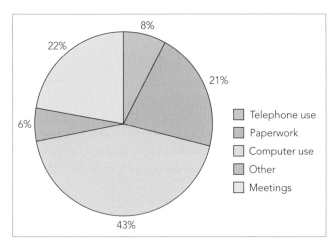

Figure 5.28 Activity in academic staff offices. Source: Parkin et al. (2006)

This is consistent with findings in corporate work environments where utilization levels of 35–40 per cent are common.

Demands for administrative space in higher education have grown. Examination of statistics from the Universities Statistical Record and the Higher Education Statistics Agency suggests that expenditure on administration and central services grew from about 6 per cent of total higher education spending in the early 1980s to about 13 per cent by 2006, reflecting the creation of essentially new functions such as quality assurance, marketing and external fundraising, and widening participation work; and the provision of a wider range of services in established areas such as finance, research administration and student support of various kinds (SMG 2006b: 13).

The SMG predicted that there would probably be further growth in demand for administrative space, with students becoming more demanding users of administrative services: the introduction of variable tuition fees in 2006 undoubtedly accelerated this trend. Other administrative services, related to more market-oriented higher education organizations, would also demand more space (p. 14).

This report also notes that new buildings offer an opportunity to collocate administrative functions in ways that improve efficiency, save space and offer an enhanced service to academic staff and students. In one case, a space reduction of about one-third was reported when administrative functions were relocated from dispersed small offices to a single, large, open-plan office with an adjoining 'one-stop shop' for students (p. 15). HEFCE's *Space Management Guidelines for the HE Sector* (University of Newcastle upon Tyne 2002, quoted in SMG 2005c) had noted that, in contrast typically to academic space management, administrative space was not subject to detailed review in order to create efficiency gains. There are, therefore, some efficiencies to be obtained from better use of administrative space, but these savings are likely to be offset by new administrative functions. The overall picture is likely to be one of slow expansion of administrative space (SMG 2006b: 14).

This pattern of space use has a number of consequences:

● Buildings are often dark and uninviting – central corridors receive very little natural light.

● There is very little choice in how or where staff work. The individual office is expected to provide suitable accommodation for individual work and research as well as tutorials and other meetings with both staff and students.

● Increasing use of two-person shared offices is likely to increase levels of disruption and frustration with the work environment caused by visitors or telephone calls and internal circulation problems caused by the amount of furniture and ancillary equipment in such a restricted space.

● There is little opportunity for interaction/communication between staff within departments.

● Student–staff interaction is also sub-optimal. Students need to queue to see staff in their office and there are few opportunities for informal collaboration or interaction within the departmental area.

● Larger offices containing meeting tables and/or sofas are often unavailable for use by other staff who may require meeting space for larger groups.

- Administrative staff may find it hard to know who is present in the department at any time.

- Staff are placing themselves at risk by not being visible while in their office and by locking themselves into their office with students and other visitors (DEGW 2005: 35–6).

Innovation in the academic workplace

In *Promoting Space Efficiency in Building Design,* the SMG (2006a) related changes in space use in HEIs to trends in the corporate office sector. It noted that:

> many organisations have embarked on projects to increase space efficiency through strategies of reducing the average size of enclosed offices and desks in open-plan areas, eliminating all solo offices and introducing office 'hotelling' for mobile staff. Much importance is also placed on reducing the space taken up by filing and document storage through the use of high density storage, efficient filing furniture, electronic filing and knowledge management. Some of these solutions are applicable to the HEI sector though not widely used as yet.
>
> (p. 9)

It also noted that many HEIs, particularly those with a significant international status, now benchmark themselves against these other sectors rather than against each other and are moving away from 'best in university class' buildings. For instance, when delivering a scientific research building, a university may benchmark itself against a leading private sector laboratory; when delivering a faculty building it may look to review what it is providing against British Council for Offices fit-out guidelines (ibid.: 11).

One of the consequences of looking outward to best practice in other sectors has been that the trend for open-plan work environments, which has been seen in most other sectors for a number of other years, is slowly emerging in HE. To some extent this transition reflects build cost – due to expanding numbers, many universities can no longer afford to provide their staff with the large cellular offices that have until recently been prevalent in HE facilities. Perhaps more significantly, it also reflects a growing recognition of the importance of informal interaction and collaboration between researchers.

This development is most apparent in the work environments provided for researchers. In 2006, Parkin et al. published the results of an 18-month EPSRC-funded study that investigated how research environments can be better designed to support the activities of their occupants. From a series of case studies of UK academic research environments, they found that communication was seen as fundamental to the research process. Informal,

impromptu communication was particularly valued, with the design of research facilities being viewed as playing a key role in fostering chance interactions. The provision of settings for more structured formal discussion was also regarded as important for interaction with colleagues and with visitors.

The quality of the environment, in terms of basic heat, light levels and ventilations, was regarded as imperative for research environments and access to natural light and views was also valued. The provision of storage at, or close to, the desk was also seen as important to their work as was space for researchers to relax, eat, drink and reflect on their work away from their desk.

Researchers expressed a requirement for a quiet environment where they are working on concentrated tasks such as writing papers. Visual privacy was also rated as important with researchers tending to dislike working where they could be overlooked by people walking past.

Open-plan environments, where individual work areas are not separated by full height walls or partitions, may be most suited to people who are working as an interdependent team, or who are working on similar projects. For these individuals it is useful to be able to have a high level of awareness of what their co-workers are doing so that they can share information and ideas, and coordinate their actions. Overhearing conversations can play an important role in this. The increased information flow that open team environments afford enables teams to produce higher quality work, and to make faster decisions than working in enclosed settings (ibid.: 3).

Parkin et al. also note that open-plan work settings are also associated with increased noise and distraction – one of the main complaints that knowledge workers have with open-plan environments is of being distracted by their colleagues' telephone calls and impromptu meetings. Exposure to noise from other people's conversations has been found to impair performance on concentrated tasks such as reading. Consequently, they felt that open-plan environments may not be so advantageous for people whose work involves the performance of individual, complex tasks (ibid.: 3).

One of the case studies in the study, the Research Club pilot at Loughborough University, queried the practicability of hot desking in a research setting. Most of the PhD students who occupied the club space adjusted quickly to not having allocated desk space and said that, given the choice between the more elaborate, higher-quality environment that the department was able to provide because of desk sharing and having an allocated desk in a more traditional research room they would choose a desk-sharing regime.

Previously the research environment has attempted to replicate the individual-centred workspace provided for academic staff. While students have usually shared offices with several others, individual workstations have tended to be partitioned off from the room with high panels, to create cubicles. Several institutions have moved away from this model, replacing cubicled facilities with more open, group-centred work settings (ibid.: 4). The study discusses the benefits of this move, but does sound a note of caution, however, suggesting that a workspace design that functions very well in one sector may not be appropriate for another. Even at the level of individual organizations in the same field, seemingly minor differences between their work-practices can mean that workspace requirements are quite different. The study suggests that any workplace solution proposed should be evaluated in terms of resource efficiency, the satisfaction and performance of its occupants and the extent to which it communicates the organization's values (ibid.: 3–4).

The authors also note that employees' satisfaction with their workplace can have a significant impact on organizational churn – the rate at which workers and technology are relocated in the work environment in a given period. The work environment is one of the strongest influences on individuals' decisions about whether to stay in a job, with several studies finding a correlation between satisfaction with the physical environment and job satisfaction. The benefits of increased performance can be equally tangible and Parkin et al. cite Oseland's 2001 assertion that achieving a 2–5 per cent increase in employees' performance can, in some cases, cover the entire cost of providing the workspace in the commercial sector (ibid.: 3).

The development of new workplace solutions is often linked to major new building or refurbishment projects where the individual academic office may be replaced with a shared office for perhaps three to six staff (SMG 2006a: 14). The SMG space efficiency study (ibid.) suggested that these shared offices need to be accompanied by a set of conveniently located small and medium-sized rooms, which can be used for meetings and small-group teaching.

They suggested that this arrangement may be particularly appropriate when academic staff are out of their offices a great deal – for example because of high class-contact hours, visits to students on work placements, professional practice of various kinds, or specialist facility-based research work. The acceptance of shared offices may be further enhanced if good common-room facilities are provided as part of the restructuring. A reception area with secretarial staff and other facilities may also be part of this redesign. They felt that this arrangement of space is likely to produce some net space savings, although if adequate teaching, meeting and support service space is also provided, the savings will normally be modest (ibid.: 13).

In its review of 15 case studies of recent refurbishment, expansion, upgrading or new builds in higher education institutions, the SMG's view is that reduction in 'ownership' of space is one of the keys to more flexible planning and the space efficiencies that brings:

> While acknowledging the strong sense of territory in academic departments, users need to be encouraged to appreciate that the move towards multidisciplinary courses, the increase in central booking of teaching space and the pervasiveness of information technology, will make it easier for rooms to be used for many different types of teaching and learning by several faculties. Generically designed rooms can easily be reassigned to different departments. Local amenity space for both staff and students, such as coffee shops, breakout areas and wireless-enabled computer zones, are examples of versatile spaces. Versatility may involve higher capital cost for more equipment or finishes, which must be justified by improved utilisation.

(ibid.: 15)

In 2007, Drivers Jonas undertook a detailed analysis of office accommodation across University College London (UCL 2007) as part of a broader review of resource allocation across the university. Six departments were selected for detailed analysis (finance, law, history, epidemiology, psychology, archaeology) as they varied in size, location, type of space occupied and their approach to space management.

Office space made up the majority of total space of three of the five academic departments (that is, excluding finance) and, of the other two, accounted for almost 50 per cent of the total space.

The average amount of space per person also varied considerably across the departments (Figure 5.29), both for academic and non-academic use. History had the most space per person (approximately 25 square metres net internal area for both academic and administrative staff) but, to some extent, this could be explained by the nature of the building they occupied. Epidemiology was the most efficient, with academic staff occupying approximately 8 square metres each and administrative staff occupying approximately 5 square metres. The biggest difference between space provision for academic and administrative staff was found in the law department.

The authors of the review suggested that some form of central booking/ownership for office space would be desirable to reduce the amount of space used solely by one department, thus reducing space costs. It is unlikely that this suggestion would have been favourably received by the departments in question. They noted that there:

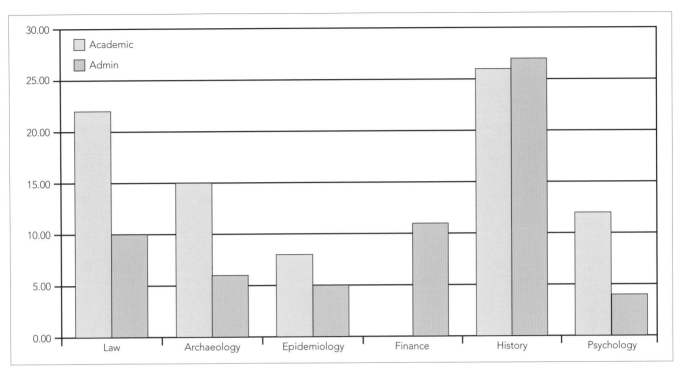

Figure 5.29 Average space/person (square metres). Source: UCL (2007: 7)

seems to be a strong affront to giving up individual offices. This is an issue within the higher education sector as a whole with academia often being very traditional. Lecturers expect a single office and to be able to store their own books and papers in their office. However, modern working practices and the pressure of the cost of space, especially in central London, dictate a need for change.

(UCL 2007: 28)

In terms of the use of the space provided, the authors felt that utilization of the academic and administrative workspace could be increased by encouraging flexible work practices such as hot desking/desk sharing, flexible working patterns including home working and the use of mobile technology and open-plan offices (ibid.: 28).

In January 2008, the Scottish Funding Council and the University of Strathclyde commissioned DEGW to undertake a research project exploring effective working environments in further and higher education (SFC 2008). The scoping document for this study, *Effective Spaces for Working in Higher and Further Education*, noted that HE appears to be one of the last places to adopt a more modern, flexible approach to working environments and that few completed successful examples exist. It also noted that further education institutions are already adopting more open working environments in new developments and they wanted to know

whether these are working and whether the lessons learned can be applied to higher education.

The project sponsors felt that considerable benefits could be gained from modern academic workplaces in terms of sustainability, quality, cost and team working – they also cautioned that if they fail in effectiveness, the consequences could also be severe (ibid.: 4–5).

The study evaluated a number of academic workplaces across the UK and developed a number of generic workplace options within the same overall space allocation that varied in the level of provision of enclosed offices, the range of support settings available and the size of workgroups. These workplace models were described as studies, quarters, clusters, hubs and clubs (Figure 5.30), providing a range of workplace options that provide varying amounts of private and collaborative workspace within a departmental area to support different work patterns. These models also vary considerably in terms of their construction costs and their ability to support higher densities of occupation over time. The research team stated that an appropriate workplace solution should be developed based on an in-depth understanding of the work activities of the people involved in the workplace projects and a change management strategy should be developed to ensure that their views are heard and, wherever possible, are incorporated into the workplace design.

	Studies	Quarters	Clusters	Hubs	Clubs
Privacy	● ● ●	● ●	● ●	●	● ●
Concentrated work	● ● ●	● ●	● ●	●	● ● ●
Team work	●	●	● ● ●	● ● ●	● ●
Informal interaction	● ●	● ● ●	● ● ●	● ● ●	● ● ●
Supporting higher densities	●	●	● ●	● ●	● ● ●
Ability to reconfigure teams	●	●	● ● ●	● ●	● ●
Cost efficiency (construction)	●	● ●	● ●	● ● ●	● ●

- Studies score well in terms of the privacy and the support of concentrated working but poorly for the support of team working and informal interaction. Study environments also tend to be inflexible over time and more expensive to construct because of the number of internal walls and the services implications of the divided space.

- Quarters support individual, concentrated work in small group areas but are less suitable for team or group working – the spaces are suited more for companionship and informal interaction rather than collaboration. Zoning of the space and the provision of owned, individual work settings makes it more difficult to increase densities or reconfigure the work environment.

- Clusters support collaborative working and informal interaction most effectively through the provision of work setting clusters, with individual, concentrated working being best supported in small study enclosures throughout the space. Increased densities can be supported through the use of shared work areas and the introduction of touch-down work settings.

- Hubs also support collaborative and team-based working most effectively through work setting clusters and a generous provision of shared work areas and social settings. Good design and the landscaping of the environment is necessary to avoid noise and negative perceptions of 'traditional' open-plan work environments.

- Clubs provide a range of work settings able to support both individual and collaborative working for a more mobile population of academic and administrative staff who are willing to adopt mobile working practices. The predominance of shared work settings makes the environment well suited for handling increased densities or reconfiguration as the occupancy requirements change.

Figure 5.30 Summary of five academic workplace models. Source: DEGW (2008a)

Each of these models was rated by the research team in terms of its ability to provide privacy and to support concentrated individual work, team or group work and informal interaction. The ability to increase densities within the space or to reconfigure the space to support changing requirements as well as relative construction costs were also assessed.

The future academic work environment was further explored in a subsequent study published in 2009 by Loughborough University, *The Case for New Academic Workspace* (Pinder et al. 2009). This 18-month study of new academic workspaces in the UK aimed to distil lessons learned from them (both positive and negative) and to offer guidelines for future implementation. The study described the challenges of academic workspace design in the twenty-first century and outlined various strategies and spatial arrangements that can help higher education institutions and their academic members achieve their goals.

The researchers found that academic workspaces are changing due to changing academic practices and priorities, new information technologies, financial pressures and environmental considerations. They also found that the most successful buildings and workplace solutions are part of wider organizational change and were developed with the active engagement of all the stakeholders in the project (p. 1).

They state that there has been little or no evidence published concerning the impact of new academic workspaces on lecturers and researchers, despite many higher education institutions in the UK undertaking post-occupancy evaluations after capital projects. However, the Loughborough study suggested that higher education institutions in the UK are seeking, and in some cases realizing, a variety of benefits from their new academic workspaces, including:

- improved organizational outcomes (such as attracting grants/aiding recruitment)
- increased user satisfaction
- effective working
- cultural change
- flexibility
- better space utilization
- a raised organizational profile (p. 10).

Many of the academics who had moved into open-plan accommodation, reported having more opportunities for interaction with their colleagues, compared to when they were working in cellular offices, where it was not uncommon to spend the entire day in isolation. This was widely considered to have had a positive impact on the sense of community, making work a more enjoyable place to be, as well as making it easier to share knowledge.

However, one of the disadvantages of shared environments that occupants reported is a lack of auditory privacy, which makes it difficult to hold conversations without disturbing their colleagues. The researchers felt this highlighted a need to distinguish between environments that foster encounters and those that support collaborative working (p. 13). Some of the difficulties the academics faced:

> could be attributed, at least in part, to a reluctance to take advantage of the auditory privacy provided by the additional work settings. The reasons for this included the lack of portable technology, which for some occupants necessitated any conversations for which they needed to access their computer to be held at their desk, and also a lack of change management ... Another reason was the inconvenience of relocating to another workstation. As one interviewee explained, 'It is easier said than done to move all your stuff'.
>
> (p. 14)

Workspace is evidently a contentious issue in many universities: in his 2010 *Times Higher Education* article, 'Space to think', Matthew Reisz investigates some of the reasons why it is such a hot topic:

> Space touches on just about all the tension points within universities. Offices and working environments are crucial measures of status, but they also have a much more tangible impact on quality of life. If individual academics feel uncomfortable about the partnerships their university enters into, they can ignore them most of the time. In so far as buildings express corporate values, they are inescapable.
>
> (Reisz 2010)

Reisz discusses both positive and negative examples of open-plan work environments in the context of wider organizational change in universities. The Blizard Building at Queen Mary, for example, was, he says, specifically designed 'to change the ways researchers worked, by bringing small groups of medical researchers together in one big open-plan environment for 300 people, although with individual, more private spaces on a raised ground floor and more discrete seminar rooms in the centre'. He quotes Philip Ogden, Senior Vice Principal of the College: 'People had not thought about how they worked before, so it led to an intellectual engagement in what could be. It is both architecturally innovative and allows people to work in more flexible ways and to reform into different teams as new research grants come in' (ibid.).

He also quotes a Liverpool academic who had concerns about the impact of more open work areas on both staff and students:

> It's a huge luxury having our own rooms to use (or not) as we see fit. That is very costly for an institution. Gradually, inexorably, it will be phased out. Much more work will be done at home; research, too, will be done at home, using online resources. But for those whose home circumstances don't make it easy to maintain a good working space, that represents a deterioration in working conditions. Worse for students, too, who inevitably would see less of their tutors.
>
> (ibid.)

Reisz concluded that the reaction to changes in the academic workplace will vary across the sector. 'When it comes to changing people's working spaces, they are always going to respond in highly individual and often unpredictable ways.'

Alexandra Den Heijer (2011a) undertook a review of estates management practices in Dutch universities for her PhD thesis, published in 2011. She believes that there have been many reasons over the last decade to reconsider the traditional 'single-occupancy cellular office' for academic staff, including:

- the transition from specialized monodisciplinary to multidisciplinary, interdisciplinary, more collaborative research

- the impact of information and communication technology on work activities and place independency of academic staff

- the low occupancy rates of academic offices – also as a consequence of the ICT developments – of 15 to 20 per cent at Dutch universities, according to Dutch campus managers and expressing the average percentage of used workplaces during the semester

- financial pressures on the resources spent on the campus, with decreasing funding for higher education in general

- carbon reduction commitments, goals to reduce the ecological footprint

- the importance of (re)build[ing] a community on campus, accommodating groups instead of individuals and stimulating physical contact (and serendipity) on the increasingly virtual campus (ibid.: 217).

Den Heijer reviewed 'new workplace' projects in Dutch universities and came to the conclusion that practice shows how hard it has been in the past decade to transform the traditional academic office into a more activity-related, collaborative, more interactive working environment that still allows concentrated work. She quotes the research undertaken by Van der Voordt (1999) at Delft University of Technology – two cases that exemplified a resistance to culture change that resulted in smaller (still territorial) offices. Projects at other (Dutch) universities show that it is easier to reduce the territorial office in size than it is to move to non-territorial concepts.

Den Heijer was directly involved in the creation of a new space for the Faculty of Architecture at TU Delft in the Netherlands to replace a building completely destroyed by fire in May 2008. Within six months a heritage building was refurbished to create a new 30,000 square metre facility for 3,300 students and more than 800 employees. Even with the addition of two new glasshouse extensions to the buildings this was a reduction of 15 per cent in gross floor area from the previous building (Figures 5.31–5.33).

Implementing the new workplace solution

An important step in the implementation process for new workplace strategies is the development of a change management strategy to oversee the social and cultural change process as the organization moves from old to new ways of working – or, at the very least, from an old environment to a new environment. Until recently these strategies focused on assisting organizations to deal with change relating to the physical environment and new working

patterns resulting from it. Now, as organizations seek to implement hybrid working environments involving both physical elements and the introduction of new systems and technologies, the combined impacts of space, technology and social organizational changes have to be considered.

If change management is not an integral part of the project, there is a risk of major unrest and dissatisfaction within the affected groups that may manifest itself in many different ways (SCUP 2009). In the UK, this disquiet periodically makes an appearance in press headlines: the *Times Higher Education Supplement* has in its time offered 'Open plan risk to collegiality', 'Staff angered by proposed open-plan site', 'Say goodbye to the office' and 'Open plan or open warfare' (ibid.).

A review of the change management literature in the 2003 HEFCE Good Management Practice Project *Effecting Changing in HE* concluded that:

> reading much of the management literature would suggest that change can be a planned and orderly process – if only the right rules and procedures are followed. In reality change, and especially large scale change, defies logical rules and simple management actions. Complexity theory and a view of organisations as complex adaptive systems, attempts to consider some of the realities and arguably provides the best model for change in a HE setting.
>
> (ibid.: 27)

In chaos and complexity theory, formulated in the 1990s, organizations are typically viewed as complex adaptive systems and effects of change difficult to predict. The emphasis of change interventions is therefore on creating the conditions for beneficial change to occur (p. 29). The report quotes Stacey (1996):

> Most textbooks focus heavily on techniques and procedures for long-term planning, on the needs for visions and missions, on the importance and the means of securing strongly shared cultures, on the equation of success with consensus, consistency, uniformity and order. [However, in complex environments] the real management task is that of coping with and even using unpredictability, clashing counter-cultures, dissensus, contention, conflict, and inconsistency. In short the task that justifies the existence of all managers has to do with instability, irregularity, difference and disorder.
>
> (Stacey 1996, in ibid.: 40)

The *Effecting Change in HE* research team developed a generalized change model that drew heavily on complexity theory to create the IDEAL model of change management (influences, decisions, enable,

The design team at the Faculty of Architecture, TU Delft tried to create as much usable area as possible, including making functional use of circulation space. New concepts with more flexible use of space ensure improved occupancy and frequency rates. Less territory for individual users and specific user groups provided much more flexibility and facilitates more users in the building. It is also very flexible for the rapid changes in the student population and flexible labour force with many visitors and guest professors.

The workplace concept for the building is that all activities of employees are supported in different parts of the working environment with identical facilities and high-quality furniture. The new workplace concept assigned less territory to individuals, and more to groups which supported their dynamic workforce of guest professors, mobile workers, temporary staff and part-time employees (Den Heijer 2011a: 219). This met the need for a home base, but prevented employees from claiming their own workplaces that are vacant for most of the time.

Simultaneously, the improved academic workplace was designed to better support the various activities: meetings, concentration, phone calls, informal consultations with students. The office concept includes fully functional workplaces – according to

health and safety standards – plus meeting rooms, 'silent rooms', space for informal consultations, living rooms and more territorial areas for support staff – distinguishing front and back offices (ibid.: 394).

In summary there was less owned space and more shared facilities, quantity of space was traded for quality that was more intensively used and ICT allows place independency – for staff students and employees to study and work at the most meaningful places – the best place to work for them.

After a year of use, in September 2009, an assessment of occupancy rates showed an average 22 per cent use of the 470 workplaces. This assessment was repeated in September 2010 and showed a utilization rate of 27 per cent. As a result of this, the number of workstations was reduced to 396 with the saved space being reallocated for use as studio space for students. The average size of the workplace is 11.2 square metres usable floor area – excluding meeting space and these workplaces are available for a flexible workforce of more than a thousand employees, equal to 462 fte (data January 2011). This means that in 2011 there is 0.86 workplace available per fte (ibid.: 397).

Source: Den Heijer (2011a)

Figure 5.31 Faculty of Architecture, TU Delft

Figures 5.32–3 Faculty of Architecture, TU Delft

achieve, leadership), which suggests the idealized model of change begins by looking at the external influences, moves on to making some key decisions, enables the change to take place and supports those responsible for achieving the change. All this requires leadership. Two additional factors are important at all stages of the process: culture and communication.

This is, as the name suggests, ideal – in reality:

- change is complex with the various stages in the cycle inter-related. In any change process there needs to be constant reference back and forwards between the different stages in the cycle

- it is often hard to say where one stage of the cycle ends and another begins

- managers are rarely afforded the luxury to sit and plan change in this manner

- different people may have different responsibilities for different stages

- other activities outside of those directly affected by the change will have an impact – change does not occur in isolation

- the resources (time, financial, human and so on) are rarely sufficient to allow unfettered application of the cycle

- complex changes require alternative perspectives and approaches (ibid.: 30–1).

The research team also noted that it is much easier to effect change if there is already a climate of change (one in which change is expected and a natural part of the way in which the organization works) and if past changes have been broadly positively received. In many areas, a climate of change does already exist and it can be controlling the pace of change, which is important. In others, getting any form of change accepted can present a major hurdle (ibid.: 102).

STUDENT CENTRES

Lewis described the rise of student centres in his 2003 article in the *Chronicle of Higher Education*, 'Forget classrooms. How big is the atrium in the new student center?' He noted that the student centre was not part of the traditional university, which preserved the basic building types of its monastic roots: the dormitory, the refectory, and the library. In the late nineteenth century, there was a great explosion of new and specialized building types, including

the laboratory and the gymnasium and there also came the first student union, Houston Hall, built in 1894 by the University of Pennsylvania. He described this as a 'robust Jacobean pile, part clubhouse and part country estate, it was an Anglophiliac reverie, every possible surface liberally panelled with oak. Its great achievement was to wed two distinct ideas, domesticity and masculinity, in a single architectural solution of great conviction' (ibid.).

Houston Hall was widely imitated during the following decades, with each university adapting the model to suit its own culture and requirements. According to Lewis, a century passed before a fundamental rethinking of the model occurred, once again at Houston Hall. Robert Venturi remodelled the building in 1980 (he did so again more recently), giving it linoleum floors, eye-popping signage, and a jaunty welter of neon, reminiscent of the commercial highway strip, which Venturi had praised previously in *Learning From Las Vegas* (1972). The new model acknowledged that student centres were being opened to outside concessions and franchises, and that their essential character was, increasingly, commercial rather than institutional.

Lewis is critical of the current generation of student centres, which he considers as 'extroverted to the point of exhibitionism' when compared with the previous generation's essentially private student halls:

> Having lost its sense of being a rather oversized living room, the student center has assumed something of the impersonal quality of a visitors' center at a national park, or a bus terminal – buildings whose task it is to orient strangers. And, in truth, the student center is designed in large measure for strangers. It must serve not only college students but also prospective students. And while it is the former who will use the building regularly, it is the latter who, in the scheme of things – even though many will visit it no more than once – matter most.

> The essence of the modern student center is to be a recruiting instrument, a fact that pardons its many infelicities: its self-consciousness, its nervous unctuousness, its relentless transparency. If its character is shaped by the world of commercial architecture, that is because it is itself an advertisement. It is the principal highlight of the standard college tour, along with the fitness center. And it communicates exceptionally well.

> (Lewis 2003)

Lewis is not alone in his disquiet about the transformation of student centres and other university facilities in the 1980s and 1990s. Salah et al. noted in their 2006 article 'The role of higher education in America: A spa or a smörgåsbord?' that higher education institutions offer more attractive facilities, movie theatres, students' lounges and online classes to attract prospective students while continuing to cut academic programmes, faculty positions and traditional classes:

> In short, universities have moved away from the austerity of the disciplined spa to the glitzy presentation of casino buffets. 'Forget the ivory towers of academia' Semuels (2004) claimed, 'Today's college kids are demanding student centers full of frills and amenities, from a glass atrium, a sports bar, a movie theater and 24-hour study lounge to a wide array of fast food options.'
>
> (ibid.)

The importance placed by universities on the student centre in the recruitment and retention of students was highlighted in a 2010 report by Ashley Wineki at the University of Kentucky, *The Makeup and Utilization of University Student Unions*.

The University of Kentucky has adopted a business plan aimed at the university becoming a top 20 research institution by 2020. This plan highlights the importance of student retention and stressed the need to 'Improve programs and services that have an impact on the undergraduate experience and improve retention and graduation rates.' The University of Kentucky Student Center houses student programming and services geared towards enhancing the student experience on campus and is regarded as a core part of the university's recruitment and retention strategy.

> The University of Kentucky Student Center 'strives to serve as a "living room" for the campus through providing facilities, services, conveniences and programs for the University community which enhance their daily lives on campus and afford them the opportunity to learn, know, and understand one another through informal association outside the formal classroom'.
>
> (Wineki 2010)

Rickes, in an article in *Planning for Higher Education* (2009), noted that the needs and expectations of the millennial students are different from the preceding generations of students. He suggests that they seek outlets in extracurricular and co-curricular activities. While athletic facilities were constructed in response to the demands of Gen Xers, he notes the assertion of Howe and Strauss (2007) that there is a need for a new 'extracurricular infrastructure' that includes technology-rich space for art, student clubs, theatre, and music to meet the needs of millennials. He believes that this is reflected in the building boom in the construction of student centres over the last decade. Because libraries are now offering amenities that used to only be found

in the student centre, student centres are now differentiating themselves through the provision of a wider set of amenities and programmes that may also overlap with academic, sports and recreational facilities (Rickes 2009: 7–17).

The boom in student centres is also related to the widespread shift towards a more student-centred pedagogy on campus. In his article 'The serious matter of informal learning' in 2009, Jamieson noted that while universities have developed only a relatively small percentage of their formal classrooms to accommodate the shift towards a student-centred pedagogy, there is considerable evidence that universities are now treating the issue of informal learning much more seriously.

He cited the appearance of social hubs and internal 'student streets' within buildings that feature a mix of functions expected to promote both social and learning-related activity as evidence of this along with the creation of comprehensive student centres that provide key administrative and course support along with information technology access and other services (Jamieson 2009: 18–25).

Hamilton (2009) characterized the merging of the traditional functions of student unions and recreation centres as the emergence of fusion buildings, facilities that combine the traditionally separate functions of student unions and recreation centres:

> Rather than representing a complete break with tradition, fusion buildings are instead a natural next step in the evolution of college and university architecture. Because they cater more closely to contemporary lifestyles, expectations, preferences, and technology needs, fusion buildings often provide an institution with a competitive advantage. Fusion buildings respond to both the unique needs of today's student body and the goals of the institution as a whole, goals that include generating revenue and promoting social interaction and cohesion.
>
> (pp. 44–51)

Fusion buildings have emerged as part of a recent larger trend of greatly expanded investment in student-life facilities. Supporting all aspects of student life on campus, these facilities encompass everything from food service to social space to programmed activity space. Hamilton considered the Johnson Center at George Mason University (1996) to be an early example of a 'fusion building' in that it combined the functions of a library with the activities more traditionally found in a student union. By inserting the library into the centre of student study, meeting, eating and commercial space, the Johnson Center made visiting the library a more compelling social experience, breaking the barrier between the purely academic and the purely social – and breaking traditional boundaries in the functional organization of buildings (Hamilton 2009).

The Belmont University Beaman Student Life Center/Curb Event Center opened in 2003, creating an integrated student-life zone on the north campus to balance the historic academic core to the south. Designed to be the focus of student life on campus, this 205,000 square foot building includes a 5,000-seat multifunctional arena, full intercollegiate locker rooms, offices, weight training facilities and therapy areas.

The arena is linked to a student recreation centre, made up of a fitness centre, an auxiliary gymnasium, activity rooms, racquetball/squash courts and a climbing wall. The student recreation centre is in turn linked to a student-life centre that contains student government offices, meeting rooms, lounges, a game room, a convenience store and a juice bar. The Department of Student Affairs is also located in the building, along with commercial space that complements the 'student village' feel of the existing stores and businesses. An 800-car parking structure is also linked to the facility.

The new Student Centre at the London School of Economics, due to open in 2013, is the first new building on campus for more than 40 years. The centre will house the students' union (including events venue, pub, learning cafe, exercise studio, roof terrace coffee/juice bar, fitness centre, media centre, activities space, advice and representation centres), multifaith prayer centre, student residences, a sales and marketing office and the LSE Careers Service (LSE 2012).

Food service offerings in student centres and across campus are expanding both geographically and in the diversity of the offering. Differentiated food service in campus buildings is used to create destinations and reasons for students and staff to leave their own buildings and venture into other parts of the campus. The integration of food service into buildings such as the library and learning resource centres also clearly signals a transition towards a more learner-centred campus model where the aim is to support the students' tastes and timetables.

The Steam Cafe at MIT, for example, was explicitly designed as a physical and virtual spatial experiment that serves up 'great food and community interaction'. The cafe arose as a collaborative venture of students from the School of Architecture and Planning in partnership with MIT Dining and the Sodexho Corporation. Steam uses 'open source' problem solving to bring people together to discuss and improve the venture – an ongoing creation of food and space that reflects and inspires a community where patrons are encouraged to submit recipes on the Steam Cafe Web site (http://steamcafe.mit.edu/). Each booth in the cafe consists of a table

that users can relocate for special functions and open-box benches that allow for many seating configurations. Up to six people can use a booth when the cafe is busy, or a student can lie down for a nap on a booth bench during quiet times (Francisco 2006).

In many universities, the main food service offerings may be grouped together into food courts with either in-house catering choices delivered through differentiated serveries but sharing a common kitchen and prep area or through a number of external franchise holders who may rent space from the student centre or university.

The importance of food to the total student experience is recognized by the Aga Khan University's Faculty of Arts and Sciences (FAS) in east Africa. A November 2010 concept note on food services states:

> The student population in Arusha will be diverse, both in terms of country and region of origin and in terms of economic status. Preparing and eating food together is one of the best ways for the student body to get to know each other, learn about and respect both the differences and similarities within the group, and develop a shared set of values about the value of learning and the need to understand and respect the connection between all of life, and the environment that sustains this connection.
>
> (FASAKU 2010b: 2)

The intention is that food preparation and cooking will be integrated into a culinary arts programme that will form part of the core academic curriculum. This programme will investigate the intersections of food, science and cultural studies, as well as the critical analysis of eating practices and the broader cultures of consumption (ibid.: 3).

The Kimmel Center for University Life at New York University opened in 2003 and serves as the primary location for the university's student services offices. The building also houses the Skirball Center for the Performing Arts (860-seat performance space), the Shorin Music and Dance Performance Centre (rehearsal rooms and dance studio), the Rosenthal Pavilion and the Eisner and Lubin Auditorium (400-person meeting and events spaces). Other amenities in the centre include lounges, open access computing facilities, several art galleries and a range of catering outlets including fine dining and a food court.

A site next to the Kimmel Center has been developed as NYU's Global Center for Academic and Spiritual Life, to include spaces for religious observance, offices for NYU's Chaplains' Circle, classes, music rehearsals and conferences. The creation of this centre provides a communal home for students' religious and spiritual lives as well as providing academic space in the core campus (NYU 2012).

The 98,000 square foot Diana Center at Barnard College in New York was completed in 2010. The arts complex, designed by Weiss/ Manfredi, was conceived as an innovative nexus for artistic, social and intellectual life at the college and was described by the Chair of the Barnard Board of Trustees as 'a renaissance building, suitable for studying, painting, acting, eating, learning and relaxing' (Lampert-Gréaux 2009).

The building contains the college's architecture and painting studios, a 500-seat performance space, black box theatre, cafe, dining room, reading room, classrooms and exhibition galleries. The building also provides conference facilities for the college and has been designed to encourage interaction with the public. The building's green roof has been used to create a 2,800 square foot ecological learning centre for Barnard's biology and environmental science students as well as an additional social space for students (archdaily 2010).

Some universities also provide dedicated areas or buildings to offer specific support to the graduate student community. These facilities may range in size from dedicated, restricted access rooms within the academic library through to major facilities that house postgraduate research facilities and faculty as well as social and support facilities. A 2002 feasibility study for a proposed Graduate Center at the University of Virginia noted that:

> Not one square foot of space is presently dedicated to the collective activities of the graduate and professional student community at the University of Virginia ... The University's post-graduate students are one of our richest resources. Their contributions to the academic, scholarly and teaching mission of this University cannot be underestimated. If our purpose is to continue as a leading public university and one of the top 25 research institutions in the US, we must support efforts to recruit the highest quality graduate candidates and then provide them with a high-quality graduate experience that rivals our peer institutions.
>
> (UV 2002)

The Research Commons at the University of Cape Town (2008) is a facility for graduate students and academic staff that is located in a secluded part of the library. Funded by the Carnegie Corporation, the Research Commons provides study desks, computer workstations, seminar rooms, a lounge and coffee space and lockers for graduate students. The commons is staffed by library staff who provide research support.

Despite the success of fusion buildings on campuses across the US and elsewhere, Hamilton (2009) noted there are a number of impacts and challenges inherent in their development:

- Size and scale: because it aggregates numerous activity spaces, some of which can be quite large, a fusion facility can easily become the largest building on campus, out of scale with the campus as a whole. A campus simply may not have space for a building on that scale.

- Future expansion is more complicated in facilities serving multiple functions, especially given that internal relationships and access points are often also more complex in these facilities. For example, the needs of recreation facilities, which frequently incorporate a single point of access to allow for supervision and control, and student union facilities, which require multiple points of access and less direct control of entry and departure, are often in direct opposition.

- Funding in mixed-use projects often draws from different sources for the different components. For the project to be successful, the funding must be available at the time the facility is designed and built, which does not always happen.

- Economic viability of catering outlets is a major factor: distributed catering facilities operating over extended hours may suit the needs of staff and students but they may make some commercial units uneconomic to run, particularly out of term time when the number of students is significantly reduced. Commercial operators may require subsidies or reduced rentals to cover these quiet periods (2009: 44–51).

ACADEMIC INNOVATION CENTRES AND BUSINESS INCUBATORS

The fostering of innovation and creativity is seen by policy makers in knowledge-based economies as a way of securing competitive advantage and of supporting sustainable economic growth.

The Cox Review of Creativity in Business (2005) in the UK, for example, stated that 'for UK plc to succeed in tomorrow's competitive world, we have to base our success on design, innovation, creativity, exploitation of technology and speed to market. There is no other attractive, viable future for the UK economy' (Cox 2005).

A similar theme was echoed in the manifesto of the 2009 European Year of Creativity and Innovation: 'The world is moving to a new rhythm. To be at the forefront of this new world, Europe needs to become more creative and innovative' (EC 2009).

To encourage innovation and creativity, centres of innovation and business incubation have been created to 'hot house' or accelerate the development of new ideas and concepts into new products or services. As Margaret Wheatley (2012) states: 'Innovation is fostered by information gathered from new connections; from insights gained by journeys into other disciplines or places, from active, collegial networks and fluid, open boundaries. Innovation arises from ongoing circles of exchange, where information is not just accumulated or stored, but created. Knowledge is generated anew from connections that weren't there before.'

The first business incubators concepts were introduced as early as the late 1950s (Rong, 2007) but it was during the 1980s and 1990s that the most intensive wave of development took place. The provision of innovation support was further enriched by fast development of virtual incubators/innovation centres and support networks following the widespread use of internet and increasing importance of IT-based, online collaboration and knowledge sharing systems.

Innovation centres were defined in 2006 by the Open Futures group (established as part of a European Union Framework programme on collaborative working environments) as workplaces specifically designed to encourage creative behaviours and support innovation. Open Futures suggested that innovation centres should:

> emphasize the dislocation of innovation processes from day to day activity, eliminate organizational hierarchy, encourage participation, focus on collaboration, face-to-face communications, mind/body and physical activity including play rather than on technology.
>
> (Fmlink 2012)

First-generation innovation spaces have tended to either be design or technology led. In 'design-led' centres, described as the 'New economy funky office' by Van Meel and Vos (2001), the main aim seems to be to utilize gimmicks and flashy design to emphasize the difference from conventional office space. Examples of this type of space have included inflatable rooms, cars and surfboards suspended in office areas and living grass floors in boardrooms.

The goal of technology-rich workspace, however, tends to be to show off the occupants' mastery of information technology and leading-edge positioning. Technology spaces enabled with 'kinetic walls', odour projection and sophisticated audio-visual ('war-room') systems are examples of these types of spaces. Often, however, these high-technology installations give insufficient consideration to the nature and diversity of human face-to-face communications or the need to develop a sound business case for their purchase and operation.

Future centres are 'special working environments that help organizations and people break out of patterns and routines, see issues from multiple perspectives, and choose effective courses of action. They are high-touch, technology-enhanced learning spaces, which enable people to create, develop, prototype, and communicate ideas, strategies, plans, solutions and actions' (FutureCentres 2010).

Future centres support their users and clients with facilitated activities in physical, virtual, cognitive and emotional space. They are user-centric, people-centred working environments purposely designed to enable users to collaborate in thinking about, questioning, designing and prototyping the future. They facilitate organizations to create innovative solutions to issues that matter to them by prototyping new policy, products, services and work relationships. They provide dedicated working environments, methods, tools, facilitation, and the appropriate context for furthering organizational, technological, social and societal innovation (FutureCentres 2010).

Successful innovation spaces are generally created through the integration of a number of elements including: the design of the space; the artefacts and physical objects within the space; the innovation processes that take place with the space; and the overall user experience. The goal of an innovation-focused space should be to create memorable, collaborative and immersive experiences for participants. This may involve the use of advanced technologies but may equally include gaming, theatre and other people-centred activities.

The important role of universities in supporting innovation at a local, regional and national level has long been recognized. As the UK government's Business Link website states:

> The commercial exploitation of new ideas is vital to the survival and prosperity of British businesses. If you can get new products to the market faster than your rivals, you will become more competitive. Academic research can often help businesses develop new ideas or enhance existing ones.
>
> One way that businesses can develop new ideas is to form relationships with universities and other research institutions. Your business can benefit commercially from research into processes and technologies relevant to your activities, while universities and colleges gain new sources of funding, and researchers achieve a better understanding of industry needs.
>
> (Business Link 2012)

In the UK, a range of mechanisms has been established to support the development of academic and commercial partnerships including a UK-wide Knowledge Transfer Partnerships (KTP) scheme, for example, which aims to help businesses to gain knowledge and expertise from universities, colleges or research/technology organizations. Through the scheme, an area where strategic change is required within a business is identified, an appropriate a higher education institution, further education college or research organization with the right expertise is selected and a one-to-three-year project is established where a recently qualified person is recruited to work in your business on the project.

University innovation centres (UICs) have also been established in five regions to focus on existing strengths in skills, innovation and enterprise and to provide a model for effective cooperation between businesses and higher education establishments. The aims of the UICs include:

- improving knowledge transfer between industry and higher education institutes

- encouraging small businesses to participate in the generation and exploitation of knowledge

- stimulating private sector research and development (R&D)

- being at the heart of regional cluster development

- helping universities to play a central role as catalysts of growth.

Each UIC focuses on a sector of strategic importance to the region it is based in and is open to both industrial and academic users. The South West UIC, for example, based at the University of Bristol, focuses on communications, computing and content technologies and aims to unite the key industrial and academic research already taking place in the region. The university also provides incubation space, entrepreneurship support and technical facilities for businesses emerging from the centre (Business Link 2012).

While university innovation support may be entirely programme or research driven, it also frequently involves bringing academic and commercial organizations into a shared space – either on campus or in a science or business environment linked to the academic institution. These university-linked innovation centres can also serve as community hubs for dispersed organizations or for small and medium-sized enterprises (SMEs) belonging to a particular market sector or geographic location where the university provides business or research support, often in partnership with a regional development agency.

The potential impact of these centres on new businesses and for the local and UK economy has been assessed by UKBI (UK Business Innovation), an international membership and best practice body for organizations and professionals actively involved in enterprise, innovation and sustainable economic growth. Their research shows that an average incubator unit is home to around 30 client businesses, generating an average of 167 jobs (FTE), with 60 per cent of them operating 'outreach' services to other companies, micro-businesses and the local community. UKBI (2012) cites one university business incubation environment where 'over £120 million of early stage funding were raised recently and 1,000 jobs created'.

UKBI also found that business incubators have an average success rate of 98 per cent of businesses succeeding whilst in the business incubator (compared to a national average of less than 30 per cent of all small and medium-sized companies registered) and 87 per cent surviving after five years (ibid.).

The range of services and facilities offered by an innovation hub/incubation centre depends on the nature of the facility but could include:

- low-cost, flexible office space with standard service offering (telephony, internet access) provided on an easy-in, easy-out basis, with flexible short-term contracts

- a variety of shared support facilities such as meeting and project rooms, conference facilities, reception, touchdown work areas and visitor areas

- specialist spaces including wet laboratories, R&D facilities and state-of-the-art technology

- stimulating and creative work environments designed to inspire, foster cross-disciplinary collaboration, knowledge sharing and support collaboration between academic and commercial partners

- a range of business services and support including reception and secretarial services, bookkeeping, business and intellectual property advisory services and facilities management

- access to finance through entrepreneur grants systems, publicly funded or private sponsorship, network of business angels, venture capital funds, investors

- physical and virtual access to a variety of knowledge and support networks, such as the affiliated academic community, other entrepreneurs and businesses operating in related sectors/industries

- virtual knowledge pool comprising libraries, thematic networks, data repositories and community groups for entrepreneurs to exchange information

- wider neighbourhood network (business and science parks, industrial clusters, academic campuses) (ibid.).

In academic innovation centres in the UK, Finland and the US (Figures 5.34–5.40) spaces are now being created at a range of scales, activities – and ambitions. Figure 5.41 illustrates the diversity of these spaces in terms of both the level of university engagement and the scale of the enterprise that is supported. University-linked innovation spaces vary greatly in terms of scale, range of settings, services and technology available within the space and the level of university engagement with the activities that go on within the space. At one extreme, the innovation centre can be seen as an independent business incubator that brings revenue to the institution through rentals and perhaps short-term overflow space for research teams or newly created university business start-ups. At the other extreme, the innovation centre can provide a spatial focus for the integration of research and business on campus and create opportunities for students at all levels to work on 'real-world' problems with people from other parts of the institution and beyond.

BOX is a 220 square metre space in the heart of the London School of Economics' (LSE's) central London campus, conceived as a space to provide innovation and knowledge transfer services to a tightly linked, university-business network. Originally funded by EDS (Electronic Data Systems), it served as a laboratory for exploring decision making and collaboration processes for both public sector and commercial organizations with academics and students from a number of academic departments. These processes were facilitated through a diverse range of workshops featuring various tools and techniques such as LEGO Serious Play, an experiential process designed to enhance innovation and business performance.

A key feature of the design was the 'Cabinet of Wonder', a wall holding visible and invisible treasures that enable the viewer to see the world in a multitude of ways. The Cabinet of Wonder used light, sounds and artefacts to intrigue as well as encourage discussion and original thinking.

The space was also used by academics linked to the BOX research programme as a community club space to inhabit, communicate, and explore ideas and BOX hosted a significant number of internal LSE seminars and workshops, as well as collaborative policy development events for both governmental and non-governmental organizations. While the EDS sponsorship has ceased, BOX is still a key LSE meeting and innovation space.

Source: http://www.educause.edu/learningspacesch23

Figure 5.34 BOX, London School of Economics (LSE)

Design Factory opened in 2008 and is a 3,000 square metre work environment that enables creative work, knowledge sharing and experience exchange. The space is designed for flexible use and can be reconfigured to support a wide range of activities from large lectures and presentations to intensive workshops and the development of product prototypes. The open layout and the wide range of shared facilities including kitchen and eating areas are designed to encourage open communication and spontaneous encounters between Aalto faculty and staff, students and business start-ups.

Design Factory develops creative ways of working, spatial solutions and enhanced interdisciplinary interaction to support world-class product design in educational, research and practical application contexts. It is one of three factories on campus (Media, Service and Design factories) that were established to support the development of an 'Aalto passion-based, student centric learning culture' as well as improving the quality of research and education at the university. All three factories serve as experimental platforms as well as showrooms and sources of inspiration for all the parties involved.

For students, the Design Factory provides holistic learning experiences solving real-life challenges in multidisciplinary teams often involving international partnerships. In terms of engagement with industry, the Design Factory website states that 'the Factory is an innovative environment for finding, incubating, and realizing new ideas together with leading scholars, top future talent, and a mixture of other companies.' The site also suggests that the Design Factory is a good way to recruit future staff members.

The Design Factory also has links to Aalto Venture Garage, a free 700 square metre co-working space and seed accelerator for Baltic & Nordic entrepreneurs located in an adjacent building. Anyone is able to use the main hall of the Garage as work and development space for business start-ups. Aalto Venture Garage is part of the Aalto Centre of Entrepreneurship (ACE) which coordinates all activities related to technology transfer, intellectual property management, start-up companies and the teaching and research of growth entrepreneurship at Aalto University. The Aalto Entrepreneurship Society ('The Aaltoes') also uses the Garage to host many of its events.

Programmes at the Venture Garage include 'Start-up Sauna' that brings promising start-ups from different cities from around the Baltic Rim for an intense mentoring and development programme and the 'Summer of Start-ups' – a ten-week programme targeted at students and researchers from Finland, Northern Europe and the rest of the world.

Sources: http://designfactory.aalto.fi/about/; http://aaltovg.com/about/; http://aaltoes.com/

Figure 5.35 Design Factory, Aalto University, Helsinki, Finland

Figure 5.36 Design Factory, Aalto University, Helsinki, Finland

The Hasso Plattner Institute of Design at Stanford was founded in the School of Engineering in 2004. The Institute is known on campus as the d.school, and brings students and faculty from different backgrounds together to develop innovative, human-centred solutions to real-world challenges.

The d.school serves as a university-wide hub for innovation where students from engineering, the arts, medicine, education, law and the social sciences come to take classes together and work on projects. The d.school currently works with around 350 students each year.

Courses and curriculum are based on the design thinking process, drawing on methods from engineering and design and combining them with ideas from the arts, tools from the social sciences and insights from the business world. Students are typically immersed in an experiential learning environment and cycle rapidly through a series of steps including observation, brainstorming, synthesizing, prototyping and implementing. Classes at the d.school are taught by teams made up of a multidisciplinary mix of faculty and leaders from industry.

The d.school has had several homes on campus since its creation. From its first home in a one-room trailer on the outskirts of the campus, it moved a number of times before occupying a new 35,000 square feet home in 2010 in the heart of the Stanford campus.

The school intentionally uses the design and configuration of spaces to support learning and research activities and to 'practice what it teaches' with design thinking by prototyping and iterating in rapid cycles to each new space, all with the intention of learning how environments can drive a culture of innovation. The school believes that space can be used as a tool to fuel the creative process by encouraging and discouraging specific behaviours/actions and by creating venues for emotional expression and physical negotiation. Furniture elements such as mobile screens, foam blocks and quickly reconfigurable 'T walls' are used to create a dynamic teaching and research environment. The physical prototyping lab, for example, is located next to its digital counterpart to facilitate building, photographing, and printing – deliberate juxtapositioning of a messy, low-tech space with a pristine, high-tech one designed to add a jolt.

Sources: http://dschool.stanford.edu/our-point-of-view/; http://dschool.stanford.edu/wp-content/uploads/2011/03/dschool_TWALL1.pdf

Figure 5.37 The d.school, Stanford University, US

Figure 5.38 The d.school, Stanford University, US

The Media Lab at MIT was founded in 1985 – a degree-granting graduate programme in Media Arts and Sciences (MAS) and a diverse research programme located in the Wiesner Building on MIT's East campus, designed by I.M. Pei. The building houses an experimental theatre, sculpture gallery, film and video auditorium for 200, video production facilities, computer studios and 44,000 square feet of flexible loft space that can be configured to meet the needs of the individual programmes and research projects.

The guiding concept of the original Media Lab was that most of the exciting work in science occurs at the boundaries between disciplines, a 'place where people from different backgrounds – not only sciences, but the arts – would bump into one another and sparks of creativity would fly'. In 2009, the Media Lab expanded into a new, six-floor building with approximately 163,000 square feet of laboratory, office and meeting space designed by the Tokyo-based architectural firm of Maki and Associates. The new Media Lab building has been designed to support innovative research that cuts across traditional disciplinary boundaries.

The building provides an atrium with exhibition and social spaces, a theatre, large meeting spaces and conference facilities, dining and catering spaces and seven labs that range in size from 5,000 to 8,500 square feet. Each lab consists of a common research areas surrounded by mezzanine offices: 'Instead of being designed around technical systems and equipment as in many older MIT laboratories, they put the people first – providing lots of natural light, operable windows, views, and sociability.'

> The goal is to make everyone's work visible to everyone else. From the central atrium, you can look into the labs of half a dozen different research teams. Labs are wide open: senior offices wrap around the top of a double-height shared space. They work like the ateliers of art schools, each with a master and a team of acolytes.
>
> (Campbell 2009)

Sources: http://www.bondbrothers.com/experience/news.cfm?year=2009; http://www.media.mit.edu/about; http://www.media.mit.edu/files/overview.pdf; http://expansion.media.mit.edu/factsheet-mlexpansion.pdf

Figures 5.39–40 Media Lab, MIT, US

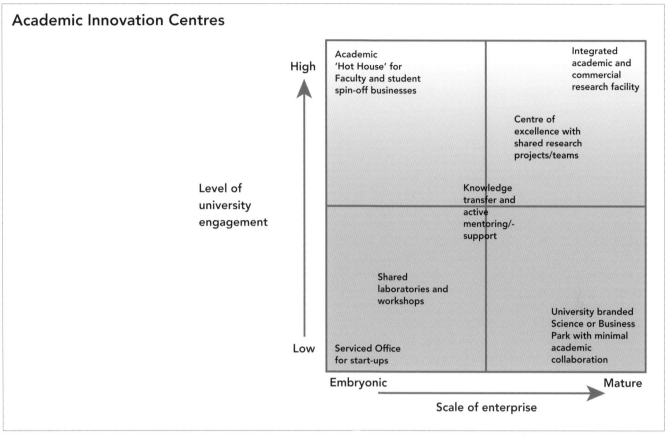

Figure 5.41 Diversity range in university innovation centres

STUDENT HOUSING

Moving away from home and living with other students is an important part of the university experience for many students. The way in which they live during this time – on or off campus, in dormitories, in residential colleges or apartments – varies widely from university to university depending on availability and cost options as well as on their stage of study.

From the institution's point of view, having the students living on or near campus is a fundamental part of the development of a learning community, providing opportunities for students to interact with each other and with faculty and to share knowledge.

Residential colleges have their origins in the UK at Oxford and Cambridge universities, although the model has now spread widely to many other parts of the world. In an *Inside Higher Education* article, 'Hogwarts U', Robert O'Hara (2006) describes the expansion of residential colleges as permanent, cross-sectional, faculty-led societies that bring the educational advantages of a small college into the environment of a large university. He considers this to

be 'one of the most substantive structural reform movements in higher education today, and it promises to repair a half-century of destructive bureaucratic centralization'.

A review of the learning and teaching experience at Manchester University in 2007 noted that residential student communities facilitate student engagement in rich, interactive learning, although it acknowledged that this can also be achieved in other kinds of learning communities. Alan Gilbert (2007), president and vice chancellor of the University, concluded that 'the kinds of multi-layered, close-knit, highly-interactive learning communities that good university colleges and halls of residence create are likely to remain among the hallmarks of any great undergraduate educational experience'.

The Warden of Rhodes House, Oxford, Dr Donald Markwell (2010), cited research by Daniel (2008) that looked at the educational attributes of some of the world's 'top 50' universities and found that the majority of the top ten universities have over 90 per cent of their undergraduates living on campus and that many more institutions have high percentages of students in residence or have students living in university-run accommodation very close to the campus. Daniel also stated that one of the benefits of this is that 'colleges can be used to introduce innovative educational programs and to target particular segments of the potential student market'.

The provision of high-quality housing is also becoming an important element of the competition between universities for prospective students. Changing student expectations are forcing universities to upgrade and expand their housing options. This shift in priorities was described by Martin and Allen in a 2009 article that appeared in *Planning for Higher Education*.

> Where Spartan facilities might once have been adequate, amenities now abound, particularly in new residence halls. The once-prototypical double room located off a double-loaded corridor with ganged bathrooms has given way to a suite or apartment with a private or semi-private bath. New residence halls typically offer a variety of common areas, including lounges, fitness centers, and coffee bars, to help students connect with one another. Of course, institutions not only compete among themselves to provide superior housing options, but also with private developers creating off-campus residences. Whether institutionally or privately developed, students expect to be enticed with supportive and enriching residential environments. In particular, breaking down anonymity by providing opportunities for social and academic engagement is especially important in large residential projects.
>
> (pp. 34–43)

Some institutions are also facing political pressure to house more of their student body on campus because of the impact of students on the surrounding community, either because of driving up house prices and rent levels for the local population or because of concerns about the creation of student ghettoes. There is also increasing expectation that new housing schemes on campus or at the campus edge also contain amenities that provide a public benefit (ibid.: 42).

Increasingly, student housing is being provided by commercial developers or organizations such as housing associations. Developments can be in direct partnership with the institution where the arrangement provides the institution with undergraduate and graduate student housing 'off balance sheet', thus preserving a greater proportion of capital budgets for non-residential institutional missions and those that are in competition to the institutions (ibid.: 41). In the marketplace, student accommodation is seen as a good investment with an above average yield on the investment.

An article in the *Daily Telegraph,* for example, on 5 September 2011, 'Want 10%? Try student housing investment', stated that student property decreased risk in a commercial property portfolio. 'The yield is attractive, plus it offers diversification. Other commercial property has been hit by the downturn, but student housing, because of the demand, has stayed strong. It's a defensive investment' (*Telegraph* 2011). The article also discussed the establishment of an investment fund that will buy existing student accommodation from universities in the UK and leasing it back to them over a 35-year period.

Where student accommodation is run by commercial providers, the terms of contract for residents may change from paying for academic terms to having to sign a 50-week contract that also includes the summer vacation and other academic breaks, whether they are using the room or not, since the provider's financial obligations and maintenance commitments continue throughout the year and loading these onto the academic terms would make the accommodation charge per week less competitive with other providers.

This change of contract period can have an impact on the university associated with the accommodation, where the student housing was traditionally used during vacation periods for university or commercial conferences to generate additional 'third stream' income for the institution. With 50-week contracts in place, the university would need to make arrangements with both the accommodation provider and the individual students renting the rooms – considerably more complicated and often impracticable.

Commercial student housing providers may also provide general student housing that is available to students from any academic institution in the area. UNITE, for example, is the UK's largest developer and manager of purpose-built student accommodation with 120 properties across the UK housing around 40,000 students (UNITE 2012).

Students are increasingly expecting to live in a comfortable and engaging environment. As Sarah Schweitzer reported in the *Boston Globe*: 'Gone is the era when cinder block walls, polyester couches, and triples were dorm de rigueur. College students today are arriving on campuses with ratcheted-up expectations for the aesthetics and comforts of their homes-away-from-home. And increasingly, colleges are scrambling to meet student expectations in the hope of luring top applicants' (2008: 1).

The traditional double undergraduate room has been replaced by a wide range of options that vary in size, living arrangement and cost. UNITE, for example, offers twin rooms with en-suite facilities, studios and flats with three to six bedrooms and shared kitchen and living areas. Accommodation options are also classified as 'basic' (most affordable), 'classic' (general provision) or 'premium' where rooms may be larger with more storage, a larger bed or good views and cost more per week to rent.

High-speed internet, high-quality furniture and enhanced building amenities include social lounges, fitness centres and cafes are common. Schweitzer described current student housing projects at MIT that include the provision of dance studios and music practice rooms complete with grand piano and Northeastern University's LaundryView system that allows students to check on the status of their laundry via computer or they can use a laundry service that, for a fee, will pick up, wash, fold and deliver laundry back to a dorm in a day's time (ibid.: 1).

University administrators say the changes simply mirror what students have grown up with – homes that are more spacious, and with more technology than those of students even a decade earlier. 'Society has changed,' said Karen Nilsson, senior associate dean for student life with a focus on residential life at MIT. 'These students who have had their own rooms, their own bathrooms all their lives. They are going off to college and looking for those kinds of things' (ibid.: 1).

Residential colleges often also include academic space as well as social and amenity space. Oxford colleges, for example, provide accommodation, meals, common rooms, libraries, sports and social facilities, and pastoral care for their students and are also responsible for students' tutorial teaching and welfare (Oxford University 2012).

The residential accommodation may be located above ground-floor learning spaces and other shared amenity spaces. The University of Dayton, for example, in 2004 opened 'ArtStreet', a combined living and learning space that includes housing for 56 students – junior and seniors of all majors – in a series of interconnected two and three-storey buildings that suggest a village street. Shared spaces include a cafe, an amphitheatre, rehearsal rooms, several activity rooms and gallery spaces, a screening room, meeting spaces for classes and groups and a new studio for the campus radio station (ArtStreet 2012). Activity programmes and workshops are available for residents and also for other Dayton students. ArtStreet also hosts local, national and international visiting visual and performing artists for residencies at the university.

Student housing can be segregated by sex or educational stage (freshmen, juniors, seniors, postgraduate) or can be mixed. In addition, it is common practice to include a number of faculty or postgraduate students in undergraduate accommodation blocks to provide a degree of pastoral care to students. At MIT, full-time graduate students can apply to become graduate resident tutors and their role is 'to foster a positive living environment for, and

to build a community atmosphere among, undergraduates in MIT residence halls. This responsibility includes encouraging personal growth, providing outlets for managing stress, and facilitating positive interpersonal relationships. GRTs are also responsible for implementing community standards, enhancing security, and promoting mutual respect between and among the residents they serve' (MIT 2012). In return for at least ten hours' interaction with students, the tutors receive a free room for the 12 months plus a small monthly stipend.

In addition, MIT has a number of housemasters who live in the campus houses, participate in student life and act as the representative of the wider institute within the community of student residents. They also provide leadership within the houses so that residential life will reinforce the institute's educational mission (ibid.).

The mixing of faculty and student accommodation is taken even further in a new development by a private developer for Barnard College in New York. The new development combines 92 beds of student housing, 26 units of faculty housing, 25 affordable apartments and a non-profit day-care facility. In keeping with Barnard's liberal philosophy, the student and faculty units are mixed together on the same floors rather than being segregated on different floors, with students and faculty sharing common spaces such as the laundry room, lounge and terraces. Student accommodation is provided in multi-bedroom suites of up to six students, each with a bathroom and kitchen: faculty accommodation consists of conventional one, two and three-bedroom apartments (Barnard College 2012).

Academic functions and housing are combined in the University of Michigan's North Quadrangle Residential and Academic Community. This $175 million, 360,000 square foot complex opened in 2010 and provides accommodation for approximately 450 upper undergraduate students. The 10ten-storey residence hall building is primarily new build, although it incorporates the entrance of the Ann Arbor High School Public Library that was previously on the site.

Accommodation includes double and triple suites with shared bathroom and living area and single, double and triple rooms. There is a lounge on each floor plus a main living room and kitchen on the tenth floor. Student amenities include a marketplace-style dining facilities and cafe and shared social and informal work areas. The complex includes classrooms, studios and offices for five information and communications-related university programmes and the intention is that 'students and faculty flow seamlessly from classrooms and hallways to faculty offices and living areas' (UM 2012).

The aim of the North Quad is to provide an innovative experience that connects upper-level undergraduate students to their community and the outside world. The quad is home to International Impact, a theme community focused on multiculturalism, as well as two academic learning communities: the Global Scholars Program and the Max Kade German Program. In addition to residential spaces and classrooms, North Quad also includes offices for the School of Information, Communication Studies, Screen Arts and Cultures, the Language Resource Center and the Sweetland Writing Center (ibid.). Academic facilities to support these programmes include classrooms, multimedia spaces, screening rooms, a language resource centre and a student lounge that is also used as a classroom during the day.

Student housing can also form part of larger mixed-use developments. The Nido student housing business established by the US private equity firm Blackstone Group (Nido means 'nest' in Spanish and Italian) currently operates three student housing complexes in London (Figures 5.42 and 5.43) and it has another scheme under development in Barcelona (Worldarchitecture 2006; Nido 2013).

On a larger scale, the first phase of the National University of Singapore's University Town (UTown) opened in 2011 and this project expands student accommodation to the point where the key issue becomes the creation of a sustainable urban community (National University of Singapore UTown 2012). The village is on a 19-hectare site, a former golf course, linked by bridge to the Kent

---

Nido's first London Project in Kings Cross included the re-use of two existing office towers and the addition of a podium block. Its second London development, in Spitalfields, is marketed as the world's tallest student accommodation. The 34-storey, 105 metre tall development will provide housing for 1,200 undergraduate students in a mix of en-suite studios, two-bedroom studios and shared apartments. Amenities include common rooms on every floor of the building, a mix of lounges and study rooms and a lounge on the first floor that contains flat screen TVs and games areas. A fitness centre on the 33rd floor is free for residents and has floor-to-ceiling views of the London skyline.

Some 50,000 square feet of classroom space in the development has been leased by a university/commercial joint venture to provide foundation courses for international students wishing to access undergraduate and post-graduate studies at the partner universities.

Their third London development is described by Nido as a 'boutique residence' in Notting Hill that will provide accommodation for 277 students in a range of unit types above a ground floor of support services, retail and office space.

Figure 5.42 Nido, Spitalfields, London UK

Figure 5.43 Nido, Spitalfields, London UK

Ridge campus of the university. At the ground-breaking ceremony to initiate the project the prime minister of Singapore, Lee Hsien Loong, stated that University Town will be 'a vibrant centre of learning and creative inquiry ... not an ivory tower, but an intellectual community integrated into our society, and connected to the world' (Newshub 2008).

UTown will eventually house 6,000 students in eight residential colleges and graduate residences. The new campus is modelled on universities such as Oxford and Cambridge where students live, learn and socialize under the same roof as professors. Undergraduate student accommodation in the residential colleges is a mix of single rooms and shared six-person suites. Each college

is also equipped with facilities such as theme rooms, multipurpose halls, dining halls, student lounges and common lounges (National University of Singapore UTown 2012).

The Education Resources Centre (ERC) is the focal point for the UTown development and will contain a library, research facilities and computer labs, lecture theatres, seminar rooms, e-learning cafes and clusters of study spaces. Other student amenities include bookshops, retail outlets and a range of food outlets and cafes.

The EduSports Complex will be the hub of sporting, educational and cultural activities at UTown and this will house additional lecture theatres and seminar rooms, sporting facilities including a swimming pool, gym, competition hall, training hall, fitness centre, dance theatre and music practice rooms. An open plaza in the complex called the Forum will be a central gathering point for students and visitors.

UTown will also be home to the Campus for Research Excellence and Technological Expertise (CREATE) and the Asia Research Institute. CREATE is a 60,000 square metre campus launched by the National Research Foundation that will house the research centres of the Massachusetts Institute of Technology, the Swiss Federal Institute of Technology (ETH) Zurich, the Technion-Israel Institute of Technology, the Technical University of Munich (TUM) and the Hebrew University of Jerusalem, along with around 1,000 researchers (National University of Singapore U Town 2012).

SPORTS FACILITIES

Sport is important to almost all universities but levels of provision – of sports teams, the integration with the academic programme and the investment in facilities – vary hugely from sport to sport, institution to institution and region to region. In general, however, sport plays a central role in campus student life, creating communities of interest and skill as well as contributing towards institutional identity and community engagement. Organized sports also provide an opportunity to continue contact with university alumni and generate income for the institution.

The relationship between sport and academic and life success was stressed by Sport England in its 2009 document, *Higher Education and Community Sport: A Partnership Plan:* 'it is essential that higher education sport can articulate and demonstrate not only the contribution it can make to the student experience but more importantly the significant contribution it can make to academic achievement, gaining transferable skills and improving the employment prospects of students'.

The level of provision of sports facilities on campus or in the surrounding area also varies widely depending on the location of the institution (central city sites tend to be space constrained with limited opportunities for sports facilities), institutional and academic mission (e.g., undergraduates at Emory University in Atlanta are required to take four physical education courses) and financial resources.

There may also be government requirements for a minimum level of sports facilities provisions for universities of various sizes to achieve university registration. In Kenya, for example, the Universities (Establishment of Universities) (Standardization,

Accreditation and Supervision) Rules, 1989 state, 'A university shall have or shall have access to at least one standard athletics track enclosing a football pitch, at least one standard lawn tennis pitch, one standard volleyball pitch, one standard badminton or tenniquoit pitch and one standard netball court' (Kenyan Universities 1989: 32), whereas in the UK each institution is autonomous and the level of provision is dependent on the location of the institution and their overall university mission.

As the UK *Complete University Guide* states:

> The range and quality of student sports clubs, facilities and classes available will be a revelation. Most universities offer a full range of traditional (British) sports such as football, rugby, netball, badminton, tennis and squash, and Oxford and Cambridge are only two of the universities at which rowing has a high profile. Many also provide less common sports such as archery, American football, caving, fencing, gliding, hot air ballooning, motor sports, sub-aqua, triathlon, ultimate Frisbee and windsurfing.
>
> The list is varied and constantly changing in response to students' needs and expectations. In addition, there will be opportunities to take part in a wide range of 'lifestyle' or fitness activities from aerobics to Tai Chi to working out in modern, well-equipped fitness studios that in many universities are every bit as good as those in the trendiest commercial fitness club – but much better value for money … The scale and range of taught recreation programmes varies from one university to another, with some offering over 100 classes a week. They provide an ideal opportunity to grasp the basics of a sport or a range of activities both cheaply and without any long-term commitment.
>
> (Complete University Guide 2012)

There are also very strong links between university sport and national and international sporting competition: the UK has rapidly developed an elite sporting infrastructure in the past few years with a range of sports institutes and initiatives designed to nurture the country's future sports stars and many of the best facilities located at universities (ibid.).

The amount of space provided to house indoor sports facilities varies widely across the UK but the recommended amount per FTE student is 1.1 square metre (Littlefield 2007).

The Australasian Association of Higher Education Facilities Planners (AAHEFP) *Space Guidelines* report (Edition 2) states that student services space including sports and fitness facilities should constitute approximately 4–8 per cent of the total non-residential space which is typically about 0.4–0.8 square metre per FTE student (2009: 5).

While intramural and recreational sport is considered an important element of student life in the UK, Europe and Australasia it goes much further in the US, where university sports teams play a central role in the national sporting scene through college football and other sports.

On campus, alumni and other donors frequently fund the construction and operation of major sports facilities that enable colleges to attract and retain the best athletes and athletic coaches and hopefully to secure prestigious national championships. Swarthmore College, for example, is a small college near Philadelphia with a very strong academic reputation for both research and teaching (student/faculty ration of 8:1). The undergraduate student body consists of approximately 1,500 but their sports facilities are extensive and include, according to its website (www.swarthmore.edu/):

- 12 outdoor and three indoor tennis courts

- six full-length indoor basketball courts

- ten outdoor playing fields

- an athletic events centre with seating for 1,800

- an indoor field house for team practices during inclement weather

- an outdoor eight-lane, 400-metre Versaturf track

- an indoor 215-metre banked Tartan track

- a ten-lane-by-ten-lane, indoor swimming pool with electronic timing system

- five squash courts with spectator galleries

- new fitness centre with aerobic and Med-X equipment

- a professionally staffed sports medicine facility with three full-time trainers.

Harvey Mudd College (www.hmc.edu/) is a small undergraduate college located in Claremont near Los Angeles. Predominantly an engineering, mathematics and science college and regularly ranked in the top 20 colleges in the US, it is also a member of the Claremont Universities Consortium which enables the colleges to share specialist resources including sports facilities.

Harvey Mudd College, Claremont McKenna College and Scripps College are associated in a joint programme of intercollegiate athletics, intramural and recreational activities, physical education

and club sports known as Claremont-Mudd-Scripps (CMS). CMS facilities include a football field, gymnasium (an aerobic fitness room, a weight room with both free weights and a Nautilus system), a soccer field, a lacrosse field, a nine-lane, 400-metre track, a baseball field, a softball field, an aquatics centre with a competition pool for swimming, diving and water polo, nine tennis courts, volleyball courts, and numerous intramural and recreational fields.

Emory University is a considerably larger, top-20 research university located in Atlanta, Georgia with a student body of approximately 13,000 (7,000 undergraduate, 6,000 postgraduate and professional). Undergraduates are required to take four courses in physical education and students are able to participate in a wide range of intramural and club sports.

Emory's 'athletics for all' principles date from the 1890s, when the school president of the time prohibited intercollegiate sport competition on the grounds of the 'cost of intercollegiate athletics programmes, the temptation to gambling and the distraction to scholarship' (emory.edu). At the same time, he established the first intramural sports programme in the US and had extensive sports facilities developed on campus to support recreational sport. On campus sports facilities include:

- two Olympic-sized pools

- large arena serving basketball, volleyball, badminton and fencing

- eight outdoor and four indoor tennis courts

- 400-metre outdoor and 200-metre indoor tracks

- racquetball and squash courts

- two climbing walls

- two dance studios

- weight and cardio fitness equipment and a strength conditioning room.

The main campus also features four irrigated athletic fields, along with the Blomeyer Health Fitness Center for faculty and staff only. Other facilities include a state-of-the-art college ballpark, soccer field with space for 1,000 spectators and a 'natatorium' which is home to Emory's nationally ranked varsity swimming and diving teams (Emory 2012).

There is very little, if any, correlation between size of institution in the US and the level of sports facilities provision on campus. The level of provision is largely determined by the aspirations of the institution and by the size of the academic endowment that will fund the development and operation of the sports facilities. A recent survey by the *Chronicle of Higher Education* compared the size of the athletic endowment to the overall academic endowment for the ten universities with the largest athletic endowments. The size of sports endowments varied from $46,139,000 at Ohio State University to $212,000,000 at the University of North Carolina at Chapel Hill, which equates to $485,126 per athlete (*Chronicle of Higher Education* 2009).

Sports facilities are also given high priority in campuses in other parts of the world. The University of Cape Town in South Africa, for example, is the highest ranked African university in both the THE-QS World University Rankings and the Shanghai Jiao Tong Academic Ranking of World Universities. Sports facilities at the university include an artificial hockey field, an indoor sports complex and extensive tennis, squash, soccer, rugby and cricket facilities. The university rowing club is one of the best equipped university clubs in South Africa and the university also has mountain climbing facilities, an L26 Keelboat and sailing dinghies, an ocean-going dive boat, and a water-ski boat (UCT 2012b).

There are a large number of student-run and professionally coached sports clubs (including team sports, individual sports, extreme sports and martial arts) on campus and students are actively engaged in promoting sport in the local communities and within their clubs on campus. Scholarships are available to potential students who have represented their country in any sport at a national schools or age-group level (UCT 2012b).

The design of new university sports facilities generally follows best practice for the sport concerned, particularly in terms of facilities for competitive sports. There is also a trend to create more blended facilities that either include elements of sport and fitness within academic buildings on campus or introduce formal and informal learning spaces into the sports facilities.

The top floor of the new Li Ka Shing Center for Learning and Knowledge at the Stanford School of Medicine, for example, includes a range of study and social spaces for the medical students including a fitness centre that lets 'students squeeze in a workout between classes or laboratories ... with limited time at their disposal, students need an easily accessible retreat that nurtures a sense of community. This blended space puts work and play under one roof – a home away from home' (LKSC 2012).

Access to wireless networks and the provision of cafe and other social spaces within sports centres allow the spaces to also be used for informal learning and group study. Classrooms in the centres may support the competitive teams but may also be timetabled

spaces for sports-related academic programmes. At the 3,000 square foot Arthur 'Buster' Browning, M.D. Athletic Training and Education Center at the University of North Florida, for example, the classrooms support the athletic training programme for more than 250 UNF student-athletes and are also used as a clinical training site for the University's Certified Athletic Training Program in the College of Health (UNF 2012).

Universities that have faculties or departments of sports science frequently use the institution's sports facilities as a key teaching and research resource and may make significant investments in motion tracking and physiological testing equipment to support their programme.

The University of Stirling in Scotland announced in early 2011 that it was investing £750,000 to create 'world-class sports-science and sports medicine facilities' at the university. The development at the existing sports centre will include the creation of two new sports performance assessment laboratories that will be shared by the university and the SportScotland Institute of Sport. The new centre will also include an analytical lab; a consultancy room for doctors and nutritionists; a pilates space and three treatment areas for physiotherapy. Equipment will include a state-of-the-art treadmill worth more than £100,000 (Stirling 2011).

Another university that has also recently partnered with an external organization to create sports-related learning and research facilities is Florida State University which has medical, exercise science, nutrition, sports psychology and athletic training programmes. It announced a partnership in May 2011 with the Tallahassee Orthopedic Clinic, a healthcare provider, to create the Institute of Sports Sciences and Medicine: 'The institute will lead interdisciplinary research and educational outreach programs focused on the development of elite-level athletic and human performance – including an emphasis on long-term health and the prevention and treatment of athletic injuries such as concussions' (FSU 2011). To support the institute's research and clinical activities a Human Performance Laboratory is being constructed near the Florida State University track-and-field complex.

As the complexity of the sports science and related programmes and research increases, there is a requirement for more specialized equipment and facilities that require a controlled environment and substantial investment. At this point, universities often concentrate their expertise and resources into specialized sports-related research centres back on the main campus. The Centre for Sport and Exercise Science at Sheffield Hallam University in the UK (SHU 2012), for example, includes biochemistry, biomechanics, physiology and psychology laboratories, environmental chambers able to simulate any world climate and sports engineering facilities including high-speed video motion capture and analysis and prototyping workshops. Additional expertise is provided through research and teaching partnerships with other academic departments including engineering and business.

The provision of sports facilities at a university is driven by a range of factors including government regulation, the availability of space on or near campus, the economic resources available to the institution through endowments or other sources, the priority placed on sports facilities by the institution as a student recruitment and retention tool and the role of sports-related activities within its academic programme. The interplay of these factors has led to a wide diversity of sports facilities at universities that shows little correlation with the size or location of the institution.

CHAPTER 6

Business and cultural spaces

INTRODUCTION

Third stream learning spaces can be loosely, but usefully, divided between those that occupy the borderland between the workplace and formalized education and those that exploit the andragogic potential of existing cultural spaces. Here innovation is found in – sometimes radically – reallocated function rather than modified space. For the most part the forms remain limited but the uses change – classrooms become meeting rooms, library spaces become community hubs, entire colleges are given over to industry for the acquisition and accreditation of professional and vocational qualifications. Some are new spaces – or new as learning spaces: Tent City, coffee shops, village and community halls, retirement communities, extended roles for museums and galleries. What they have in common is their emergence in response to society's increasing hunger for learning at all stages and in all areas of modern life.

Facilities catering to the needs of the first group – vocational and professional activities – would traditionally be re-badged existing spaces, with little in the way of custom-built accommodation. In fact this is still very widely the case. Many organizations run internal training courses utilizing their own meeting rooms, conference facilities or production areas. These courses may use internal trainers or they may bring in training specialists from external organizations, including universities. Professional bodies without their own educational facilities – or who want to achieve a wider geographic reach – may accredit training organizations, colleges or universities to deliver the courses on their behalf: they may buy in time in established conference centres. The space itself is modified only by change of use.

Many organizations use commercial conference and meeting venues for the delivery of their corporate education and training programmes, often in venues with residential components. These may include large country houses converted into education centres, conference centres attached to hotels and purpose-built conference centres – such as the Cotswold Conference Centre in the UK, a dedicated conference venue with 89 bedrooms on a 370-acre property, its many activities and amenities blurring the line between learning and leisure (Cotswold Conference Centre 2012).

Custom-built spaces do, of course, exist: innovation centres and knowledge transfer spaces, simulation-based learning for precise applications (military, medical), and sometimes distance-based using technology. The military, for instance, because in its various forms it covers such a wide age, expertise and social range, has had to come to terms with a very generous reading of learning. The UK army maintains a clear distinction between training and education, in colleges that induct school leavers into the service, impart officer skills, pass on specific skills from catering to helicopter piloting, and prepare service people for a civilian life. Medical skills are developing so rapidly – the widely quoted half-life of five years for biomedical knowledge (Lindsay et al. 1974) – that new ways of learning have had to be found to cope with the accelerating rate of change.

A handful of large corporates are establishing their own internal universities or focusing on leadership development and soft skills with associated learning spaces. In 1973, Domino's Pizza in the US founded the College of Pizzarology at its headquarters in Ann Arbor, Michigan to train potential franchisees (Domino's Pizza 2012) – or, as Thomas Dicke (1992) puts it in *Franchising in America: The Development of a Business Method 1840–1980*: 'apply batch production techniques to franchisee training'. The most well-known training institution within the fast food industry, however, is undoubtedly McDonald's now worldwide Hamburger University (HU) (Figure 6.1).

But blending and layering are the norm: school-children taking university courses while still at school and professionals meeting their CPD obligations at university (blending); schools using university laboratories and universities running courses specifically for business (layering).

The changing role of public libraries, museums and galleries, however – the cultural spaces now adumbrating the learning landscape – is already resulting in some fundamental shifts in the space itself.

In 2003, the Department of Culture, Media and Sport in the UK published *Framework for the Future: Libraries, Learning and Information in the Next Decade*, setting out the government's vision for the development of public libraries during the following

Books on management and leadership sit on a shelf at McDonald's Corp's Hamburger University in Shanghai, China: Illinois-based McDonald's has 1,300 stores in China. In 2011, according to the McDonald's school's official newsletter, Harvard University's record low acceptance rate of 7 per cent compared favourably with McDonald's management training programme in Shanghai, where the selection rate was less than 1 per cent (Bloomberg 2011a).

Hamburger University began in 1961 in a McDonald's restaurant basement in Elk Grove Village, Illinois with 15 graduates in the first class. In 1983, the company invested $40 million in a 130,000 square foot facility on an 80 acre campus at its corporate offices in Oak Brook, Illinois. This industry-leading facility includes 13

teaching rooms, 12 interactive education team rooms, three kitchen labs, state-of-the-art service training labs and a 300-seat auditorium.

There are 19 full-time professors at the Hamburger University with international restaurant operations expertise who deliver the McDonald's training curriculum using a combination of classroom instruction, hands-on lab activities, goal-based scenarios and computer e-learning modules. Hamburger University interpreters can provide simultaneous interpretation, and the faculty has the ability to teach in 28 different languages including Spanish, German, French, Japanese and Mandarin Chinese.

Sources: Bloomberg (2011); McDonald's (2012)

Figure 6.1 McDonald's Hamburger University, Shanghai

decade. The framework concentrated on libraries' roles in developing reading and learning, digital skills and services, community cohesion and civic values:

> Public libraries provide a learning network that supports formal education but also extends far beyond it. Reading, literacy and learning are inextricably linked. The selfmotivated learning which libraries promote is central to the creation of a lifelong learning culture in which people expect and want to learn throughout their lifetime.
>
> (DCMS 2003: 8)

In the same year, a report by the Commission for Architecture and the Built Environment (CABE), *Better Public Libraries* (2003) stressed the importance of innovation and creativity in the design of public libraries. It stated that public libraries were 'facing enormous challenges as the population and demographic mix changes more rapidly than ever before, as Information and Communications Technology (ICT) reconfigures the very nature of physical space, communications and movement in both the village and the city, as education moves out of the institutions to inflect the whole of society, and as leisure, recreation and personal development increasingly fuse in a more individualistic culture'.

New and extended uses will require a different architecture and different settings to support the diverse activities – a point also made by a 2004 report from CABE, *Building Futures: 21st Century Libraries* (CABE 2004), which looks at the design implications of the changing role of libraries:

> The developing role of the library has created a set of new and complex challenges for those delivering library buildings and services. The libraries of the 21st century are no longer simply familiar repositories for books. They have changed and expanded, been rethought and redesigned. Libraries now provide an increasing range of different services, using a multitude of media, and reach a more diverse audience than ever before.
>
> (p. 4)

Spatial implications for the changing role of museums and galleries are, if anything, even more stark. In *Learning to Live: Museums, Young People and Education*, Bellamy and Oppenheim (2009) state that until relatively recently 'learning' was marginalized in the museum sector, and 'culture' sidelined in the education sector. They believe, however, that in the past few years both sectors have made a concerted effort to engage with one another:

> Although museums make a valuable contribution to formal learning, and offer vital alternative ways of learning that complement the formal education system, they are more than an adjunct to it; museums are places of excitement and wonder, that can inspire interest and creativity in all children and young people, and an awareness of the wider world and their place in it, in ways which neither parents nor teachers can provide and that might otherwise remain untapped.
>
> (p. 10)

In tandem with his observation that 'museum education ... is as old as museums' (Hein 2006: 161), George Hein also notes that 'collections of objects, even collections carefully classified, organized, and preserved, are not necessarily primarily educational – the world includes many fine private collections. As soon as these objects are in a public museum, however, they are incorporated within a broadly educational project, though not one that is necessarily effective' (Hein 2011: 34).

The almost universal recognition that visitors need active engagement for understanding (Hein 2006: 171) has led to the introduction of interactive components in exhibits, not only in the science centres and children's museums, but also in history and art museums. Activity centres, resource rooms, and direct links to virtual extensions for exhibits have become standard components of most major museums and galleries.

BUSINESS AND EDUCATION

The interconnectedness of business and education was acknowledged in the UK by the establishment in 2008 of the Training Gateway, set up to support UK universities' involvement in corporate, vocational and executive training by creating a 'one-stop shop' for middle and senior managers and technical specialists from UK training providers. When it was created, it represented every UK university and more than 70 further education colleges but since then its remit has been expanded to work with UK-based private training providers and consultants, bringing the total number of training providers represented to more than 2,600 and the number of courses to over 100,000. To date, the organization has promoted over 1,800 training and educational partnership business opportunities worth over £200 million from around the world across a range of business sectors.

The Northants Engineering Training Partnership (NETP), for example, is a company formed by the University of Northampton with four industrial companies in 1989, designed to create a pool of industry-ready engineers. The NETP partners provide paid industry placements each year for a number of engineering students studying at the University of Northampton which allows the students to apply their skills and gain industry experience. The partner employers gain assistance with projects and may also identify potential future employees for later recruitment. Since the launch of the partnership, the partner companies have provided over 450 placement opportunities and the employment rate among graduates who have taken part in the scheme is in excess of 90 per cent, with many finding employment with one of the partner companies.

The NETP assists in curriculum development, ensuring that engineering courses at the university remain current and relevant to industry, and also supports the wider engineering student body, school and college students and engineering companies through a variety of events and activities including industry talks and visits.

Collaboration between the academic provider and the commercial organization can extend beyond the provision of a tailored training programme. In June 2011, Arup, international design consultants and engineers, signed an agreement with the University of Salford to collaborate in a number of areas including critical city infrastructure, building retrofit, sustainability and 3D city modelling and Building Information Modelling (BIM). Academics from the School of the Built Environment at Salford will work with the designers, engineers and technical experts at Arup to develop new research and to create new courses and training. The partnership will also be used to increase collaboration on bidding for funding and knowledge exchanges between industry and academia (Salford 2012).

The relationship between the academy and the workplace can, of course, be a minefield, as the experience of Buckinghamshire New University and the London School of Economics and Political Science (LSE) in the UK testified, in their dealings, respectively, with bed manufacturer Dreams and the Gaddafi dynasty. Buckinghamshire's vice chancellor pointedly insisted that it was better for employers to partner with universities than to award their own qualifications – a clear reference to the McDonald's University (THE 2008). And the Woolf inquiry into the LSE's relationship with the Gaddafi regime made the stern comment that the 'London School of Economics was guilty of multiple failures of governance and management in its links with the deposed Gaddafi regime' [which resulted in the resignation of the Director of the School] – before concluding that 'the acceptance of a £2.2 million contract to train Libya's elite civil servants, for example, was "clearly of merit" and a service the school should be performing' (THE 2011a). An amount of £705,000 is outstanding and a provision is likely to be necessary against the outstanding debt (LSE 2011): the damage to the institution's reputation is less quantifiable.

The academy and professional education

Many professions require accreditation or additional qualifications to enable people to practice or gain membership of the

appropriate professional body. These qualifications range from certificate courses based on the completion of online or face-to-face training through to extensive postgraduate courses that may take several years to complete. (To become an actuary, for example, work is combined with part-time study for the Institute of Actuaries or the Faculty of Actuaries examinations and qualification will usually take three to six years.)

Professional bodies without their own specialized educational facilities – or that want to have a wider geographic reach – may accredit third-party bodies to deliver the courses on their behalf. Holborn College in Greenwich, London is a typical example of the many private colleges in the UK offering both degree and professional qualification courses – a range of business and law qualifications specially designed for full-time study in the UK, and undergraduate and postgraduate degrees from a number of UK universities. Finance and accountancy qualifications at Holborn College are provided in partnership with Kaplan Financial (Kaplan Financial 2012), which also has a Law School, an Open Learning business (with degrees awarded by the University of Essex), a continuing professional development (CPD) business providing management courses in finance, law and business management (Kaplan Hawksmere 2012) and a Business School (Kaplan Business School 2012) (degrees awarded by the University of London).

BPP is another major provider of financial, law and other professional qualifications in the UK. The company was founded in 1976, listed on the Stock Exchange in 1986 and became part of the Apollo Group in 2009 when it was acquired for just over $600 million (THE 2010). The Apollo Group, a market-listed US company, also owns the University of Phoenix, a private institution offering degrees through distance learning to more than 400,000 students in 2011 from more than 200 locations across the US, internationally (40 states, the District of Columbia, Puerto Rico, Canada, Mexico, Chile and the Netherlands) and online. This is a reduction in student enrolment of around 30 per cent from 2010, which has been attributed to operational changes amid criticism of high debt loads and low job prospects for University of Phoenix students (Warner 2011). Other changes include allowing students to try classes before officially enrolling and recruiter training programmes that are designed to improve student retention and completion rates. The projected income for the Apollo Group in 2012 is between $4.1 billion and $4.3 billion (Bloomberg 2011b).

BPP now has 2,000 staff and 40 locations worldwide with more than 6,500 students in business and law schools and over 30,000 accountants undertaking training courses. BPP's core professional education business is supported by BPP Learning Media, the BPP University College of Professional Studies (Four Law Schools and a Business School). Through MPW, BPP also operates three sixth form colleges in London, Birmingham and Cambridge and offers GCSE and A-level courses to full-time students and Easter revision courses to pupils registered at other schools.

In 2007, BPP became the first private company in the UK to be granted the power to award higher education degrees (the two other private universities are charities). The BPP College of Professional Education began by offering the legal practice course and bar vocational course as masters degrees and award the graduate diploma in law as an honours degree. Masters degrees in commercial law and other areas of corporate practice are also offered from the four law school locations across the England. The Business School based in London offers masters degrees in accounting, finance, insolvency, taxation, actuarial science, marketing, management and human resources (BBC 2007b).

Degrees are offered either by face-to-face learning at the BPP campuses, fully online or a combination of the two. The BPP Business School in London City consists of 14 air-conditioned, technology-equipped training rooms over two floors. As well as lecture theatres and classrooms, there are business break-out areas, a comprehensive business library and a student cafe: 'The atmosphere is professional and business-focused, making it the perfect place to study' (BPP 2013).

With the 2012 change in UK fee structures for higher education, BPP is pricing its degrees competitively against the rest of the UK higher education market with the launch of an enhanced degree programme, with a career and employability benefits package built in to all undergraduate degrees and £5,000 per year for a three-year degree and £6,000 per year for a two-year degree, compared with the £9,000 per year charged by many UK universities from 2012 onwards.

BPP's goal is to increase the number of its own undergraduates tenfold by undercutting publicly funded universities after 2012, when it will be able to charge up to £9,000 a year. In 2011, BPP had just over 1,000 undergraduates. The Chief Executive, Carl Lygo, stated in the *Guardian* in June 2011: 'We want to offer a radical, high-quality alternative, with classroom-hours contact which is in small groups' (Shepherd 2011).

More controversially, in 2011 BPP launched an initiative to help run at least ten publicly funded universities. When reported by the *Guardian* in June 2011, talks with three universities were said to be at a 'serious stage', but commercial negotiations were yet to begin. Under the BPP model, 'universities would control all academic decisions, while BPP would be responsible for managing the campus estate, IT support, the buying of goods and services and other "back office" roles. BPP would not hold equity in the universities' (ibid.).

Lygo stated that his firm stood to make tens to hundreds of thousands of pounds from working with each institution, but that it would be 'too radical at the moment' to bid to take over a university. He also predicted that universities could save a quarter of their costs if they agreed to BPP running the commercial side of their operation, money they could invest in the academic side:

> We have got a lot of universities in the UK and not all are in a strong financial position ... There is an opportunity for the private sector to help the higher education sector to achieve its goals. By working in partnership, the private provider would add expertise in the back office functions. Most universities are running at high costs and don't properly utilise their buildings. The private sector is better at procurement because they are keener at negotiating better prices.
>
> (ibid.)

BPP does face its own challenges as the UK higher education market goes through major changes. In November 2010, the Apollo Group wrote off more than a quarter of the purchase value of for-profit provider BPP because of uncertainty surrounding the UK higher education market's future. BPP's operating loss for 2010 was almost $190 million, most of it a result of the write-off. In a note on the accounts relating to the impairment charge, Apollo stated that the company has revised its forecast for BPP because of the ongoing recession and increased uncertainty as to when these conditions will recover. Apollo also, however, forecast a significant increase in revenue over the long term from BPP University College (THE 2010).

The possibility of a private business acquiring a public university in the UK continues to be discussed. An article in the *Times Higher Supplement* in October 2011 quoted Glynne Stanfield, a partner in the education group at international law firm Eversheds, as predicting that a private equity firm or private higher education provider will buy a UK university in whole or part within the next six months. He went on to suggest that private equity firms or 'trade buyers' (established private higher education providers) could buy out a university in its entirety and thus gain its degree-awarding powers. Alternatively, and more likely according to Stanfield, a private equity firm or trade buyer could buy a stake in a university, providing the institution with working capital in return for using its degree-awarding powers overseas (THE 2011). In fact, the College of Law, a private education provider, was sold in April 2012 to Montague Private Equity for around £200 million, and while legal and education policy experts at the time thought it unlikely that private companies would take over traditional universities entirely in the near future – 'Russian oligarchs won't be getting their hands on Cambridge quite yet' – they did foresee some university activities soon being financed with private cash (Swain 2012).

The THE article also noted that private equity firm Warburg Pincus – the biggest stakeholder in Bridgepoint Education, which operates Ashford University and the University of the Rockies in the US – attended round-table meetings in December 2010 and January 2011 with David Willetts, the UK universities and science minister, along with private providers including BPP, Laureate, Pearson and the ifs School of Finance.

Despite the entry of major international private providers, professional education continues to also be delivered through 'mainstream' higher education institutions, such as the Møller Centre in Cambridge (Figures 6.2 and 6.3). Edge Hill University, Ormskirk, UK is the country's largest provider of professional development courses for teachers (Edge Hill University 2012) – with, in 2011, more than 13, 000 part-time and 803 full-time postgraduate students and 8,685 full-time and 5,404 part-time undergraduate students.

At Edge Hill, professional qualification courses are fully integrated into the activities of the main campus and there has been £130 million of investment in the facilities on the main campus during the last decade. The most recent project has been the completion of a new £14 million Student Hub building (2011). Other projects have included the creation of the West campus that houses the Learning Innovation Centre (2000), the Faculty of Education Building (2004), the Centre for Media, Information Systems and Technology (2004), the Management Centre and the Faculty of Health and Social Care (2007). Other projects have included the construction of the Wilson Centre for Sports Psychology and physiology (2001), the Performing Arts Centre (2005), the Business and Law School (2009), the refurbishment of the old Business School to create Social and Psychological Sciences Building (2009) as well as the construction of new accommodation blocks for students (2009 and 2010) and the new gymnasium (2010).

While commercial professional education providers may gain degree-awarding powers, it is unlikely that they will be in a position to take the long-term view that a university needs to take, investing in facilities that both support the developing academic programme and enhance the learning, teaching and research experience at the institution.

Specialized training

Many professional development courses can take place in general teaching spaces such as classrooms and lecture theatres – but some courses require more specialist facilities. In these cases the professional body may choose to partner with an academic institution to

The Møller Centre is a wholly owned subsidiary of Churchill College, University of Cambridge – a dedicated venue for continuing professional development, set up with the aim of creating strong links between the university and industry. It aims to support its clients in the acquisition of knowledge 'for professional development and personal and business success in an executive environment'.

Figure 6.2 Møller Centre, Cambridge, UK

Figure 6.3 Møller Centre, Cambridge, UK

deliver these specialized courses or it may choose to develop its own purpose-built educational centre.

The British Airways Flight Centre at Cranebrook, near Heathrow, provides a wide range of technical training related to all aspects of flying for both British Airways and global airline customers. The centre includes 15 full-flight simulators and four fixed-base simulators covering both Boeing and Airbus aircraft types – and in its mix of rigorous professional and technical training and accessibility to corporate event parties (including simulated crash landings) perfectly exemplifies the blending of learning and entertainment.

Ground school instructors provide aircraft-type technical courses. Computer-based training (CBT) is used in conjunction with daily sessions in the fixed-base simulators (FBS). Each session is conducted using the scans, procedures and checks relevant to the client airline and pilots are tested every three days to monitor their progress. Aircraft conversion courses for pilots normally last 10–11 days depending on type and recent experience, after which time they move on to the full-flight simulator phase of training.

Cabin simulators and door trainers are available for a range of Boeing and Airbus aircraft and flights crews can receive fire and smoke training both in simulator and in a specialist fire, ground and smoke chamber; wet drills include lifejacket and life raft operation in water, slide descent and door operation training.

As well as providing advanced technical training for the world's airlines, the centre is courting the corporate conference, training and entertainment markets: 'Pick from our selection of full motion flight simulators, cabin simulators and conference facilities for an amazing experience, all supported by British Airways pilots and instructors. Combine this with full banqueting facilities, private function rooms and plenty of free on-site car parking for your tailor-made event' (BAFT 2012).

The aim of the Wolfson Surgical Skills Centre is to improve training for surgeons and patient care, both in the UK and internationally, combining advanced simulator training with hands-on experience. The clinical skills unit was opened in 2009, made up of three main teaching areas.

● The skills area is designed for bench-top models using both plastic and tissue. Eight workstations can accommodate up to 30 people.

● The minimal access area (which can also be used for critical care training) contains a range of laparoscopic equipment with all services supplied through boom arms.

● The team skills training theatre comprises a fully equipped operating theatre, recovery area, control room and observation and debrief room. A life-like mannequin can be programmed to deliver emergency scenarios which will be used in theatre team training. Participants' actions can be recorded and discussed in debrief sessions.

The college also has a number of purpose-built conference and seminar rooms, including two audio-visual presentation-enabled lecture theatres seating 300 people and 125 people respectively.

All of the centre's tables are fully interconnected by monitors so that up to 50 surgeons can learn collaboratively at once.

The key learning spaces in the centre are the dissection workshop and the clinical skills unit. The dissection workshop:

● simulates the operating conditions of a modern hospital with dissection tables with integrated services to accommodate up to 36 participants

● -incorporates state-of-the-art audio-visual facilities with each dissecting table provided with a mounted screen for close-up viewing of procedures

● includes large, wall-mounted plasma screen to facilitate links to other lecture areas in the college, or externally to other national or international venues

● has two smaller demonstration rooms for small group work.

Sources: http://www.rcseng.ac.uk/media/medianews/college-opens-state-of-the-art-surgical-training-centre; http://www.rcseng.ac.uk/education/facilities

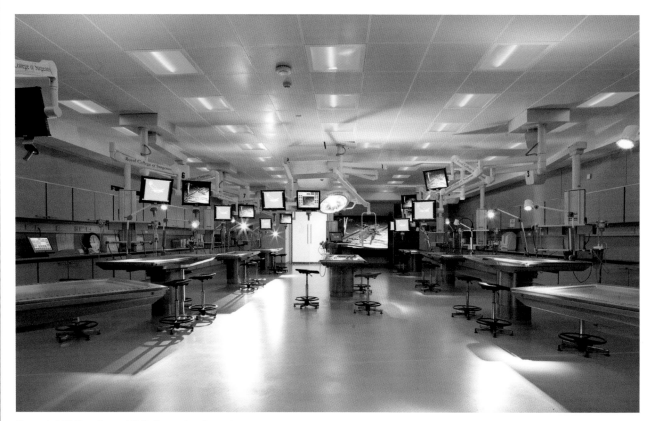

Figure 6.4 Wolfson Surgical Skills Centre, London, UK

Team-building opportunities available at the flight centre include a simulated flight on a full-motion Boeing 737 cabin simulator, leading to an emergency landing and full aircraft evacuation from a smoke-filled environment including jumping down the emergency evacuation slides.

The range of simulation environments is likely to be even wider in the new £139 million Joint Services College at a 250-acre site at Desertcreat on the outskirts of Cookstown, Northern Ireland. The college, for which approval has recently been given, will provide integrated training facilities for the Police Service Northern Ireland, Northern Ireland Prison Service and the Northern Ireland Fire and Rescue Service when it becomes operational in 2015.

The facilities to be provided include academic classrooms, ICT suites, simulated learning suites, practical training areas, live fire rescue, public order, district command, emergency situation, driver training, prison environment, mock courts, residential environment, rural training and marine rescue training areas as well as conference facilities, fitness facilities and accommodation (PSNI 2012). Other facilities will include dog kennels, firearms ranges, combined operational and fire training facilities together with a parade ground (Desertcreat 2012).

The Perkins + Will-led winning submission for the project includes the creation of a 'college hub' that will contain the principal shared programme spaces: exhibition gallery, sports and lecture halls, an auditorium and the campus canteen. This hub provides access to a north–south pedestrian axis that links student and staff accommodation, classrooms, locker facilities, administration, faculty and staff offices and the practical training buildings (Worldarchitecture 2012).

In 2007, the Royal College of Surgeons opened the first phase of its new surgical training centre at its building in Lincoln's Inn Fields in London. This centre was part of the 'Eagle Project', the goal of which was to provide the UK with a world-leading surgical training centre by 2010 (RCS 2012).

The £3 million Wolfson Surgical Skills Centre takes advantage of the latest technology and the opportunities presented by the Human Tissue Act 2004 which, for the first time, allows surgeons to practise surgical techniques on donated human bodies before taking their skills into the hospital operating theatres (Figures 6.4 and 6.5) (Junior Dr 2007).

A different approach is taken to surgical simulation at Imperial College School of Medicine in London (Figures 6.6 and 6.7). A team led by Dr Roger Kneebone has been exploring the concept of distributed simulation. The goal of the research project was to recreate only key elements of the surgical environment in a low-cost, portable and immersive simulation environment that could be used to train surgeons and widen access to high-fidelity simulation. By combining a realistic simulation of the operating theatre environment with professional actors in the roles of patients and team members, it would be possible to train surgeons how to deal with real-world stressful situations such as uncooperative patients or ineffective surgical teams.

The simulation environment – the Igloo – is designed to be entirely controlled from a laptop using custom-made computer interface that allows a trainer to control the heart rate of the patient and background noise (which was found to be invaluable in enhancing the realism experienced by the surgeon), and to capture video streams from three separate camera perspectives, and audio from the microphone.

The Igloo is designed to fit in a suitcase and can be easily transported, creating low-cost simulation environments in any hospital or health clinic (BUPA 2011):

> The portable operating suite means simulation can be carried out in local settings where it's most needed – teams don't need to travel elsewhere to do simulated training. This kind of training allows surgical teams to experience what it means to operate on a seriously wounded patient and get valuable practice, without any real danger.
>
> (Imperial 2010)

The Igloo has also been used at science fairs to help to recruit future doctors and surgeons. As one spectator at the Cheltenham Science Fair in 2010 stated: 'Amazing. I loved the fake operation with all the blood. It taught me a lot about being a doctor and I'm going to be one, one day' (ibid.).

Professional education environments range from a simple online training package through to conventional classroom and lecture environments either provided by a higher education institution or private provider through to specialist technical environments that are used to ensure that members of a profession maintain their knowledge and skills to an appropriate level.

As more people reinvent or refresh their professional skills during their working lives, professional educational facilities will be increasingly important – because of their impact on the individual and the economy overall and because of the revenue opportunities that they offer to service providers.

The National Skills Academy Creative & Cultural (NSA C&C) is the rather unwieldy title of one part of a national network of Skills Academies, with a membership of over 230 theatre and live music employers and 20 colleges throughout England. It exists to 'recognise, develop and improve skills opportunities for those entering the creative and cultural sector and those already employed within it' (http://nsa-ccskills.co.uk/what-we-do). The performing arts and music sector is already of great economic significance in the UK and predicted to grow by more than 40 per cent by 2020. For the industry to meet this potential, the availability of a highly skilled technical workforce is fundamental: the NSA C&C aims to provide a single, collective standard for skills development in the sector, built on industry-endorsed careers advice, entry routes and apprenticeships.

A new focal point for the organization, the Backstage Centre (Figures 6.8 and 6.9), offers practical and extended training and

rehearsals in a bespoke environment that offers full-scale venue-style training opportunities. Designed and specified by experts in the theatre, music and live events industry, the £13 million performing arts academy, in a new cultural industries business zone in Purfleet, east of the City of London, provides a dedicated meeting point for technicians, producers, creative teams and learners of all ages and at every stage of their careers – from world-renowned international artists to young people taking their first career steps.

The academy will become an important national and local training facility that will help meet the UK's anticipated need for 30,000 skilled backstage and technical theatre staff by 2017.

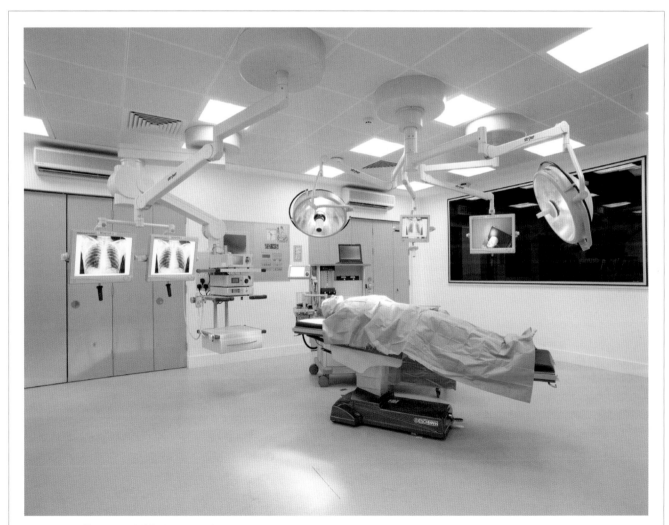

Figure 6.5 Wolfson Surgical Skills Centre, London, UK

Imperial's search for a surgical simulation environment resulted in a portable operating theatre, known as the Igloo, that inflates in just three minutes. Pop-up furniture (photographs on exhibition stands), lighting and sound all help to make the environment within the Igloo realistic, enabling doctors to practice their clinical and team-working skills without any risk to patients. A custom overhead LED operating lamp with built-in camera and microphone captures the action so teams can review their performance and make improvements.

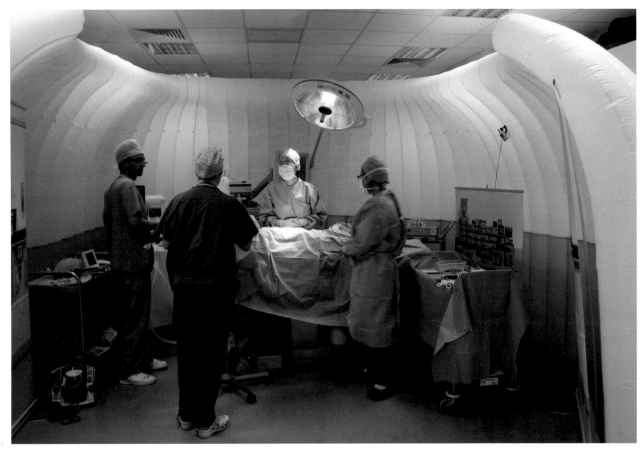

Figure 6.6 Imperial College School of Medicine, London, UK

CULTURAL SPACES AND LIFELONG LEARNING

In the UK, the 2009 government White Paper *The Learning Revolution* (DIUS 2009) firmly set lifelong learning in the context of a progressive relationship between learning and democratic action. It accounts for the consolidation of a national system of public libraries and museums in the rise of local government, and traces the development of classes in dressmaking, boot repair, cookery and physical education – and institutions such as Birkbeck College in London, Ruskin College in Oxford and the Mechanics' Institutes, where workers gained formal qualifications often unavailable at school:

Universities developed programmes to make learning available to the wider community and with the arrival of the BBC, first radio and then television developed educational programmes with massive reach. Hundreds of thousands of students signed up to Open University courses and more than two million people a week eavesdropped on OU programmes on the BBC in the 1990s.

(p. 49)

Public libraries

Public libraries – publicly owned and supported by taxes, open to any citizen who desires to use them, and containing a wide range of material, both popular and scholarly (SDSAB 2006) – have

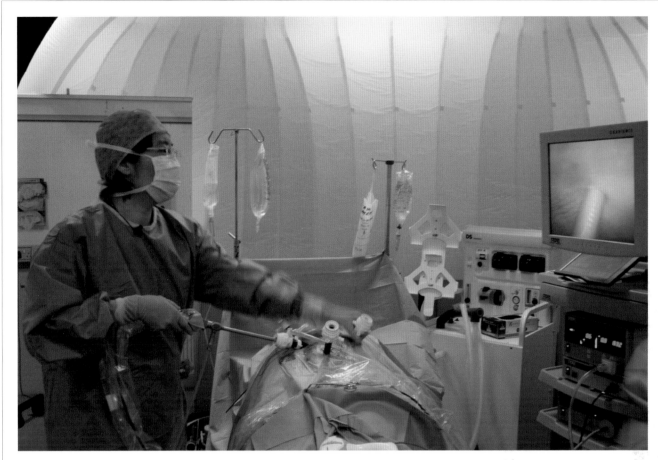

Figure 6.7 Imperial College School of Medicine, London, UK

only been in existence since the nineteenth century but now, according to the International Federation of Library Associations and Institutions (IFLA) in its report on lifelong learning (IFLA 2004) number 267,219 worldwide, including 797 in Africa, 37,063 in Asia, 20,081 in North America, 3,942 in South America and 205,336 in Europe. In the UK, the Chartered Institute of Library and Information Professionals (CILIP) state that in 2008/2009 there were 4,517 public libraries in the UK and that an estimated 58 per cent of the population have a library card (CILIP 2010).

In the UK, the Public Libraries Act became law in 1850. While this Act enabled the financing of the construction of libraries through taxation, it was limited to a maximum of a half penny in the pound and then only if two-thirds of the local rate payers agreed. The money raised through this taxation also could not be used to purchase books. Amendments to the Act in the 1850s raised the maximum rate that could be levied to one penny and enabled the purchasing of books for the new libraries using this revenue.

The limits on financing made it impossible for local authorities to provide libraries without the support of wealthy patrons who generally supported the construction of libraries in their own area although Andrew Carnegie financed more than 380 libraries across Britain.

By 1900 there were 295 public libraries in Britain. However, it was not until the rate limit was abolished in 1919 that a truly comprehensive and free library service was possible (Spartacus Educational 2013).

In parallel with the development of publicly funded libraries, other forms of public access libraries also emerged. The London Library was founded in 1841 by Thomas Carlyle and is still in operation today. Carlyle's founding vision was 'for an institution which would allow subscribers to enjoy the riches of a national library in their own home' (London Library 2012). Early members included Thackeray, Gladstone, Dickens and Elliot. The library currently contains more

The National Skills Academy's Backstage Centre is equipped to accommodate the rehearsal and production needs of large-scale theatre and opera productions – and also has an advanced educational role, providing accreditation and training in the backstage skills required by the theatre and live music sectors. It will offer young learners the chance to experience real-time training with some of the world's best bands and theatre companies in a large-scale industry-standard venue, strengthening their skills and giving them the practical experience of working in a real-world environment.

Source: http://www.thurrockgazette.co.uk/news/8933117.Work_starting_on___13_million_National_Skills_Academy_in_Purfleet/

Figure 6.8 Backstage Centre, Purfleet, UK: tension wire grid above the sound stage

Figure 6.9 Backstage Centre, Purfleet, UK: lighting desk

than one million books from the sixteenth century to modern works and periodicals in more than 50 languages. Membership is open to everyone and in 2012 an individual membership costs £445 p.a.

Boots the Chemist ran a lending library in the UK from 1899 to 1966. By 1938 they were issuing 35 million books a year nationwide and during the Second World War there were more than one million subscribers: Boots were buying books at the rate of 1,250,000 a year (Wilson nd).

Subscription libraries became less popular during the late 1950s and early 1960s, possibly because of the lower cost of paperbacks, the growing investment in public libraries and other sources of entertainment. Increasing commercial pressures also made companies look more closely at the use of sales space in stores for libraries. In 1961, UK newsagents W.H. Smith closed their libraries and Boots took over their subscribers but by 1965 the announcement was made that the Boots Booklovers' Libraries, now with only 121 branches and 140,000 subscribers, were also to close. The last branches closed in February 1966 (Infoscience 2011).

The American Library Association (ALA) – at variance with the IFLA figures above – estimates that there are a total of 121,785 libraries of all kinds in the US today. Of these, 9,250 are public libraries operating out of 16,698 central and branch library buildings (ALA 2012). To put this in perspective, Phillip Torrone, senior editor of MAKE magazine, notes that there are around 10,000 Curves International Fitness locations, 17,000 Starbucks locations, and 32,000 McDonald's locations (MAKE 2012).

In America, small private libraries had existed from early colonial times. Colleges, Churches or individual ministers and doctors often owned these collections and in some cases they were accessible by the people living in the surrounding area. In 1668, for example, John Harvard bequeathed a recently founded college around 280 books and an endowment. The school was so grateful 'it adopted his name and went on to build a fair reputation for itself' (SDSAB 2006).

In 1731, Benjamin Franklin created a 'subscription library' as a way of sharing books among members of a literary society. This was incorporated in 1742 as the Library Company of Philadelphia and you could only join the library by buying stock in the company. Other forms of social library emerged including the Athenaeum – a gentlemen's club with reading materials and the mercantile library. The mercantile library was frequently funded by contributions from wealthy benefactors and was typically aimed at middle-class young men, 'to promote orderly and virtuous habits, diffuse knowledge and the desire for knowledge, improve the scientific skill' and create good citizens.

Circulating libraries were also opening across America from the late 1700s. These were often housed in book or print shops and rented out books and popular materials including the latest novels. By the 1830s, School Districts were also creating libraries, funded through taxes, to provide reading materials for the schools in their district.

Aspects of all three types of libraries were combined in the US in the first truly public libraries. In 1849, New Hampshire became the first state to pass a law permitting local taxes to support public libraries. The Boston Public Library, opened in 1854, is usually considered the 'real' first public library and it included within its statement of purpose that 'Every citizen has the right of free access to community-owned resources' (SDSAB 2006).

In 1876, the American Library Association held a conference to promote the library interests of the country. One of the participants at this conference was Melvil Dewey (1851–1931) who went on to lead the ALA in 1890 (with the election slogan of 'the best reading for the largest number at the least cost') and to begin the standardization of libraries across the US – in many ways creating much of the look and feel of the modern library. His innovations included the Dewey Decimal Classification Systems, extended opening hours, reference departments, author and subject catalogues, arrangement of books on shelves by classification, overdue fines and circulation records for books.

The number of public libraries in the US expanded rapidly at the end of the nineteenth century and public libraries were established in cities such as Los Angeles (1889), New York (1895), New Orleans (1896) and Brooklyn (1897). By 1900, reference departments and open shelving for books were standard and a system of interlibrary loans to meet the special needs of scholars and students was established The first children's libraries were founded in the 1890s, and by 1908, circulation of materials to children accounted for around one-third of total library lending.

Andrew Carnegie played a significant role in this expansion across the country. By 1920, the Carnegie estate had donated $50 million to erect 2,500 library buildings, including 1,700 in the US – by far the most sustained and widespread philanthropic enterprise ever devoted to libraries (Straight Dope Science Advisory Board 2006).

Libraries also increasingly supported the waves of immigrants arriving after the 1890s and the role of the libraries began to include adult education – helping to socialize immigrants and teach the customs and expectations of US society.

Financial support for libraries was curtailed during the Depression, but the demand for services grew and libraries had to innovate to continue to deliver their role with reduced budgets. In 1941, President Franklin Roosevelt issued a proclamation supporting libraries as 'essential to the functioning of a democratic society' and 'the great tools of scholarship, the great repositories of culture, and the great symbols of the freedom of the mind' and after the war, the Library Services Act was passed in 1956, allowing federal funding for libraries and the further expansion of the US public library system (Straight Dope Science Advisory Board 2006).

The UK and US library experience

Attendance figures at many UK public libraries have been declining for several decades, despite growing demand for books and information (Audit Commission 2002). To reverse the trend, the 2002 UK Audit Commission report recommended libraries rethink services from the user's point of view, providing more of the books and information services that people want and improve accessibility by opening at times that suit people, sharing facilities with other services and using the internet. Libraries also need to ensure that services are easy and pleasant to use – learning, in particular, from bookshops that they need to build awareness among non-users of the services that libraries offer. The Audit Commission also noted that over one-half of library services use buildings that are poorly located or in poor condition.

The 2003 DCMS report *Framework for the Future: Libraries, Learning and Information in the Next Decade* set out a long-term and wide-ranging programme for the development of public libraries and stressed the vital role that public libraries play in supporting education at all levels from early childhood through formal education and lifelong learning and literacy skills development. It stated that libraries offer neutral welcoming community space and support active citizenship and they hold enormous stocks of material including books, DVDs, videos, CDs and computer software. Investment in information technology has equipped all public libraries with internet access and libraries operate as community centres of formal and informal learning, promoting reading across all ages and providing access to information and advice:

> Libraries have a central role to play in ensuring everyone has access to the resources, information and knowledge they need – particularly those groups in society who will otherwise be disadvantaged, including people who are less affluent and people with literacy problems.
>
> (DCMS 2003: 6)

The report made the point that libraries are increasingly working with schools to provide planned programmes of reader development to enrich and enhance the curriculum and creating a national network of homework clubs and summer reading programmes, and that this involvement in learning continues into further and higher education. As participation rates in further and higher education climb so, the report notes, will the demand from students for study space and support materials. 'Public libraries can play a critical role as study centres for people engaged in distance learning programmes ... where libraries provide both access to equipment and staff trained in learner support, and for students returning home in university vacations' (ibid.: 8).

Better Public Libraries (CABE 2003), concentrating on the importance of innovation and creativity in the design of public libraries, takes the space implications further.

As public libraries are being reinvented to help them meet the rapid social and technical changes of the twenty-first century, they are increasingly seen as the shared ground in an increasingly diverse society, beacons of learning where the whole community can feel a connection. They also provide the vital link to our digital future (ibid.: 2–3). In the future, individual libraries will develop their own bespoke programmes and services priorities based on the specific needs of their users and will increasingly be developed in partnership with other services such as further education, local government services, nursery facilities, housing offices and other cultural facilities including art galleries and performance spaces. These partnerships will serve to spread the costs of capital investment and maintaining the programme which needs-based assessment requires (ibid.: 6).

Reading development and literacy are likely to become even more central to what libraries offer communities and libraries will become key communications centres for mobile populations. Children's services will grow in importance as the library becomes a secure, electronic safe haven in the city, virtual library services will be provided 24 hours a day and electronic links between homes and libraries will increase. The role of librarians will change from being custodians of culture to knowledge navigators (ibid.: 5).

CABE noted that adaptability of internal design, circulation, access and hours of services will be a key factor in building layout and design and that long stay use of libraries for study purposes will require friendly and efficient support services such as toilets, catering and recreational quiet zones:

> Library architecture and design is adopting a more domestic or 'club' feel, with armchairs, sofas, coffee machines, and rooms

and spaces available for group meetings and discussions. In Scandinavia the public library is often referred to as 'the living room in the city' or 'the town salon', and the re- discovery of the library as the civic heart of the community is likely to continue.

(ibid.: 8)

The changing role of libraries is further explored by CABE in *Building Futures, 21st Century Libraries* (CABE 2004) and finds they have 'successfully rejuvenated themselves into places where you are as likely to meet a friend for coffee, do your homework, find out more about the history of the local community or take part in an activity, as borrow a book' (CABE 2004: 5). A key element of this rejuvenation has been the rise of information and communications technology. Initially this was thought to herald the end of the public library but ICT is now integral to their future success with all of the new library buildings of the past decade in the UK containing large numbers of computer terminals, technology suites, seminar rooms, and hot-desking email stations.

This vision of the future library has learning firmly at its heart:

> Now, and in the foreseeable future, people will need to upgrade their skills or learn new ones many times in the course of their working – and even domestic and recreational – lives. Education will no longer be a once and for all operation at the outset of life, but a continuous process of adaptation, self development and vocational re-skilling that will go on until people are well into their eighties, and even beyond
>
> (ibid.: 6)

Despite the acknowledgement of the increased role that public libraries were playing, however – both as a community hub and as an important support for both formal and informal learning – all was not well. In April 2004, an article by John Ezard in the *Guardian* reported on the publication of a study by Tim Coates which suggested that 'Britain's once-proud public libraries, founded 154 years ago as "the university of the street", are starting to die on their feet ... They stock too few new books, are not open at times that suit the public and are burdened with too many expensive administrators' (Ezard 2004). The report also stated that during the previous ten years the number of library users has fallen by 21 per cent, the number of books borrowed has fallen by 35 per cent and the national cost of the service has risen by 39 per cent. The findings of the report led to the government calling a high-level meeting to try to find answers to what was seen as a gathering crisis.

In 2008, the Museums, Libraries and Archives Council (MLA) published *Framework for the Future MLA Action Plan for Public Libraries – Towards 2013*, which stated:

individuals and communities are entitled to excellent public libraries that are integrated with other local services and responsive to local needs; offering books, information and learning resources on the high street and online for everyone at all times.

(MLA 2008: 1)

Libraries should support well-being, encourage reading, spread knowledge, contribute to learning and skills and help to foster identity, community and a sense of place for people of all ages, backgrounds and cultures through integration with local education, culture, arts and service providers. They should offer resources, books, essential information and materials that meet local needs for all people.

(MLA 2008: 2)

To achieve the action plan, the MLA planned to work with local government, national agencies, professional bodies, chief librarians and cultural leaders to advocate the relevance of public libraries and highlight the advantages of integrated provision in response to local needs and promote 'best practice', innovation and community engagement, especially in relation to local authority priorities, and support improvements in learning, information and reading services.

Unfortunately the MLA was not able to see implementation of the action plan through to 2013. In July 2010, the UK government announced the abolition of the MLA after a review of 'arms length bodies' across the government, to enable DCMS to focus its resources on frontline, essential services and ensure greater value for money. Many of the functions of the MLA were transferred to the Arts Council of England.

The reduction in library attendance numbers in the UK has continued. It was reported in the *Independent* in 2009 that the number of borrowers had dropped by 20 per cent during the period 2002/2003 to 2007/2008 and attendance was down by 2.6 per cent over the previous year. The number of full-time library staff had also reduced by 6.5 per cent and there had been an 11 per cent reduction in book stock. Forty libraries closed across Britain in 2006/2007 alone (Akbar 2009).

The decline in attendance numbers for public libraries is by no means universal. The Institute of Museum and Library Services analysis of service trends in US public libraries, for example, found that during the period 1997 to 2007 per capita visits increased every year during the study period, growing steadily from 4.13 in 1997 to 4.91 in 2007, an increase of 19 per cent. During the same period, per capita circulation increased by 12 per cent. The report noted that this growth in demand for library services occurred

even as people increasingly turned to the internet to meet their information needs. Internet availability at US public libraries rose sharply between 2000 and 2007, increasing by 90 percept on a per capita basis (Henderson 2009).

Access to information technology has been a key element of the continued popularity of US public libraries as well. 'Opportunity for All: How the American Public Benefits from Internet Access at U.S. Libraries', a Gates Foundation and Institute of Museum and Library Services-funded research project published in 2010, found that 77 million Americans – 2 per cent of the US population – use public library computers and internet access. A much higher percentage of people below the poverty line – 44 per cent – rely on it (Spotlight 2010). More than three-quarters of these users also had internet access at home, work or elsewhere (Becker and Crandall 2010).

More than 32 million visitors reported using library computers for a variety of educational activities: doing their homework, searching for and applying to graduate educational development (GED) and graduate programmes, completing online courses and tests, and even applying for financial aid.

Becker and Crandall (2010) also noted that the increase in internet availability in libraries has impacted the librarian's job and mission:

Librarians have begun serving as informal job coaches, college counselors, test monitors, and technology trainers for the growing number of patrons navigating government aid, the job market, and all levels of education on library computers. Many librarians have embraced this change as a natural extension of their role as highly trained information guides. They now offer beginning and advanced computer classes, host job training seminars, and provide countless patrons one-on-one computer training.

(p. 4)

Bennett (2009) also acknowledges the powerful impact technology has on the library and on the design of library spaces:

The transformation of information from a scarce commodity to a superabundant commodity has driven three paradigms in the design of library space. These are the reader-centered, book-centered, and learning-centered paradigms. The first two competed inconclusively with one another throughout most of the twentieth century. Revolutionary changes in information technology have only recently made a third design paradigm possible, one focused on intentional (autonomous) learning. This paradigm frees us from a schoolwork approach to learning and from mere trafficking of information. The challenge before us is to align space design with the transformational character of intentional learning.

(p. 181)

With every space in the library becoming an information-rich space, the design challenge for future libraries is more about the connection between space and learning rather than with the interaction of readers and books.

Some key library projects

Public library construction or refurbishment projects in recent years have incorporated a wide range of individual and group learning settings enabled, where appropriate, with information technology, to support the diverse activities now taking place in libraries.

Peckham Library, London Borough of Southwark, London, UK

Designed by Alsop and Störmer and completed in 2000, this was an influential library project in the UK. The iconic architecture, described as 'a large green boggle-eyed cartoon monster on seven insect-like legs' on the H2G2 website (H2G 2012), houses 60,000 books, a meeting room 'pod' (hired to local organizations and businesses), a study area 'pod', a children's play area 'pod', staff offices, the Southwark Local History Library, and the One Stop Shop for council information and advice (Livingplaces 2012). The library organizes a wide range of activities including baby and toddler sessions, teenage and adult reading groups, Manga Clubs for 10 to 16 year olds and a family learning and homework help club (Peckham Library 2012).

Idea Store, Tower Hamlets, London, UK

Tower Hamlets in London developed the Idea Store concept to bring together Tower Hamlet's programmes for library renewal, the support of lifelong learning and community renewal of inner-city areas and deliver its library, learning and information services. The first Idea Store was opened in Bow in 2002 and four more have been opened in the borough since that time. As well as the traditional library service, the Idea Stores offer a wide range of adult education classes, along with career support, training, meeting areas, a crèche, cafes and arts and leisure pursuits.

The intention is that all the Idea Stores will be located at the heart of the main local shopping centres, beside (or even inside) the supermarkets. It was felt that each store, attracting large numbers of users, would bring great benefits to their shopping centre and breathe new life into local retail (Idea Store 1999).

Dr Martin Luther King Jr Library, San José, California, US

This 47,500 square metre joint-use library (Figures 6.10–6.12) opened in 2003 and is shared by the City of San José and the San José State University (SJSU). The collections comprise 1.3 million volumes and users include 30,000 students, faculty members and staff from SJSU, and 918,800 San José residents.

The library includes traditional central public service desks, segregated spaces for some age groups (children, teens) and open stacks of print materials. The library building is situated on one corner of the SJSU campus and has two entrances, one from the city and one from the university. The library acts as 'a gateway from the city of San José into SJSU. It invites community users to explore not only the library itself but also the wider university, including events, courses, and degree programs' (Peterson 2005: 57).

Rotterdam Public Library, Rotterdam, the Netherlands

The Rotterdam Public Library consists of the central library, 23 district branches and two mobile libraries. The 24,000 square metre central library was designed by Van den Broek and Bakema and was completed in 1983 and refurbished by them between 1999 and 2004. The library collection includes over one million books, CD-ROMs, DVDs and videos, 1,600 magazine and newspaper titles, 300,000 CDs and the same number of LPs in the Central Discotheque (Bibliotheek 2012). The central library also contains the Erasmus Collection – the world's largest collection 'about' and 'of' Erasmus and his works (Erasmus 2012). The Erasmus Centre 'aims to foster communication between the public and academia, university and city, the past and the present, and between Erasmus, his books, and his readers'.

The central library also houses a library theatre that stages cabaret performances and literary activities, a cafe-restaurant with bar, a ticket purchasing outlet for city events, a city information centre and a central discotheque where you can borrow music that is run in partnership with an independent music store. Several of the branch libraries are located in public schools and library staff have organized extended school (after school) programmes in their libraries (Infotoday 2010).

Seattle Public Library, Seattle, US

In 1998, Seattle voters approved a $291 million Libraries for All programme to rebuild and renew the Seattle Public Library (SPL) (Figures 6.13 and 6.14). A major element of the programme was the redevelopment of the Seattle Central Library. The $166 million new library, designed by OMA/LMN, was completed in 2004: the 'stunning steel and glass building has grand public spaces, cityscape views, an all-red meeting room floor and 30 miles of books arranged in the only Books Spiral in the world. Some of the innovative artwork includes a celebration of world languages built into hardwood flooring, talking video sculptures along an escalator, and a real-time look at what Seattle is reading that floats across plasma display screens' (SPL 2012).

The Libraries for All programme was completed in 2008. An evaluation of the impact of the programme produced some impressive statistics. Annual circulation of books and materials was up 94 per

Planners of the King Library provided space in the library for five types of user activity: information seeking, recreation, teaching/learning, connection and contemplation. It was recognized that some library patrons would make use of all five types of space; others use only one or two.

Information seeking was seen as a common pursuit in both public and academic libraries and is a paramount function in King Library. Public library customers look for information important to their work and personal lives – for example, information on sources of small-business grants. Academic users do curricular-based research, such as searching for scholarly articles for coursework. Information seeking requires good print and electronic collections and excellent reference and technical services staffs. To support these activities the library has a merged reference desk where both academic and public librarians provide reference assistance.

A wide range of spaces is provided in the library to support individual and group study as well as to create neutral spaces where public and university groups can meet. Group study spaces, library classrooms, computer labs and public service desks (e.g., reference, adult services, Teen Center and Cultural Heritage Center desks) all support both formal and informal learning. There is also a number of dedicated spaces such as the California Room and the Children's Education Resource Center, where parents, teachers and education students gather for dialogue, programmes and displays of curricular resources.

During the first year of operation visits to the King Library increased by almost 70 per cent compared with the number of visits to both libraries in the previous year and patrons of the public library increased their use of the print and media collections by 38 per cent (compared with the previous year's use in the former building) and university users increased their borrowing more than 100 per cent in the same time period.

Source: Peterson (2005)

Figure 6.10 Dr Martin Luther King Library, San José, US

Figures 6.11–12 Dr Martin Luther King Library, San José, US

cent – more than 9.3 million books and materials circulated in 2007, up from 4.8 million items in 1998. Library usage increased by 158 per cent with 11.6 million in person and virtual visitors in 2007, compared to 4.5 million in 2000. Library card registration had also increased by 53 per cent during this period.

In its first year of operation, the new central library was also associated with $16 million in net new spending in Seattle, because of the number of out-of-town visitors who came to see the new building.

Worcester Library and History Centre, UK

The Hive – Worcester Library and History Centre, designed by architects Feilden Clegg Bradley Studios – is the first joint use library in the UK: a public library and a university library (Figure 6.15). It emerged from a partnership between the University of Worcester and Worcestershire County Council to replace a range of provisions previously located across the city, uniting them in a single location to create an innovative new typology which exploits the synergies between the services provided to benefit and inspire users and staff (De Zeen 2012)

The vision was to create the first purpose-built, joint-use library in Europe where the city library collection is seamlessly integrated with the university collection to create a single resource for all users. Co-location with the County Archive and Local History Centre has furthered this ambition. The central location lent itself to the inclusion of a service centre for the local authority which, in addition to meeting the immediate needs of Worcester residents, encouraged them to explore the resources on offer at the Hive.

This vision for an agglomeration of public services under one roof is not unique – the rebranding of public libraries as 'Idea Stores' advertised their potential to provide a broader community resource. The integration with higher education is, however, a first in the UK.

Canada Water Library, London Borough of Southwark, UK

In late 2011, the Canada Water Library in South London was opened (in the same borough as the Peckham Library). Billed as London's new 'Super-library' the £14 million building, designed by CZWG Architects, contains 40,000 books, a cafe, meeting rooms, evening class space, 70 computers (40 fixed computers, 30 laptops for hire), wi-fi facilities and a purpose-built 150-seat theatre. There is direct access from the library to the adjacent tube station.

The library's inverted pyramid shape is designed to be a 'library as a living room' and to act as a 'civic hub' for the community.

The architect, Piers Gough, of CZWG architects, described the four-storey building as 'a park for the mind where users can learn and have space to think … I think of a library as a Pandora's Box of possibilities where you go looking for something or you come across something you didn't know you were going to come across' (This is London 2012).

Economic realities

While there have been undoubted successes with libraries embracing new roles and delivering a wide range of services supporting both formal and informal learning – the exemplar projects detailed in this chapter and the tool libraries, hackerspaces and fab labs shown in Chapter 2 to be responding to technological change – this has not been sufficient to isolate public libraries from the effects of the current economic environment and widespread government cutbacks in many parts of the world

The impact of the UK coalition government's Comprehensive Spending Review of November 2010 in England had by September 2011 already led to proposals for changes to the library service: it was estimated that around 400 libraries were currently under threat, had closed or left council control since 1 April, out of around 4,612 in the UK. Similar pressures on the library services also exist in the other parts of the UK.

A briefing note by the Carnegie Foundation at the time stated that responses to the cuts had varied, with some local authorities proposing deep cuts in library services, some creating new business structures to reduce the costs of taxation and rates, some turning to Private Finance Initiative to fund developments: others were experimenting with the use of volunteers and developing a model for community managed services (McDonald 2011: 5).

There were protests against disproportionate cuts to library services in various parts of the UK: in 2011, for example, it was reported that Doncaster Council had been asked to make 8.9 per cent savings but were proposing over 50 per cent cuts to the library budget (BBC 2011). Nationally, 11 February was designated as 'Save our libraries day' with an estimated 100 events taking place across England and many more in Scotland.

Financial pressures were also having an impact on public systems in the US:

> Dwindling tax dollars are forcing libraries to close branches, cut hours and end programs just as more people are turning to them for services … Cities are making tough choices, says Chris Hoene, director of policy and research at the National League of Cities. As people lose income or curb spending, income

tax and sales tax revenue falls. Local officials must choose between core services, such as police and fire protection, and services such as libraries and parks.

(*USA Today* 2009)

In 2010, *Newsweek* reported the American Library Association's view that the majority of the country's library systems were having

to make cuts and 'many of those cutbacks are quite devastating' despite the fact that libraries are experiencing increased demand (*Newsweek* 2010).

There has been considerable protest against the library cutbacks in the US. The Losing Libraries website, for example, is mapping various types of cuts, staff layoffs and furloughs, reduced services

Seattle Central Library houses more than one million books, movies (DVDs) and music CDs. It also contains a language centre with books, movies (DVDs) and music CDs to borrow in Spanish, Chinese, Vietnamese, Russian and East African languages, 400 free public computers and English as a Second Language (ESL) and citizenship resources including classes, books and DVDs. Equal access programmes provide resources for the blind, low vision, deaf and hard of hearing and there are classes

for children, teens and adults in multiple languages including author readings, lectures and book groups. An auditorium, meeting rooms and a training room are available for public use, in addition to defined areas for children and teens, a number of special collections areas and a coffee shop and gift shop.

Source: http://www.spl.org/locations/central-library/
cen-about-the-central-library

Figure 6.13 Seattle Central Library, Washington, US

Figure 6.14 Seattle Central Library, Washington, US

and hours and more that are happening to public libraries in the US. As the authors of the site state: 'Public libraries in the U.S. are in trouble. A LOT of trouble. We hope this map will help raise public awareness about the devastating cuts to libraries and assist libraries in similar circumstances to counteract cuts' (Losing Libraries 2012).

The author of the US Liberal Policies section of the about.com website goes even further and states that:

> the closure and severe limitation of public libraries is a travesty to a democratic society. And it's often a death knell

of democracy ... the public library plays an essential role in allowing all people to pursue the American Dream. Equal access to information is a basic right in a democratic society. And providing each child with the ability to read, a place to do homework and access to learning about his or her world is both a responsibility and source of pride in the US.

(about.com 2012)

In August 2011, the Local Government Group (LGG) in the UK published the findings of the first phase of the government's Future Libraries programme which they had initiated with the MLA prior to its abolition in 2010. *Future Libraries: Change, Options and How to Get*

The principal library is at second floor level where the six perimeter roof cones imply separate 'reading rooms', each of which provides a subtly different environment with contrasting views and light, accentuated by contrasts in colours used for floors and furniture. Book stack heights are varied to provide differing degrees of enclosure and acoustic environment. Even within this floor plate users can choose a study setting to suit their preferences.

The architecture reflects the library's aspiration to be accessible – it is deliberately populist in style and highly transparent in the hope that this will encourage the broadest range of visitors. It is designed to foster whole-life learning for the entire community, to promote social inclusion by access to education and inspiration and to be a catalyst for social mobility.

Source: Feilden Clegg Bradley Studios (2012)

Figure 6.15 Worcester Library and History Centre, UK

There described some of the approaches that councils are pursuing to develop, plan and implement change in their public library systems. The emerging delivery models reflected local needs and included:

- delivering the service network in different ways through co-location or new, non- traditional outlets and service points

- using external providers such as trusts and charitable companies, other councils or through the private sector

- sharing services with other councils to varying degrees of integration

- empowering communities to do things in their own way (LGG 2011: 4).

The overall goal of the change programmes described in the report was to improve the provision of library services while achieving cost reductions. The discussion on 'service location' included the collocation of libraries in shops, sports centres, village halls and children's centres, enabling services to share costs, extend opening hours and provide a more accessible service: there was no mention of the potential role of libraries in supporting both formal and informal education through collocation with schools, colleges or through the services offered in the libraries. The report does, however, note that 'libraries can contribute to a wide range of better outcomes for communities – from children and young people to older people, health and wellbeing and stronger communities to access to education, skills and employment' (ibid.: 19).

The Carnegie Foundation's November 2011 briefing paper on public libraries acknowledged the financial pressures making an impact on library services in the UK and reaffirmed the importance of public libraries in:

offering a neutral welcoming community space, holding large stocks of material and access to IT facilities, providing a venue for a wide range of services, such as supporting literacy through adult education or children's activities, and providing the services of trained librarians who can help members of the public find the information or resources they need. They have considerable scope to contribute to individual and community wellbeing, and address social exclusion.

(McDonald 2011: 5)

The Carnegie Foundation will be producing a report exploring how the public library service can support access to knowledge in the twenty-first century and to outline models of library provision that will meet the needs of the future in relation to:

● the challenge of reductions in public spending

● changing ways of accessing knowledge

● being a delivery agent for other local and central government services

● a central hub for community activity maintaining its traditional role in supporting reading, learning and literacy (ibid.: 8).

This report will also consider library buildings and those aspects that will contribute to making libraries attractive and supportive as well as the role of librarians in the twenty-first century.

Museums and galleries

The introduction of more formal education programmes in museums, galleries and other cultural institutions came relatively late to the world of collection and display and can – certainly in the US – be linked, according to George Hein, to the rise of progressive education policies in the late nineteenth and early twentieth centuries:

Museum education and progressive education both arose at the same historical period, approximately a century ago, and share not only a common history but also common features. Both emphasize pedagogy based on experience, interaction with objects, and inquiry. They also share a social vision of serving the entire society, including underserved audiences.

Progressive education principles included the broadening of the school curriculum beyond traditional subjects, the broadening of school responsibility to include concern for children's health and well being, as well as their intellectual and moral needs, the introduction of new pedagogies based on a better understanding of childhood development and a belief in the democratization of learning – that everyone should share in the benefits of the new sciences and the arts.

(2006: 164)

For John Dewey (1859–1952) – of whom it was said no philosopher, including Plato, examined education 'so long and so carefully' (Hawkins 1968: 25) – progressive education stressed practical experience as the basis for intellectual analysis and his vision of the 'ideal school' included libraries and museums in an organic whole in which life-experiences and specialized experiences such as reading and museum visits were unified. Dewy believed that the 'experience' in museums was valuable, but, by itself, not a complete life-experience. Like knowledge in books, it may be 'harmful as a substitute for experience,' but 'all-important in interpreting and expanding experience' (Hein 2004: 418).

Museums should be part of the active learning network of any school: 'we want to bring all things educational together; to break down the barriers that divide the education of the little child from the instruction of the maturing youth; to identify the lower and the higher education, so that it will be demonstrated to the eye that there is no lower and higher, but simply education' (Dewey 1897, quoted in Hein 2004: 413–27). For Dewey, regular museum visits, along with other kinds of field trips were a core element of the educational programme rather than a special once-a-year activity. He also believed that museums should be an integral part of any educational setting, and that the most desirable museums were those used for educational purposes and are associated with life activities outside the museum (ibid.: 419).

These principles were embraced by early museum educators such as Anna Billings Gallup (1872–1956) who joined the Brooklyn Children's Museum as curatorial assistant in 1902 and later became curator-in-chief. Her goal was to create a museum that, 'through its collections, library, curator and assistants will attempt to bring the child, whether attending school or not, into direct relation with the most important subjects that appeal to the interest of children in their daily life, in their school work, in their reading, in their games, in their rambles in the fields, and in the industries that are being carried on about them or in which they themselves later may become engaged' (Hein 2006: 166).

While progressive education fell out of favour in the 1940s and 1950s in the US, the 1960s saw renewed interest in progressive schools of all kinds: museums, especially children's museums, began to develop exhibits and programmes closely modelled on progressive practices. Education resurfaced as a central focus and museum education matured into an acknowledged profession

– supported by a growing literature in the field, graduate degree programmes in museum education, professional positions for museum educators, large, standing committees for educators within major professional museum organizations (international, national and regional), and journals dedicated to museum education (Hein 2011: 340).

Four London museums

A review of the education offer at four of London's main museums and galleries – the British Museum, the Victoria and Albert Museum, the National Gallery and the Natural History Museum – clearly illustrates the diversity of approach, in terms of space, programme and level of engagement with formal education.

British Museum

Education activities at the British Museum are centred on the Clore Education Centre which is located on the lower level of the Great Court. The centre consists of the:

- BP Lecture Theatre
- Hugh and Catherine Stevenson Theatre
- Raymond and Beverly Sackler seminar room
- Studio, used for art and craft activities
- Claus Moser seminar room
- Ford Centre for Young Visitors
- Samsung Digital Discovery Centre (British Museum 2012).

The Clore Education Centre has enabled the museum to expand its educational role and the museum now runs a daily programme of lectures, film and videos, as well as conferences, concerts and other performances related to cultural festivals or special exhibitions. Five additional multipurpose rooms are also used by the museum for other programmes including informal 'drop-in' sessions and courses for the general public and teacher training.

Victoria and Albert Museum

The Sackler Centre at the Victoria and Albert Museum (V&A) opened in 2008 – the V&A's centre for public learning through creative design and the arts, inspired by the museum and the breadth of its collections. It provides a space for debate on the current issues of design and its place in society, alongside opportunities to learn new, traditional and digital skills: 'every visitor to the V&A will be given the opportunity to take the knowledge and inspiration they get from our collections, and use it for creative practice in the Centre' (http://www.vam.ac.uk/content/articles/s/sackler-centre-for-arts-education-at-the-vanda/).

The centre is made up of an auditorium (for debates, lectures, talks, conferences, live performances and outside broadcasts), seminar rooms for courses, and design, digital and art studios for residencies, workshops, courses and drop-in programmes.

The V&A's programmes for schools, students, families, young people and adults utilize the museum's collections and staff, the expertise of creative professionals, and the skills of museum visitors and residents. The residency programme gives designers, writers, makers, musicians and artists of all kinds the opportunity to have a studio in the museum for six months. Two studios in the Sackler Centre provide space for four six-month residents each year, and a further fully equipped studio in the new ceramics galleries offers space for resident ceramicists. Using these studios as a base, residents have access to the V&A's resources, including the extensive collections, curatorial and conservation expertise, practical art, design and digital media workshops in the centre and experienced educational and outreach staff (http://www.vam.ac.uk/content/articles/s/sackler-centre-for-arts-education-at-the-vanda/).

National Gallery

At the National Gallery, educational programmes include services for adults, families and school children (including lectures, films, guided tours, study days to complement exhibitions), short talks, short courses and workshops, holiday activities and continuing professional development courses for primary and secondary school teachers. The education department runs an extensive outreach programme of talks and workshops.

Digital services include ArtStart, the National Gallery's interactive multimedia system that allows visitors to explore the collection for information on every painting in the gallery through the use of high-quality touch-screens on which every painting can be examined in detail via a 'zoom-able' image. The system also includes in-depth explorations of 30 of the collection's most popular paintings by means of video and audio clips. The 'Themes and Tours' section of the system allows paintings to be explored by topic, ranging from 'drunkenness and debauchery' to 'Impressionism' (http://www.nationalgallery.org.uk/visiting/artstart-interactive-guide). ArtStart can also help visitors plan their visit with pre-set themes tours or visitors can select up to ten paintings and a route map is created to help with the journey around the gallery.

Programmes for university and college students include 'Talk and draw' sessions where students join with an artist to explore a painting in two different ways and then make their own response by making a drawing with the materials provided.

Tailor-made tours and talks also form part of general adult learning programmes and a 'Keys to Creativity' toolkit is 'for anyone who would like to add a bit of creativity to their visit to the National Gallery'. On application, all visitors are allowed to sketch in the galleries using pencil, graphite and felt pens and oil and other paints (http://www.nationalgallery.org.uk/learning/inspired-by-the-collection/keys-to-creativity).

The National Gallery has also developed the 'Articulate' project, funded by Deutsche Bank, that aimed to support London schools that were under-performing in literacy to implement the National Literacy Strategy and improve the attainment of young people. Using the National Gallery's collections as a starting point, students worked closely with authors, poets, scriptwriters, playwrights and journalists in a series of masterclasses to develop their writing skills, exploring the variety of ways that images can be used to encourage different styles of writing. The work produced at the Gallery was continued and developed with English departments back at school (http://www.nationalgallery.org.uk/articulate/).

The three-year project created a sustained period of contact with targeted schools which gave the students a purpose to write that stimulated their imaginations and motivated them and helped the schools develop their confidence in accessing and using cultural institutions such as the National Gallery and embedding the project into the practice of the school.

The authors of an evaluation into the first three years of the programme felt that its success clearly reflects wider findings about the power of learning in museums and galleries: 'Enjoyment was a clear factor in the experiences of teachers and students. Previous studies have shown that teachers consider enjoyment to act as a catalyst to a range of other learning outcomes. If students enjoy their experience at the museum or gallery they are more motivated to learn. The importance of an emotional or personal connection to learning was also highlighted' (http://www.nationalgallery.org.uk/articulate/pub/pdf/articulate1.pdf).

The findings of the programme evaluation 'therefore point to the National Gallery as making a strong contribution to the creation of a "rich and tangible learning environment" ... providing enjoyable, effective and stimulating pathways to learning for all [young people]' (Hooper-Greenhill 2006: xv).

Natural History Museum

The Natural History Museum (Figures 6.16 and 6.17) has education activities and resources aimed at each educational stage of schooling from five years and upwards with activities at the museum complemented by lessons at the school both before and after the visit. The educational programme has recently been expanded with the opening of the Darwin Centre, the museum's scientific research and collections facility which consists of a central bank of laboratories and specimen storage facilities surrounded by a spiral path of interactive exhibits exploring various aspects of the natural sciences and the research process (Natural History Museum 2013).

Outreach programmes

As well as providing a wide range of education programmes on site, many universities, galleries and cultural institutions also have outreach educational programmes where individual artefacts and curated exhibitions are lent to external institutions including schools and smaller regional museums that can be accessed by schools and the wider community.

The Alberta Foundation for the Arts (AFA), for example, has supported a provincial travelling exhibition programme since 1981 with a mandate 'to provide every Albertan with the opportunity to enjoy visual art exhibitions in their community' (http://www.affta.ab.ca/travelling-exhibition.aspx). The programme is a collaboration between three regional galleries and one arts organization who provide both the curated exhibitions and the educational support material to help educators integrate the visual arts into the school curriculum. Each year more than 300,000 Albertan's visit nearly 100 exhibitions across the region in local community centres, schools, colleges and other public venues.

Venues select exhibitions from the TREX (TRavelling EXhibitions) catalogue. A description of each exhibition is provided along with a contents list, the associated educational resources, the number of crates the exhibition is transported in and the number of feet of wall space required to hang the exhibition. Exhibitions are booked on a monthly time slot. Schools and other venues pay an administration charge of $75 per exhibition and all shipping and insurance costs are covered by the AFA programme (http://www.affta.ab.ca/travelling-exhibition.aspx) (AFA 2011).

The Scottish Arts Council has taken the process even further by building on the long history of mobile libraries supporting schools and communities in rural areas. The Travelling Gallery is a unique, self-contained, custom-built mobile art gallery, which brings contemporary art exhibitions into communities throughout Scotland. The Travelling gallery visits schools, as well as high streets, community centres, shopping centres, art centres, hospitals and colleges across the region.

The Travelling Gallery was established by the Scottish Arts Council (SAC) in 1978 and the first vehicle was a converted double-decker bus that was staffed by a lone curator/driver. The project was successful and in 1983 the SAC commissioned a custom-built

The science theatre is used for a wide range of educational programmes including a number of set piece multimedia presentations and demonstrations – an immersive 'cocoon experience', interactive film (narrated by Sir David Attenborough), an animal adaptation feature, an interactive 'variety' science show, an exploration of the role the museum plays in the wider community and lectures on science techniques.

There are over 300 researchers and curators, at the Natural History Museum with access to more than 70 million specimens, of which 800,000 are type specimens. Eighty PhD students are also based at the museum, undertaking research with the students registered with a British university from which they receive the postgraduate degree.

There are also two Masters courses run at the museum: an MSc Taxonomy and Biodiversity and an MRes Biosystematics which is a one-year research-based postgraduate course run jointly by Imperial College London and the Natural History Museum. Students on the MRes course are trained in research techniques in systematics, taxonomy, evolutionary biology and bioinformatics as a stepping-stone to a PhD or research-related career.

Source: Natural History Museum (2103)

Figure 6.16 The Natural History Museum, London: world-class science and research

Figure 6.17 The Natural History Museum, London: extensive and engaging schools programme

vehicle which was used for the next 25 years. In 1996, the City of Edinburgh Council took over the running of the Travelling Gallery with funding from the SAC. In 2006, the Travelling Gallery was granted around £300,000 of funding to research, develop and build a new vehicle to replace the gallery: the new bus went into operation in 2007 (SAC 2007).

The new gallery is a custom-built single-storey wheelchair accessible unit and the interior of the gallery is a carpeted single rectangular space with natural light entering through roof panels and a narrow window at the rear of the gallery, with additional lighting provided by a suspended lighting track. The exhibition programme explores concepts and technologies which are representative of current trends in international, contemporary art and the exhibitions range from specially commissioned one and two-person installations to themed group shows and visionary collaborations.

Educational institutions may also be established and based within or near the museum or galleries where the collection forms an important element of the learning, teaching and research experience. The Museum School in San Diego was established in 1998 as a partnership between the Children's Museum/Museo and the San Diego Unified School District – a tuition-free, public charter school that serves students from all over San Diego in Kindergarten up to sixth grade. A central part of the learning and teaching approach for the school is experiential, project-based learning and the school utilizes the resources available at local museums and within the wider San Diego community (Museum School 2012).

The Museum School is located in a facility next to the museum. Its flexible floor plan is designed both for direct instruction (an entire class) and for cooperative learning groups of from three to five children. Major exhibitions at the museum, such as 'Design Worlds-Diseño Mundos' – the most comprehensive exhibition about design in the US created specifically for children – are incorporated into the curriculum. During the planning period for this year-long exhibition, for example, students designed and built desks to use throughout the school year. This project employed basic design principles intended to enhance the students' maths and motor skills, while at the same time their classroom work informed the museum staff and the curators of 'Design Worlds-Diseño Mundos' during the final months of planning and building the exhibition (Fowler 1998).

Museum, school and higher education integration
The integration of school and museum has also been extended further into both high school and higher education. The Henry Ford Academy of Manufacturing Arts & Sciences, for instance, is chartered by Wayne County RESA (Regional Educational Service Agency) and set on the premises of Henry Ford Museum & Greenfield Village, Dearborn, Michigan. The museum and Ford Motor Company are the founding partners of the academy, which is 'committed to an intensive use of innovative instructional technologies and employing the theme of manufacturing as a lens through which to develop an interdisciplinary curriculum that would meet state and national academic standards' (Pittman and Pretzer 1998).

When it opened in 1997 – as a four-year public high school academy for 400 students in grades 9 to 12 – the school was believed to be the first major collaborative effort of its type, involving a global corporation, a not-for-profit cultural organization and the public schools system.

The new school builds on earlier educational programmes started by Henry Ford. The Ford indoor/outdoor museum and the Greenfield Village School opened in 1929 and at its height enrolled more than 400 students in grades 1 to 12. Greenfield Village operated as an independent school as well as a museum for the visiting public until the school closed in 1969.

Much of the core learning space for the academy is located within the museum exhibit area. Classrooms have been constructed in the museum space using glazing and aluminium shop front systems that provide both acoustic separation of the classroom spaces and security for the students and teachers. The academy's offices and ninth-grade learning studios are within full view of hundreds of thousands of visitors a year.

The rest of the school is located in Greenfield Village, which consists of farms, fields and historic buildings. Non-historic structures such as an old restaurant and arcade have been converted into learning studios, project rooms, staff offices and a cafeteria.

The integration between museum and academy extends as far as a cafeteria that is shared by museum employees and students. There were concerns from staff about noise, so schedules were devised to ensure that there were no more than 35 students in the cafeteria at one time and that they are supervised by staff while dining.

The teachers for the academy are recruited both from industry and education and teachers are encouraged to develop lesson plans that draw on the resources of the internet, the museum and Ford Motor Company, as well as more traditional sources. Ford company employees serve as 'academic coaches' and project experts:

> Students use museum artefacts and exhibitions for analysis, inspiration, and association. For example, students in math class used the museum structure itself as a resource, making estimates and calculations of geometrically symmetrical window, wall, and ceiling areas as well as irregular exhibit spaces. Clear plastic covers on light switches and security boxes provide opportunities for science and technology lessons. Emphasizing the 'muse' in 'museum,' students in the language arts class found a spot in the museum and recorded their impressions of the environment, once in prose and once in poetry. Students produced brass candlesticks using early 20th-century machine tools and calculated tool speeds, feed rates, and mechanical advantage in the historic Greenfield Village machine shop as part of their study of physics. A discussion in civics began in front of the chair Abraham Lincoln was sitting in that fateful night at Ford's Theater.
>
> (Pittman and Pretzer 1998)

The School Museum of Fine Arts in Boston, Massachusetts (also known as the Museum School or SMFA) is an undergraduate and graduate college that specializes in the visual arts. It is affiliated with the Museum of Fine Arts in Boston and offers undergraduate and graduate degrees programmes through Tufts University and North-eastern University (SFMA 2012).

The school's main campus is next to the Museum of Fine Arts and most classroom space is located there, as well as the Cafe des Arts, the library, the school's store and the Grossman Gallery. Other studio spaces for graduate and post-Baccalaureate students as well as classrooms, workshops, the writing centre and the registrar's office are located in the Mission Hill Building about a quarter of a mile from the main building. The school also shares on-campus housing at the Artist's Residence Hall with the Massachusetts College of Art.

One of the unusual aspects of SMFA is that there are no grades in studio classes; credit is awarded through a 'review board', which is a review of all of the art work that a student has done during the semester. Review boards are led by two faculty members, one of whom is the students' choice, and two fellow students. Students have many opportunities to exhibit their work each year in the various galleries and spaces that are available to students in the SMFA Buildings as well as in the Museum of Fine Arts itself (http://www.smfa.edu/about-smfa).

Museum/education partnerships

The impact of partnerships between museums and educational partnerships was explored in a 2004 UK report commissioned by the Department of Culture, Media and Sport (DCMS) and undertaken by the Research Centre for Museums and Galleries based at the University of Leicester (RCMG) to evaluate 12 National/Regional Museum Education Partnerships 2003–4 (RCMG 2004). The report found that museums inspire powerful and identity-building learning in children, young people and community members. They:

- inspire learners across all age ranges

- are sites of enhanced achievement, going beyond what learners think they can do

- engage both boys and girls

- stimulate vulnerable pupils and those that find learning difficult

- target and motivate disadvantaged individuals and groups effectively

- provide resources for all curriculum areas, and for inter-disciplinary themes

- respond effectively to primary, secondary, FE and HE curricula

- complement formal education when pupils are off curriculum (hospital schools, pupils who are refugees).

The authors of the report also found that students were very enthusiastic about museums – and sometimes more confident about the impact of the museum experience on their learning than their teachers were.

Of the teachers surveyed, 85 per cent stated that their visit was directly linked to the delivery of the national curriculum. Themes they identified included history, science and technology, geography, art, citizenship and personal, social and health education, literacy/English and cross-curricular studies. The report also found that teachers who were working with science-based themes were the least confident about using museums, and the least likely to use them in a broad- based way: this was felt to be a significant development opportunity for museums in the future.

Stated barriers that limited the use of museums by teachers included transportation difficulties, levels of administration and risk assessment, perceived curriculum constraints, getting replacement cover for teachers in secondary schools and a lack of knowledge about what it is possible and realistic to expect museums to do linked to limited communication with the museums concerned.

The evaluation concluded:

> clear evidence of impact on learning has been found across the whole range of individuals, groups and communities as part of both formal and informal learning. In addition, it is clear that there is a potential for using museums to engage with children and young people who are often not reached, or stimulated, by more conventional methods of teaching. Museums can work effectively with both special needs and vulnerable groups and also with the mainstream.

> The challenge now is to find the structures and the means to use the power to inspire learning and to build identities more effectively and more consistently. The research found barriers to the realisation of this power in those aspects of museum culture that marginalised educational work, in the capacity of museums to respond to the demands of ambitious educational programmes, and in the limited expectations of museum users and partners who did not know how to maximise the learning potential of museums.

> (ibid.)

Beyond museums and galleries

Institutions other than museums and galleries are also working more closely with educational establishments: national parks, botanic gardens and wildlife reserves. The Eden Project, for example (Figures 6.18 and 6.19) is an educational charity and visitor attraction in Cornwall in the UK owned and operated by the Eden Trust – a limited company and UK registered charity. It was built in a 160-year-old exhausted china clay quarry near St Austell and was one of the Landmark Millennium Projects to mark the year 2000.

A programme of research funded by the Calouste Gulbenkian Foundation has been examining the social role and relevance of contemporary botanic gardens. One of the research projects, commissioned by Botanic Gardens Conservation International (BGCI) and undertaken by the Research Centre for Museums and Galleries (RCMG) at the University of Leicester specifically looked at the future role of botanic gardens.

The authors of the report state that the botanic garden community is now more aware of the need for their social relevance, of working in partnership with their local communities and addressing contemporary concerns such as climate change. However, they feel that the full potential of botanic gardens in this field remains unrealized (RCMG 2010: 2).

Collectively they offer a range of educational experiences, from academic, specialist courses to lifelong learning opportunities for school and community groups. They also engage in research of local and global socioeconomic importance, developing medicines and hardier crops, methods of seed storage and conservation strategies.

The study found that while many botanic gardens are well established as educators in a formal sense, their role as informal learning environments, frequently involving practical, multisensory engagement with plants and sites, is less well documented.

Yet, as custodians of living plant collections that are often displayed in an informal, relaxed way, they are ideal environments in which to demonstrate how important plants and people are to each other. Botanic gardens can enable links between urban society and the natural world to be re-established, providing education and

---

The Eden Project includes the world's largest greenhouse – two huge adjoining domes that house thousands of plant species and more than one million plants. Each dome emulates a natural biome – one a tropical environment and the other a Mediterranean environment.

The Education Centre – the Core – opened in September 2005, providing the project with a wide range of interactive displays, classrooms and exhibition spaces designed to help communicate the central message about the relationship between people and

plants. In the evening, the Core becomes an arts venue hosting live acts and DJs throughout the year.

More than 50,000 pupils and students of all ages visit the Eden Project every year from across the UK and Europe for workshops linked to the National Curriculum, in a range of subjects including geography, art, science (biodiversity, biology, botany, conservation, ecology, and horticulture), architecture and sustainability.

Source: http://www.edenproject.com/come-and-visit/whats-here/the-core

Figure 6.18 The Eden Project, Cornwall, UK

Figure 6.19 The Eden Project, Cornwall, UK: Core Education Centre

physical engagement with our surroundings: 'By raising awareness of issues of social and environmental justice among their audiences and local communities, botanic gardens can also support more wide ranging action on global moral issues' (ibid.: 5).

The authors noted that there is considerable variation around the extent to which education is embedded in the culture of the respective botanical gardens and found limited evidence of research into learning experiences in the botanic gardens. They found that successful programmes take a lifelong and holistic approach to learning and can have a major impact on their partici-pants, boosting knowledge and enhancing social well-being and self-esteem.

Impact of increasing financial pressures

Despite the evident educational and social benefits of museums, there are increasing financial pressures on schools in many locations that make visits to museums more difficult or

unaffordable. An article in the *Observer* in the UK, for example, on 8 May 2011 was headlined 'School trips to museums are a thing of the past as budget cuts bite'. The author, Daniel Boffey, reported that thousands of children are missing out on trips to Britain's museums and galleries even though educational visits have been shown to help raise standards, improve behaviour and aid personal development. Cuts to school budgets have meant that schools can not afford to pay for supply teachers to cover staff away on the museum visit:

> The Office for Standards in Education (Ofsted) says school trips can 'contribute significantly to the raising of standards'. Funding for schools, however, has been squeezed in real terms since the coalition came to power and critics claim headteachers have been put under pressure to reduce 'non-essential' spending, including on supply teachers required to cover lessons for colleagues engaged on visits.

(Boffey 2011)

Parents were, in some cases, being asked to contribute towards the costs of hiring supply teachers as well as the cost of the school trip. Boffey also noted that the current education secretary, Michael Gove, had dismissed a recent recommendation from the House of Commons Schools Select Committee to ensure that each pupil had at least one trip every term.

Bellamy and Oppenheim (2009), reviewing the provision of education spaces in museums, concluded that museums have responded to the needs of children and young people by creating children's projects and spaces, developing education programmes, and bringing schools in: 'It is once again recognised that museums' learning programmes can grow out of and are underpinned by museums' scholarship – offering the public the chance to engage with collections and contribute to knowledge of them – rather than threatening museums' academic focus or reputation' (p. 12).

They cited the Science Museum's relaunched Launchpad, for example, which attracted 1.2 million visitors in its first year, and the new British Galleries at the Victoria & Albert museum, with their participative exhibits and interactive areas, as examples of good practice. However, they ask whether this is sufficient.

> The task ahead, surely, is not merely to provide some facilities which meet the needs of children and young people, but to see them as partners with equal rights in museums, and in dialogue with them treat them as equal participants in determining what museums offer.
>
> (p. 11)

The challenge for the future is to find new and financially sustainable ways that museums and galleries can continue and develop their involvement in all levels of education – to move away from the notion of the annual school museum visit towards one where museums and galleries are part of an integrated network of learning spaces used by schools, colleges and universities as a fundamental part of their learning and teaching approach.

The goal should be to return, in some way, to the pioneering vision of Dewey. The timetable for the Laboratory school he established in the 1890s is instructive.

> an hour and a half was set aside on Monday mornings for trips to the Field Columbian Museum. ... The younger children had a plot of ground ... where they often went to observe seasonal changes in nature. Older children went to the university laboratories to such instruments as the interferometer and spectroscope. There were also longer trips – to the quarry

on Stoney Island where glacial markings were observed, to the cotton mills in Aurora to see the spinning of cotton, and others to Ravinia to see the clay bluffs, to Miller Station to see the sand dunes and desert and to Sixty-third street and the city limits to see a typical prairie area.

> (Hein 2004: 418)

Real lifelong learning – retirement communities linked to academic institutions

The rise of the distributed workplace in the corporate sector (Harrison et al. 2004) is offering opportunities for academic institutions to capitalize on their existing estates by, among other initiatives, creating mixed academic and business campuses (Harrison and Dugdale 2004). This blurring of the boundaries between the corporate and the academic worlds opens up new possibilities for the coming together of living and learning that include linking retirement communities to academic institutions: the goal, after all, is lifelong learning.

In 2006, an article in *Planning for Higher Education*, the journal of the Society for College and University Planning (SCUP), looked in detail at the growing trend in the US for university-linked retirement communities and its relationship with social housing trends in Europe and showed that it provided a way for universities to earn revenue at the same time as enhancing the quality of life of both students and staff (Harrison and Tsao 2006: 20). The article pointed out that the growing proportion of older people worldwide presents challenges for society as a whole, but opportunities for higher education institutions (ibid.: 21).

Increasing numbers of these older people are participating in adult education. In the UK, research from the Learning and Skills Council (LSC) has shown that more 'over 60s' are signing up for part-time courses – of the 3.5 million people undertaking education and work-based learning, 7 per cent (237,000) are now over the age of 60 (Ford 2002). Research also confirms that such participation brings health, social inclusion and quality of life benefits (Smithers 2000). In the US, the percentage of adults aged 55 and over participating in educational activities has increased sixfold within 15 years, from 5.7 per cent in 1984 (Manheimer et al. 1995) to 37.9 per cent in 2001 for 55 to 64 year olds, and to 21.4 per cent for those age 65 and above (National Center for Education Statistics 2003).

At a conservative estimate, 14 million Americans aged 55 and over are pursuing lifelong learning by participating in work and non-work-related learning activities through formal and informal adult education programme providers.

In a presentation at the University of North Carolina at Greensboro, Professor Leon Pastalan of the University of Michigan described higher education's role in an active retirement: 'People are no longer satisfied with a condo and a golf course. They are looking for more value and meaning' (2001: 6).

College-linked retirement communities already exist at more than 60 US campuses and this figure is predicted to increase significantly over the next two decades as many of the nation's 76 million baby boomers reach retirement age (Alexander 2003).

In her 2003 *New York Times* article 'Prime time: how the baby boomers will revolutionize retirement and transform America', Alexander cited Marc Freedman's 2002 book of the same name. Freedman suggested that, at the very least, these communities could provide a revenue generator for universities and a pleasant way for older people to while away their days – and, at best, they will satisfy the baby boomers' increasing appetite for lifelong education (Freedman 2002).

The nature of the relationship between the retirement community and the university varies – some communities include alumni; some have informal ties to university programmes and others offer residents access to university healthcare services and gerontology experts as well as courses. There is also a range of factors driving universities to develop retirement communities associated with their campuses:

- a mutually empowering relationship between colleges/universities and campus retirement communities – older adults are an invaluable human resource, contributing to the diversity of campus life and in turn benefiting from the opportunities to explore learning, working, and leisure while ageing

- property development and financial considerations – collegiate retirement communities have great potential to add land value and generate revenues from the sale or lease of land and facilities

- demand from alumni, retired faculty and staff – University Commons at the University of Michigan, conceived as an active adult residential community on campus in which residents could continue their affiliation with the university; faculty and staff members established the University Condominium Association, purchased land from the university, and collaborated with Blue Hill Development, a local developer, to make the idea a reality

- demand from developers – joint ventures between universities and developers have acknowledged the allure of 'big name'

colleges lined with a large potential market of alumni, retired faculty and staff members

- a response to the social challenge of increased life expectancy – the majority of older adults are healthy, vigorous, and capable of taking on new challenges after the end of their working life; the low expectations and empty roles traditionally associated with retirement are no longer always relevant. Colleges and universities have traditionally been agents of social change by contributing to the solution of major problems encountered both within their local community and in wider society. Recognizing the new social challenges resulting from increased longevity, some universities are attempting to develop new models for retirement and lay the foundations for attitudinal change (Tsao 2008).

Existing retirement communities can be broadly categorized in terms of two main variables: the level of university involvement in the community and the level of care provided to the residents. 'Low level' university involvement could include the sale or lease of a site to a developer or operator of commercial retirement communities. 'High level' university involvement can be defined as closer integration of the community into the academic and social life of the institution – externally or internally. High-level involvement suggests that the university has considered in some detail the potential benefits of developing a community.

A 'low level' of care would be 'independent living', where residents are in relatively good health and require no medical or social support on a daily basis (Box 6.1). If medical care is required, it may be provided in-house in a medical centre or procured externally (e.g., through third-party health insurance companies). A 'high level' of care can be described as 'assisted living', where a wide range of health and social services are provided, up to and including Alzheimer's long-term care and hospice care for the terminally ill (Box 6.2).

Retirement community, Arusha, Tanzania

The Harrison and Tsao research cited above (2006 and 2008) underpinned the planning for the creation of a retirement community in the Aga Khan University's Faculty of Arts and Sciences campus in east Africa currently under development in Arusha, Tanzania (Figure 6.20). The proposal is for a retirement community integrated into the core FAS campus to provide, among other things, a major pastoral care resource to support the core curriculum students who will be coming to the campus from diverse backgrounds. If participation in mentoring programmes were to be made a condition for residency in the community, a 400-unit community could provide 400–600 mentors for the 800 core curriculum students.

A wide range of shared facilities would be provided for community residents including shared dining rooms, club rooms and libraries, digital cinema, computer resources centres and workshops, seminar and meeting rooms and a fitness centre. While residents would be able to be completely self-sufficient within their own units, they would be encouraged to participate actively in the life of the community, including student and community mentoring projects and educational and cultural activities.

While the emphasis should be on providing accommodation for recently retired people seeking educational challenges and willing to mentor others, it is likely that the community would also include a significant number of residents still actively engaged in employment in some way, working on consulting projects or continuing to manage their businesses virtually for parts of the year. The name of the community would probably focus on wellbeing and work–life balance rather than retirement.

Residents would benefit in a number of ways from this community existence – a unique living experience blending living, learning, working and service and with access to a wide range of cultural and learning experiences. They would also be part of an international community with shared values about the importance of education and of giving back to the community. For the university, the retirement community could provide a significant pastoral care resource and a substantial 'knowledge and expertise bank' providing guest lecturers and members of research teams on FAS and community-based research projects. Residents' business experience could also support FAS innovation and business incubation activities.

Box 6.1 University Commons – independent living

University Commons consists of 92 apartments and townhouses aimed at University of Michigan alumni or retired faculty over the age of 55. As well as individually owned units, the community provides 17,000 square feet of common space including a large lecture and recital facility, dining room and commercial kitchen, library, crafts workshop, fitness centre and seminar rooms.

The community hosts a regular schedule of lectures, classes, seminars and music performances. Residents can attend classes and events at the nearby campus. All the learning spaces and living units are connected to MERIT, the university's higher education internet network (Rose 2002).

Box 6.2 The Village at Penn State – assisted living

At the Village at Penn State, residents pay an entrance fee ranging from $166,100 to $361,700, with a second-person fee of $10,900 for lifetime use of an apartment. A monthly service charge is levied on top of the entrance fee, depending on the size of the apartment. Residents have priority access to university cultural and sporting events, university classes on a space-available basis, and transportation to campus for group activities, presentations, workshops and activities. The fee also covers utility charges (except telephone and cable television), scheduled housekeeping and linen service, 20 meals per month, and delivery of the daily university newspapers. Residents are also entitled to 'priority access to on-site assisted living and skilled nursing care at virtually no increase in the monthly service fee' (The Village at Penn State 2005).

Figure 6.20 Mt Meru: possible retirement outlook from Aga Khan University's Faculty of Arts and Sciences, Arusha, Tanzania

PART 3
Developing a community learning model

CHAPTER 7

The blending of institutions

Part 2 has shown graphic evidence of the extent of change across the learning landscape, with schools and institutions of further and higher education responding in varying degrees to the demands of technological, legislative, social and pedagogic pressures and an array of new interstitial areas from libraries to conference centres widely and imaginatively extending learning far beyond the academy.

These demands – and the communities from which they spring – have changed dramatically, as Part 1 made clear: connecting and empowering students through technology, undergoing a constant cycle of changing pedagogical styles and their impact on learning settings, meeting a cascade of government initiatives and unforeseen (and sometimes unforeseeable) events, blurring the distinction between physical and virtual learning spaces and even linking activities *without* settings.

The complexity of this change has required an equally complex spatial response which has only sometimes been forthcoming. Do those projects that seem to be the most successful – evincing greater flexibility, mobility, agility, value and resilience to change – reveal usable (and scaleable) lessons in the ways in which they have responded to this array of new challenges? Do they show characteristics that can account, in any systematic way, for their success?

It is immediately apparent that in each of the sectors we have looked at – schools, higher education and beyond – there is wide evidence of a move towards the spatial, societal, generational and pedagogical blending of all aspects of learning into one seamless experience: institutions blending with other institutions, institutions creating two separate institutions in a symbiotic relationship and even, occasionally, institutions creating hubs in networks.

Three exemplars illustrate this tendency and point up some of its benefits. In Christchurch, NZ, the Discovery 1 and Unlimited Paenga Tawhiti (UPT) schools inserted education into another space type, mixing abilities and using the city itself as a learning resource. In Helsinki, Finland, the Design Factory in Aalto University brought together the faculty, students and the business world in the process of design. In London's Natural History Museum, researchers and curators work side by side with PhD and MA students accredited to a British university for work carried out at the museum.

DISCOVERY 1/UNLIMITED PAENGA TAWHITI, CHRISTCHURCH, NZ

Discovery 1 School is a special character, state-funded primary school in Christchurch, New Zealand, that has been in operation for more than ten years. It was originally set up in underused space above a department store, with students directing and managing their own learning based on their interests. Learning could take place anywhere with no restriction of curriculum, place, time, style or subject, and learning goals agreed by students, staff and parents. Its sister school, UPT, was based on a similar pedagogical model. Community mentors and businesses supplemented learning resources (Figure 7.1).

The 6.1 magnitude earthquake in New Zealand's oldest city in February 2011 killed 185 people and largely destroyed the city centre, with 1,400 buildings irreparably damaged. Post-earthquake, the Christchurch regeneration plan aims to give the city the feel of a university campus, set round the River Avon (Gayle 2012). The declared aim is to build the city centre as a series of hubs featuring related activities – a health precinct anchored by a hospital, a justice precinct with courts and a police station. This offered the possibility of rebuilding the city's education facilities as the heart of the city. A Ministry of Education report, published in October 2012, insists that 'a strong education network is vital for the renewal of greater Christchurch' and recognizes that the earthquakes 'while devastating, have provided an opportunity beyond simply replacing what was there, to restore, consolidate and rejuvenate to provide new and improved facilities that will reshape education, improve the options and outcomes for learners, and support greater diversity and choice' (NZ Ministry of Education 2012: 1).

It seems that this opportunity will only be taken up in a limited way. The new public library, for instance, *is* being relocated to the main square but since the old library did suffer $8 million worth of damage this move hardly constitutes a bold philosophical initiative: the initiative does create networks of learning spaces but makes no real connection with city or university amenities.

Discovery 1 is a primary school that was originally established in underused space over a department store in the centre of Christchurch, NZ. The flexible attitude towards ownership of space indicates that Discovery 1 was clearly offering a distributed learning model of space use, with students using the city facilities for sports, libraries and recreation, and students, of mixed age, working at home. Children travelled in groups between learning settings during the day, with older children unescorted, though provided with mobile phones in case of problems. Discovery 1's sister school, Unlimited Paenga Tawhiti, is a co-educational state secondary school that was also established in space above a nearby block of shops, providing secondary level education based on a similar model: mixed abilities, using the city as a learning resource, learning taking place without restriction of curriculum, place, time, style or subject and with learning goals agreed by students, staff and parents. In 2011, UPT was planning to open its central city space as a 24-hour learning centre for the community. Before this could happen, both schools were completely destroyed by the 2011 Christchurch earthquake.

Figure 7.1 Discovery 1, Christchurch, NZ

Discovery 1 is to be merged with Unlimited Paenga Tawhiti, which will create opportunities to create an integrated learning experience covering years 1 to 13.

The consultation document for the proposed merger says that the ministry 'would expect a merged school would want to work with all learners in its community' (ibid.: 5). Although it is reassuring to know that all spaces will be 'upgraded to meet the "Sheerin Core" modern environment standard – which has a strong focus on heating, lighting, acoustics, ventilation and ICT infrastructure upgrades' (ibid.: 5) – there is no suggestion that Discovery and Unlimited's slice of the government's $1 billion ten-year budget 'to enhance education outcomes across greater Christchurch' is the first step to creating a much broader community of learning across Christchurch.

The Design Factory is a 3,000 square metre innovation space housed in a redundant engineering workshop building at Aalto University in Helsinki. Work is interdisciplinary – science, engineering and business – and researchers take over the space to work on specific design and development projects. The space provides access to prototyping workshops as well as work and meeting spaces. A growth entrepreneurship programme, Bootcamp, run four times a year, offers start-up companies the opportunity to build up their product and test their ideas in a competition: winners receive €5,000 in seed funding, exclusive coaching and workspace.

Figure 7.2 Design Factory, Aalto University, Helsinki

DESIGN FACTORY, AALTO UNIVERSITY, HELSINKI, FINLAND

The Design Factory is one of three 'factory' projects at Aalto University – Media, Service and Design – serving as experimental platforms, showrooms and sources of inspiration. The university is committed, says Design Factory director Kalevi 'Eetu' Ekman, to developing and cultivating a 'passion-based, student centric learning culture' and in essence the Design Factory is 'a place where students, teachers, researchers and industry partners can interact under the same roof' (Aalto Design Factory 2012). It is, he claims, 'the symbiosis of the state-of-the-art conceptual thinking and cross-disciplinary hands-on doing. It leads a way towards a paradigm shift in education and business by providing a constantly developing collaboration environment for students, researchers and business practitioners'. This sounds a lot like true blended learning (Figure 7.2), with the design itself taking place on campus – compared with, say, the Blizard experience in Queen Mary, London, which is a good example of a flexible research facility, *layering* science and the community: there are no children actually *in* the labs.

Opened in 2008, the Design Factory is made up of a 3,000 square metre work environment that enables creative work, knowledge sharing and experience exchange. The spaces are all designed for flexible use and can be reconfigured to support a wide range of activities from large lectures and presentations to intensive workshops and the development of product prototypes. The open layout and the wide range of shared facilities including kitchen and eating areas are designed to encourage open communication and spontaneous encounters between Aalto faculty and staff, students and business start-ups.

For students the Design Factory provides holistic learning experiences solving real-life challenges in multidisciplinary teams often involving international partnerships. In terms of engagement with industry, the Design Factory website states that 'the Factory is an innovative environment for finding, incubating, and realizing new ideas together with leading scholars, top future talent, and a mixture of other companies'. The site also suggests that the Design Factory is a good way to recruit future staff members.

The Design Factory also has links to Aalto Venture Garage (Aaltovg 2012) which is a 700 square metre open source co-working space and seed accelerator for Baltic & Nordic entrepreneurs located in an adjacent building. Anyone is able to use the main hall as work and development space for business start-ups. Aalto Venture Garage is part of the Aalto Centre of Entrepreneurship (ACE) which coordinates all activities related to technology transfer, intellectual property management, start-up companies and the teaching and research of growth entrepreneurship at Aalto University. The Aalto Entrepreneurship Society ('The Aaltoes') also uses the Garage to host many of its events (Aaltoes 2012).

Programmes at the Venture Garage include 'Start-up Sauna', bringing together promising start-ups from different cities from around the Baltic Rim for an intense mentoring and development programme, and the 'Summer of Start-ups', a ten-week programme targeted at students and researchers from Finland and Northern Europe as well as the rest of the world (Aalto Venture Garage 2012).

NATURAL HISTORY MUSEUM, LONDON, UK

The Natural History Museum in London has a remarkable array of collections and links its science and research mission – 'to explore the diversity of the natural world and the processes that generate this diversity ... use the knowledge gained to promote responsible interaction with the natural world' – with a wide education commitment (Figure 7.3).

This means that not only is the museum a highly regarded research institute but that school activities, linked to key stage levels, engage children with the big ideas of science and nature in an inspiring location. This is extended to family activities such as self-led museum trails, hands-on activities and shows and talks, and adult activities for informal learners – lifelong learning. Relationships with community groups have led to free, tailor-made programmes based on the collections and include physically handling the specimens.

In partnership with a network of museums with natural history collections – Oxford University Museum of Natural History, the Manchester Museum, Great North Museum: Hancock, Stoke-on-Trent Museums, Leeds Museums and Galleries, Peterborough Museum and Wollaton Hall (Nottingham Museums and Galleries) – the museum runs a Real World Science programme aimed at enriching and enhancing science teaching and learning at upper primary and secondary levels. Activities include facilitated discussions with leading research scientists, science shows and practical workshops.

Real World Science (RWS) learning activities aim to engage and inspire secondary school students to study science further, to pursue a science-related career, or gain confidence as a scientifically literate individual who feels more prepared to discuss scientific issues. RWS learning activities are based on certain guiding principles and beliefs: developments must meet audience, organizational and strategic needs; authenticity enhances engagement; inspiration and aspiration lead to transformation; multiple approaches to delivery are needed to cater for a diverse range of learners; partnership fosters professional practice.

Academic, school and private visitors and researchers engaged in structured and informal courses of study and inquiry are served by one of the world's key science institutions. Interactive exhibits allow visitors to follow up areas of interest by linked computer access after the museum visit is completed.

Figure 7.3 The Natural History Museum, London

CHAPTER 8

A conceptual learning landscape

These institutions are blurring and extending their boundaries in ways that go far beyond the exploitation of digital technology to facilitate time management – one traditional view of blending – and begin to aspire to something rather more ambitious: creating communities of learning at the heart of a conceptual learning landscape.

Policy initiatives in many parts of the world have stressed the importance of creating integrated learning strategies in the community to break down the boundaries between traditional silos, promoting learning communities, learning development partnerships, regional development organizations and the creation of learning cities and regions and islands. There have also been examples of business-academia collaboration, as recommended by the Lambert review in the UK: the Finnish professional services company Hubconcept, for example (Hubconcept 2012), which specializes in planning, development and management of regional innovation ecosystems and hubs around the world, has combined infrastructure development and innovation processes into one package put together by developers and architectural masterplanners to meet emerging city and ecosystem needs (Figure 8.1).

The Hubconcepts framework aims to be a concrete tool for combining infrastructure development and innovation processes into one package: the real-estate developers can combine innovation process architecture to their master plans from the beginning of the planning process, improving their ability to meet the emerging needs for building sustainable innovation cities and ecosystem. The work method helps developers, regional planners, political decision makers and core hub organizations to identify core issues, determine compelling value propositions and create a shared vision for the regional development in a global setting. Using common terminology, best practice tool-sets and readily available reference material drawn from leading innovation environments, the framework is designed to make a dramatic improvement in development times and processes.

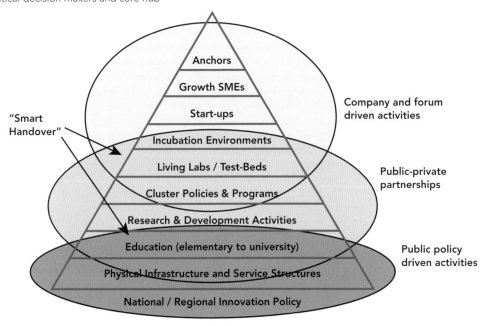

Figure 8.1 A Finnish hub concept. Source: Hubconcept 2012

And there has undoubtedly been innovation in terms of the creation and sharing of community learning resources, such as joint school, community and academic libraries and public libraries sharing local government office space. In the US, charter schools are using spare capacity in public schools and, in the UK, universities are sharing their facilities with schools and academies (Figures 8.2 and 8.3).

But this innovation within building types has only rarely extended to cross-cultural partnering between building types. What the three exemplars discussed in Chapter 7 seem to reveal is that the *degree* of blending is a factor in their success: so that we can equate success with blending. But it is equally clear that what they represent, in the face of the possibilities open to them, is only one, rather constrained, aspect of the learning landscape. This more

The UCL Academy, designed by architects Penoyre and Prasad, represents both a 'stage not age' community approach to learning and a new phase in the sponsorship of academies in the UK. The emphasis is on interdisciplinary and problem-based learning, with a 'superstudio' concept developed specifically to support this vision. The idea of the superstudio is the formation of a group of linked teaching spaces that will encourage children to move between activities – to work collaboratively and across disciplines. The studios bring together traditional classrooms, small and large seminar rooms and open learning spaces to create a dynamic learning space that can accommodate a

range of teacher- and student-led activities at the same time. There will be five of these superstudios in the UCL Academy – one exclusively for foundation year students and the others level-based. As sponsor, UCL will provide a comprehensive programme of activities – visits to UCL, lectures and masterclasses by academics in curriculum subjects and access to the university's extensive resources, such as its laboratories and libraries.

Source: http://www.uclacademy.co.uk/the-ucl-academy/the-ucl-superstudios.php

Figure 8.2 UCL Academy

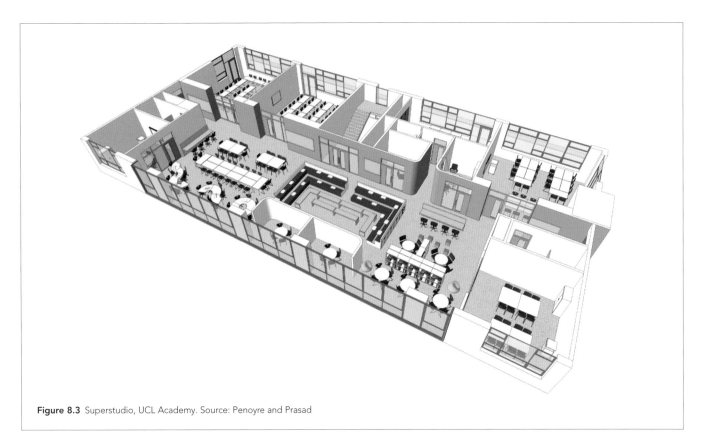

Figure 8.3 Superstudio, UCL Academy. Source: Penoyre and Prasad

unbounded view of learning asks the widest questions – what is the community? Who are the stakeholders? What is the time frame that can be realistically accommodated? And – since the most spatially innovative ideas are meaningless without equally potent innovation in procurement and space utilization – what are the constraints: money (capital and running costs), pedagogical vision and the totality of resources available (including virtual resources)?

We can certainly build on these institutional successes: four more ambitious projects move even further from the formless, disconnected learning landscape we noted in Chapter 1 towards a clustered, hub-shaped landscape which puts learning at the centre of the community. They ask, at a variety of scales, how extensive – how inclusive – can that landscape be?

BRIDGE SCHOOL, XIASHI – A VILLAGE CONNECTION

The Bridge School in Xiashi, in Fujian Province, China, bridges two parts of a village on either side of a small stream (Figures 8.4 and 8.5). The structure is created by two steel trusses that span the creek with the space between them housing the functions of the school. Suspended from the structure and running below it is a pedestrian bridge for the people of the village to use (Aga Khan Development Network (AKDN) 2012; Li Xiaodong 2012).

Small and modern in design, with no reference to the area's traditional building style, the school has nonetheless become the physical and conceptual centre of what was a declining village.

The Bridge School was designed to form a bridge between two ancient tulou – traditional fortress-like, circular structures – erected on either side of a small river. The modern structure blends into the landscape and also succeeds in joining the bulky forms of the two historic structures through a linear lightweight sculpture that floats above the river. According to architect Li Xiaodong, the building is conveying 'the most important lesson

a child can learn: life is transient, not one second of it similar to the next'. For the architect, the award-winning structure 'achieves unity at many levels: temporal unity between past and present, formal unity between traditional and modern, spatial unity between the two riverbanks, social unity between one-time rival communities-as well as unity with the future'.

Source: www.lixiaodong.net

Figures 8.4–5 Bridge School Xiashi, Fujian

Placed in such a way that it addresses its surroundings, the Bridge School connects the disparate parts of the village for the first time, providing a central, social space. The broader social aspect of the project was part of the brief, which was developed with the school principal and head of the village to answer community needs rather than simply those of a primary school. A public library separates the two classrooms and the ends of each classroom, or the two ends of the school can be opened up, creating open stages at either end of the building that are integrated with the public spaces outside. The stage at the northern end can be used for performances, with the *tulou* (Fujian roundhouses) as a backdrop. The result is a project that has successfully invigorated the entire community, encapsulating social sustainability through architectural intervention – in recognition of which it was one of the winners of the 2010 Aga Khan Award for Architecture (AKDN 2012).

NEW ORLEANS NEXUS CENTRES – EDUCATION AT THE HUB

As well as disaster, Hurricane Katrina in New Orleans brought in its wake the possibility of a fresh start – rebuilding the city for the community. By 2010, a total of $3 billion had been allocated to public building projects that would implement a far-reaching plan for the systemic renovation and rebuilding of community programmes and infrastructure. Six domains of community life were identified for what was called 'nexus planning' – the physical domain, encompassing the city's built and natural resources; the cultural domain, including ethic, religious and aesthetic diversity; social needs, including health and human services; the economy, to maintain a healthy balance between financial, human and environmental capital; organizational programmes and services, covering everything from families to clubs; and educational assets (Figure 8.6). This avowedly compendious domain was to 'include everything from early childhood to primary, secondary, community college, university, adult education and workforce training programmes and services' (Bingler 2010: 2).

Overseen by the Louisiana Recovery Authority, Nexus planning will allow sharing of community resources, with Nexus centres conceived of as places where a wide range of programmes and services are effectively sited, coordinated and administered in a way that addresses the needs of the people who most need them. Community programming, planning and design will be the responsibility of community trusts representing all stakeholders as they struggle with the challenge of delivering 'more transformational change' (ibid.: 3).

> With the student population down to nearly half of pre-storm totals, a recently completed school facilities master plan will

finance the rebuilding of some 85 schools. At a minimum, each of these school sites will become a community school, with gymnasiums, auditoriums and school libraries open to the community at nights and on weekends. Furthermore, many of the school sites will also become community 'nexus' centres where parks, community gardens, parenting centres, healthy grocery stores, farmer's markets and other community-centred programmes will be co-located.

(ibid.: 1)

Each Nexus centre could contain public open space, centres for K–12 education, career and technical training, adult learning, multimodal information access, community fitness, visual and performing arts and other social services. With sites located within a short walking distance of all housing areas in the city, this plan would also be more environmentally and socially sustainable: 29 per cent of New Orleans residents do not have access to private transportation.

Some of these community-based ideas are beginning to take root in projects across the US: the Baker-Ripley Neighborhood Center in Houston, Texas, is a $25 million complex of five buildings on a four-acre site – a school, credit union, health clinic, meeting hall and space dedicated to art and artists (Figure 8.7). In the most densely populated neighbourhood in Texas, in southwest Houston, this development is putting into practice the idea of providing a single source for a variety of services, with learning at the heart (Crocker 2010).

HUME GLOBAL LEARNING VILLAGE

The importance of learning in cities of the future has led international educational think-tank the PASCAL International Observatory – from its four regional bases at RMIT University, Melbourne, the University of Glasgow, the University of South Africa, Pretoria and Northern Illinois University – to set up PASCAL International Exchanges (PIE) to provide for online exchanges of ideas and experience between cities around the world relevant to fostering lifelong learning and building inclusive learning communities (http://pascalobservatory.org/about/who-we-are).

At present, ten cities across five continents are participating in PIE – Glasgow, Bari, Kaunas, Cork, Bielefeld, Dar es Salaam, Dakar, Hong Kong, Hume and Vancouver, with others expected to join. The approach involves each city preparing a short stimulus paper providing an overview of key themes and issues, to be posted online for discussion.

The recovery and long-term redevelopment of New Orleans and the Gulf Coast region in the wake of the August 2005 category five Hurricane Katrina called for simultaneous planning in a wide range of disciplines. Because of the complexity of the endeavour, a nexus approach presented itself as an appropriate managerial, programmatic and physical planning model, integrated in design and execution. Early on, education was seen as one of the basic support systems, along with health, social, cultural, transport and other needs, and came to be the heart of community programming.

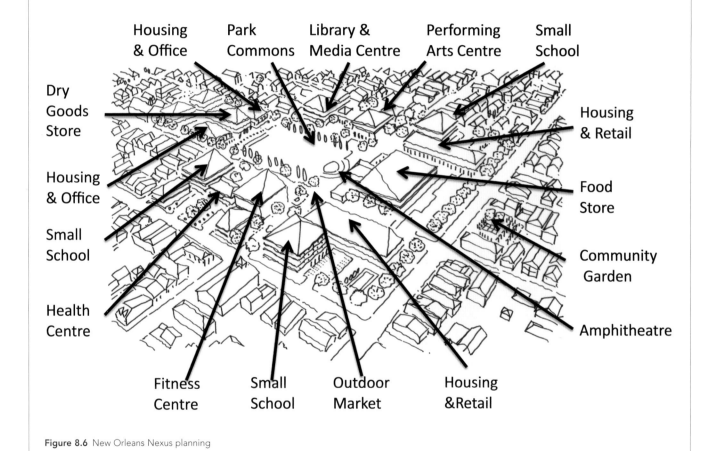

Figure 8.6 New Orleans Nexus planning

The Hume Global Learning Village in Victoria, Australia (Box 8.1), appears to be working towards a three-hub strategy with local neighbourhood projects supported by resources in these hubs – embedding a culture of learning within the community, strengthening pathways to learning, employment and shared prosperity and strengthening the Hume Global Learning Village by expanding and consolidating the commitment of its partners through collaborative planning, community engagement and advocacy for learning (Hume 2009). In common with many of the cities participating in the project, Hume has been faced with problems arising from population growth, diversity and exclusion and is addressing them with a major long-term intercultural heritage project conducted from 2001 to 2013 aimed at achieving these goals by 2030.

As well as concentrating on growth, diversity and exclusion, the Hume plan acknowledges the necessity of building community understanding and support and has experimented with a number of strategies to secure community interest – there is a purpose-built Global Learning Centre to project the image of learning in the community and a periodic publication, *Imagine, Explore, Discover*, that deals with community stories and images of learning in a wide range of contexts. Organizations, families and individuals are encouraged to become members of the village: in 2010 membership totalled 800.

Since 2003, the village has been sustained by a series of innovations that have both advanced its ideas and demonstrated their

In the Baker-Ripley Neighborhood Center in southwest Houston, Texas, a school forms a key element in community building.

Source: http://www.chron.com/news/houston-texas/article/Neighborhood-center-helps-Gulfton-area-find-its-1585590.php

Figure 8.7 Baker-Ripley Neighborhood Center, Houston, Texas

Box 8.1 Hume Global Learning Village, Victoria, Australia

The Hume Action Plan set out three main goals, all of which are aimed at driving a community-learning agenda for the city. The first was to embed a culture of learning in the community – to develop confident learners, support families, widen intergenerational and intercultural learning and to foster a confident and active community. Indications that this had been achieved would include increased preschool attendance, library membership and employment rates and decreased youth disaffection. Goal two was to strengthen pathways to learning – encouraging and supporting learners (including mature learners) and developing close links with employers. Success indicators here would be increased employment and particularly local employment, and decreased youth unemployment and 'disengagement'. The final goal was to strengthen the learning village by expanding and consolidating the commitment of its partners through collaborative planning, community engagement and advocacy for learning. Here success would be marked by increased broadband connections and membership of the learning village accompanied by high scores for the project as a means of providing positive learning outcomes.

benefits to the community – including an IdeasLab in the Learning Centre. Supported by the Victorian Government, Hume City Council and, critically, leading international organizations in the field of IT, this building up of partnerships of stakeholders is a key element in developing a shared vision of the city, building social capital, economic benefits and widening access to lifelong learning. Changing roles have been found for the library as a re-entry gateway to learning, and also as a means of enhancing self-esteem in disengaged young people. The time frame for the project is generous: the strategic approach works in a succession of three-year bands beginning in 2003, in a wider plan taking the village up to 2030.

LEARNING TOWNS – DUMFRIES

Scotland's Curriculum for Excellence model led to the Senses of Place: Building Excellence project (2008), with five architectural practices developing school design concepts with local authorities, schools and pupils and coming up with five major themes – big spaces, enterprise, outward-looking design, science and active learning. This in turn led to the Senses of Place: Learning Towns initiative, in which the same architectural practices looked at these concepts in the context of real towns, with the aim of unlocking their learning potential.

Asked to provide a strategy to support Dumfries schools (Figure 8.8), the practices first came up with a whole-school strategy and then a whole-town strategy:

> In our 'Whole School Exemplar' we explored the potential of the 'L-shaped classroom' as a means of allowing different learning experiences to operate simultaneously. In this next phase of the project we will investigate how a desire for individual learning, group learning and community interaction could manifest spatially in the Scottish townscape and allow a similar flexibility in programme.
>
> (Cassels 2009: 3)

As the report by Architecture and Design Scotland states:

> Scottish towns are often proliferated by untended open 'voids'. In situations where potentially valuable townscape assets are positioned on the edges of such spaces they cannot be appreciated and are often negatively interpreted by both locals and visitors. The interface, setting and usability of these sites present an intriguing opportunity to experiment with new interventions. For pupils, who spend time out of doors in the

margins of inside and outside space the interfaces and voids between the buildings are a critical territory for exploration.

> (ibid.: 3)

In Dumfries, the report claims, the opportunities exist for designers to weave the interior and exterior landscape of the school into the wider landscape, creating, in the words of the exhibition accompanying the Sense of Place: Learning Towns report, 'a town based on a deep understanding of how learning could underpin the sustainable growth of the town and the lives of its communities' (http://www.learningtowns.org/).

> Our aim, within the brief we have been set is to explore the meaningful and strategic differentiation of the urban landscape in order to provide an exciting range of new learning opportunities for all ages.
>
> (Cassels 2009: 3)

In reality, when the plans to revamp future education provision went out to public consultation in July 2012, the learning town proposal focused on the creation of a single new school for senior secondary pupils that also contains an FE college and an HE satellite campus (http://www.bbc.co.uk/news/uk-scotland-south-scotland-18726837). This may, as Director of Education Colin Grant said, be interpretable as 'a ground-breaking, innovative project that could benefit everyone if it goes ahead. Dumfries could be first in Scotland to begin to be more flexible with our school structure and take full advantage of other educational opportunities on our doorstep' (BBC News, 6 July 2012). It is, however, some way short of the total learning community implicit in the idea of a 'learning town'.

The Crichton Campus, however, on the outskirts of the town (Figure 8.9), embodies many of the more ambitious ideas proposed by the Learning Towns initiative. Dumfries and Gallow College, University of Glasgow, University of West of Scotland, Open University, Crichton Carbon Centre and Scottish Agricultural College all have a presence on the campus and in addition to these classic educational resources there is a business park, a conference and events centre, a hotel and church.

This is beginning to meet some of the requirements of a learning community, matching educational and economic life on one site. Plans are in progress for a research institute and – bringing in the Learning Towns initiative more directly – using an upper secondary school to feed the campus, with a nearby site to be developed as an innovative model of low carbon housing supported by the town's Sustainable Communities initiative (http://www.crichtonfoundation.org/the-crichton-campus).

Dumfries and Galloway Council in Scotland is one of a number of authorities considering the single-school solution as a model for secondary schools – and current proposals could make it the first town in Scotland to use such a structure.

Dumfries is currently served by four secondary sites – Dumfries Academy, Dumfries High School, Maxwelltown High School and St Joseph's College. The idea is to take advantage of other educational opportunities in the town – particularly the further

and higher education available at the Crichton site. Educational partners envisaged include the college and the university and also local businesses. Director of Education Colin Grant acknowledged that there were no clear indications when such a school would be built – but was confident that 'somewhere in the country at some stage people will begin to consider whether having separate primary, secondary, college and university is the best for that locality'.

Source: BBC Scotland (2011)

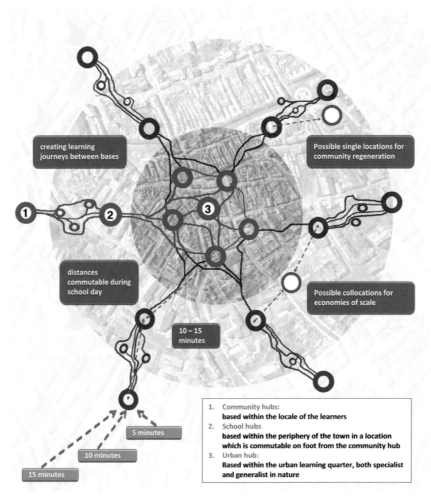

creating learning journeys between bases

Possible single locations for community regeneration

distances commutable during school day

Possible collocations for economies of scale

10 – 15 minutes

5 minutes

10 minutes

15 minutes

1. Community hubs:
   based within the locale of the learners
2. School hubs
   based within the periphery of the town in a location which is commutable on foot from the community hub
3. Urban hub:
   Based within the urban learning quarter, both specialist and generalist in nature

Figure 8.8 Dumfries Learning Town, Scotland. Source: Architecture Design Scotland

Current projects in or near the Crichton Campus include a research institute to focus on rural issues around health and wellbeing, Dumfries Learning Town's Schools Innovation Initiative and a low carbon housing development. Dumfries and Galloway Council has launched plans to streamline educational opportunities through Dumfries Learning Town's Schools

Innovation Initiative, which could see an upper secondary school for Dumfries established to feed the campus. The Ladyfield site to the west of the Crichton Campus is also to be developed as an innovative model of low carbon housing supported by the Sustainable Communities Initiative.

Source: Crichton Foundation (2013)

Figure 8.9 Crichton Campus, Dumfries, Scotland

CHAPTER 9
Creating a learning matrix

These variously linear, discrete and hub structures show that wider, more generously conceived communities of learning are achievable – and, moreover, that the scale of the ambition is not linked to the scale of the project. The Xiashi Bridge links two halves of a small village, Hume and Dumfries are learning towns, Nexus makes learning the centre of an entire city learning landscape. The move is conceptual, not to do with scale: but it does require a change of mindset, in which individual, community and societal benefits are balanced to produce increased efficiency, effectiveness, happiness and lifelong learning. For the owner, benefits are better use of the resource, whether it is a church hall, a university or an office development.

Both blended institutions and the more ambitious learning communities show evidence of the importance of interconnectedness,

with the learning institution at the centre of the community. The creation of neighbourhood Nexus schools in New Orleans post-Katrina illustrates this theme perfectly: the political will now exists to plan a whole city's learning environment so that it is accessible, useful and relevant to all. In this case, the easily imaginable – but unimagined – city-wide provision of spaces as though people mattered links hubs and neighbourhood centres in a web that will be not just strong and flexible but resilient. One of the key lessons of New Orleans is that the blending that occurred in the wake of the disaster stemmed from the urgent need to service activities – which have trumped organizationally imposed spatial boundaries and privileged connectedness over zones of special interest.

What we should be aiming for as an ideal may not, however, be a hub structure at all, but a matrix – not one to many but many to all,

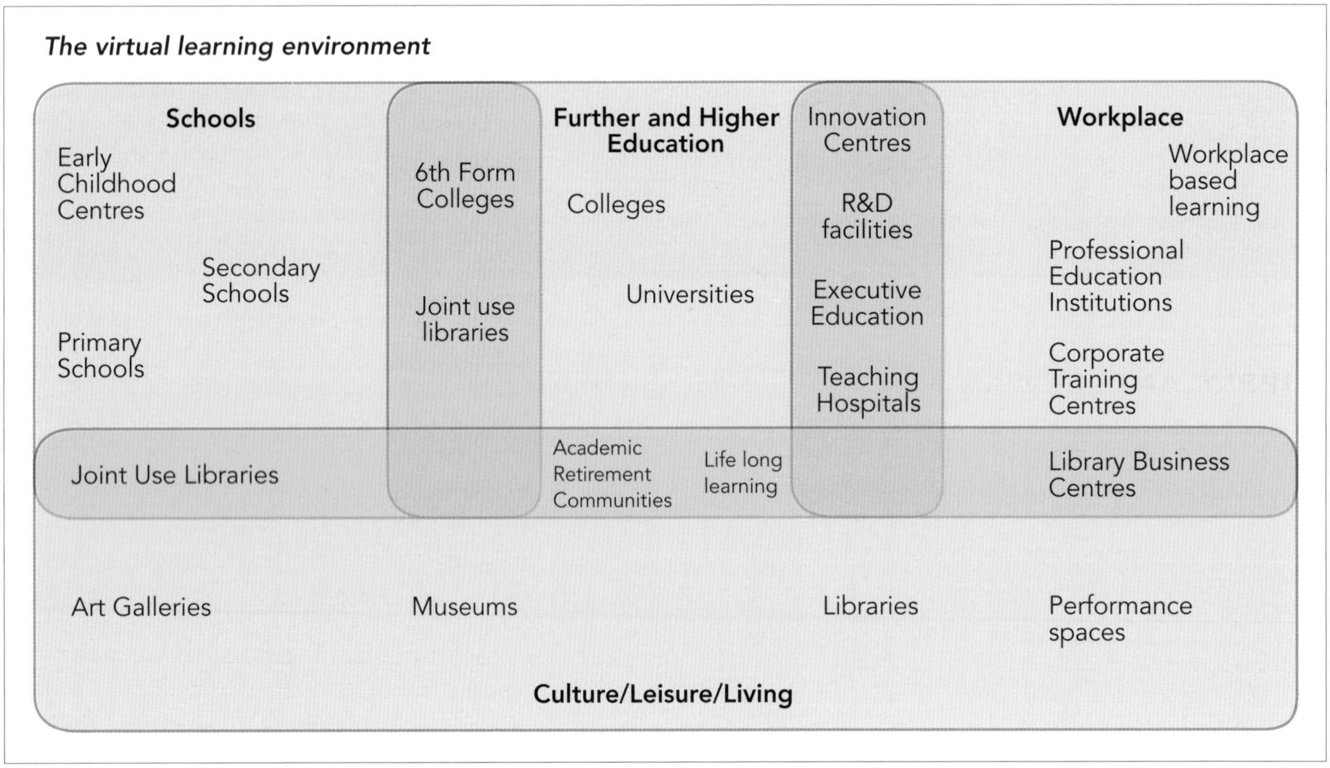

Figure 9.1 Creation of learning centred communities

linking neither resources nor users but needs, linking settings and activities. Something that will match the diverse range of different institutions (nodes) and reflect the increased complexity shown in Part 1 – ratcheted demands caused by shifts in technology, learning theory, policy and world events (Figure 9.1).

We have to audit the possible nodes in terms of resources rather than relationships – which will be promiscuous. And, critically, these nodes, figures in a (learning) landscape, represent undifferentiated stakeholders – a cake-icing collective requiring access to resources in exactly the same way as a university vice-chancellor. Demand will be driven by the activity and by how and where the stakeholders want to carry it out.

The challenge for any designer or provider of learning environments committed to the creation of such a matrix is therefore to create an events-based rather than a space-based identity and produce a strategy to deliver it. This means defining the learning landscape in the widest and most generous way possible – withholding the rush to provide physical accommodation until an entire learning strategy is in place. In effect, this requires a briefing process that takes into account in the first instance activities – what the learning (and total learning) community requires – and only then negotiates the square foot utilization of budgetary and departmental allowances.

Setting the community vision in this wide and cross-boundary way allows us to create a delivery strategy that will achieve the best outcome at the most appropriate scale: a conceptual learning landscape not bounded by place. A number of techniques are at our disposal in making a systematic move into this landscape – creating an inventory of requirements, resolving the physical/virtual organizational dilemma and mapping inventoried supply and demand limitations on to each other in the form of projects, complete with real-world procurement figures.

SUPPLY AND DEMAND

Broadly these tools and processes can be divided into those that help to define and communicate the 'demand' for learning in terms of learning objectives, activities and processes and those that define and evaluate the 'supply' of physical and virtual learning resources – where the learning will take place (Figure 9.2).

Conceptualizing the design briefing process in this way has been used extensively by DEGW in consulting projects and is described at length by Alistair Blyth and John Worthington in *Managing the Brief for Better Design* (2010). They make it clear that such a

process must be based on a deep understanding of both sides of the demand and supply equation. On one side lie the learning community's aspirations, learning objectives and activities, together with the location of all the stakeholders (teachers, researchers, students, support networks). On the other, an appropriate set of physical and virtual learning settings based on factors such as location, condition, building and space configuration and the availability of IT tools to support individual and collaborative learning tasks.

The matching of demand and supply is seen as an iterative process with ongoing analysis of how the physical and virtual learning settings are supporting the learning process and the achievement of the educational goals. As needs change, so too must the combination of physical and virtual learning settings: the learning landscape must be agile enough to handle these changes. As Blyth and Worthington point out: 'The rate at which organizations change seems often to be much faster than the ability of the real estate to catch up' (ibid.: 12). This concentration on demand rather than space is in itself indicative of a changed mindset – allowing stakeholders the right to create the demand which space then supplies.

Looking at the learning outcomes first in this way is firmly in the tradition of work developed to establish strategies for distributed work in the commercial, corporate and government workplace – SANE in 2002, *The Distributed Workplace* in 2004 (Harrison et al. 2004), *Working Without Walls* and *Working Beyond Walls* (Allen et al. 2004; Hardy et al. 2008). One key theme of these workplace research initiatives could be summarized as: You don't have to do everything at your desk (and in fact you can't). The learning landscape is wider and more volatile, but this corporate space strategy is suggestive of a useful approach and offers valuable and transferable insights: in learning communities the key message could translate as: You don't have to do everything in a classroom (and in fact you shouldn't). Embracing this much wider landscape means that each learning node – library user, university researcher, school student (or cake icer) – can take its place on an innovatory trajectory that makes the landscape as a whole much more resilient in meeting changing demands.

SANE (Sustainable Accommodation for the New Economy) looked at the combined impact of the new economy on place, people and process, with the objective of enabling space designers, technology developers and other professionals concerned with the workplace to move from a location-centric to a location-independent approach. The overall aim of the project was the provision of a unified framework of space environment, human environment and processes and tools modelling for the creation of sustainable, collaborative workplaces for knowledge workers across Europe, encompassing both virtual and physical spaces.

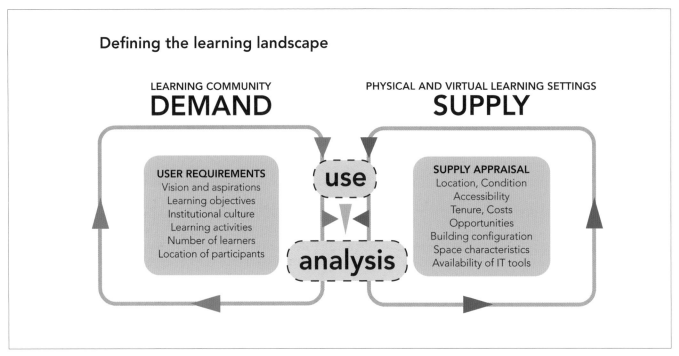

Figure 9.2 Matching supply and demand

The space environment modelling was undertaken by architects DEGW, who in 2000 developed a distributed workplace model (Figure 9.3) that would form the basis for much of the SANE research. This initial model attempted to incorporate the increasing congruence between physical and virtual work environments, acknowledging the impact that information and communications technologies have had on the work process of most individuals and organizations. It also examined the continuum between public and private space and produced novel solutions to their integration into workplaces. It divided workplaces into three conceptual categories according to the degree of privacy and accessibility they offered, each composed of a number of different types of work settings, the relative proportion of each forming the character of the space. Each of the physical work environments had a parallel virtual environment that shared some of the same characteristics. When designing accommodation strategies, organizations would increasingly need to consider how the virtual work environments would be able to support distributed physical environments and how the virtual environments could contribute to the development of organizational culture and a sense of community when the staff spend little or no time in 'owned' facilities.

The distributed workplace model contained several key principles, among them:

● the central notion of privacy or access as a descriptor of work locations or work settings

● the grouping of a number of different types of work settings into a workplace with a distinctive character

● the idea of increasing congruence between physical and virtual workplaces.

This model was subsequently developed further to take into account the importance of the boundaries between virtual and physical spaces. This more robust model emphasized the importance of hybrid work environments, based on the tripartite split of private, privileged and public spaces, and applied at two scales of focus – the virtual and the physical workplace – and also the larger scale environment in which knowledge work takes place, from the office building up to the scale of the entire city. This model proved fertile in leading to a richer understanding of how places for work function, how they fit into their wider environmental context and how humans experience space. It has now been applied productively in real-world consultancy projects, helping organizations improve their strategy for the provision and use of office space.

It became evident, however, that there was a gap between the level of focus of this model and the factors that needed to be taken into account when making decisions about what kinds of workplaces should be provided and what kinds of knowledge work they best accommodated, remembering that 'workplace' includes both physical spaces and virtual worksettings, mediated by technology. In fact, a new term, workscape – the combination of virtual and real

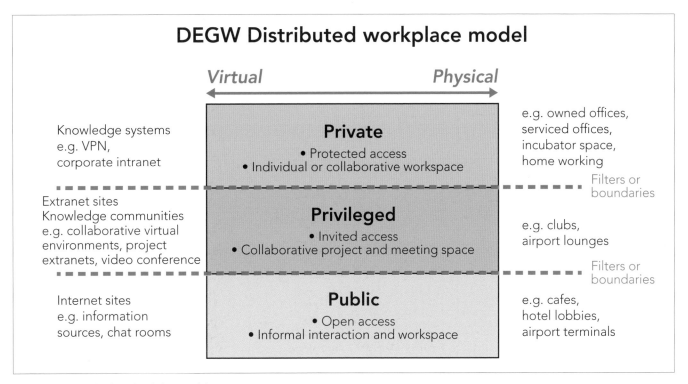

Figure 9.3 DEGW distributed workplace model

work settings within a work arena, located in a work environment – came to be adopted to mark how complex, and fluid, the once straightforward concept of workplace had become. Not only had the knowledge work activities themselves to be considered, but they had to be seen in the widest possible business and organizational context. In addition, the activities were clearly mediated by a variety of factors that would interact with the characteristics of specific workscapes en route to the eventual choice of a workscape.

A third and final model (Figure 9.4) demonstrated this more obvious and explicit relationship between knowledge work activities (the layers of what we do) and the workscape (the layers of where we do it). Not only does this comprehensive space environment model provide a methodology for the provision of a workscape – virtual or physical – appropriate to any organization – but it also reveals the extent to which any organization has a complex story to tell, made up of the work its people do, and where and how they do it (Harrison et al. 2004). To a large extent, the success of the organization is bound up with its success in telling that story – in focusing the terms of that story in its physical fabric.

Implementation of this distributed workplace strategy of course proved to be heavily dependent on an in-depth understanding of organizational culture, work process and group and individual communications requirements. The more significant the change

envisaged, the more essential to support the planned strategy with a workplace change management programme and to ensure effective communications and collaboration within and between teams of knowledge workers. This has been a major area of research in areas such as organizational psychology and computer-mediated communications (Computer Supported Cooperative Work: CSCW – Schmidt 2011) and has resulted in theories such as social presence theory – where social presence can be defined 'as the degree to which a medium is perceived to convey the actual presence of communicating participants' (Short et al. 1976) – media richness theory and media synchronicity theory (Box 9.1).

BUILDING ON A WORKSPACE ENVIRONMENT MODEL

The SANE space environment model sought to provide a template for the selection of distributed work environments – if work can take place anywhere, how should an individual or an organization determine where particular work activities should be located? This model can be adapted to apply to the creation of appropriate learning landscapes, taking into account the social and political as well as the organizational context in which the activity will take place.

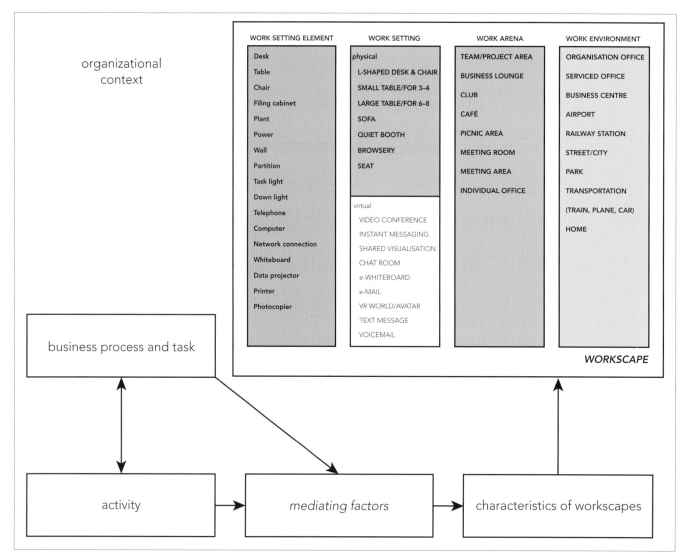

Figure 9.4 SANE space environment model – moving from activities to workscapes

Government policy can constrain or require changes to the learning landscape – increased emphasis, for example, on vocational learning, may require the enhancement of technical facilities at schools and colleges or the development of apprenticeship-based learning at the workplace or cuts to local education budgets may force closure of school or community libraries. At the organizational level, culture, history and aspirations all have a part to play in defining the boundaries of what is possible when making choices about the future learning landscape.

Instead of the business processes and tasks of Figure 9.4, this revised model would consider learning objectives and tasks, which would have to include diverse organizational and individual goals for the formal or non-formal learning activities which may relate

to the attainment of qualifications, the realization of individual ambitions or the achievement of institutional targets for student numbers or income. The objectives would be achieved through the participation in a range of learning activities that may be individual or collaborative, face to face or mediated through technology. Just as in the workplace model, a variety of mediating factors would have an impact on the selection of an appropriate environment for these activities to take place (Box 9.2).

In the same way that the particular mediating factors of activities can be identified, learning landscapes can be seen to vary across certain dimensions or characteristics that can then be used to define their suitability for particular activities (Box 9.3). It can be seen that the critical factors determining the most appropriate

Box 9.1 Communications theories

Media richness theory

Media richness theory claims that different communications media can be classified as lean or rich, according to their ability to convey knowledge and information. Task performance will be improved when task needs are matched to a medium's ability to convey information (Daft and Lengel 1986). Media capable of sending 'rich' information (e.g., face-to-face meetings) are better suited to equivocal tasks (setting goals, where there are multiple interpretations for available information), while media that are less 'rich' (e.g., computer-mediated communication) are best suited to tasks of uncertainty (where there is a lack of information).

The classification scheme proposed by media richness theory ranks face-to-face as the richest communication medium, and electronic media in general as relatively lean – the term refers to the extent to which the communication medium can provide immediate feedback, the number of cues and channels utilized, the back channelling cues, and the socioemotional content in a communication session (ibid. 1986). One way, therefore, in which to assess communications media is in terms of the extent to which they facilitate social presence.

There are two fundamental communication processes in action here: conveying information and converging on a shared interpretation. Media richness theories emphasize the need to converge, with conveyance of information left to tasks of uncertainty. But conveying information and converging on a shared meaning are equally critical for both tasks of equivocality and uncertainty. Without adequate conveyance of information, individuals will reach incorrect conclusions. Without adequate convergence, the group cannot move forward. Knowledge must be communicated in order to reduce task equivocality, whereas information must be communicated in order to reduce task uncertainty (ibid. 1986).

Media synchronicity theory

The richness theory was developed – according to Dennis and Valacich (1999: 2) – to theorize which media should prove most effective for a given situation, rather than to help managers choose appropriate communications strategies and media. For that purpose they proposed a media synchronicity theory, which looks beyond Daft and Lengel's richness theory to take a physical vs virtual stance on communication performance – on the state 'in which individuals are working together at the same time with a common focus' (Dennis et al. 1998) – and to act as a predictor of performance. In this theory, every group communication process is composed of two fundamental communication processes – conveyance and convergence – that are necessary to reach a group outcome. The goal of conveyance is to enable the most rapid exchange of information among the participants as possible, and to enable them to effectively process this information and arrive at their individual interpretations of its meaning. The goal of convergence is to enable the rapid development of a shared understanding among group members.

For Dennis and Valacich the key to effective use of media is the matching of media capabilities to the fundamental communication processes required to perform the task – because most tasks require individuals to convey information as well as converge on shared meanings, and media that excel at information conveyance are often not those that excel at convergence. Choosing a single medium for any task may prove less effective than choosing a medium or set of media which the group uses at different times in performing the task, depending on the current communication process (convey or converge).

The impact of these theories goes beyond the need to select appropriate levels of technology, reaching into all aspects of the process of analysis, discussion and sharing of insights that makes up the entire learning landscape and informs its design: Voigt makes this link overt in his 2008 paper, 'Education design and media choice' (Voigt 2008; Clark 2001).

Media synchronicity theory in physical and virtual communication space

According to media synchronicity theory there are five important media characteristics (immediacy of feedback, symbol variety, parallelism, rehearsability and reprocessability). No medium is richest on all media characteristics, and the relationships between communication processes and media capabilities will vary between established and newly formed groups, and will change over time.

Immediacy of feedback: the extent to which a medium enables users to give rapid feedback on the communications they receive. It is the ability of the medium to support rapid bidirectional communications.

Symbol variety: the number of ways in which information can be communicated which Dennis and Valacich refer to as the 'height' of the medium. Some information is easier to convey in one format than another and verbal and non-verbal symbols enable senders to include information beyond the words themselves when the message is transmitted. The cost to compose a message or to process an incoming message using some symbol set may impose a delay cost or a production cost that alters the way in which the sender creates messages or reduces the understanding of the receiver. The lack of verbal and non-verbal symbols can have significant effects on social perceptions and in general when verbal and non-verbal symbols are removed there is a loss of social presence such that the people with whom one is communicating become less like real people with whom one is communicating and more like objects.

Parallelism: the number of simultaneous conversations that can exist effectively – the 'width' of the medium. Dennis and Valacich note that with traditional media such as the telephone, only one conversation can effectively use the medium at one time whereas in contrast many electronic media can be structured to enable many simultaneous conversations to occur. However, as the number of conversations increases, it becomes increasingly difficult to monitor and co-ordinate the conversations.

Rehearsability: the extent to which the media enables the sender to rehearse or fine tune the message before sending – some media enable the sender to carefully edit a message while it is being sent to ensure that the intended meaning is expressed exactly, with no extraneous information.

Reprocessability: the extent to which a message can be re-examined or processed within the context of the communication event.

Dennis and Valacich reviewed the capabilities of a number of communication media using these characteristics and called them relative trait salience of selected media.

location for a particular learning activity are not found solely within the nature of the activity itself. Instead, they are part of the surrounding organizational context and are impacted by a wide range of mediating factors. In Figure 9.5, the relationship between learning activities and learning environments is depicted conceptually as a set of circles, each one embedded within the other. Activities take place within a learning setting (which may have a virtual as well as a physical aspect), which is located within a learning arena, which exists within an environment.

The same activity can be supported by a number of different learning environments (work settings and arenas), and conversely, a particular arena or environment can support a variety of different activities. For example, a discussion about a book, a collaborative activity, can take place round a meeting table (physical work setting) in a seminar room (work arena) within an academic building in a university (learning environment) but the activity could equally be carried out at a table and benches in a picnic area within a park.

Furthermore, if some of the participants are physically distant, the session might be achieved through the use of virtual learning environments, videoconferencing or within a virtual world. If this is the case, the use of a virtual work setting may mean that the specific physical work setting and work arena are of somewhat less relevance (Figure 9.6).

Coupled with a comprehensive mapping of available community resources and an understanding of the characteristics of the required learning landscape, the physical and virtual components of the appropriate landscape may then be selected.

In some cases, the learning landscape will have to be defined before the learning activities are known. A critical element of the briefing process for new buildings or the refurbishment of existing buildings is to plan for changes in educational mission, pedagogy and technology over time. Blyth and Worthington (2010) refer to this as futureproofing, which 'enables the organization to address how change might impact on the built environment whether it be

Box 9.2 Mediating factors

Learning mediating factors may include:

- the number of participants

- the geographical distribution of participants

- the choice of individual or group activity

- the degree of concentration needed, and conversely, the degree of interruption that would be tolerated: it should be noted that this can in some cases depend almost as much on the preferences of the individual(s) involved as on the activity

- duration (minutes versus hours versus days): this influences the decision as to whether it is worthwhile changing location in order to fulfil this activity

- how intermittent or continuous the activity is: the more intermittent the activity is, the more the other activities carried out between times will need to be taken into account when choosing the most appropriate learning locations. A mix of different intermittent activities will almost certainly require more resources in the immediate vicinity than continuous single activities

- the importance placed by the participants and wider stakeholders on the activity and the task of which it is part – for

example, when distant parties are weighing up the options of a face-to-face or virtual meeting, this will affect whether the participants in the activity are prepared to tolerate slightly less than optimal conditions for the activity, given the compensations in time-saving, cost and environmental damage brought by avoiding travel

- predictability – if activities are unpredictable, one needs to have available all the resources necessary for the activity, which may include rapid virtual or physical access to colleagues or information

- formality – degree of formality appropriate to the activity and learning task. This will also be affected by the formality of the institution as a whole – that is, the organizational context

- the relationship needed with participants for successful activity (such as needing trust or familiarity).

Other mediating factors may also include the organizational preferences based on institutional identity, history and financial structure and the enduring and temporary preferences and personal circumstances of the individual learners engaged in the activities which may affect the convenience and desirability of particular learning locations and ways of learning.

Box 9.3 Characteristics of learning landscapes

Accessibility to people (the learning community)

Accessibility is about how easily an individual can access other people in his or her learning community either face to face or virtually.

Accessibility to information and data.

This characteristic describes how easily an individual in a workspace can access documents, other reference material and electronic information. Virtual work settings will generally offer

high accessibility to information held electronically, but other forms of data and information may be inaccessible in a virtual work setting.

Boundary control

This can be defined as the individual person or group's control of the community's access to them, when they are in a learning arena or environment. There will be times when concentration and isolation are needed as part of the learning process. Some environments will not be able to provide this effectively so the individual or group may seek other places that offer this control.

Physical control

In the physical realm, boundary control can be implemented at the level of the building or at the level of the learning arena or learning setting, by either physical enclosure or through protocols (e.g., high screens around the work table reduce casual interruptions by others, shutting the door to an individual room can indicate that you do not wish to be disturbed).

Boundary control may discriminate between classes of people (e.g., students may have access to only certain floors of the building). Boundary control can also be achieved by geographical distance (working at home or elsewhere), and the accessibility limitations of this can be overcome by means of virtual environments and the use of communications tools.

There are various other implications of the means chosen for achieving boundary control in the physical realm. Physical enclosure can also define, or come to be seen as defining, personal territory and so may reinforce feelings of ownership, attributions of status and particular kinds of behaviour. Communication may become more formal, relying on systems of communication such as memos and e-mails rather than informal, ad hoc interaction. In addition, though, physical enclosure sometimes enables the individual to control noise and their own concentration level.

Virtual control

Just as a building allows members of the organization access to internal spaces through a series of controlled boundaries, so, in a similar way, protocols can be established for virtual space. This can reinforce people's membership of and sense of belonging to a learning community. Boundary control can be achieved by removing oneself from chains of communication which automatically creates effective distance from other participants. This distance may be total (on/off) or partial, if email and voice filters are used to create levels of virtual boundary control.

Technology-enabled learning landscapes

In the traditional approach to designing learning environments, a direct link was drawn between activities and the physical learning setting that best support them. With technology-enabled learning landscapes, the dominance of the physical setting may be eliminated by the use of technology to cross boundaries of space and time, enabling a learner on one side of the globe to leave messages (text, voice, avatar or video), share documents, develop ideas (using, for example, electronic whiteboards) or 'meet' (via video-conference, telepresence or within a virtual world) with other participants on the other side of the globe. A decision about what is the 'best' setting for a particular learning activity is likely to involve consideration of the virtual settings through which that learning activity can also be carried out, either substituting for or mediating the face-to-face presence of others.

in terms of the location of buildings, work patterns or impact of information and communications technologies' (p. 12).

In all cases, however, the learning landscape must be defined in terms of its detailed elements – physical and virtual learning settings, learning arenas and learning environments (Figure 9.7).

While no straightforward relationship exists between each learning activity and the selection of locations in which it can most effectively take place, this adaptation of the SANE workspace environment model to the learning landscape produces a template that suggests one way of approaching the matching of event and environment (Figure 9.8).

PHYSICAL AND VIRTUAL LEARNING RESOURCES

As well as creating a demand profile for the sorts of learning settings, arenas and environments that will make up the total learning landscape we also, of course, have to understand what physical and virtual learning resources are available to support the individual and the institution.

Learning Landscapes in Higher Education (Neary et al. 2010) moves from the big idea of the university and the spaces that embody the idea to a set of tools that show how to deliver that physical landscape.

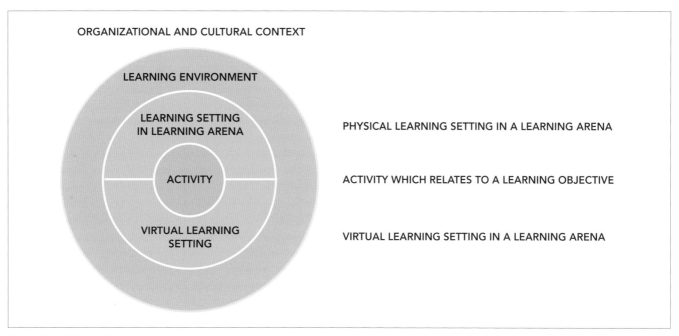

Figure 9.5 Activities in the learning landscape

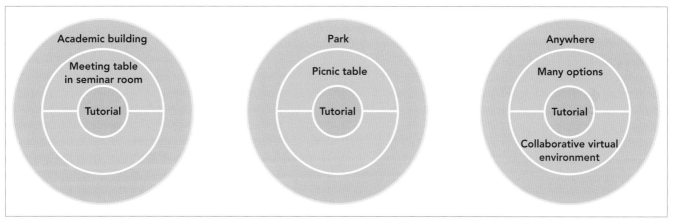

Figure 9.6 Selection of appropriate learning environment

The book was the outcome of a long-term project that was conceived as:

> a response to those in higher education who are concerned that decision making about the development of the learning and teaching environment is not as effective as it could be. Learning Landscapes offers the higher education community a practical and conceptual framework to consider the ways in which learning and teaching spaces are being designed and developed. This notion of 'community' extends to all who work

in universities: academics, support and professional staff, as well as existing and potential students.

(ibid: 4)

In the foreword, John Worthington, reprising his ideas on core space, flexible space and just-in-time space, makes the point that 'in the commercial sector, in response to an increasingly competitive environment, organizations in both the public and the private sectors are embracing new ways of working. They recognize the rigidity of a real-estate portfolio composed entirely of owned and

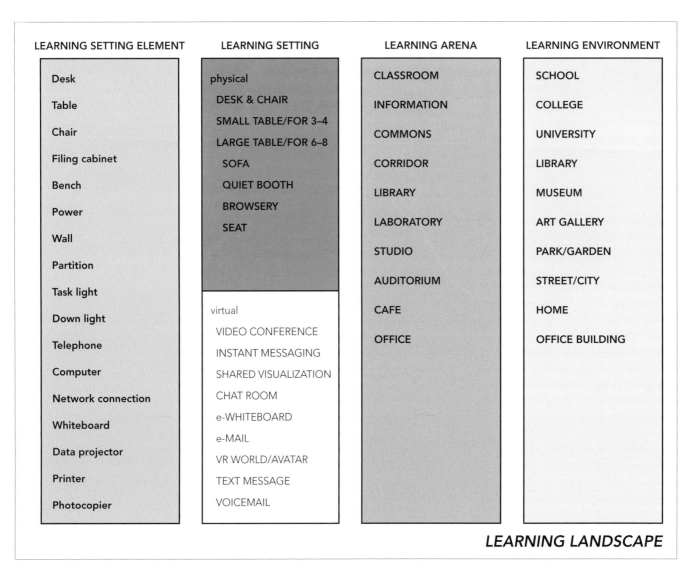

LEARNING SETTING ELEMENT	LEARNING SETTING	LEARNING ARENA	LEARNING ENVIRONMENT
Desk	physical	CLASSROOM	SCHOOL
Table	DESK & CHAIR	INFORMATION	COLLEGE
Chair	SMALL TABLE/FOR 3–4	COMMONS	UNIVERSITY
Filing cabinet	LARGE TABLE/FOR 6–8	CORRIDOR	LIBRARY
Bench	SOFA	LIBRARY	MUSEUM
Power	QUIET BOOTH	LABORATORY	ART GALLERY
Wall	BROWSERY	STUDIO	PARK/GARDEN
Partition	SEAT	AUDITORIUM	STREET/CITY
Task light		CAFE	HOME
Down light	virtual	OFFICE	OFFICE BUILDING
Telephone	VIDEO CONFERENCE		
Computer	INSTANT MESSAGING		
Network connection	SHARED VISUALIZATION		
Whiteboard	CHAT ROOM		
Data projector	e-WHITEBOARD		
Printer	e-MAIL		
Photocopier	VR WORLD/AVATAR		
	TEXT MESSAGE		
	VOICEMAIL		

LEARNING LANDSCAPE

Figure 9.7 Defining the learning landscape

purpose-designed buildings' and proposes a move to the greater flexibility of 'a mixed portfolio'. 'Such a strategy increases financial flexibility, reduces risk, and opens up new opportunities' (ibid.: 6).

At a time when universities, as he points out, are under 'severe financial pressure and faced with rapidly changing demands', there's a strong incentive to learn from the commercial property sector 'by questioning whether new purpose-built buildings are always the answer and assessing the opportunities to intensify the use of the building stock by innovative timetabling, and sharing resources with non-academic partners' (ibid.: 6).

Learning Landscapes provides a set of tools designed to bring the academic, estates and other key stakeholder interests together in one integrated process (Box 9.4). They emerged from a

collaboration between DEGW, a major international design company, and 11 British universities between February 2008 and December 2009, funded by the Higher Education Funding Council for England (HEFCE), the Higher Education Funding Council for Wales (HEFCW) and the Scottish Funding Council (SFC), to find 'ways in which the academic voice can be more fully articulated within the decision making processes at all levels of the design and development of teaching and learning spaces' (ibid.: 7).

The research looked at the relationship between campus planning and specific exemplary teaching and learning spaces in the participating universities and particularly at the way in which these exemplary spaces were integrated into an overall campus plan. From a series of case studies the research then derived a set of development tools: mapping the campus profile to fit the vision

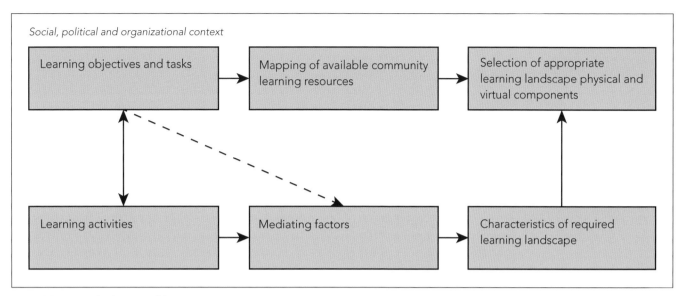

Social, political and organizational context

| Learning objectives and tasks | Mapping of available community learning resources | Selection of appropriate learning landscape physical and virtual components |

| Learning activities | Mediating factors | Characteristics of required learning landscape |

Figure 9.8 Learning landscape model

Box 9.4 *Learning Landscapes in Higher Education*: five tools to deliver the physical learning landscape

The tools are derived from issues that emerged from the campus profiling exercises and the case studies. The tools are set up to support academics, estates professionals and other key stakeholders in responding progressively to these issues. The tools are informed by academic literature on design and its relationship with educational psychology and the social sciences.

Campus mapping profiles: designed as prototype mapping tools to carry out research at the level of each university campus. This profiling device has enabled colleagues from all parts of the university to engage in a situational analysis of the relationship between the vision and mission of the university with its built environment. The output provides a strong visual impression of the estate's performance, identifying areas for potential interventions.

Teaching with space in mind: based on a key point emerging from the research – that the most effective teaching and learning spaces are based on ideas that are evidence-based and research-informed. Designs for teaching and learning spaces need to be informed by pedagogical principles, rather than being estates-led. This tool can be used to develop the educational brief for a particular project.

Pragmatics of place: provides an insight into the preoccupations of space planners and space managers in higher education. Based on the urban design principles of efficiency, effectiveness and expression, the tool reveals the theoretical and practical aspects of estates activities in a way that is intellectually stimulating and very pertinent to academics engaged as part of a learning space client group. The tool attempts to counteract some of the negative stereotyping revealed by the case study research.

Talking our futures into being: based on the problem, identified in the research, of the nature and purpose of client project groups, and how to fulfil the roles and responsibilities as a member of such a group. This tool is written without recourse to any building or design jargon and in a language that is engaging and inspirational.

The idea of the university: designed to enhance the academic voice in relation to the way in which teaching and learning spaces are conceptualized. Within this tool the academic voice moves beyond cost-benefit analysis to encourage debates and discussions grounded within the academic literature on the role and nature of higher education. The progressive ideas expressed in this literature might negate some of the more conservative tendencies expressed by academics and students in the case study research.

Source: Neary et al. (2010: 33)

and mission of the university with its built environment; designing teaching and learning spaces with pedagogical principles, rather than the university estate, in mind; building on urban design principles of efficiency, effectiveness and expression to create a 'pragmatics of place'; identifying and informing the client in such a way that they can create the future they themselves desire; and designing to achieve the highest ideals of the institutions without being shackled at too early a stage by such restrictive considerations as cost-benefit analyses.

The campus mapping tools in Neary et al. (2010) look at university spaces in terms of efficiency, effectiveness and expression (identity) measures and as a means of supporting 'work across professional boundaries, between academics, support services, other key stakeholders and students' they are undoubtedly valuable. We would go further – towards the idea of every learning group having its own manifesto and pedagogies and a view on where that learning can take place. It is now necessary to go well beyond the campus boundaries to consider all the available resources in terms of what learning activities they could support and how access to them can be gained (through purchase, rental, partnerships or sharing or use of public amenities or cultural institutions). This should result in more intensive use of existing learning assets and an increased appreciation of the valuable role of cultural institutions including community libraries, museums and art galleries can play in the support of lifelong learning.

As the boundaries continue to blur between learning and working, living and leisure, there will be opportunities to form new relationships and create new space types to support blended learning in its widest sense – where the learning 'demands' are overlaid on the 'supply' of community learning resources to create true learning-centred communities.

Illustration credits

1.2	Space for Personalised Learning, Creative Commons Licence	**5.6**	North Carolina State University
1.3	Aga Khan University	**5.7**	Alison Bourdon
1.4	Andrew Harrison	**5.8**	Massachusetts Institute of Technology
2.4	Courtesy of the University of Abertay, Dundee	**5.9**	University of Melbourne, first published in The University of Melbourne Voice, 2007
2.5	Courtesy of the University of Abertay, Dundee	**5.10**	University of Melbourne, first published in The University of Melbourne Voice, 2007
2.6	www.heppell.net		
2.7	www.heppell.net	**5.11**	© 2012 Regents of the University of Minnesota. Photographs used with permission.
2.8	Space for Personalised Learning, Creative Commons Licence		
2.9	DEGW	**5.12**	Abilene Christian University/ Jeremy Enlow
2.10	DEGW	**5.13**	Abilene Christian University/ Jeremy Enlow
2.11	John Collie, Reproduced with permission of Christchurch Art Gallery Te Puna O Waiwhetu	**5.14**	Norm Shafer
		5.15	Spaces That Work Ltd/ Robert Baker
3.4	Richard Keith Wolff	**5.16**	Aga Khan University
3.5	Richard Keith Wolff	**5.17**	Markus Kauppinen
4.2	Parsons Brinckerhoff/ Keith Paisley	**5.18**	Markus Kauppinen
4.3	Parsons Brinckerhoff/ Keith Paisley	**5.19**	UMSL / August Jennewein
4.4	Sydney Centre for Innovation in Learning	**5.20**	Queen Mary, University of London/Morley von Sternberg
4.5	Sydney Centre for Innovation in Learning	**5.21**	Queen Mary, University of London/Morley von Sternberg
4.6	Sydney Centre for Innovation in Learning	**5.22**	Queen Mary, University of London/Morley von Sternberg
4.7	EIW Architects	**5.23**	Aalto University
4.8	EIW Architects	**5.24**	Aalto University/ Sami Perttilä
4.9	Chicago History Museum	**5.26**	Keith Hunter Photography
4.10	Richard Wheeler	**5.27**	Sketch Studio London
4.11	David Trood	**5.31**	MVRDV/Rob't Hart
4.12	David Trood	**5.32**	MVRDV/Rob't Hart
4.13	Torben Eskerod	**5.33**	MVRDV/Rob't Hart
4.14	Rosan Bosch Studio/ Kim Wendt	**5.34**	Chris Gascoigne Photography
4.15	Rosan Bosch Studio/ Kim Wendt	**5.35**	Aalto Design Factory/ Kai Kuusisto
4.16	© dRMM Architects	**5.36**	Aalto Design Factory/ Kai Kuusisto
4.17	Space for Personalised Learning, Creative Commons Licence	**5.37**	d.school/ Scott Witthoft
4.18	© Alex de Rijke.	**5.38**	d.school/ Joel Simon
4.19	Fiordland Kindergarten	**5.39**	Andy Ryan
4.20	Studio Twenty Seven Architecture/ Hoachlander Davis Photography	**5.40**	Andy Ryan
		5.42	Nido Student Living
4.21	Studio Twenty Seven Architecture/ Hoachlander Davis Photography	**5.43**	Nido Student Living
		6.1	Getty images
4.22	Studio Twenty Seven Architecture/ Hoachlander Davis Photography	**6.2**	Courtesy of The Møller Centre – management training and conference centre in Cambridge, UK
5.5	Wikimedia Commons, uploaded by HBS1908 (http://commons.wikimedia.org/wiki/File:Inside_a_Harvard_Business_School_classroom.jpeg#file). Creative commons Licence.	**6.3**	Courtesy of The Møller Centre – management training and conference centre in Cambridge, UK
		6.4	Royal College of Surgeons

Illustration credits

Bibliography

Aalto Design Factory (2012) http://designfactory.aalto.fi/about/. Accessed 30 April 2013.

Aalto on tracks (2012) http://aaltoontracks.com/. Accessed 30 April 2013.

Aalto on waves (2012) http://www.aaltoonwaves.com/. Accessed 30 April 2013.

Aalto Venture Garage (Aaltovg) (2012) http://aaltovg.com/about/. Accessed 30 April 2013.

Aaltoes (2012) http://aaltoes.com/. Accessed 30 April 2013.

Acker, S.R. and Miller, M.D. (2005) 'Campus learning spaces: investing in how students learn', Educause Center for Applied Research Research Bulletin, vol. 2005, issue 8, 12 April. Retrieved from: http://net.educause.edu/ir/library/pdf/ERB0508.pdf

Aga Khan Development Network (AKDN) (2010) '2010 cycle award winners'. Retrieved from: http://akdn.org/architecture/awards.asp?tri=2010. Access 8 May 2013.

Akbar, A. (2009) 'The big question: how are public libraries changing, and what does their future hold?', The Independent, Tuesday 29 September. Retrieved from: http://www.independent.co.uk/arts-entertainment/books/features/the-big-question-how-are-public-libraries-changing-and-what-does-their-future-hold-1794725.html.

Akinsanmi, B. (2008). 'Optimal learning environments: societal expectations, learning goals and the role of school designers', Designshare. Retrieved from: http://www.designshare.com/index.php/articles/optimal-learning-environments-societal-expectations-learning-goals-and-the-role-of-school-designers/.

Alberta Foundation for the Arts (2011) 'Travelling exhibition program 2011/2012 booking calendar', Alberta Foundation for the Arts. Retrieved from: http://prairiegallery.com/wp-content/uploads/2011/05/TREX-booking2011_M05.pdf.

Alexander, C. (1976) A Pattern Language: Towns, Buildings, Construction, Centre for Environmental Structure Series, Oxford: OUP.

Alexander, K. (2003) 'Grandparents are returning to college, to retire', New York Times, 11 May.

Allen, J. (2005) 'GlaxoSmithKline pioneers flexible lab design: setting the stage for modern research', Tradeline, 28 June. Retrieved from: http://www.tradelineinc.com/reports/2005-6/glaxosmithkline-pioneers-flexible-lab-design. Accessed 3 May 2013.

Allen, T., Bell, A., Graham, R., Hardy, B. and Swaffer, F. (2004) Working Without Walls, London: OGC and DEGW.

American Association of School Librarians (AASL) (2012) 'AASL Crisis Toolkit'. Retrieved from: http://www.ala.org/aasl/aaslissues/toolkits/crisis#role.

American Institute of Architecture Students (AIAS) (2002) Taskforce on Studio Culture, report to AIAS. Retrieved from: http://www.aias.org/website/download.asp?id=314.

American Institute of Architecture Students (AIAS) (2008) Toward an Evolution of Studio Culture, report of the second AIAS task force on studio culture. Lessons Learned, Best Practices and Guidelines for an Effective Studio Culture Narrative. AIAS. Retrieved from: http://www.aias.org/website/download.asp?id=312.

American Library Association (ALA) (2012) 'Fact Sheet 1: Number of Libraries in the United States'. Retrieved from: http://www.ala.org/tools/libfactsheets/alalibraryfactsheet01.

American Library Association (ALA) 2011) 'State of America's Libraries: a report of the American Library association', American Libraries Special Issue. Retrieved from: http://www.ala.org/news/sites/ala.org.news/files/content/mediapresscenter/americaslibraries/state_of_americas_libraries_report_2011.pdf.

Anderson, D. (2011) 'Learning beyond the university: the Utopian tradition', in A. Boddington and J. Boys (eds) Reshaping Learning; A Critical Reader: The Future of Learning Spaces in Post-compulsory Education, Rotterdam, Boston, Taipei: Sense Publishers.

Apple (2008) 'Apple Classrooms of Tomorrow—Today. Learning in the 21st Century: background information', Apple, April. Retrieved from: http://ali.apple.com/acot2/global/files/ACOT2_Background.pdf.

Architecture Design Scotland (ND) 'Senses of Place: learning towns', DEGW Pamphlet. Retrieved from: http://www.ads.org.uk/resources/4472-senses-of-place-learning-towns-conference. Accessed 14 July 2013.

archdaily (2010) http://www.archdaily.com/97256/the-diana-center-at-barnard-college-weiss-manfredi/. Accessed 8 May 2013.

Arkitema Architects Hellerup School (2012) http://www.arkitema.com/Laering+Learning/Projekter/Hellerup+Skole.aspx. Accessed 8 May 2013.

ArtStreet (2012) http://artstreet.udayton.edu/about/index.html. Accessed 8 May 2013.

Asher, A., Duke, L. and Green, D. (2010) *The ERIAL Project: Ethnographic Research in Illinois Academic Libraries*. Retrieved from: http://www.academiccommons.org/commons/essay/erial-project.

Association for Learning Technology: Learning environments (2012) http://wiki.alt.ac.uk/index.php/Learning_environments#Extending_the_learning_environment_into_informal_settings. Accessed 8 May 2013.

Atherton, J. S. (2011) 'Teaching and learning; physical layout'. Retrieved from: http://www.learningandteaching.info/teaching/layout.htm.

ATL: The Education Union (nd) 'Standards for education premises'. Retrieved from: http://www.atl.org.uk/health-and-safety/work-environment/standards-education-premises.asp.

Audit Commission (2002) 'Building better library services', Audit Commission. Retrieved from: http://ebookbrowse.com/acklibrariesbr-pdf-d78363077.

Austin, S. and Harrison, A. (2009) 'The evolving academic workplace: efficient, effective and supportive', SCUP 44 conference presentation. Retrieved from: http://www.scup.org/page/annualconf/44/concurrent?pc_65475_page=2.

Australasian Association of Higher Education Facilities Planners (AAHEFP) (2009) *Space Planning Guidelines Edition 2,* Australasian Association of Higher Education Facilities Planners. Retrieved from: http://www.tefma.com/uploads/content/26-SpaceGuidelines.pdf.

Australia School Library Association (ASLA) (nd) 'Research findings on the value of libraries'. Retrieved from: http://www.asla.org.au/research/.

Bafitis, P.A. (2007) 'Multiuse dorm for New York', *Student Housing Business.com.* 2 July. Retrieved from: http://www.studenthousingbusiness.com/voices/1542-cathedral-gardens-multiuse-dorm-new-york-student-housing-news.html.

Baker, S. (2010) 'Huge BPP write-off announced as Apollo prophesies bleak short-term future for private demand', *Times Higher Education,* 18 November. Retrieved from: http://www.timeshighereducation.co.uk/story.asp?sectioncode=26&storyCode=414308&c=1.

Baraldi. S. (2010) 'Making the classroom a play-ground for knowledge', in Mäkitalo-Siegl et al. (eds) *Classroom of the Future: Orchestrating Collaborative Spaces*, Rotterdam, Boston, Taipei: Sense Publishers, 87–114.

Barnard College (2012) http://www.studenthousingbusiness.com/voices/1542-cathedral-gardens-multiuse-dorm-new-york-student-housing-news.html. Accessed 8 May 2013.

Barr, R. and Tagg, J. (1995) 'From teaching to learning – a new paradigm for undergraduate education', *Change*, November/December: 13–25. Retrieved from: http://ilte.ius.edu/pdf/barrtagg.pdf.

Barrett, P. and Zhang, Y. (2009) 'Optimal learning spaces: design implications for primary schools', Salford Centre for Research and Innovation in the built and human environment (SCRI). Retrieved from: http://www.oecd.org/dataoecd/38/47/43834191.pdf.

Barrett, P., Zhang, Y., Moffat, J.and Kobbacy, K. (2013) 'A holistic, multi-level analysis identifying the impact of classroom design on pupils' learning', Building and Environment 59 (2013) 678-689. Elsevier.

Bath Ventures Innovation Centre (2012) http://www.bath.ac.uk/bathventures/forbusiness/innovationcentre.html. Accessed 8 May 2013.

Battles, M. (2004) *Library: An Unquiet History,* London: Vintage.

BBC (2007a) April. http://news.bbc.co.uk/1/hi/education/6541251.stm. Accessed 8 May 2013.

BBC (2007b) September. http://news.bbc.co.uk/go/pr/fr/-/1/hi/education/7012203.stm. Accessed 8 May 2013.

BBC (2008) 12 April. http://news.bbc.co.uk/1/hi/7343027.stm. Accessed 8 May 2013.

BBC (2009) 'DIY gadgetry', Saini, A., 19 June. Retrieved from http://news.bbc.co.uk/1/hi/magazine/8107803.stm. Accessed 8 May 2013.

BBC (2011) http://www.bbc.co.uk/news/uk-england-12239388. Accessed 8 May 2013.

BBC (2011a) 'UK university reviews funding from Libya', 22 February, 2011. Accessed 12 May, 2013. http://www.bbc.co.uk/news/education-12537155.

BBC Education (2010) http://www.bbc.co.uk/news/education-10682980. Accessed 8 May 2013.

BBC Scotland (2011) 'Dumfries "learning town" vision examined', 26 June 2011. Retrieved from: bbc.co.uk/news/uk-scotland-south-scotland-13925967. Accessed 13 July 2013.

BBC Wales (2011) http://www.bbc.co.uk/news/uk-wales-16036749. Accessed 8 May 2013.

Becker, L. (2006) 'Globalisation and changing practices for academic librarians in Australia: a literature review', *Australian Academic and Research Libraries*, 37, 2 (June).

Retrieved from: http://www.alia.org.au/publishing/aarl/37.2/globalisation.pdf.

Becker, S. and Crandall, M.D. (2010) 'Opportunity for all: how the American public benefits from internet access at US libraries', Institute of Museum and Library Services (IMLS-2010-RES-01). Washington, D.C. Retrieved from: http://www.gatesfoundation.org/learning/Documents/OpportunityForAll.pdf

Beichner, R. (nd) 'The SCALE-UP project: a student-centered active learning environment for undergraduate programs', North Carolina State University. Retrieved from: http://www7.nationalacademies.org/bose/Beichner_CommissionedPaper.pdf.

Beichner, R., Bernold, L. and Dail, P. (1999) 'Case study of the physics component of an integrated curriculum', *Physics Education Research: A Section of the American Journal of Physics,* 67, 7 (July). Retrieved from: http://www.ncsu.edu/per/Articles/04IMPEC_AJP.pdf.

Bellamy, K. and Oppenheim, C. (2009) *Learning to Live: Museums, Young People and Education,* Institute for Public Policy Research and National Museum Directors' Conference. Retrieved from: http://www.nationalmuseums.org.uk/media/documents/publications/learning_to_live.pdf.

Bello, M. (2009) 'U.S. libraries on borrowed time?' *USA Today,* 1 February. Retrieved from: http://www.usatoday.com/news/education/2009-02-01-libraries_N.htm.

Benn, M. (2011) *School Wars: The Battle for Britain's Education,* London and New York: Verso.

Bennett, N., Andreae, J., Hegarty, P. and Wade, B. (1980) *Open Plan Schools,* Windsor: Schools Council Publishing/NFER.

Bennett, S. (2003) 'Libraries designed for learning', Council on Library and Information Resources, Washington, D.C. November. Retrieved from: http://www.libraryspaceplanning.com/assets/resource/libraries-designed-for-learning.pdf.

Bennett, S. (2009) 'Libraries and learning: a history of paradigm change', *Libraries and the Academy,* 9, 2: 188.

Bennett, S. (nd) 'Designing for intentional learning'. Retrieved from: http://www.libraryspaceplanning.com/assets/resource/Designing-for-Intentional-Learning.pdf.

BER (2009) http://www.deewr.gov.au/Schooling/BuildingTheEducationRevolution/Pages/default.aspx. Accessed 7 May 2013.

Berglund, E. (ed.) (2009) *Growing by Degrees: Universities in the Future of Urban Development,* London: Building Futures/RIBA. Retrieved from: http://www.buildingfutures.org.uk/assets/downloads/GROWING_BY_DEGREES___RIBA_Building_Futures_Web_Download.pdf.

Berk & Associates (2005) 'The Seattle Public Library Central Library: economic benefits assessment', Berk & Associates, July. Retrieved from: http://www.spl.org/Documents/branch/CEN/SPLCentral_Library_Economic_Impacts.pdf.

Berry, M. (2002) 'Healthy school environment and enhanced educational performance: the case of Charles Young Elementary School Washington DC', *The Carpet and Rug Institute,* 12 January. Retrieved from: http://www.carpet-health.org/pdf/CharlesYoungElementary.pdf.

Beyer Blinder Belle Architects & Planners LLP (2009) 'Building UB: the comprehensive physical plan', The University at Buffalo: the State University of New York. Retrieved from: http://www.buffalo.edu/ub2020/building_ub/building_ub.html.

bibliotheek (2012) http://www.bibliotheek.rotterdam.nl/EN/Information/aboutthelibrary/Pages/about.aspx. Accessed 8 May 2013.

Bingler, S. (2010) 'Rebuilding for the community in New Orleans', CELE Exchange 2010/14, OECD.

Biox (2012) 'Stanford University. Hotel space in the Clark Center: a new way to start new projects', unpublished paper, no date. Retrieved from: http://biox.stanford.edu/clark/images/Hotel_policies.pdf.

Birdsong, L. (2010) 'The Innovative Dutch libraries, universities, and research institutes in the netherlands', *Information Today,* 18, 2 (March). http://www.infotoday.com/searcher/mar10/Birdsong.shtml

Blankinship, D. G. (2010) 'Libraries fading as school budget crisis deepens', *The Boston Globe,* 24 June. Retrieved from: http://www.boston.com/news/nation/articles/2010/06/24/libraries_fading_as_school_budget_crisis_deepens/?rss_id=Boston.com+--+Latest+news.

Blaschke (2012) http://www.irrodl.org/index.php/irrodl/article/view/1076. Accessed 22 April 2012.

Blizard (nd) Blizard Institute, Barts and The London School of Medicine and Dentistry http://www.icms.qmul.ac.uk/. Accessed 22 April 2012.

Bloomberg (2011a) 'Getting into Harvard easier than McDonald's', *Bloomberg News.* Retrieved from: http://www.bloomberg.com/news/2011-01-26/getting-into-harvard-easier-than-mcdonald-s-hamburger-university-in-china.html.

Bloomberg (2011b) http://www.bloomberg.com/news/2011-10-19/apollo-fourth-quarter-profit-sales-top-analysts-estimates-1-.html. Accessed 22 April 2012.

Blyth, A. and Worthington, J. (2001; 2nd edn 2010), *Managing the Brief for Better Design,* London and New York: Routledge.

Boddington, A. and Boys, J. (eds) (2011) *Reshaping Learning; A Critical Reader: The Future of Learning Spaces in Post-compulsory Education,* Rotterdam, Boston, Taipei: Sense Publishers.

Boffey, D. (2011) 'School trips to museums are a thing of the past as budget cuts bite', *The Observer,* Sunday 8 May . Retrieved from: http://www.guardian.co.uk/education/2011/may/08/school-field-trip-funding-threat.

Bolstad, R. and Gilbert, J. (2008) *Disciplining and Drafting, or 21st Century Learning? Rethinking the New Zealand Senior School Curriculum for the Future,* Wellington: NZCER Press.

Bonanno, K. (2011) 'Do school libraries really make a difference?', *InCite*, 32, 5 (May): 5. Retrieved from: http://www.schoollibrarymanagement.com/articles/do-school-libraries-really-make-a-difference/.

Bonge, L. (2002) 'Designing flexibility', *American School and University*, September. Retrieved from: http://asumag.com/mag/university_designing_flexibility/.

Bosch, P. (2011) 'What Starbucks taught us about redesigning college campuses', *Fast Company,* 11 March. Retrieved from: http://www.fastcodesign.com/1663380/what-starbucks-taught-us-about-redesigning-college-campuses.

Boys, J. (2011) *Towards Creative Learning Spaces: Rethinking the Architecture of Post-compulsory Education,* London and New York: Routledge.

BPP (2013) http://www.bpp.com/about-bpp http://www.bpp.com/contact-us/press--media.aspx http://www.bpp.com/about-bpp/our-structure.aspx http://news.bbc.co.uk/go/pr/fr/-/1/hi/education/7012203.stm http://www.bpp.com/courses/degree-programmes.aspx http://www.bpp.com/contact-us/uk-study-centres/bpp-business-school-london-cit.aspx http://www.bpp.com/contact-us/press--media.aspx. Accessed 22 April 2012.

British Airways Flight Centre (BAFT) (2012) http://www.ebaft.com/corpent/corpent.htm. Accessed 22 April 2012.

British Council for School Environments (BCSE) and Morgan Ashurst (2008) *Family Guide to School Environments,* BCSE/Morgan Ashurst. Retrieved from: http://www.bcse.uk.net/downloads//476_broch2070_MA_BCSE_Morgan_Ashurst_FINAL_print.pdf.

British Library (2007) 'British Library Digital Centre: preliminary business case', unpublished paper, British Library.

British Library (2010) '2020 vision project: trends in the library environment', internal discussion document. British Library, February. Retrieved from: http://www.bl.uk/aboutus/stratpolprog/2020vision/searchdiscoverydelivery2.pdf.

British Library (2012) 'Growing knowledge: the British Library's strategy 2011–2015', British Library. Retrieved from: http://www.bl.uk/aboutus/stratpolprog/strategy1115/strategy1115.pdf.

British Museum (2012) http://www.britishmuseum.org/about_us/the_museums_story/great_court.aspx. Accessed 22 April 2012.

Brophy, P. (2007) *The Library in the Twenty-First Century,* London: Facet Publishing.

Brown, M. (2005) 'Learning spaces', Oblinger, D. and Oblinger, J. (eds) *Educating the Net Generation,* Educause. Retrieved from: http://net.educause.edu/ir/library/pdf/pub7101.pdf.

Bryant, M. (2011) 'First look inside London's £14m new super-library', London Evening Standard.co.uk, 22 November. Retrieved from: http://www.thisislondon.co.uk/standard/article-24012594-first-look-inside-londons-pound-14m-new-super-library.do.

Bucks Free Press (2012) http://www.bucksfreepress.co.uk/news/2193112.0/. Accessed 22 April 2012.

Buie, E. (2007) 'You're never too old to learn', *FE Focus,* 26 October. Retrieved from: http://www.tes.co.uk/article.aspx?storyCode=2453579.

Building Design (BD) (2012) BD Online http://www.bdonline.co.uk/news/michael-gove-in-new-attack-on-award-winning-architects/5012674.article. Accessed 22 April 2012.

Building Futures, 21st Century Libraries. Commission for Architecture and the Built Environment (CABE) and Royal Institute for British Architects (RIBA) in collaboration with Museums Libraries and Archives Council (MLA) (2004). Retrieved from: http://www.buildingfutures.org.uk/assets/downloads/pdffile_31.pdf.

BUPA (2011) 'Up, up and away', *BUPA World,* February. Retrieved from: http://194.75.37.236/bupaintlhome/partner/for-providers/provider-news-march-2011/global-news-march-2011.

Burke, C., Gallagher, C., Prosser, J. and Torrington, J. (2008). 'The view of the child: explorations of the visual culture of the made environment', in Tom Inns (ed.) *Designing for the 21st Century. Interdisciplinary Questions and Insights.* London: Ashgate.

Business Link University Innovation Centres (2012) http://www.businesslink.gov.uk/bdotg/action/detail?itemId=1084780139&r.i=1075067605&r.l1=1073858796&r.l2=1073859020&r.l3=1074415859&r.s=sc&r.t=RESOURCES&type=RESOURCES. Accessed 22 April 2012.

Campbell, R. (2009) 'Media Lab aims to elevate transparency', *The Boston Globe*, 6 December. Retrieved from: http://www.boston.com/ae/theater_arts/articles/2009/12/06/mit_media_lab_elevates_transparency/.

Carlson, S. (2012) 'Colleges and developers find common ground to build student housing', *The Chronicle of Higher Education,* 12 February. Retrieved from: http://chronicle.com/article/CollegesDevelopers-Find/130739/.

Carr, D. (2007) 'Machinima and education', Futurelab, September. Retrieved from: http://archive.futurelab.org.uk/resources/publications-reports-articles/web-articles/Web-Article794. Accessed 25 April 2013.

Caserotti, G. (2012) 'Questioning the answer', *Libraries and transliteracy,* 27 February. Retrieved from http://librariesandtransliteracy.wordpress.com/.

Cassidy, R. (2006) 'Rethinking workplace design', *Building Design and Construction* (BDC). http://stage.bdcnetwork.com. Accessed 8 May 2013.

Cassels, S. (2009) 'Dumfries learning town, executive summary', Architecture and Design, Scotland, Lisa Mackenzie Consultancy.

Cayman Islands Government (2008) 'Moving young minds', World Ministerial Seminar on Technology in Education, 8 January.

CELE (2010) 'Can the physical environment have an impact on the learning environment?', CELE Exchange 2010/13, Peter C. Lippman, JCJ Architecture, New York. OECD. Retrieved from: http://www.oecd.org/dataoecd/50/60/46413458.pdf.

CELE (2011) 'Schools of the future initiative in California', CELE Exchange 2011/7. OECD.

Centre for Research on Adaptive Nanostructures and Nanodevices (CRANN) (2012), Trinity College, Dublin. Retreived from: http://www.crann.tcd.ie/index.

Chartered Institute of Library and Information Professionals (CILIP) and the Museums Libraries and Archives Council (MLA) (2007) 'Designed for Learning: School libraries', MLA/ CILIP. Retrieved from: http://www.cilip.org.uk/sitecollectiondocuments/PDFs/policyadvocacy/Findoutmore.pdf.

Chartered Institute of Library and Information Professionals (CILIP) (2012) 'The primary school library guidelines', CILIP. Retrieved from: http://www.cilip.org.uk/filedownloadslibrary/groups/ylg/primaryschool_guidelines_2002.pdf.

Chartered Institute of Library and Information Professionals (CILIP) (2010) 'How many libraries are there in the UK?', CILIP. Retrieved from: http://www.cilip.org.uk/membership/enquiry-service/top-enquiries/pages/numberoflibraries.aspx. Accessed 25 April 2013.

Chartered Institute of Library and Information Professionals (CILIP) and Department of Education and Skills (DES) (nd) 'School libraries – making a difference', CILIP/ DES. Retrieved from: http://www.schoollibrariesadvocacy.org.uk/toolkit/making_a_difference.pdf.

Chronicle of Higher Education (2009) 'How do athletics endowments measure up?', *Chronicle of Higher Education,* 20 July. Retrieved from: http://chronicle.com/article/Athletics-Endowments-vs/47396/.

CILASS (2008) 'Learning spaces', CILASS Briefing Paper 003, University of Sheffield, May. Retrieved from: http://www.shef.ac.uk/content/1/c6/09/37/83/J24045_Briefing.pdf.

Civica (2011) 'Libraries, the community hub and service needs in the online age', Civica, March. Retrieved from: http://www.civica.co.uk/system/production/downloads/000/000/131/original/Library%20and%20Learning%20Roundtable%20Event%20White%20Paper%20-%20March%202011.pdf.

Clark, H. (2002) *Building Education: The Role of the Physical Environment in Enhancing Teaching and Research.* London: Institute of Education, University of London.

Clark, R. E. (ed.) (2001) *Learning from Media: Arguments, Analysis, and Evidence,* Greenwich, CT: Information Publishing Age.

Claxton, G., Lucas, B. and Webster, R. (2010) *Bodies of Knowledge: How the Learning Sciences Could Transform Practical and Vocational Education,* London: Edge Foundation.

Clay III, E.S. (2009) 'The partnership between public libraries and public education', *Virginia Libraries,* April–June, pp 11–14. Retrieved from: http://scholar.lib.vt.edu/ejournals/VALib/v55_n2/pdf/clay.pdf.

CLEAPSS (2006) 'Improving school laboratories?', report for the Royal Society of Chemistry on the number and quality of new and re- furbished laboratories in schools. CLEAPSS, October. Retrieved from: http://www.rsc.org/images/Labsreport_tcm18-65943.pdf.

Clyde, L.A. (1981) 'The magic casements: a survey of school library history from the eighth to the twentieth century', Ph.D. thesis, James Cook University, Australia, 1981. Retrieved from: http://eprints.jcu.edu.au/2051/.

Collini, S. (2012) *What Are Universities For?* London: Penguin Books.

Collins, P. (2004) 'Meeting room configurations: guidelines for meeting room seating arrangements', Jordan Webb. Retrieved from: http://www.midwest-facilitators.net/downloads/meeting_room_configurations_v5.pdf.

Commission for Architecture and the Built Environment (CABE) (2003) *Better Public Libraries,* London: CABE. Retrieved from: http://webarchive.nationalarchives.gov.uk/20110118095356/http://www.cabe.org.uk/files/better-public-libraries.pdf.

Commission for Architecture and the Built Environment (CABE) (2004) *Building Futures, 21st Century Libraries,* CABE and Royal Institute for British Architects (RIBA) in collaboration with Museums Libraries and Archives Council (MLA).

Commission for Architecture and the Built Environment (CABE) (2005) 'Picturing school design: a visual guide to secondary school buildings and their surroundings using the Design Quality Indicator for Schools', CABE. Retrieved from:

http://webarchive.nationalarchives.gov.uk/20110118095356/
http://www.cabe.org.uk/files/picturing-school-design.pdf.

Commission for Architecture and the Built Environment (CABE) (2006) 'Assessing secondary school design quality', research report, CABE. Retrieved from: http://webarchive. nationalarchives.gov.uk/20110118095356/http://www.cabe. org.uk/files/assessing-secondary-school-design-quality.pdf.

Commission for Architecture and the Built Environment (CABE) (2010a) *Creating Excellent Primary Schools: Guide for Clients*, CABE. Retrieved from: http://webarchive.nationalarchives. gov.uk/20110118095356/http://www.cabe.org.uk/files/ creating-excellent-primary-schools.pdf.

Commission for Architecture and the Built Environment (CABE) (2010b) 'Our school building matters: how to use investment in the fabric of your school to inspire learning', CABE. Retrieved from: http://www.designcouncil.org.uk/Documents/Documents/ Publications/CABE/our-school-building-matters.pdf.

Commission for Architecture and the Built Environment (CABE) and Building Futures (2004) *21st Century Schools: Learning Environments of the Future*, CABE/ Building Futures. Retrieved from: http://webarchive.nationalarchives.gov. uk/20110118095356/http://www.cabe.org.uk/files/21st- century-schools.pdf.

Complete University Guide (2012) http://www. thecompleteuniversityguide.co.uk/single.htm?ipg=6366. Accessed 25 April 2013.

Computer Clubhouse (2012) http://www.computerclubhouse.org. Accessed 25 April 2013.

Cotswold Conference Centre (2012) http://www. cotswoldconferencecentre.com/index.asp?id=144. Accessed 25 April 2013.

Council for Learning Outside the Classroom (2012) http://www. lotc.org.uk/what-is-lotc/. Accessed 25 April 2013.

Council on Library and Information Resources (CLIR) (2008) *No Brief Candle: Reconceiving Research Libraries for the 21st Century*, CLIR, August. Retrieved from: http://www.clir.org/ pubs/reports/pub142/reports/pub142/pub142.pdf.

Cox, G. (2005) 'Cox review of creativity in business: building on the UK's strengths', HM Treasury, report by Sir George Cox delivered November 2005. Retrieved from: http://www. hm-treasury.gov.uk/d/Cox_review-foreword-definition-terms- exec-summary.pdf.

Craddock, N. (2007) 'The rise of the super lab', *Laboratory News*. 8 November. Retrieved from: http://www.labnews.co.uk/ feature_archive.php/2546/5/rise-of-the-super-lab.

Crichton Foundation (2013). 'The Crichton Campus'. Retrieved

from: http://www.crichtonfoundation.org/the-crichton- campus. Accessed 13 July 2013.

Crocker, R. (2010) 'Neighborhood center helps Gufton area find its way', *Houston Chronicle*, 22 December. Retrieved from: http:// www.chron.com/news/houston-texas/article/Neighborhood- center-helps-Gulfton-area-find-its-1585590.php.

Cunnane, S. (2011) 'Time to budge up, for your budget's sake', *Times Higher Education*, 23 June. Retrieved from: http://www.timeshighereducation.co.uk/story. asp?storyCode=416591.

Curtis, G., Hammond, M., Hawtin, R., Ringland, G. and Yapp, C. (2011). 'Academic libraries of the future: scenarios beyond 2020', JISC. Retrieved from: http://www.futurelibraries.info/ content/system/files/scenarios_beyond_2020_reportwv.pdf.

Curtis, G. (2011) 'Academic libraries of the future final report', Curtis + Cartwright. Retrieved from: http://www. futurelibraries.info/content/system/files/LotFFinalreport.pdf.

d.school (2011) 'T Wall', Institute of Design, Stanford University. Retrieved from: http://dschool.stanford.edu/wp-content/ uploads/2011/03/dschool_TWALL1.pdf.

d.school (2012) 'd.school, Stanford University'. Retrieved from: http://dschool.stanford.edu/our-point-of-view/.

Daft, R.L. and Lengel, R.H. (1986). Organizational information requirements, media richness and structural design *Management Science*, 32, 5: 554–71.

Dalton, P., Elkin, J. and Hannaford, A. (2006) 'Joint use libraries as successful strategic alliances', *Library Trends*, 54 4: 535–48. Retrieved from: http://www.thefreelibrary. com/Joint+use+libraries+as+successful+strategic+allianc es.-a0147824995.

Darmody, M., Smyth, E. and Doherty, C. (2010) 'Designing primary schools for the future', The Economic and Social Research Institute, Dublin. Retrieved from: http://www.esri.ie/ UserFiles/publications/RS16/RS016.pdf.

Davies, S. (2008) 'Taking stock: the future of our public library service', Unison. Retrieved from: http://www.unison.org.uk/ acrobat/17301.pdf.

Day, W. (2009) 'Office space: how will technology affect the education office environment?', *American School and University*, 81, 10: 28–31. Retrieved from: http://asumag. com/Construction/technology/technology-education- office-200905/index1.html.

De Gregori, A. (2011) 'Reimagining the classroom: opportunities to link recent advances in pedagogy to physical settings', NJIT Center for Building Knowledge. Retrieved from: http://mcgraw-hillresearchfoundation.org/wp-content/

uploads/2011/10/Reimagining_the_Classroom_ DeGregoriFINAL.pdf.

DEGW (2005) *The Changing Finnish Goverment Workplace: The development of new workplace guidelines.* DEGW. http://www.senaatti.fi/tiedostot/DEGW_2005.pdf. Accessed 10 May 2013.

DEGW (2006–8) unpublished research data.

DEGW (2008a) 'Future Academic Library case studies', unpublished DEGW research paper.

DEGW (2008b) 'Campus concepts report', The University at Buffalo, the State University of New York.

DEGW (2009) Unpublished presentation.

DEGW (nd) Unpublished project data.

Delanty, G. (2001) *Challenging Knowledge: The University in the Knowledge Society,* Buckingham and Philadelphia: The Society for Research into Higher Education and Open University Press.

Den Heijer, A. (2011a), *Managing the University Estate,* Delft: Eburon Academic Publishers.

Den Heijer, A. (2011b) 'Rethinking the academic workplace: opportunities of a crisis', PowerPoint presentation at SCUP 46, TU Delft, 26 July. Retrieved from: http://managingtheuniversitycampus.files.wordpress.com/2011/03/july-26-2011-scup-c226-adh-hand-out.pdf.

Dennis, A.R. and Valacich, J.S. (1999), 'Rethinking media richness: towards a theory of media synchronicity', paper delivered at 32nd Hawaii International Conference on System Sciences.

Department for Business, Innovation and Skills (BIS) (2011) 'Higher education: students at the heart of the system', BIS, June. Retrieved from: http://c561635.r35.cf2.rackcdn.com/11-944-WP-students-at-heart.pdf.

Department for Children, Schools and Families (DCSF) (2004a) *Building Bulletin 98: Framework for Secondary School Projects.* DCSF.

Department for Children, Schools and Families (DCSF) (2004b) *Building Bulletin 77: Designing for Pupils with Special Educational Needs and Disabilities in Schools.* DCSF.

Department for Children, Schools and Families (DCSF) (2007) *Project Faraday. Compendium of Exemplar Designs.* DSCF. Retrieved from: http://www.partnershipsforschools.org.uk/documents/library/BSF-archive/Faraday_exemplars_1.pdf.

Department for Children, Schools and Families (DCSF) (2008) *Project Faraday: Exemplar Designs for Science,* Department for Children, Schools and Families. Retrieved from: http://www.partnershipsforschools.org.uk/documents/library/BSF-archive/Faraday_exemplars_1.pdf; http://www.partnershipsforschools.org.uk/documents/library/BSF-archive/ProjectFaraday_Part2.pdf.

Department for Children, Schools and Families (DCSF) (2009) *Food Technology Spaces in Secondary Schools: A Design Guide,* DCSF. Retrieved from: http://www.data.org.uk/generaldocs/DCfS%20design%20guide%20for%20Food%20Rooms-1.pdf.

Department for Culture, Media and Sport (DCMS) (2003) *Framework for the Future: Libraries, Learning and Information in the Next Decade,* DCMS. Retrieved from: http://www.healthlinklibraries.co.uk/pdf/Framework_for_the_Futures.pdf.

Department for Education and Employment (DfEE) (1990/99) *Building Bulletin 71. The Outdoor Classroom: Educational Use, Landscape Design and Management of School Grounds,* Her Majesty's Stationery Office. Retrieved from: https://www.education.gov.uk/publications/eOrderingDownload/112710611.pdf.pdf.

Department for Education and Employment (DfE) (1999) *The National Curriculum Handbook for Primary Teachers in England.* www.nc.uk.net http://www.educationengland.org.uk/documents/pdfs/1999-nc-primary-handbook.pdf. Accessed 9 May 2013.

Department for Education and Skills (DfES) (2002) *Building Bulletin 95: Schools for the Future. Designing for Learning Communities.* The Stationery Office TSO. Retrieved from: http://www.archive2.official-documents.co.uk/document/reps/bulletin95/bulletin95.pdf.

Department for Education and Skills (DfES) (2003) *The Future of Higher Education.* DfES. http://www.bis.gov.uk/assets/BISCore/corporate/MigratedD/publications/F/future_of_he.pdf. Accessed 9 May 2013.

Department for Education and Skills (DfES) (2003a) *Classrooms of the Future.* DfES, 2003. Retrieved from: http://www.education.gov.uk/publications/eOrderingDownload/DfES%200162%20200MIG504.pdf

Department for Education and Skills (DfES) (2004) *Schools for the Future – Exemplar Designs: Concepts and Ideas.* DfES. Retrieved from: http://www.partnershipsforschools.org.uk/documents/library/BSF-archive/compendium.pdf.

Department for Education and Skills (DfES) (2004a) *Schools for the Future – An Inspirational Guide to Remodelling Secondary Schools.* DfES. Retrieved from: http://www.partnershipsforschools.org.uk/documents/library/BSF-archive/Transforming-schools-combined.pdf.

Department for Education and Skills (DfES) (2004b) *Building Bulletin 81: Design and Technology Accommodation in Secondary Schools: A Design Guide,* The Stationery Office (TSO). Retrieved from: http://www.effefftee.co.uk/assets/files/Design_Tech_Part1.pdf

Department for Education and Skills (DfES) (2004c) *Building Schools for the Future: A New Approach to Capital Investment*. DfES. Retrieved from: http://webarchive.nationalarchives. gov.uk/20130401151715/https://www.education.gov. uk/publications/eOrderingDownload/DfES%200134%20 200MIG469.pdf.

Department for Education and Skills (DfES) (2005) *Harnessing Technology: Transforming Learning and Children's Services*. http://webarchive.nationalarchives.gov.uk/20130401151715/ https://www.education.gov.uk/publications/standard/Depar tmentalobjectivesandprogress/Page1/DFES-1296-2005. Accessed 10 May 2013.

Department for Education and Skills (DfES) (2005a) *Building Schools for the Future: Consultation on a New Approach to Capital Investment*, DfES. http://webarchive.nationalarchives. gov.uk/20130401151715/https://www.education.gov. uk/publications/eOrderingDownload/DfES%200134%20 200MIG469.pdf. Accessed 30 April, 2013.

Department for Education and Skills (DfES) (2005b) *Schools for the Future – Inspirational Design for PE and Sports Spaces*. DfES. Retrieved from: http://www.partnershipsforschools.org. uk/documents/library/BSF-archive/ExtendedServices.pdf.

Department for Education and Skills (DfES) (2006) *Schools for the Future – designing schools for extended services*. DfES. Retrieved (Parts One and Two) from:

Department for Education and Skills (DfES) (2006a) *Schools for the Future – Designing School Grounds*. DfES. Retrieved from: http://www.partnershipsforschools.org.uk/documents/library/ BSF-archive/Transforming-schools-combined.pdf.

Department for Education and Skills (DfES) (2006b) *Better Buildings, Better Design, Better Education. A report on capital investment in education*. DfES.

Department for Education and Skills (DfES) (2006c) *Learning Outside the Classroom Manifesto*, DfES. http://webarchive. nationalarchives.gov.uk/20130401151715/; https://www. education.gov.uk/publications/standard/publicationDetail/ Page1/DFES-04232-2006 Accessed 10 May, 2013.

Department for Education and Skills (DfES) (2007) *Better Buildings, Better Design, Better Education. A report on capital investment in education*. http://dera.ioe.ac.uk/7713/1/ Better%20Education%20v2.pdf. Accessed 9 May 2013.

Department for Education and Skills (DfES) (nda) *Building Bulletin 99: Briefing Framework for Primary School Projects*, DfES. Retrieved from: http://media.education.gov.uk/assets/files/ pdf/b/building%20bulletin%2099%20-%20briefing%20 framework%20for%20primary%20school%20projects.pdf.

Department for Education and Skills (DfES) (ndb) *Building Bulletin 98: Briefing Framework for Secondary School Projects*, DES. Retrieved from: http://media.education.gov.uk/assets/ files/pdf/b/building%20bulletin%2098%20%20briefing%20 framework%20for%20secondary%20school%20projects.pdf.

Department for Innovation, Universities and Skills (DIUS) (2009a) *The Learning Revolution*, London, The Stationery Office. Retrieved from: http://www.bis.gov.uk/assets/biscore/ corporate/migratedD/publications/L/learning_revolution.

Department for Innovation, Universities and Skills (DIUS) (2009b) Government White Paper, DIUS March 2009.

Deschenes, S., Arbreton, A. and Little, P. (2010) *Engaging Older Youth: program and city-level strategies to support sustained participation in out-of-school time*. Harvard Family Research Project. Retrieved from: http://www. hfrp.org/out-of-school-time/publications-resources/ engaging-older-youth-program-and-city-level-strategies-to-support-sustained-participation-in-out-of-school-time.

Desertcreat (2012) http://www.keppiedesign.co.uk/index.php/ services/architecture/desertcreat-college. Accessed 24 April 2013.

Design Council (2005) 'Learning environments campaign prospectus: from the inside looking out', Design Council.

Dewey, J. (1897) 'My pedagogic creed', *School Journal* 54 (January): 77–80.

De Zeen (2012) 'The Hive by Feilden Clegg Bradley Studios', *De Zeen Magazine*, 10 April. Retrieved from: http://www.dezeen. com/2012/04/12/the-hive-by-feilden-cleggbradley-studios/.

DfE (2013) http://www.education.gov.uk/inthenews/speeches/ a0077948/michael-goves-speech-to-the-policy-exchange-on-free-schools. Accessed 9 March 2013.

Dicke, T. (1992) *Franchising in America: The Development of a Business Method, 1840–1980,* Chapel Hill, NC: University of North Carolina Press.

DIUS (2009) *The Learning Revolution*, Government White Paper, March.

Dodd, J. and Jones, C. (2009) 'Articulate: an evaluation of the National Gallery's secondary school literacy project 2008-2009', Research Centre for Museums and Galleries (RCMG), September. Retrieved from: http://www2.le.ac. uk/departments/museumstudies/rcmg/projects/articulate/ articulateSummary.pdf.

Dodd, J. and Jones, C. (2010) 'Towards a new social purpose: redefining the role of botanic gardens', Research Centre for Museums and Galleries/Botanic Gardens Conservation International London. Retrieved from: http://www.bgci. org/files/Worldwide/Education/Social_inclusion/social%20 inclusion%20report.pdf.

DOE (2011) 'Review of education capital', DOE, James, S.

Domino's Pizza (2012) http://www.referenceforbusiness.com/history2/60/Domino-s-Pizza-Inc.html. Accessed 9 March 2013.

Donkai, S., Toshmori, A. and Mizoue, C. (2011) 'Academic libraries as learning spaces in Japan: toward the development of learning commons', Asia-Pacific Conference Library & Information Education & Practice, 2011 proceedings. Retrieved from: http://fim.uitm.edu.my/aliep2011/images/stories/pdf/practice.pdf.

Donovan, J.J. (1921) School Architecture: Principles and Practice, New York: Macmillan.

Doorley, S. and Witthoft, S. (2012) Make Space: How to Set the Stage for Creative Collaboration, Hoboken, NJ: Wiley & Sons.

Dori, Y.J. and Belcher, J. (2004) 'How does technology-enabled active learning affect undergraduate students' understanding of electromagnetism concepts', Journal of the Learning Sciences, 14, 2. Retrieved from: http://web.mit.edu/8.02t/www/802TEAL3D/visualizations/resources/TEAL_JLS_10_2004.pdf. Accessed 25 April 2013.

Douglas, J. and Wilkinson, S. (2010) 'School Libraries: A plan for improvement'. Museums, Libraries and Archives Council. Retrieved from: http://www.literacytrust.org.uk/assets/0000/5718/School_Libraries_A_Plan_for_Improvement.pdf.

Downes, S. (2012) http://www.downes.ca/post/53825. Accessed 9 March 2013.

Drivers Jonas (2007) 'University College London Office Space Utilisation Part 1', Drivers Jonas. Retrieved from: http://www.ucl.ac.uk/estates/space/UCL%20Office%20Utilisation%20Study.pdf.

Dubhthaigh, R. and Barter, T. (2006) 'Food for thought: a service based approach to embedding innovation', Innovation RCA, Royal College of Art, London.

Duderstadt, J. (1997) 'The future of the university in an era of change', The Association of the Collegiate Schools of Planning, Georgia Institute of Technology College of Architecture 7 March. Retrieved from: http://milproj.dc.umich.edu/publications/change/download/change.pdf.

Duderstadt, J., Wulf, W. and Zemsky, R. (2007) 'Envisioning a transformed university', Issues Online in Science and Technology. Retrieved from: http://www.issues.org/22.1/duderstadt.html.

Dugdale, S. (2009) 'Space strategies for the new learning landscape', Educause Review, March/April. Retrieved from: http://www.educause.edu/EDUCAUSE+Review/EDUCAUSEReviewMagazineVolume44/SpaceStrategiesfortheNewLearni/163820.

Dugdale, S. and Long, P. (2007) 'Planning the informal learning landscape', ELI Webinar 12 March. Retrieved from: http://net.educause.edu/ir/library/pdf/ELIWEB073.pdf.

Duggan, F. (2004) 'The changing nature of the studio as an educational setting', CEBE Transactions, 1, 2 (December): 70–6. Retrieved from: http://www.cebe.heacademy.ac.uk/transactions/pdf/FionaDuggan.pdf.

Duggan, F. and Dugdale, S. (2003) 'The distributed university sustained by convenient technology and meaningful space', SCUP July.

Dvir, R. (2006) 'Knowledge city, seen as a collage of human knowledge moments', in Carillo, F. (ed.), Knowledge Cities: Approaches, Experiences, and Perspectives, Burlington, MA: Butterworth Heinemann. Retrieved from: http://innovationecology.com/papers/knowledge%20city%20human%20moments%20dvir1.pdf.

Dvir, R., Garcia, T., Ozores, F. and Shwartzberg, Y. (2007) 'The future center as a catalyzer for innovation ecology in science & technology parks', paper for IASP conference, Barcelona 2007. Retrieved from: http://innovationecology.com/papers/Future%20Center%20for%20Science%20and%20Tech%20Parks.pdf.

E&SC (2007) 'Sustainable schools: are we building schools for the future?', seventh report of session 2006–07 vol. 1, House of Commons Education and Skills Committee.

EC (2009) http://ec.europa.eu/education/lifelong-learning-policy/doc/year09/manifesto_en.pdf. Accessed 9 March 2013.

The Eden Project (2012) 'The Core', Eden Project. http://www.edenproject.com/come-and-visit/whats-here/the-core. Accessed 9 March 2013.

Edge Hill University (2012) http://www.edgehill.ac.uk/about/history http://www.edgehill.ac.uk/study/courses/education/pd http://www.edgehill.ac.uk/about/profile/people http://www.edgehill.ac.uk/study/courses/education/pd/courses http://www.edgehill.ac.uk/study/courses/education/pd/scienceDevelopmentCentre http://info.edgehill.ac.uk/EHU_eprospectus/Health/ http://www.edgehill.ac.uk/about/developments/recent. Accessed 9 March 2013.

Educational Facilities Laboratories (EFL) (1966) 'Profiles of significant schools: schools without walls', Educational Facilities Laboratories. Retrieved from: http://archone.tamu.edu/CRS/engine/archive_files/EFL000.1417.pdf.

Education Scotland (2004). Retrieved from: http://www.educationscotland.gov.uk/thecurriculum/whatiscurriculumforexcellence/howwasthecurriculumdeveloped/processofchange/timeline.asp.

Educause Learning Initiative (ELI) (2011) '7 things you should know about the modern learning commons', ELI, April 2011. Retrieved from: http://net.educause.edu/ir/library/pdf/ELI7071.pdf.

Edwards, B. (2000) *University Architecture*, London: Taylor & Francis.

Ellis, W. (2010) 'iTEC designing the future classroom: project overview', *European Schoolnet*. Retrieved from: http://itec.eun.org/c/document_library/get_file?p_l_id=10307&folderId=15051&name=DLFE-653.pdf.

Emory College of Arts and Sciences (2012) http://www.college.emory.edu/home/about/history.html. Accessed 9 March 2013.

EMS (2010) 'Performance in higher education estates', *EMS annual report 2011*. HEFCE.

The Erasmus Centre for Early Modern Studies (2012) Rotterdam Central Library http://www.erasmus.org/. Accessed 9 March 2013.

ERIAL (2012) http://www.academiccommons.org/commons/essay/erial-project. Accessed 9 March 2013.

European Commission (EC) (2009) 'European ambassadors for creativity and innovation manifesto'. ec.europa.eu/education/lifelong-learning-policy/doc/.../manifesto_en.pdf. Accessed 9 March 2013.

Evanshen, P. and Faulk, J. (2011) *A Room to Learn: Rethinking Classroom Environments*, Silver Spring, MD: Gryphon House Inc.

Ezard, J. (2004) 'British libraries could shut by 2020', *Guardian* Wednesday 28 April. Retrieved from: http://www.guardian.co.uk/uk/2004/apr/28/books.highereducation.

Faculty of Arts and Science, Aga Khan University (FASAKU) (2010a) 'Concept note on science spaces', unpublished paper. November.

Faculty of Arts and Science, Aga Khan University (FASAKU) (2010b) 'Concept note on food services', unpublished paper. November.

Faculty of Arts and Science, Aga Khan University (FASAKU) (2010c) 'Concept note on the East Africa Innovation Hub', unpublished paper. December.

Fazackerley, A., Smith, M and Massey, A. (2009) 'Innovation and industry: the role of universities; Policy Exchange'. Retrieved from: http://www.policyexchange.org.uk/images/publications/innovation%20and%20industry%20-%20the%20role%20of%20universities%20-%20nov%2009.pdf.

Fearn, H. (2009) 'Grand designs on hold until future of learning is clear', *Times Higher Education,* 28 May. Retrieved from: http://www.timeshighereducation.co.uk/story.asp?storyCode=406725&sectioncode=26.

Fearn, H. (2009) '"Excellence"? Aye, there's the "hub"', *Times Higher Education,* 31 December. Retrieved from: http://www.timeshighereducation.co.uk/story.asp?storyCode=409716&sectioncode=26.

Fearn, H. (2010) 'The colour of money', *Times Higher Education*, 10 June. Retrieved from: http://www.timeshighereducation.co.uk/story.asp?storyCode=411971.

Feilden Clegg Bradley Studios (2012) *Education, Architecture, Urbanism: Three University Projects*. Retrieved from: http://fcbstudios.com/practice.asp. Accessed 13 July 2013.

Felder, R. and Soloman, B. (2002) 'Learning styles and strategies'. http://www2.ncsu.edu/unity/lockers/users/f/felder/public/ILSdir/styles.htm. Accessed 9 March 2013.

Ferguson, J. and Owen, M. (2012) *The Australian*, 6 March. http://www.theaustralian.com.au/national-affairs/state-politics/after-the-revolution-the-bailouts/story-e6frgczx-1226289873281. Accessed 9 March 2013.

Fielding, R. (2006) 'Learning, lighting and color: lighting design for schools and universities in the 21st century'. Retrieved from: http://www.designshare.com/articles/1/133/fielding_light-learn-color.pdf.

Fielding, R. and Nair, P. (2005) 'The language of school design: design patterns for 21st century schools', DesignShare.

Fielding, R., Lackney, J. and Nair, P. (2006) 'Master classroom: let Leonardo da Vinci, Albert Einstein, and Jamie Oliver show you the future', *Edutopia Magazine*, June. Retrieved from: http://www.designshare.com/index.php/articles/master_classroom.

Fink, I. (2003) 'Class laboratories space use and utilization', *Facilities Manager Magazine*, 19, 6 (November/December). Retrieved from: http://www.org/FacilitiesManager/article.cfm?ItemNumber=1507&parentid=1506.

Fink, I. (2004) 'Research space: who needs it, who gets it, who pays for it?', *Planning Higher Education* 33, 1. Retrieved from: http://www1.scup.org/PHE/FMPro?-db=PubItems.fp5&-lay=ART&-format=read_full.htm&-error=error.htm&ID_pub=PUB-EXJZAZi3DNEWMZo88q&t_Pub_PgNum=5&-SortField=t_Pub_PgNum&-Find.

Fink, I. (2005) 'Offices on campus', *Facilities Manager Magazine*, 21, 3 (May/June). Online version, p. 2.

Finkelstein, A. (2010) 'Nation's biggest landlord runs into tough sales market', World Property Channel. Retrieved from: http://www.worldpropertychannel.com/us-markets/commercial-real-estate-1/general-services-administration-gsa-ralph-conner-moira-mack-office-of-management-budget-old-orchard-light-station-manitowoc-breakwater-light-3547.php. Accessed 9 March 2013.

Fisher, K. (2010) 'Technology-enabled active learning environments: an appraisal', CELE Exchange 2010/7. OECD. Retrieved from: http://www.oecd.org/dataoecd/33/38/45565315.pdf.

Fisher, K., (2005) 'Linking pedagogy and space: proposed planning principles'. Department of Education and Training [Victoria], section 2.09. Retrieved from: http://www.eduweb.vic.gov.au/edulibrary/public/assetman/bf/Linking_Pedagogy_and_Space.pdf.

Fisher, K. (2007) 'Ne(x)t gen learning environments', in Scottish Government, *Building Excellence: Exploring the Implications of the Curriculum for Excellence for School Building* (pp. 19–28). Edinburgh: The Scottish Government. Retrieved from: http://www.scotland.gov.uk/Resource/Doc/207034/0054999.pdf.

Florida State University (2011) 'Institute of Sports Sciences and Medicine kicks off'. http://www.fsu.com/News-Archive/2011/May/Institute-of-Sports-Sciences-and-Medicine-kicks-off-at-Florida-State. Accessed 9 March 2013.

Fmlink (2012) 'Molding the workplace to support innovation and creativity'. Retrieved from: http://fmlink.info/article.cgi?type=Magazine&title=Molding%20the%20workplace%20to%20support%20innovation%20and%20creativity&pub=RFP%20Office%20Space&id=31082&mode=source. Accessed 9 March 2013.

Forbes (1997) *Forbes Magazine,* 3 October.

Ford, L. (2002) 'More Older People Returning to College', *Guardian,* 3 October. Retrieved from: http://www.education.guardian.co.uk/further /story/0,,804081,00.html.

Fowler, G. (1998) 'The museum school: a model for educating through the arts', Museums and the Charter School Movement, *Museum News,* September/October. Retrieved from: http://www.aam-us.org/pubs/mn/MN_SO98_MuseumCharter.cfm.

Francisco, S. (2006) 'MIT Steam Café', in Diana Oblinger (ed.) *Learning Spaces*, Educause. Retrieved from: http://www.educause.edu/learningspacesch27.

Freedman, M. (2002) *Prime Time: How Baby Boomers Will Revolutionize Retirement and Transform America,* New York: PublicAffairs.

FutureCentres (2010) http://resilientcommunities.org/wp-content/uploads/2010/04/FutureCentres.pdf. Accessed 9 March 2013.

Futurelab (2006) 'Savannah Project', Futurelab. Retrieved from: http://archive.futurelab.org.uk/resources/documents/project_flyers/savannah.pdf.

Futurelab (2008) 'Reimagining outdoor learning spaces: primary capital, co-design and educational transformation', Futurelab. Retrieved from: http://www2.futurelab.org.uk/resources/documents/handbooks/outdoor_learning_spaces2.pdf.

Futurelab (2012) http://www.futurelab.org.uk/resources/publications-reports-articles/web-articles/Web-Article794. Accessed 9 March 2013.

Gallagher, L. (2010) 'Live simulated surgery at Science Festival show', *Imperial College News,* 11 June. Retrieved from: http://www3.imperial.ac.uk/newsandeventspggrp/imperialcollege/newssummary/news_11-6-2010-17-25-5.

Galloway, J. (2007) 'A 21st-century pencil case', *Guardian,* 9 January. Retrieved from: http://www.guardian.co.uk/education/2007/jan/09/elearning.technology1.

Gaston, P. (2010) *The Challenge of Bologna: What United States Education Has to Learn from Europe, and Why It Matters that We Learn It,* Virginia: Stylus Publishing.

Gayle, D. (2012) Mail Online 30 July. Accessed 1 November 2012.

Gibbons, S. (2007) *The Academic Library and the Net Gen Student: making the connections*, Chicago: ALA Editions.

Gibson, V. and Luck, R. (2004) *Flexible Working in Central Government: Leveraging the Benefits*. London: Office of Government Commerce.

Gil, N. (2009) 'The BSF programme: teacher involvement in design (A)', Manchester Business School, The University of Manchester. Retrieved from: http://www.php.portals.mbs.ac.uk/Portals/49/docs/ngil/BSF%20Case%20Study%20Online%20Post.pdf.

Gilbert, A. (2007) 'Positioning the University of Manchester as a premium provider of world class undergraduate education', briefing paper for 2007-08 review of teaching, learning and the student experience, August. Retrieved from: http://www.manchester.ac.uk/medialibrary/staffnet/briefing_paper_ug_education.pdf.

Gilbert, J., (2005), *Catching the Knowledge Wave? The Knowledge Society and the Future of Education,* Wellington: NZCER Press.

Gill, J. (2009) 'Office size shows who measures up', *Times Higher Education,* 12 February. Retrieved from: http://www.timeshighereducation.co.uk/story.asp?storyCode=405324.

Gillard, D. (2011) *Education in England: A Brief History*. Retrieved from: http://www.educationengland.org.uk/history/chapter02.html#01.

Gillie, C. (2012) SN/SP/6484. Standard Note to Members of Parliament by Social Policy Section.

Gordon, D. (2010a) 'Multipurpose spaces', National Clearinghouse for Educational Facilities, October. Retrieved from: http://www.ncef.org/pubs/multipurp.pdf.

Gordon, D. (2010b) 'Teacher workspaces', National Clearinghouse for Educational Facilities, October, p. 1 Retrieved from: http://www.ncef.org/pubs/teacherspace.pdf.

Gove (2011) YouTube video uploaded by Department for Education.

Graham, G. (2002) *Universities: The Recovery of an Idea,* Thorverton, UK: Imprint Academic.

Gray, C. (2010) 'Alternative education spaces in Mexico', *CELE Exchange* 2010/11, OECD. Retrieved from: http://www.oecd.org/dataoecd/13/15/46380847.pdf.

Green, A. (1992) *Education and State Formation: The Rise of Education Systems in England, France, and the USA,* Basingstoke: Macmillan.

Green, H. and Hannon, C. (2007) *Their Space: Education for a Digital Generation,* London: Demos. Retrieved from: http://www.demos.co.uk/files/Their%20space%20-%20web.pdf.

Greenstein, D. (2009) 'Libraries of the future', *Inside Higher Education*, 24 September.

Guardian (2012a) 'Academies to become a majority among state secondary schools', 5 April. http://www.guardian.co.uk/education/2012/apr/05/academies-majority-state-secondary-schools. Accessed 9 May, 2013.

Guardian (2012b) 'Michael Gove faces rebellion over no-curves school plan', 31 December. http://www.guardian.co.uk/education/2012/dec/31/michael-gove-rebellion-no-curves-schools. Accessed 9 May .

GVA Grimley (2010) *Further Complications: Further Education Estate Management in the Age of Austerity,* GVA Grimley.

H2G2 (2012) The Peckham Library http://h2g2.com/dna/h2g2/A1043164. Accessed 9 March 2013.

Hackerspaces (2012) http://hackerspaces.org/wiki/Hackerspaces. Accessed 9 March 2013.

Häggström, B. (ed.) (2004) 'The role of libraries in lifelong learning', final report of the IFLA project under the Section for Public Libraries, IFLA, 2004. Retrieved from: http://archive.ifla.org/VII/s8/proj/Lifelong-LearningReport.pdf.

Hamilton, C. (2009) 'Fusion building: new trend with some old roots', *Planning for Higher Education,* 37, 2: 44–51. Retrieved from: http://www1.scup.org/PHE/FMPro?-db=PubItems.fp5&-lay=ART&-format=read_full.htm&-error=error.htm&ID_pub=PUB-DWPkJe1BbJR5yFkPZN&t_Pub_PgNum=44&-SortField=t_Pub_PgNum&-Find.

Hanna, D. and Kirby, C. (2008) 'Integrating mission and classroom design', SCUP 43 PowerPoint presentation, SCUP. Retrieved from: http://www.scup.org/asset/55173/SCUP-43_20080722_CC-65.pdf.

Hardy, B., Graham, R., Stansall, P., White, A. Harrison, A., Bell, A. and Hutton, L. (2008) *Working Beyond Walls: The Government Workplace as an Agent of Change,* London: OGC and DEGW.

Hargreaves, G. (2011) 'Higher education faces "maelstrom"', BBC Radio 4 broadcast 24 June. Retrieved from: http://news.bbc.co.uk/today/hi/today/newsid_9521000/9521628.stm.

Harris, S. (2010) 'The Place of Virtual, Pedagogic and Physical Space in the 21st Century Classroom', Sydney Centre for Innovation in Learning, 2010. Retrieved from: http://scil.com.au/documents/stephen-harris_virtual-pedagogical-physical-space.pdf

Harrison, A. (2006) 'BOX', in Diana Oblinger (ed.) *Learning Spaces*, Educause. Retrieved from: http://www.educause.edu/learningspacesch23.

Harrison, A. (2007) 'Working to Learn: design in educational transformation', Fourth Annual Founders' Lecture, November 2006, DEGW.

Harrison, A. and Cairns, A. (2008) *The Changing Academic Workplace,* DEGW. Retrieved from: http://ipddirectedstudies.files.wordpress.com/2011/01/the-changing-academic-workplace-degw-27-10-08.pdf.

Harrison, A. and Dugdale, S. (2004) 'The SANE research project: its implications for higher education', *Planning for Higher Education*, 31: 33–42.

Harrison, A. and Tsao, T.–C. (2006) 'Enlarging the academic community: creating retirement communities linked to academic institutions', *Planning for Higher Education,* January – March. Society for College and University Planning (SCUP). Retrieved from: http://www.collegiateretirementcommunity.com/resources/SCUP_V34-N2-Harrison-Tsao.pdf.

Harrison, A., Andrew, P. and Bradley, S. (2010) 'Creative hubs: moulding the workplace for the innovation generation', *RFP Space*, Feb–March. Retrieved from: http://www.fmlink.com/article.cgi?type=Magazine&title=Molding%20the%20workplace%20to%20support%20innovation%20and%20creativity&pub=RFP%20Office%20Space&id=31082&mode=source.

Harrison, A., Wheeler, P. and Whitehead, C. (2004) *The Distributed Workplace,* London and New York: Spon Press, Taylor & Francis Group.

Hartley, R. (2011) 'Vocational value: The role of further education colleges in higher education', Policy Exchange, 2011. Retrieved from: http://www.policyexchange.org.uk/publications/item/vocational-value-the-role-of-further-education-colleges-in-higher-education?category_id=24.

Hartley, R. and Richmond, T. (2009) 'Simply learning: improving the skills system in England', Policy Exchange. Retrieved from: http://www.policyexchange.org.uk/images/publications/simply%20learning%20-%20jan%202010.pdf.

Harvard style classroom (2012) http://www.midwest-facilitators.

net/downloads/meeting_room_configurations_v5.pdf. Accessed 9 March 2013.

Hase, S. (2011) 'Learner defined curriculum: heutagogy and action learning in vocational training', *Southern Institute of Technology Journal of Applied Research*. Retrieved from: http://www.governmentskills.com.au/images/file_groups/10802/learner_defined_curriculumpdf.pdf.

Hastings, S. (2004) 'Staffrooms', *TES Newspaper*, 1 October. Retrieved from: http://www.tes.co.uk/article.aspx?storyCode=2036778.

Hawkins, D. (1968) 'Teacher of teachers', *New York Review of Books* (28 February): 25–29. Retrieved from: http://www.nybooks.com/articles/archives/1968/feb/29/teacher-of-teachers/?pagination=false.

Hay, L. (2010) 'Shift happens. It's time to rethink, rebuild and rebrand', *Access*, 24, 4: 5–10. Retrieved from: http://www.asla.org.au/pubs/access/commentary-24042010.htm.

Hay, L. and Todd, R. (2010) 'Report of the School libraries 21C online discussion', commissioned by School Libraries and Information Literacy Unit, Curriculum K–12 Directorate, NSW Department of Education and Training. Retrieved from: http://www.curriculumsupport.education.nsw.gov.au/schoollibraries/assets/pdf/21c_report.pdf.

Haycock, K. (2003) *The Crisis in Canada's School Libraries: The Case for Reform and Re-Investment,* Association of Canadian Publishers. Retrieved from: http://bccsl.ca/download/HaycockReport.pdf.

Hein, G. E. (2004) 'John Dewey and museum education', *Curator*, 47, 4 (October): 413–27 (at 418). Retrieved from: http://onlinelibrary.wiley.com/doi/10.1111/j.2151-6952.2004.tb00136.x/abstract.

Hein, G. E. (2006) 'Progressive education and museum education: Anna Billings Gallup and Louise Connolly', *Journal of Museum Education,* 31, 3: 161–74. Retrieved from: http://www.deepdyve.com/lp/left-coast-press/progressive-education-and-museum-education-anna-billings-gallup-and-kBj0oeFk2B.

Hein, G.E. (2011), 'Museum education', in Macdonald, S. (ed.) *A Companion to Museum Studies,* Oxford: Wiley-Blackwell.

Hellerup (2012) http://www.arkitema.com/Laering+Learning/Projekter/Hellerup+Skole.aspx. Accessed 9 March 2013.

Henderson, E. (2009) *Service Trends in U.S. Public Libraries, 1997–2007:* Research Brief No. 1, Institute of Museum and Library Services, December. Retrieved from: http://www.imls.gov/assets/1/AssetManager/Brief2010_01.pdf.

Henry, J. (2011) 'University of Wales abolished after visa scandal', *Telegraph*, 22 October. Retrieved from: http://www.telegraph.co.uk/education/educationnews/8843200/University-of-Wales-abolished-after-visa-scandal.html.

Heppell, S. (2005) http://rubble.heppell.net/heppell/tk_park/index1.html. Accessed 2 May 2013.

Heppell, S., Chapman, C. and Millwood, R. (2004) 'Building learning futures…', a research project at Ultralab within the CABE/RIBA Building Futures programme. Ultralab. Retrieved from: http://rubble.heppell.net/places/media/final_report.pdf.

Herman Miller (2008) 'Forming Places that form ideas: creating informal learning spaces', Herman Miller. Retrieved from: http://www.hermanmiller.com/MarketFacingTech/hmc/solution_essays/assets/SE_Forming_Places.pdf.

Hertzberger, H. (2008) *Space and Learning,* Rotterdam: 010 Publishers.

Hertzberger, H. and de Swaan, A. (2009) *The Schools of Herman Hertzberger*, Rotterdam: 010 Publishers.

Hickman, L. (2010) 'Is the mobile library dead?', *Guardian*, Wednesday 7 April. Retrieved from: http://www.guardian.co.uk/books/2010/apr/07/mobile-libraries.

Higgins, S., Hall, E., Wall, K., Woolner, P. and McCaughey, C. (2005) *The Impact of School Environments: A Literature Review,* Centre for Learning and Teaching, School of Education, Communication and Language Science, University of Newcastle. CfBT Research and Development. Design Council. Retrieved from: http://www.ncl.ac.uk/cflat/about/documents/designcouncilreport.pdf.

Higher Education Academy (2012) Retrieved from: http://www.heacademy.ac.uk/assets/documents/research/Learning_spaces_v3.pdf. Accessed 9 March 2013.

Higher Education Funding Council for England (HEFCE) (2003) *Development of a Methodology for Systematic Change Management to Enhance Organisational Efficiency and Effectiveness* (generally shortened to *Effecting Changing in HE*), HEFCE.

Higher Education Funding Council for England (HEFCE) (2010) 'National Student Survey: findings and trends 2006 to 2009', HEFCE. Retrieved from: http://www.hefce.ac.uk/pubs/hefce/2010/10_18/10_18.pdf.

Higher Education Funding Council for England (HEFCE) (2011) 'Performance in higher education estates: EMS annual report 2011', Higher Education Funding Council for England (HEFCE) Scottish Funding Council (SFC), Higher Education Funding Council for Wales (HEFCW), Department for Employment and Learning, Northern Ireland (DELNI). Retrieved from: http://www.hefce.ac.uk/pubs/hefce/2011/11_17/11_17.pdf.

Hille, T. (nd) 'Back to the future: what's new in school design', American Institute of Architects. Retrieved from: http://www.aia.org/aiaucmp/groups/ek_members/documents/pdf/aiab082493.pdf.

Hive (2012) 'The Hive at Queen Mary College'. http://learninglandscapes.lincoln.ac.uk/case_studies/queen-mary-college-university-of-london-the-hive/. Accessed 9 March 2013.

Hlavac, M. (2007) *Open Access for UK Schools: What Britain Can Learn from Swedish Education Reform,* Adam Smith Institute. Retrieved from: http://www.adamsmith.org/sites/default/files/images/uploads/publications/Open_Access_%5bFINAL%5d.pdf

Hoare, S. (2008) 'Saltire Centre', *Education Guardian.co.uk,* 29 April. Retrieved from: http://education.guardian.co.uk/librariesunleashed/story/0,,2275365,00.html.

Hoare, S. (2011) 'Buildings need to inspire', *Education Guardian.co.uk..* Retrieved from: http://education.guardian.co.uk/librariesunleashed/story/0,,2274826,00.html.

Hoare, S., Hoeger, K. and Christiaanse, C. (2009) *Campus and the City – Urban Design for the Knowledge Society,* Zurich: Gta Verlag.

Holder, A. (nd) 'Furniture for schools'. Retrieved from http://www.imagineschooldesign.org/uploads/media/Furniture_for_Schools.pdf.

Holleis, P., Schmidt, A., Drewes, H., Satterer, R. and Dollniger, P. (2010) 'Taking teaching beyond the classroom', in Mäkitalo-Siegl, K., Zottmann, J., Kaplan, F. and Fischer, F. (eds) *Classroom of the Future: orchestrating collaborative spaces,* Rotterdam, Boston, Taipei: Sense Publishers.

Hooper-Greenhill, E., (2006) *Companion to Museum Studies,* Oxford: Blackwell Publishing.

Horne, J. (2011) 'New schools in New Orleans: school reform both exhilarated and imperilled by success', *Education Next,* Spring. Retrieved from: www.educationnext.org.

House of Commons Culture, Media and Sport Committee (2005) *Public Libraries: Third Report of Session 2004–05 Volume I,* The Stationery Office Limited, 10 March. Retrieved from: http://www.publications.parliament.uk/pa/cm200405/cmselect/cmcumeds/81/81i.pdf.

House of Commons Debate (1997) 2 July 1997. Col 316. http://www.publications.parliament.uk/pa/cm199798/cmhansrd/vo970702/debtext/70702-21.htm#70702-21_spmin1. Accessed 30 April 2013.

House of Commons Public Accounts Committee (2009) *Renewing the Physical Infrastructure of English Further Education Colleges: Forty-eighth Report of Session 2008–09,* The Stationery Office Limited, 28 July . Retrieved from: http://www.publications.parliament.uk/pa/cm200809/cmselect/cmpubacc/924/92402.htm.

Howe, N. and Strauss, W. (2007) *Millennials Go to College,* 2nd edn, LifeCourse Associates.

Hu, W. (2011) 'Math that moves: schools embrace the iPad', *The New York Times,* 4 January 4. Retrieved from: http://www.nytimes.com/2011/01/05/education/05tablets.html?_r=1.

Hubconcepts (2012) http://www.hubconcepts.com/en/concept. Accessed 6 May 2013.

Hubinfo (2012) 'The Hub campaign for quality school libraries in Australia.' http://hubinfo.wordpress.com/background/. Accessed 8 May 2013.

Hume (2009) 'Learning together 2030 – shaping lifelong learning in Hume City'. www.hume.vic.gov.au. Accessed 30 April, 2013.

Hunley, S. and Schaller, M. (2009) 'The key to creating spaces that promote learning', *Educause Review,* 44, 2 (March/April). Retrieved from: http://www.educause.edu/EDUCAUSE+Review/EDUCAUSEReviewMagazineVolume44/AssessmentTheKeytoCreatingSpac/163797.

Hutchison, D. (2004) *A Natural History of Place in Education,* New York: Teachers College Press.

Idea Store (1999) 'A library and lifelong learning development strategy for Tower Hamlets: a joint accommodation strategy developed by the Customer Services and Education Directorates for the Arts, Leisure, Sports and Youth and Community Services Committees', April 1999, updated January 2002. Retrieved from: http://www.ideastore.co.uk/public/documents/PDF/A_Library_and_Lifelong_Learning_Development_Strategy_for_Tower_Hamlets.pdf.

IFLA (2004) *Lifelong Learning.* http://archive.ifla.org/VII/s8/proj/Lifelong-LearningReport.pdf. Accessed 8 May 2013.

IFLA/ UNESCO (2002) *The IFLA/ UNESCO School Library Guidelines, 2002.* Retrieved from: http://www.ifla.org/files/school-libraries-resource-centers/publications/school-library-guidelines/school-library-guidelines.pdf.

Illinois Institute of Technology/Institute of Design (2007) 'Schools in the digital age', Illinois Institute of Technology/Institute of Design, March. Retrieved from: http://www.id.iit.edu/media/cms_page_media/44/macarthurfinalreport1-1.pdf.

Imholz, S. and Arns, J. (2007) 'Worth their weight: an assessment of the evolving field of library valuation', Americans for Libraries Council,. Retrieved from: http://www.ila.org/advocacy/pdf/WorthTheirWeight.pdf.

Imperial College (IC) (2010) http://www3.imperial.ac.uk/newsandeventspggrp/imperialcollege/newssummary/news_11-6-2010-17-25-5. Accessed 8 May 2013.

Information Science Today (2011) 'The Boots Booklovers Library', 28 March . Retrieved from: http://www.infosciencetoday.org/library-history/boots-booklovers-library.html.

Innocent, N. (2009) 'How museums, libraries and archives contribute to lifelong learning', Inquiry into the Future for Lifelong Learning (IFLL) and National Institute of Adult Continuing Education (NIACE). Retrieved from: http://www.niace.org.uk/.

Inside Higher Education (2009) 'Libraries of the future', 24 September. http://www.insidehighered.com/news/2009/09/24/libraries Accessed 28 September 2012.

Institute of Museum and Library Services (IMLS) (2010) 'Public Libraries Survey Fiscal Year 2008', The Institute of Museum and Library Services, June 2010. Retrieved from: https://harvester.census.gov/imls/pubs/Publications/pls2008.pdf.

International Association of School Librarianship (IASL) (2008) 'School libraries make a difference to student achievement', IASL 2 April. http://www.iasl-online.org/advocacy/make-a-difference.html. Accessed 26 April, 2013.

ISL (2012) 'The ISL Programme (Innovation, Sustainabilty and Leadership)'. http://iciscenter.org/isl/. Accessed 8 May 2013.

Jamieson P. (2005) 'Positioning the university library in the new learning environment', Planning for Higher Education, 34, 1: 5–11. Retrieved from: http://www1.scup.org/PHE/FMPro?-db=PubItems.fp5&-lay=ART&-format=read_full.htm&-error=error.htm&ID_pub=PUB-D4lJghnUalOm1ZOXJ&t_Pub_PgNum=5&-SortField=t_Pub_PgNum&-Find.

Jamieson, P. (2007) Creating New Generation Learning Environments on the University Campus, Southbank, Australia: WB Research Press. Retrieved from: http://www.woodsbagot.com/en/Documents/Public_Research/WB5307_U21_FA-7_final.pdf.

Jamieson, P. (2009) 'The serious matter of informal learning', Planning for Higher Education, 37, 2. Retrieved from: http://www1.scup.org/PHE/FMPro?-db=PubItems.fp5&-lay=ART&-format=read_full.htm&-error=error.htm&ID_pub=PUB-1bqu7qIEVdryri43xC&t_Pub_PgNum=18&-SortField=t_Pub_PgNum&-Find.

Jingxia, L. (2002) 'The public library and citizens' information literacy education in China: a case study of Wuhan area, China', 68th IFLA Council and General Conference 18–24 August. Retrieved from: http://archive.ifla.org/IV/ifla68/papers/039-098e.pdf.

Johnson, L., Adams, S. and Cummins, M. (2011) 'Technology outlook for New Zealand tertiary education 2011–2016: an NMC Horizon report regional analysis', The New Media Consortium, Austin, Texas. Retrieved from: http://www.nmc.org/publications/2011-technology-outlook-nz.

Johnson, L., Adams, S., and Cummins, M. (2012) The NMC Horizon Report: 2012 Higher Education Edition. Austin, Texas: The New Media Consortium. http://www.nmc.org/publications/horizon-report-2012-higher-ed-edition. Accessed 10 May 2013.

Johnson, L., Adams, S. and Witchey, H. (2011) 'The NMC Horizon Report: 2011 Museum Edition', The New Media Consortium, Austin, Texas. Retrieved from: http://www.nmc.org/publications/horizon-report-2011-museum-edition.

Johnson, L., Smith, R., Levine, A. and Haywood, K. (2010) 'Horizon Report: K-12 Edition', The New Media Consortium, Austin, Texas. Retrieved from: http://www.nmc.org/publications/horizon-report-2010-k-12-edition.

Joint Information Systems Committee (JISC) (2006), Designing Spaces for Effective Learning: A Guide to 21st Century Learning Space Design, Bristol: JISC Development Group. Retrieved from: http://www.jisc.ac.uk/media/documents/publications/learningspaces.pdf.

Joint Information Systems Committee (JISC) (2008) '"Google Generation" is a myth, says new research', 16 January. http://www.jisc.ac.uk/news/stories/2008/01/googlegen.aspx. Accessed 26 April 2013.

Joint Information Systems Committee Conference (2009) 'Opening digital doors. Making the most of your physical learning spaces', PowerPoint presentations, JISC. Retrieved from: http://www.jisc.ac.uk/media/documents/events/2009/03/physicallearningspaces-tintopm.pdf.

Joint Information Systems Committee (JISC) (2009a) 'A study of effective evaluation models and practices for technology supported physical learning spaces'. Retrieved from: http://www.jisc.ac.uk/publications/reports/2009/learningspaces08.aspx.

Joint Information Systems Committee (JISC) (2010), 'Libraries of the future', Debate. http://www.jisc.ac.uk/librariesofthefuture. Accessed 28 September 2012. Document. Libraries of the Future. Retrieved from: http://www.jisc.ac.uk/media/documents/publications/lotfbrochure.pdf. Accessed 26 April 2013.

Jordan, E. and Ziebell, T. (2009) 'Learning in the spaces: a comparative study of the use of traditional and "new generation" library learning spaces by various disciplinary cohorts', in Radcliffe, D., Wilson, H., Powell, D. and Tibbetts, B. (eds) Learning Spaces in Higher Education: Positive Outcomes by Design, The University of Queensland. Retrieved from: http://www.uq.edu.au/nextgenerationlearningspace/proceedings.

Junior Dr (2012) http://www.drtribe.com/index.php?option=com_content&view=article&id=147:royal-college-of-surgeons-opens-new-training-centre&catid=38:surgery-news&Itemid=182K12.. Accessed 8 May 2013.

Kachel, D.E. (2011) 'School library research summarized: a graduate class project', Mansfield University, Mansfield, PA.

Retrieved from: http://libweb.mansfield.edu/upload/kachel/ImpactStudy.pdf.

Kaplan Business School (2012) http://www.kbs.org.uk/degrees/bsc-business. Accessed 8 May 2013.

Kaplan Financial (2012) http://financial.kaplan.co.uk/aboutkaplan/Pages/default.aspx; http://financial.kaplan.co.uk/TrainingandQuals/Accountancy/ACCA/Pages/default.aspx; http://financial.kaplan.co.uk/pages/default.aspx. Accessed 8 May 2013.

Kaplan Hawksmere (2012) http://www.kaplanhawksmere.co.uk/hawksmere/content.php?name=financial_cpd. Accessed 8 May 2013.

Kay, J. (2003) 'Hartford's "Learning Corridor" leads to urban revival', Michigan Land Use Institute, 16 March. Retrieved from: http://www.mlui.org/growthmanagement/fullarticle.asp?fileid=16456.

Kelland, M. (2012) http://www.futurelab.org.uk/resources/publications-reports-articles/web-articles/Web-Article794. Accessed 10 May 2013.

Kendall, P. (2010) 'The future of schools', *Telegraph*, 4 May. Retrieved from: http://www.telegraph.co.uk/culture/7658278/The-future-of-schools.html.

Kenyan Universities (1989) 'The Universities (Establishment of Universities)(Standardization, Accreditation and supervision) Rules', Government of Kenya. Retrieved from: http://www.che.or.ke/downloads/Universities%20Rules%201989%20pdf.pdf.

Kesterton, J. and Aspden, L. (2008) 'Space for learning: creating technology-rich informal learning opportunities through institutional space planning', paper presented at the Solstice Conference, Edge Hill University.

Killack, J. (1983) 'Public libraries and adult education: an historical review', *Research in Rural Education*, 2, 2: 57. Retrieved from: http://www.jrre.psu.edu/articles/v2,n2,p51-58,Killacky.pdf.

Klan, A. (2011) 'BER waste tops $1.5 billion', *The Australian*, 8 July. http://www.theaustralian.com.au/national-affairs/ber-waste-tops-15b/story-fn59niix-1226090622303. Accessed 26 April 2013.

Knight Commission (2009) 'Informing communities: sustaining democracy in the digital age', report of the Knight Commission on the Information Needs of Communities in a Democracy. The Aspen Institute. Retrieved from: http://www.knightcomm.org/wp-content/uploads/2010/02/Informing_Communities_Sustaining_Democracy_in_the_Digital_Age.pdf.

Knowles, M., Holton, E. F. and Swanson, R. A. (2011) *The Adult Learner: The Definitive Classic in Adult Education and Human Resource Development*, Oxford: Butterworth-Heinemann, Elsevier.

Koch, A. and Schwennsen, K. (2002) 'The redesign of studio culture: a report of the AIAS Studio Culture Task Force', The American Institute of Architecture Students. Retrieved from: http://www.aias.org/website/download.asp?id=314.

Kolowich, S. (2009) 'Libraries of the future', *Inside Higher Ed.*, 24 September. Retrieved from: http://www.insidehighered.com/news/2009/09/24/libraries.

Kolowich, S. (2011) 'What students don't know', *Inside Higher Ed.*, 22 August. Retrieved from: http://www.insidehighered.com/news/2011/08/22/erial_study_of_student_research_habits_at_illinois_university_libraries_reveals_alarmingly_poor_information_literacy_and_skills.

Krashen, S., Lee, S. and McQuillan, J. (2008a) 'Is the library important? Multivariate studies at the national and international Level', unpublished paper, retrieved from: http://www.kzneducation.gov.za/Portals/0/ELITS%20website%20Homepage/IASL%202008/keynote/krashenkeynotewithapp.pdf

Krashen, S. (2008b) 'The case for libraries and librarians', invited paper submitted to the Obama-Biden Education Policy Working Group, December. Retrieved from: http://www.sdkrashen.com/articles/case_for_libraries/index.html.

Kune, H. (2010) 'The reality of future centres in Europe', Intellectual Cafe presentation paper. Retrieved from: http://resilientcommunities.org/wp-content/uploads/2010/04/FutureCentres.pdf.

Labnews (2012) http://www.labnews.co.uk/feature_archive.php/2546/5/rise-of-the-super-lab. Accessed 8 May 2013.

Lambert, C. (2012) 'Twilight of the lecture', *Harvard Magazine*, March/April. http://harvardmagazine.com/2012/03/twilight-of-the-lecture. Accessed 10 May 2013.

Lambert, R. (2003) 'Review of business-university collaboration: final report', HMSO. December. www.lambertreview.org.uk. Accessed 10 May 2013.

Lampert-Gréaux, E. (2009) 'Diana Center to open at Barnard College', *Live Design*, 15 December. Retrieved from: http://livedesignonline.com/venues/diana_center_barnard_college_091512/.

Lauerman, J. (2011) 'Apollo fourth-quarter profit, sales top analysts' estimates', *Bloomberg News*, 19 October. Retrieved from: http://www.bloomberg.com/news/2011-10-19/apollo-fourth-quarter-profit-sales-top-analysts-estimates-1-.html.

Lauridsen, H. and Stone, G. (2009) 'The 21st century library: a whole new ball game?', *Serials*, 22, 2: 141–5. Retrieved from: http://eprints.hud.ac.uk/5156/1/c284571120742236.pdf.

Le, T. (2010) 'The end of education is the dawn of learning', FastCo Design, Blog entry 26 September. Retrieved

from: http://www.fastcodesign.com/1662358/
the-end-of-education-is-the-dawn-of-learning.

Leadbeater, C. (2004) *Personalisation Through Participation*, DEMOS.

Leadbeater, C. (nd) 'What's next? 21 ideas for 21st century learning', The Innovation Unit. Retrieved from: http://www.innovationunit.org/sites/default/files/What's%20Next%20-%2021%20ideas%20for%2021st%20century%20learning.pdfhttp://news.bbc.co.uk/1/hi/education/6541251.stm. Accessed 26 April 2013.

Learning through Landscapes (LTL) (2012) 'Learning through Landscapes is the UK charity dedicated to enhancing outdoor learning and play for children'. http://www.ltl.org.uk/about/about-ltl.php. Accessed 10 May 2103.

Lee, C. (2010) 'Colleges consider plan to sell and rent back campuses to survive cash crisis', *TES Newspaper,* 19 February. Retrieved from: http://www.tes.co.uk/article.aspx?storyCode=6036385.

Lee, W. (2004) 'School-university partnerships: the need for cross-level collaboration in educational reform', Ed.D. Candidate University of California, Los Angeles, escholarship, University of California, April. Retrieved from: http://escholarship.org/uc/item/9b96x05q#page-10.

Lenzner, R. and Johnson, S. (1997) 'Seeing things as they really are', *Forbes.com* 3 October.

Leung, A. and Ferris, J.S. (2008) 'School size and youth violence', *Journal of Economic Behavior & Organization,* Volume 65, Issue 2, February 2008, pp. 318–333.

Lewis, D.W. (2007a) 'A model for academic libraries 2005 to 2025', paper presented at Visions of Change, California State University at Sacramento, 26 January. Retrieved from: http://hdl.handle.net/1805/665.

Lewis, D.W. (2007b) 'A strategy for academic libraries in the first quarter of the 21st century', College & Research Libraries. Retrieved from: dea.iupui.edu.

Lewis, M.J. (2003) 'Forget classrooms. How big is the atrium in the new student center?' *Chronicle of Higher Education*, 11 July. Retrieved from: http://chronicle.com/article/Forget-Classrooms-How-Big-Is/35303.

Library Research Service (2009), 'A return on investment study of Colorado libraries', Library Research Service, March. Retrieved from: http://www.lrs.org/documents/closer_look/roi.pdf.

Lietzau, Z. and Helgren, J. (2011) 'U.S. public libraries and the use of web technologies, 2010', Library Research Services, April. Retrieved from: http://www.lrs.org/documents/web20/WebTech2010_CloserLookReport_Final.pdf.

Light, G. and Cox, R. (2001) *Learning and Teaching in Higher Education: The Reflective Professional*, London: SAGE Publications.

Lighthouse, The (2008) *Senses of Place: Building Excellence. The Toolkit and Outcomes*. Retrieved from: http://www.ads.org.uk/resources/2584-senses-of-place-building-excellence-the-toolkit-and-outcomes.

Lindsay, C.A., Morrison, J.L. and Kelley E.J. (1974) 'Professional obsolescence: implications for continuing professional education, *Adult Education* 25, 3.

Lippincott, J. (2006), 'Linking the information commons to learning', in D. Oblinger (ed.), *Learning Spaces*, Washington, DC: Educause. Retrieved from: http://net.educause.edu/ir/library/pdf/PUB7102g.pdf.

Lippman, P.C. (2002) 'Understanding activity settings in relationship to the design of learning environments', *CAE Quarterly Newsletter,* AIA Committee on Architecture for Education.

Lippman, P.C. (2003) 'Advancing concepts about activity settings within learning environments', *CAE Quarterly Newsletter,* AIA Committee on Architecture for Education.

Lissaman, C. (2011) 'Library closure threats spark campaigns across England', BBC News England. 26 January. Retrieved from: http://www.bbc.co.uk/news/uk-england-12239388.

Little, A.D. (2001) 'North West Science and Daresbury Development Study', Report to the Government Office for the North West.

Littlefield, D. (2007) *Metric Handbook: Planning and Design Data*, 3rd edn, London: Architectural Press.

Living Libraries Project (2012) Helen Hamlyn Centre, Royal College of Art http://livinglibraries.rca.ac.uk/. Accessed 8 May 2013.

Livingplaces (2012) http://living-places.org.uk/living-places-in-action/case-study-subject/culture-and-sport-infrastructure/peckham-library.html. Accessed 8 May 2013.

Li Xiaodong (2012) www.lixiaodong.net

LKSC (2012) 'Student life: human component'. Retrieved from: http://lksc.stanford.edu/students/. Accessed 8 May 2013.

Local Government Group (LGG) (2011) *Future Libraries: Change, Options and How to Get There,* Learning from the Future Libraries Programme Phase 1LGG August.

Lomas, C. and Oblinger, D. (2004) 'Learning space design in the 21st century', Fall Focus Session Summary. NLII. Retrieved from: http://net.educause.edu/ir/library/pdf/NLI0446.pdf.

Lombardi, M. (2007) 'Authentic learning for the 21st century: an overview', Educause Learning Initiative Paper 1: 2007, May. Retrieved from: http://net.educause.edu/ir/library/pdf/ELI3009.pdf.

London Library, The (2012) http://www.londonlibrary.co.uk/index. php?/history-of-the-library.html http://www.londonlibrary. co.uk/index.php?/join.html. Accessed 8 May 2013.

London School of Economics (LSE) (2011) http://www2.lse.ac.uk/ newsAndMedia/news/archives/2011/02/libya_funding.aspx. Accessed 8 May 2013.

London School of Economics (LSE) (2012) 'New student centre', http://www2.lse.ac.uk/intranet/students/campusLondonLife/ newStudentsCentre/Home.aspx. Accessed 8 May 2013.

Lopez, H and Gee, L. (2006) 'Estrella Mountain Community College: The Learning Studios Project', in Diana Oblinger (ed.) *Learning Spaces,* Educause. Retrieved from: http://www. educause.edu/learningspacesch19.

Losing Libraries (2012) http://www.losinglibraries.org/about. Accessed 8 May 2013.

Loughlin, C. (1977) 'Understanding the learning environment', *The Elementary School Journal,* 78: 124–31.

Machinima (2012) http://www.machinima.com/film/ view&id=31029. Accessed 8 May 2013.

Maclure, S. (1984) *Education Development and School Building: aspects of public policy, 1945–73.* Harlow: Longman.

Mahony, P., Hextall, I. and Richardson, M. (2011) 'Building schools for the future: reflections on a new social architecture', *Journal of Education Policy*, 26, 3: 341–60. Retrieved from: http://dx.doi.org/10.1080/02680939.2010. 513741.

MAKE (2012) http://blog.makezine.com/2011/03/10/is-it-time-to-rebuild-retool-public-libraries-and-make-techshops/. Accessed 8 May 2013.

Mäkitalo-Siegl, K., Zottmann, J., Kaplan, F. and Fischer, F. (eds) (2010) *Classroom of the Future: Orchestrating Collaborative Spaces,* Rotterdam, Boston, Taipei: Sense Publishers.

Maley-Shaw, C. (2012) 'Fiordland Kindergarten: philosophy and practice'. Letter (email) to Harrison, A.

Manheimer, R. J., Snodgrass, D. D. and Moscow-McKenzie, D. (1995) *Older Adult Education: A Guide to Research, Programs, and Policies,* Westport, CT: Greenwood Press.

Markwell, D. (2010) 'The value of university residential colleges', The Ashley Lecture.

Marmot, A. (2007) 'Evidence-based design for learning spaces', presentation at senior staff conference, University of Ulster Ballymena 10 May.

Martin, J. and Allen, M. (2009) 'Students in my backyard: housing at the campus edge and other emerging trends in residential development', *Planning for Higher Education,* 37, 2: 34–43. Retrieved from: http://www1.scup.org/PHE/

FMPro?-db=PubItems.fp5&-lay=ART&-format=read_full. htm&-error=error.htm&ID_pub=PUB-kyLhWHpI6s9Uh3G5QT&t_ Pub_PgNum=34&-SortField=t_Pub_PgNum&-Find.

Massey, A. and Munro, G. (2010) 'Higher education in the age of austerity: the role of private providers', Policy Exchange. Retrieved from: http://www.policyexchange.org.uk/images/ publications/higher%20education%20in%20the%20age%20 of%20austerity%20-%20nov%202010.pdf.

Matthews, M. (2012) 'Would you miss your school staff room?', *Guardian Professional*, Saturday 25 February. Retrieved from: http://www.guardian.co.uk/teacher-network/2012/feb/25/ school-staff-rooms-teaching.

McDonald, J. (1997) 'Lurching from fad to fad: The open plan schools were but one costly craze in a long list', *Organization for Quality Education*, December:7. Retrieved from: http:// www.societyforqualityeducation.org/newsletter/archives/ lurching.pdf.

McDonald, L. (2011) 'Public libraries briefing paper', Carnegie UK Trust, September. Retrieved from: http://www. carnegieuktrust.org.uk/getattachment/f57df5fb-a063-4690-9351-511483ad44a2/Public-Libraries-Briefing-Paper.aspx.

McDonald's (2012) http://www.aboutmcdonalds.com/mcd/ corporate_careers/training_and_development/hamburger_ university/our_faculty.html. Accessed 8 May 2013.

Meade, A. (2006) 'New Zealand: the importance of outdoor space', *Education Facilities for Young Children: PEB Exchange* 2006/5. OECD. Retrieved from: http://www.oecd.org/ dataoecd/62/33/37697238.pdf.

Menichinelli, M. (2012) 'Business models for Fab Labs', Open p2p design blog. Retrieved from: http://www.openp2pdesign. org/2011/fabbing/business-models-for-fab-labs/. Accessed 8 May 2013.

Milne, A. (2007) 'Entering the interaction age: implementing a future vision for campus learning spaces today', *Educause Review*, January/ February. Retrieved from: http://net. educause.edu/ir/library/pdf/ERM0710.pdf.

Minner, K. (2010) 'The Diana Center at Barnard College/ Weiss Manfredi', *Arch Daily*, 19 December. Retrieved from: http://www.archdaily.com/97256/ the-diana-center-at-barnard-college-weiss-manfredi/.

MIT (2011) 'MIT Media Lab at a glance', MIT Media Lab, October. Retrieved from: http://www.media.mit.edu/files/overview.pdf.

MIT (2012) Technology-enhanced active learning (TEAL). http://web. mit.edu/edtech/casestudies/teal.html. Accessed 8 May 2013.

MIT (2013a) Housing Graduate resident tutor job description. http://web.mit.edu/residence/systemdesign/grt.html. Accessed 26 April, 2013.

MIT (2013b) Housing Housemasters job description. http://web.mit.edu/residence/systemdesign/housemasters.html. Accessed 26 April, 2013.

MIT (2013c) Media Lab. http://www.media.mit.edu/about. Accessed 26 April, 2013.

Mitchell, W.J. (2004) 'Rethinking campus and classroom design', presentation at the NLII 2004 Fall Focus Session, 9 September, Cambridge, MA. Retrieved from: http://www.educause.edu/Resources/RethinkingCampusandClassroomDe/160013.

Molaro, A. (2012) 'Transliteracy, customer services and the future of reference libraries and transliteracy', 6 February. Retrieved from: http://librariesandtransliteracy.wordpress.com/.

Monaghan, P. (2001) 'The "insane little bubble of nonreality" that is life for architecture students', *The Chronicle of Higher Education*, 29 June. Retrieved from: http://chronicle.com/article/The-Insane-Little-Bubble-of/7505.

Montgomery, S. (2011) 'Quantitative vs. qualitative – do different research methods give us consistent information about our users and their library space needs?', *Library and Information Research*, 35, 111. Retrieved from: http://www.lirgjournal.org.uk/lir/ojs/index.php/lir/article/view/482/529.

Morgan, J. (2009) 'Shared space – good for collaboration or too noisy?', *Times Higher Education*, 19 November. Retrieved from: http://www.timeshighereducation.co.uk/story.asp?storyCode=409152&sectioncode=26.

Morgan, J. (2011) 'Universities could be in private hands "in six months"', *Times Higher Education,* 13 October. Retrieved from: http://www.timeshighereducation.co.uk/story.asp?sectioncode=26&storyCode=417767.

Multiverse (2012) http://www.multiverse.net/about/index.jsp?cid=5&scid=0. Accessed 8 May 2013.

Murray, S. (2010) 'Trends from the CIPFA Public Library Service Statistics 2004/05 to 2008/09', Museums, Libraries & Archives Council, 29 June. Retrieved from: http://research.mla.gov.uk/evidence/documents/MLA%20Research%20Briefing%209%20-%20CIPFA%20Library%20Trends%20FINAL.pdf.

Museum School, California (2012) http://museumschool.org/. Accessed 8 May 2013.

Museums, Libraries and Archives Council (MLA) and Chartered Institute of Library and Information Professionals (CILIP) (MLA/CILIP) (2007) 'Designed for learning: school libraries'. Retrieved from: http://www.cilip.org.uk/sitecollectiondocuments/PDFs/policyadvocacy/Findoutmore.pdf.

Museums, Libraries and Archives Council (MLA) (2008) *Framework for the Future: MLA Action Plan for Public Libraries – towards 2013*, MLA Council. Retrieved from: http://www.mla.gov.uk/what/strategies/~/media/Files/pdf/2008/library_action_plan.

Museums, Libraries and Archives Council (MLA) (2010a) 'Opening up spaces: bringing new people into museums, libraries and archives by supporting self-organised learning', MLA. Retrieved from: http://www.mla.gov.uk/what/~/media/Files/pdf/2010/news/Opening_Up_Spaces.ashx.

Museums, Libraries and Archives Council (MLA) (2010b) 'The opportunity of devolved governance for museums, libraries and archives', MLA, April. Retrieved from: http://www.mla.gov.uk/what/strategies/~/media/Files/pdf/2010/programmes/The_opportunity_of_devolution_for_museums_libraries_and_archives.

Museums, Libraries and Archives Council (MLA) (2010c) 'Role of public libraries in supporting and promoting digital participation', MLA, January. Retrieved from: http://research.mla.gov.uk/evidence/documents/public-libraries-and-digital-participation-mla.pdf.

Nair, P. (2011) 'The classroom is obsolete: it's time for something new', *Education Week,* 29 July. Retrieved from: http://www.designshare.com/images/TheClassroomisObsoleteEdWeek.pdf.

Nair, P. and Gehling, A. (2010) 'Life between classrooms: applying public space theory to learning environments', in Atkinson, D. (ed.), *Reshaping Our Learning Landscape: a collection of provocation papers.* Croydon Council.

Nair, P., and Fielding, R. (2005) *The Language of School Design: Design Patterns for 21st Century Schools,* Minneapolis: Designshare.

Nair, P., Fielding, R. and Lackney, J. (2009) *The Language of School Design: Design Patterns for 21st Century Schools,* Minneapolis: DesignShare.

Naismith, L., Lonsdale, P., Vavoula, G. and Sharples, M. (2004) 'Literature review in mobile technologies and learning', Futurelab. Retrieved from: http://www.futurelab.org.uk/sites/default/files/Mobile_Technologies_and_Learning_review.pdf.

National Center on Education Statistics (NCES) (2003) 'The condition of education 2003, NCES 2003–067', Washington, DC: US Department of Education, Institute of Education Sciences.

National Center on Education Statistics (NCES) (2011) 'The condition of education 2011 (NCES 2011–033), Indicator 3', US Department of Education.

National Center on Education and the Economy (NCEE) (2007) 'Tough choices or tough times', the Report of the New Commission on the Skills of the American Workforce. Retrieved from: http://www.skillscommission.org/wp-content/uploads/2010/05/ToughChoices_EXECSUM.pdf

National Institute of Adult Continuing Education (NIACE) (2009) 'The impact of learning as a family: a model for the 21st century', National Institute of Adult Continuing Education. Retrieved from: http://www.niace.org.uk/lifelonglearninginquiry/docs/IFLL-Sector-Paper9.pdf.

National University of Singapore (2008) 'Under one roof', *The Straits Times*, 1 February. Retrieved from: http://newshub.nus.edu.sg/news/0802/PDF/ROOF-st-1Feb-p3.pdf.

National University of Singapore U Town (2012) http://utown.nus.edu.sg/about-utown.html http://utown.nus.edu.sg/about-utown/residential-colleges.html; http://utown.nus.edu.sg/facilities-a-centres/create.html. Accessed 8 May 2013.

Natural History Museum (2013) 'Education'. Retrieved from: http://www.nhm.ac.uk/education/index.html. Accessed 13 July 2013.

Nature (2007) 'The university of the future', *Nature*, 26 April . Retrieved from: http://www.nature.com/nature/journal/v446/n7139/pdf/446949a.pdf.

Neary, M., Harrison, A., Crellin, G., Parekh, N., Saunders, G., Duggan, F., Williams, S. and Austin, S. (2010) *Learning Landscapes in Higher Education*, Centre for Educational Research and Development, University of Lincoln. Retrieved from: http://learninglandscapes.blogs.lincoln.ac.uk/files/2010/04/FinalReport.pdf.

New York University (NYU) (2012) http://www.nyu.edu/life/resources-and-services/kimmel-center/construction.html. Accessed 8 May 2013.

New York University Global Center for Academic and Spiritual Life (nd) http://www.nyu.edu/life/resources-and-services/kimmel-center/construction.html. Accessed 8 May 2013.

Newman, M. (2008) 'Staff angered by proposed open-plan site', *Times Higher Education*, 12 June. Retrieved from: http://www.timeshighereducation.co.uk/story.asp?storyCode=402353.

Newshub (2008) 'University Town, first-ever Youth Olympic Village', Newshub, National University of Singapore news portal, March. Retrieved from: http://newshub.nus.edu.sg/ke/0803/articles/pg03.php.

Newsweek (2010) 'Closing the books?', *Newsweek*, 23 August. Retrieved from: http://www.thedailybeast.com/newsweek/2010/08/23/libraries-face-increasing-budget-cutbacks.html.

Nido (2012) 'Nido student living. Blackstone's NIDO Student Living to open boutique residence in Notting Hill', press release 1 June. Retrieved from: http://www.nidostudentliving.com/__assets/asset768.pdf.

Nido (2013) 'Nido student living'. Retrieved from: http://www.nidostudentliving.com. Accessed 10 May 2013.

NZ Ministry of Education (2012) 'Discovery 1 – rationale for change', report for New Zealand Ministry of Education, 12 October. Retrieved from: http://www.discovery1.school.nz/assets/files/useful/D1%20-%20Rationale%20for%20change.pdf.

O'Connor, R. (2005) 'Studying a Sewanee education. Sewanee: The University of the South, Library Planning Task Force', final report for the Jesse Ball duPont Library, p. 73 Retrieved from: http://library.sewanee.edu/libplan/LPTF%20Final%20Draft%204-11.pdf.

O'Hara, R. (2006) 'Hogwarts U', *Inside Higher Ed.*, 28 November. Retrieved from: http://www.insidehighered.com/views/2006/11/28/ohara.

Oblinger, D. (2005a) 'Leading the transition from classrooms to learning spaces: the convergence of technology, pedagogy, and space can lead to exciting new models of campus interaction', *Educause Quarterly Magazine,* 28, 1. Retrieved from: http://net.educause.edu/ir/library/pdf/eqm0512.pdf.

Oblinger, D. (2005b) 'Is it age or IT; First steps towards understanding the net generation', Oblinger, D. and Oblinger, J. (eds) *Educating the Net Generation*, Educause. Retrieved from: http://net.educause.edu/ir/library/pdf/pub7101.pdf.

Oblinger, D. (ed.) (2006a) 'Space as a change agent', *Learning Spaces,* Educause. Retrieved from: http://net.educause.edu/ir/library/pdf/PUB7102.pdf.

Oblinger, D. (ed.) (2006b) 'Learning how to see', *Learning Spaces,* Educause. Retrieved from: http://net.educause.edu/ir/library/pdf/PUB7102.pdf.

OECD (1996) 'Lifelong learning for all', OECD Education Ministers. http://www.oecdbookshop.org/oecd/display.asp?k=5LMQCR2K9XLP&lang=en. Accessed 8 May 2013.

OECD (2009) 'Higher education – student numbers OECD countries'. Retrieved from: stats.oecd.org.

OECD (2010) 'Recognition of non-formal and informal learning', OECD. Retrieved from: www.oecd.org/document/25etc.

OECD (2011) *Designing for Education: compendium of exemplary educational facilities,* OECD.

Office for Standards in Education, Children's Services and Skills (Ofsted) (2006). *Good School Libraries: making a difference to learning,* Ofsted.

Önal, H. (2009) 'Designing tomorrow's libraries with children's views', *World Library and Information Congress: 75TH IFLA General Conference and Council proceedings*, 23–27 August, Milan, Italy. Retrieved from: http://www.ifla.org/files/hq/papers/ifla75/103-onal-en.pdf.

Orange, R. (2011) 'Doubts grow over the success of Sweden's free schools experiment,' *The Observer*, 10 September 2011. Retrieved from: http://www.guardian.co.uk/world/2011/sep/10/sweden-free-schools-experiment. Accessed 9 March 2013.

Otto, K. (1966) *School Buildings*, vol. 1, London: Illiffe Books.

Outram, S. (2009) 'Flexible Learning Pathfinders: a review of the pilots' final and interim reports', Higher Education Academy, March. Retrieved from: http://www.heacademy.ac.uk/resources/detail/flexible-learning/flexble_learning_pathfinder_review.

Oxford University (2012) http://www.ox.ac.uk/colleges/the_collegiate_system/index.html. Accessed 8 May 2013.

Padmanabhan, G. (2010) 'Classroom of the future', *The Hindu*, 27 October. Retrieved from: http://www.thehindu.com/life-and-style/metroplus/article852464.ece.

Paechter, C. (2004) 'Power relations and staffroom spaces', *Forum*, 46, 1: 33–5 (at 33). Retrieved from: http://www.school-works.org/pdf/FORUM%2046_1_web.pdf.

Palmer, M. (2011) 'Using technology to protect the future of public libraries', presentation at the London Book Fair Supply Chain Seminar 13 April. Retrieved from: http://www.bic.org.uk/files/pdfs/1104%20palmer.pdf.

Parkin, J., Austin, S. and Lansdale, M. (2006) *Research Environments for Higher Education,* Loughborough University. Retrieved from: http://www.academicworkspace.com/images/stories/PDF/ResearchEnvironmentsForHE.pdf.

Partnership for Schools (2012). DfES publications. http://www.partnershipsforschools.org.uk/library/BSF-archive/design-guidance/BSF-DfE-publications.html.

Pastalan, L. (2001) 'Higher education as part of an active retirement: possible roles for the University of North Carolina at Greensboro', presentation, 11 April. Retrieved from: http://www.uncg.edu/apl/active_retire_4-01.pdf.

Peckham Library (2012) http://www.southwark.gov.uk/info/437/libraries_and_locations/909/peckham_library. Accessed 8 May 2013.

Peterson, C.A. (2005) 'Space designed for lifelong learning: The Dr. Martin Luther King Jr. joint-use library' in *Library as Place: Rethinking Roles, Rethinking Space*, Council on Library and Information Resources Washington, D.C. February, p. 57. Retrieved from: http://www.clir.org/pubs/reports/pub129/pub129.pdf.

Pfeifer, C. and Abattoir, T. (2012) 'Triple A learning opens NMC cybercampus', *NMC Virtual Worlds,* 6 March. http://virtualworlds.nmc.org/ Accessed 25 March 2012.

Pinder, J., Parkin, J., Austin, S., Duggan, F., Lansdale, M.,

Demian, P., Baguley, T. and Allenby, S. (2009) *The Case for New Academic workspaces,* Loughborough: Department of Civil and Building Engineering, Loughborough University. Retrieved from: http://www.academicworkspace.com/images/stories/PDF/TheCaseForNewAcademicWorkspaces.pdf.

Pine, B. J., (1993) *Mass Customization: The New Frontier in Business Competition*, Harvard: Harvard Business School Press.

Pittman, W. and Pretzer, W. (1998) 'The Most Public of Public Schools', in 'Museums and the Charter School Movement', *Museum News,* September/October. Retrieved from: http://www.aam-us.org/pubs/mn/MN_SO98_MuseumCharter.cfm.

PKALAACU (2012) 'About Project Kaleidoscope'. Retrieved from: http:// pkal.aacu.org/blog/?page_id=24. Accessed 8 May 2013.

PKALLSC (2010) 'Arriving at spaces that make a difference', PKALLSC. Retrieved from: www.pkallsc.org/downloads/22.

PKALLSC (2012) 'Arriving at spaces that make a difference', PKAL LSC, 2010. Retrieved from: www.pkallsc.org/downloads/22.

Play England (2007a) 'Schools for the future: designing school grounds briefing note', Play for England, August. Retrieved from: http://www.playengland.org.uk/media/130760/psec6-schools-for-the-future-low-res.pdf.

Play England (2007b). 'Charter for children's play', Play England, updated 2009. Retrieved from: http://www.playengland.org.uk/media/71062/charter-for-childrens-play.pdf.

Private business and education (2007) 'Private business to award degrees', BBC News, Tuesday, 25 September. Retrieved from: http://news.bbc.co.uk/1/hi/education/7012203.stm.

Project Faraday (2008) *Project Faraday*, Department for Children, Schools and Families (DCSF).

PSNI (2012) http://www.psni.police.uk/new_police_college. Accessed 8 May 2013.

Public Accounts Committee (PAC) (July 2009) www.parliament.uk/business/news. Accessed 8 May 2013.

Queensland Teachers' Credit Union Limited (2010) 'Staffroom for improvement'. http://www.staffroomforimprovement.com.au/Default.aspx. Accessed 8 May 2013.

Radcliffe, D. (2009) 'A pedagogy-space-technology (PST) framework for designing and evaluating learning places', in Radcliffe, D., Wilson, H., Powell, D. and Tibbetts, B. (eds), *Learning Spaces in Higher Education: Positive Outcomes by Design*, The University of Queensland. Retrieved from: http://www.uq.edu.au/nextgenerationlearningspace/proceedings.

Radcliffe, D., Wilson, H., Powell, D. and Tibbetts, B. (eds) (2009) *Learning Spaces in Higher Education: Positive Outcomes by*

Design, The University of Queensland. Retrieved from: http://www.uq.edu.au/nextgenerationlearningspace/UQ%20Next%20Generation%20Book.pdf.

Reeder, J. (2011) 'Are maker spaces the future of public libraries?', Shareable: Science and Tech. http://shareable.net/blog/the-future-of-public-libraries-maker-spaces. Accessed 1 October 2012.

Reese, H.W. and Overton, W.F. (1970) 'Models of development and theories of development', in L.R. Goulet and P.B. Baltes (eds) *Life-span Developmental Psychology: Research and Theory.* New York: Academic Press.

Reisz, M. (2010) 'Lingua franca needed to shape cutting-edge pedagogic spaces', *Times Higher Education,* 22 April. Retrieved from: http://www.timeshighereducation.co.uk/story.asp?storyCode=411305.

Reisz, M. (2010) 'Space to think', *Times Higher Education* supplement, 13 May. Retrieved from: http://www.timeshighereducation.co.uk/story.asp?storyCode=411534.

Research Centre for Museums and Galleries (RCMG) (2004) *Inspiration, Identity, Learning: The Value of Museums,* RCMG, Leicester, September. Retrieved from: http://www2.le.ac.uk/departments/museumstudies/rcmg/projects/inspiration-identity-learning-1/Inspiration-%20Identity-%20Learning-The%20value%20of%20museums.pd.

Research Centre for Museums and Galleries (RCMG) (2010) *Towards a New Social Purpose: Redefining the Role of Botanic Gardens.* Botanic Gardens Conservation International London.

Research Libraries UK (RLUK) (2011) 'RLUK library trends', data from Sconul, the Association of Research libraries, LibQual, the International Student Barometer and CIBER, 19 March. Retrieved from: http://www.rluk.ac.uk/files/RLUK-library-trends%20tg%201.pdf.

Resnick, M. (2001) 'Revolutionizing learning in the digital age', The Internet and the University: Forum, *Forum for the Future of Higher Education and Educause.* Retrieved from: http://net.educause.edu/forum/ffpiu01w.asp.

Resnick, M., Rusk, N. and Cooke, S. (1998) 'The computer clubhouse: technological fluency in the inner city', in Schon, D., Sanyal, B. and Mitchell, W. (eds), *High Technology and Low-Income Communities,* Cambridge, MA: MIT Press. Retrieved from: http://web.media.mit.edu/~mres/papers/clubhouse-chapter.pdf.

RIBA Journal (RIBAJ) (nd) http://www.ribajournal.com/index.php/feature/article/setting_a_new_bearing/. Accessed 8 May 2013.

Richards, C. (2004) 'Personalised learning: an interview with Professor David Hargreaves, chair of Becta', Futurelab.

http://www.futurelab.org.uk/resources/publications-reports-articles/web-articles/Web-Article553. Accessed 10 May 2013.

Rickes, P.C. (2009) 'Make way for millennials! How today's students are shaping higher education space', *Planning for Higher Education,* 37, 2: 7–17.

Riva, M. (2012) http://www.growingknowledge.bl.uk/. Accessed 8 May 2013.

Robin Hood Foundation (2012) http://www.robinhood.org/initiatives/library. Accessed 8 May 2013.

Robinson, K. (2011) *Out of Our Minds: Learning to be Creative,* 2nd edn, Oxford: Capstone.

Rogers, R. (2004) 'Space for learning: a handbook for education spaces in museums, heritage sites and discovery centres', Space for Learning. Retrieved from: http://www.cloreduffield.org.uk/cms/user_files/files/space_for_learning.pdf.

Romana Cruz, N. S. (2012) 'TK Park: a haven for book lovers of all ages', *Philippine Daily Inquirer,* 10 February. http://opinion.inquirer.net/22803/tk-park-a-haven-for-booklovers-of-all-ages. Accessed 25 March 2012.

Rong, W. (2007) 'The networking system of business incubator', Shanghai Technology Innovation Centre, unpublished paper. Retrieved from: http://www.unescap.org/tid/mtg/partner_wang.pdf.

Rose, J. (2002) 'UM condos combine senior living', *Learning.* Detroit Free Press, 27 September.

Royal College of Surgeons (RCS) (2012) http://www.rcseng.ac.uk/media/medianews/college-opens-state-of-the-art-surgical-training-centre. Accessed 8 May 2013.

Royal College of Surgeons: Wolfson Surgical Skills Centre (2012) http://www.rcseng.ac.uk/media/medianews/college-opens-state-of-the-art-surgical-training-centre http://www.drtribe.com/index.php?option=com_content&view=article&id=147:royal-college-of-surgeons-opens-new-training-centre&catid=38:surgery-news&Itemid=182 http://www.rcseng.ac.uk/education/facilities. Accessed 8 May 2013.

Royal Society for the Encouragement of Arts, Manufactures and Commerce (RSA) (2012) 'Opening minds', RSA. http://www.rsaopeningminds.org.uk/about-rsa-openingminds/competences/. Accessed 8 May 2013.

Royal Society of Chemistry (RSC) (2010) 'Better science labs must be top priority for new and improved schools', 9 July. RSC. Retrieved from: http://www.rsc.org/AboutUs/News/PressReleases/2010/BetterLabs.asp.

Rudd, T., Gifford, C., Morrison, J. and Facer, K. (2006) 'What if ... reimagining learning spaces', Futurelab. Retrieved from: http://archive.futurelab.org.uk/resources/documents/opening_education/Learning_Spaces_report.pdf.

Sahlgren, G.H. (2010) *Schooling for Money: Swedish Education Reform and the Role of the Profit Motive,* IEA Discussion Paper No. 33, IEA 2010.

Saini, A. (2009) 'DIY gadgetry', *BBC News magazine* 19 June. Retrieved from: http://news.bbc.co.uk/1/hi/magazine/8107803.stm.

Saint, A. (1987) *Towards a Social Architecture: The Role of School-Building in Post-war England,* New Haven and London: Yale University Press.

Saleh, A., Lamkin, M., and Cox, D. (2006) 'The role of higher education in America: a spa or a smörgåsbord?' *Academic Leadership: the Online journal,* 4, 3. Retrieved from: http://www.academicleadership.org/68/the_role_of_higher_education_in_america/.

Salford (2012) http://www.energy.salford.ac.uk/newsitem/21. Accessed 8 May 2013.

Santos, F. (2011) 'In lean times, schools squeeze out librarians', *New York Times,* 24 June. Retrieved from: http://www.nytimes.com/2011/06/25/nyregion/schools-eliminating-librarians-as-budgets-shrink.html?_r=2&pagewanted=all.

Schmidt, K. (2010) 'Keep up the good work! The concept of work in CSW'. In M. Lewkowicz et al. (eds) *Proceedings of COOP 2010, Computer Supported Collaborative Work.* London: Springer-Verlag. Retrieved from: http://coop.wineme.fb5.uni-siegen.de/proceedings2010/15_kSchmidt_265_286.pdf

Scholastic Library Publishing (SLP) (2008) 'School libraries work!' Research Foundation paper. Retrieved from: http://www.scholastic.com/content/collateral_resources/pdf/s/slw3_2008.pdf.

Schram, H. (2011) 'Looking at people looking at animals: an international bibliography on visitor experience studies and exhibit evaluation in zoos and aquariums', EAZA Education Committee. Retrieved from: http://www.eaza.net/activities/education/Documents/2011-02-10%20Visitor%20Studies%20Bibliography%20%20V0.3.pdf.

Schratzenstaller, A. (2010) 'The classroom of the past', in Mäkitalo-Siegl et al. (eds) *Classroom of the Future: orchestrating collaborative spaces,* Rotterdam, Boston, Taipei: Sense Publishers.

Schuller, T. and Watson, D. (2009) *Learning Through Life: Inquiry into the Future for Lifelong Learning,* Leicester: National Institute of Adult Continuing Education (NIACE). Retrieved from: http://www.niace.org.uk/lifelonglearninginquiry/docs/IFLL-summary-english.pdf.

Schweitzer, S. (2008) 'The new campus crib: barracks-style dorms becoming things of the past as schools offer upscale living to lure top students', Boston.com. 27 April. Retrieved from: http://www.boston.com/news/local/articles/2008/04/27/the_new_campus_crib/?page=1.

Scott-Webber, L. (2004) *In Sync: Environmental Behaviour Research and the Design of Learning Spaces,* Society for College and University Planning (SCUP).

Scottish Funding Council (SFC) (2006) *Spaces for Learning: a review of learning spaces in further and higher education,* AMA Alexi Marmot Associates and haa design. February. Retrieved from: http://www.jiscinfonet.ac.uk/Resources/external-resources/sfc-spaces-for-learning.

Scottish Government (2007) *Building Excellence: Exploring the Implications of the Curriculum for Excellence for School Building,* Edinburgh: The Scottish Government. Retrieved from: http://www.scotland.gov.uk/Resource/Doc/207034/0054999.pdf.

Scottish Funding Council (SFC) (2008) *Effective Spaces for Working in Higher and Further Education,* Scottish Funding Council and University of Strathclyde. Retrieved from: www.exploreacademicworkplace.com.

Scottish Government (2009) *Building Better Schools: Investing in Scotland's Future,* Edinburgh: The Scottish Government. Retrieved from: http://www.scotland.gov.uk/Resource/Doc/285201/0086644.pdf.

Scottish Government (2010) *Statistical Information Relating to NPD and PPP/PFI Projects in SCOTLAND.* http://www.scotland.gov.uk/Topics/Government/Finance/18232/12308. Accessed 9 May 2013.

Seattle Public Library (2008) 'Libraries for all: a report to the Community. Seattle Public Library, 12 September. Retrieved from: http://www.spl.org/Documents/about/libraries_for_all_report.pdf.

Seattle Public Library (2012) http://www.spl.org/locations/central-library/cen-about-the-central-library. Accessed 8 May 2013.

Sheffield Hallam University: the Centre for Sport and Exercise Science (SHU) (2013) http://www.shu.ac.uk/research/cses/facilities.html#biomech. Accessed 27 April 2013.

Shepherd, J. (2011) 'Private university BPP launches bid to run 10 publicly funded counterparts', *Guardian,* Tuesday 21 June. Retrieved from: http://www.guardian.co.uk/education/2011/jun/21/bpp-private-bid-run-public-universities.

Short, J., Williams, E. and Christie, B. (1976) *The Social Psychology of Telecommunications,* New York: Wiley.

Sims, M. (ed.) (nd) 'Changing classrooms: exemplars of well designed learning and teaching spaces', The Lighthouse/Scottish Government. Retrieved from: http://www.scotland.gov.uk/Resource/Doc/91982/0097914.pdf.

Singleton, M. (2011) 'Adjusting the prescription: The School of Medicine overhauls its century-old educational approach', *University of Virginia Magazine*. Spring. Retrieved from: http://uvamagazine.org/features/article/adjusting_the_prescription/.

Smith, F., Hardman, F. and Higgins, S. (2006) 'The impact of interactive whiteboards on teacher-pupil interaction in the National Literacy and Numeracy Strategies', *British Educational Research Journal*, 32, 3: 443–57.

Smith, R. (2008) 'Technology-rich physical space design: an overview of JISC activities', JISC. Retrieved from: http://www.jisc.ac.uk/media/documents/publications/bpelearnspacev1final.pdf.

Smithers, R. (2000) 'Learning is good for your health', *Guardian*, 24 February.

Society of College, National and University Libraries (SCONUL) (2008) 'Library trends, 2007–2008 data', report by White, S. and Creaser, C. Loughborough University.

Society of College, National and University Libraries (SCONUL) (2010) 'Vision 2010', SCONUL. Retrieved from: http://www.sconul.ac.uk/publications/pubs/vision%202010.

Society for College and University Planning (SCUP) (2009) 'The evolving academic workplace: efficient, effective and supportive', Austin, S. and Harrison, A. SCUP 44 conference presentation. Retrieved from: http://www.scup.org/page/annualconf/44/concurrent?pc_65475_page=2.

Sommerlad, E., Child, C. Ramsden, C. and Kelleher, J. (2004) 'Books and bytes: new service paradigms for the 21st century library: an Evaluation of the People's Network and ICT Training for Public Library Staff Programme', Tavistock Institute. Retrieved from: http://www.biglotteryfund.org.uk/er_eval_peoples_network_evaluation_book_bytes.pdf.

Southwark (2012) http://www.southwark.gov.uk/info/437/libraries_and_locations/909/peckham_library. Accessed 3 May 2013.

Space for Personalised Learning (S4PL) (2008) 'Trends in school design', unpublished research paper.

Space for Personalised Learning (2009) 'Small-scale pilots outcomes report: West Hill', Space for Personalised Learning. Retrieved from: http://www.space4pl.co.uk/documents/CS_WestHill_Outcomes.pdf.

Space for Personalised Learning (2009a) 'West Hill Primary, Wandsworth: change management and evaluation', Space for Personalised Learning. Retrieved from: http://www.space4pl.co.uk/documents/CS_WestHill_CME.pdf.

Space for Personalised Learning (S4PL) (2010) *Space for Personalised Learning: Project Summary*, London: DCSF. Retrieved from: http://webarchive.nationalarchives.gov.uk/20110809101133/space4pl.org/.

Space Management Group (SMG) (2005a) *Drivers of the Size of the HE Estate*, UK Higher Education Space Management Project. Retrieved from: http://www.smg.ac.uk/documents/drivers.pdf.

Space Management Group (SMG) (2005b) *The Cost of Space Report*, UK Higher Education Space Management Project. Retrieved from: http://www.smg.ac.uk/documents/costofspace.pdf.

Space Management Group (SMG) (2005c) *Review of Practice Report*, UK Higher Education Space Management Project. Retrieved from: http://www.smg.ac.uk/documents/reviewofpractice.pdf.

Space Management Group (SMG) (2006a) *Promoting Space Efficiency in Building Design*, UK Higher Education Space Management Project. Retrieved from: http://www.smg.ac.uk/documents/PromotingSpaceEfficiency.pdf.

Space Management Group (SMG) (2006b) *Impact on Space of Future Changes in Higher Education*, UK Higher Education Space Management Project. Retrieved from: http://www.smg.ac.uk/documents/FutureChangesInHE.pdf.

Spartacus Educational (2013) 'Origin of public libraries'. http://www.spartacus.schoolnet.co.uk/Llibrary.htm. Accessed 3 May 2013.

Speilberger, J., Horton, C. and Michels, L. (2004) 'New on the shelf: teens in the Library', Chapin Hall Center for Children at the University of Chicago. Retrieved from: http://www.wallacefoundation.org/knowledge-center/Libraries/Documents/New-On-The-Shelf-Teens-in-the-Library.pdf.

SPICE (2011) 'School buildings: frequently asked questions', Scottish Parliament Information Centre (SPICE). dera.ioe.ac.uk/2642/1/SB11-11.pdf. Accessed 30 April 2013.

Spicker, P. (2012) 'An introduction to social policy', Robert Gordon University (RGU). Education and social policy. Retrieved from: http://www2.rgu.ac.uk/publlicpolicy/introduction/education.htm#UK. Accessed 5 February, 2012.

Sport England (2009) *Higher Education & Community Sport: A Partnership Plan*, Sport England. Retrieved from: www.sportengland.org.

Spotlight (2010) 'Spotlight on digital media and learning. One-third of U.S. population uses public library internet; social networking, education most popular', blog entry by Christine C., 31 March. Retrieved from: http://spotlight.macfound.org/blog/entry/one-third-of-u.s.-use-public-library-internet-social-networking-education-m.

Spyrou, S. (2010) 'How to relax in the staffroom as a substitute teacher', Blog entry 'Yahoo! voices', 16 May. Retrieved from: http://voices.yahoo.com/how-relax-staffroom-as-6000336.html?cat=31.

St. John, J. (2002) 'A library and lifelong learning development strategy for Tower Hamlets', London Borough of Tower

Hamlets. Retrieved from: http://www.ideastore.co.uk/public/documents/PDF/A_Library_and_Lifelong_Learning_Development_Strategy_for_Tower_Hamlets.pdf.

Stakeholder Design (nd) 'Knowledge garden', Stakeholder Design. Retrieved from: http://www.stakeholderdesign.com/html/faraday.html.

Stanfield, G. (2009) 'Developing future university structures: new funding and legal models', Universities UK. Retrieved from: http://www.universitiesuk.ac.uk/Publications/Documents/PolicyCommentary2.pdf.

Stanford University (2009) *Stanford University Space Planning Guidelines*. Retrieved from: http://lbre.stanford.edu/sem/sites/all/lbreshared/files/docs_public/DCPSM_SpaceandFurniturePlanningGuidelines_v3_April_2009.pdf.

Stanford University School of Medicine (2007) 'Defining the research facilities model of the future', Stanford University Task Force Report, May. Retrieved from: http://medfacilities.stanford.edu/space/downloads/TaskForceReport.pdf.

Stanford University School of Medicine (LKSC 2012) Li Ka Shing Center for Learning and Knowledge http://lksc.stanford.edu/students/. Accessed 3 May 2013.

Steelcase (2010) 'Learning spaces all over campus', Steelcase. Retrieved from: http://studentofthemonth.steelcase.com/downloads/360_Education_Learning_Spaces_All_Over_Campus.pdf.

Stephens, C. and Ellis, K. (2006) 'On permeability – the biology of architecture', *Project Kaleidoscope Volume IV: What Works, What Matters, What Lasts,* Project Kaleidoscope. Retrieved from: http://www.pkal.org/documents/OnPermeabilityTheBiologyOfArchitecture.cfm.

Stevenson, K. (2010) 'Educational trends shaping school planning, design, construction, funding and operation', National Clearinghouse for educational facilities. September. Retrieved from: http://www.ncef.org/pubs/educationaltrends.pdf.

Stirling (2011) http://www.sportingexcellence.stir.ac.uk/about-us/news-archive/2011/february/scottish-athletes-to-benefit-from-sports-science-investment-at-stirling. Accessed 3 May 2013.

Straight Dope Science Advisory Board (SDSAB) (2006) http://www.straightdope.com/columns/read/2236/how-did-public-libraries-get-started. Accessed 3 May 2013.

Strange, C. C. and Banning, J. H. (2001) *Educating by Design: Creating Campus Learning Environments That Work,* San Francisco: Jossey-Bass, Wiley.

Sturgeon, J. (2007) 'Lost in space: campuses find ways to escape the pinch of finite classroom space', *University Business,* March. Retrieved from: http://www.universitybusiness.com/article/lost-space.

Suarez, D. (2007) 'What students do when they study in the library: using ethnographic methods to observe student behavior', *Electronic Journal of Academic and Special Librarianship*, 8, 3 (Winter). Retrieved from: http://southernlibrarianship.icaap.org/content/v08n03/suarez_d01.html.

Sullivan, B. (2011a) 'Academic library autopsy report, 2050', *Chronicle of Higher Education,* 2 January. Retrieved from: http://chronicle.com/article/Academic-Library-Autopsy/125767/.

Sullivan, M. (2011b) 'Divine design: how to create the 21st-century school library of your dreams', *School Library Journal*, 1 April. Retrieved from: http://www.schoollibraryjournal.com/slj/home/889642-312/divine_design_how_to_create.html.csp.

Sustainable Accommodation for the New Economy (SANE) (2002) 'Sustainable Accommodation for the new economy (SANE): final space environment Model', *European Commission's 5th Framework* Contract No. IST-2000-25257, D3, v 1.1.

Sutherland, J. and Sutherland, R. (2010) 'Spaces for learning – schools for the future?', in Mäkitalo-Siegl et al. (eds) *Classroom of the Future: Orchestrating Collaborative Spaces*, Rotterdam, Boston, Taipei: Sense Publishers.

Swain, H. (2012), 'Could universities be sold off?' *Guardian*, 23 April. Retrieved from: http://www.guardian.co.uk/education/2012/apr/23/college-of-law-private-sale.

Swanström, T. and Rontu, H. (2012) 'Using virtual worlds in language learning', Teknillinen korkeakoulu/aalto University School of Science & Technology, Finland. http://in3.uoc.edu/opencms_ in3/opencms/webs/projectes/eUNoM/_resources/documents/presentation_swanstrom_ rontu.pptx. Accessed 9 May 2013.

Taipei Times (2012) http://www.taipeitimes.com/News/taiwan/archives/2012/06/17/2003535551. Accessed 3 May 2013.

Talvé, A. (2011) 'Libraries as places of invention', *Library Management,* 32, 8/9: 493–504. Retrieved from: http://www.emeraldinsight.com/journals.htm?articleid=1958868.

Taylor Family Digital Library (TFDL) (2012), Taylor Family Digital Library University of Alberta http://tfdl.ucalgary.ca/. Accessed 3 May 2013.

Teacher Support Network and the British Council for School Environments (2007) 'Teachers highlight school building problems as education experts urge Gordon Brown on BSF', press release. Teacher Support Network and the British Council for School Environments. Retrieved from: http://www.bcse.uk.net/menu.asp?id=255&l=&pid=6.

Techshop (2012) http://techshop.ws/index.html http://techshop.ws/locations.html. Accessed 3 May 2013.

Telegraph (2010) 'Future of school libraries in doubt', *Telegraph*, 3 September. Retrieved from: http://www.telegraph.co.uk/education/educationnews/7980136/Future-of-school-libraries-in-doubt.html.

Telegraph (2011) http://www.telegraph.co.uk/finance/personalfinance/investing/8741937/Want-10pc-Try-student-housing-investment.html. Accessed 3 May 2013.

Temple, P. (2007) *Learning Spaces for the 21st Century: a review of the literature*, London: Higher Education Academy. Retrieved from: http://www.heacademy.ac.uk/assets/documents/research/Learning_spaces_v3.pdf.

Temple, P. (2008) 'Learning spaces in higher education: an under-researched topic', *London Review of Education*, 6, 3: 229–41.

Tertiary Education Facilities Management Association (TEFMA) (2009) 'Space planning guidelines edition 3', TEFMA. Retrieved from: http://www.tefma.com/uploads/content/26-TEFMA-SPACE-PLANNING-GUIDELINES-FINAL-ED3-28-AUGUST-09.pdf.

Think Left (2011) 'A 21st century library service', Blog entry, 6 August. Retrieved from: http://think-left.org/2011/08/06/a-21st-century-library-service/.

Think Tank (2012) 'Think tank: East Midlands innovation strategy', http://www.lincolnthinktank.co.uk. Accessed 3 May 2013.

This is London (2012) http://www.thisislondon.co.uk/standard/article-24012594-first-look-inside-londons-pound-14m-new-super-library.do. Accessed 3 May 2013.

Thody, A. (2008) 'Learning landscapes for universities: mapping the field. Or … beyond a seat in the lecture hall: a prolegomenon of learning landscapes in universities', *Higher Education*, February. Retrieved from: http://eprints.lincoln.ac.uk/1597/1/Learning_Landscapes_Lit_Review.pdf.

Thomas, H. (2010). 'Learning spaces, learning environments and the displacement' of learning', *British Journal of Educational Technology*, 41, 3: 502–11.

Thompson, K. (2012) '7 Things you should know about MOOCs'. Retrieved from http://www.educause.edu/Resources/7ThingsYouShouldKnowAboutMOOCs/241182.

Thompson, R. (nd) 'E-learning and novel methods of teaching in Physics', PowerPoint presentation, Imperial College. Retrieved from: www3.imperial.ac.uk/pls/portallive/docs/1/54787696.PPT.

Thornburg, D. (2007) 'Campfires in cyberspace: primordial metaphors for learning in the 21st century', PhD thesis January 1996, edited October 2007.

Times Higher Education (THE) (2007) Estates Management supplement, *Times Higher Education*, 30 March. Retrieved from: http://www.timeshighereducation.co.uk/story.asp?storyCode=208448.

Times Higher Education (THE) (2008) 'Bucks New University – training partnership with retailer', 18 April 2008. http://www.timeshighereducation.co.uk/story.asp?storyCode=401453&sectioncode=26. Accessed 3 May 2013.

Times Higher Education (THE) (2010) 'Huge BPP write-off announced as Apollo prophesies bleak short-term future for private demand', 18 November 2010. Simon Baker. http://www.timeshighereducation.co.uk/story.asp?sectioncode=26&storyCode=414308&c=1. Accessed 3 May 2013.

Times Higher Education (THE) (2011a) 'Woolf returns damning verdict on LSE's Libya links'. 30 November 2011. David Matthews. http://www.timeshighereducation.co.uk/story.asp?storyCode=418287. Accessed 3 May 2013.

Times Higher Education (THE) (2011b) 'Universities could be in private hands in six months'. 13 October 2011. John Morgan. October 2011 http://www.timeshighereducation.co.uk/story.asp?sectioncode=26&storyCode=417767. Accessed 3 May 2013.

Times Higher Education (THE) (2012) 'Unplugged', 26 January. Jack Grove. http://www.timeshighereducation.co.uk/418786.article. Accessed 3 May 2013.

Tischler, L. (2010) 'The idea lab: a look at Stanford's d.school', *Fast Company*, 1 June. Retrieved from: http://www.fastcompany.com/magazine/146/the-idea-lab.html.

TK Park (2012) http://www.tkpark.or.th/tk/. Accessed 3 May 2013.

Todd, R., Gordon, C. and Ya-Ling, L. (2011) *One Common Goal: Student Learning. Report of Findings and Recommendations of the New Jersey School Library Survey Phase 2*. School of Communication and Information, Rutgers, The State University of New Jersey, September. Retrieved from: http://www.njasl.org/documents/NJASLPhase2FINALFINAL102011_000.pdf.

Tom, J., Voss, K. and Scheetz, C. (2008) 'The space is the message: first assessment of a learning studio', *Educause Quarterly*, 31, 2 (April–June). Retrieved from: http://www.educause.edu/EDUCAUSE+Quarterly/EDUCAUSEQuarterlyMagazineVolum/TheSpaceIstheMessageFirstAsses/162874.

Torrone, P. (2011) 'Is it time to rebuild & retool public libraries and make "TechShops"?', *Makezine* blog, 10 March. Retrieved from: http://blog.makezine.com/2011/03/10/is-it-time-to-rebuild-retool-public-libraries-and-make-techshops/.

Training Gateway (2012) http://www.thetraininggateway.com/aboutus. Accessed 3 May 2013.

Transliteracy.com (2012) 'Scooping transliteracy from around the world'. http://nlabnetworks.typepad.com/transliteracy/. Accessed 3 May 2013.

Tregloan, P. (2007) 'The Learning Lab Project – supporting group and collaborative learning for large classes', University of Melbourne, Australia. Retrieved from: http://www.caudit.edu.au/educauseaustralasia07/authors_papers/Tregloan.pdf.

Trinder, K., Guiller, J., Margaryan, A. and Nicol, D. (2008) 'Learning from digital natives: bridging formal and informal learning', research project report. The Higher Education Academy, May. Retrieved from: http://www.academy.gcal.ac.uk/ldn/LDNFinalReport.pdf.

Troll, D. (2001) 'How and why are libraries changing?', Digital Library Federation. Retrieved from: http://old.diglib.org/use/whitepaper.htm.

Tsao, T.–C. (2008) 'New models for future retirement: a study of college/university linked retirement communities', VDM Verlag.

UKBI Business incubation (UKBI) (2012) http://www.ukbi.co.uk/resources/business-incubation.aspx. Accessed 3 May 2013.

UNESCO/ IFLA (2001) 'School Library Manifesto', UNESCO/ IFLA. Retrieved from: http://www.unesco.org/webworld/libraries/manifestos/school_manifesto.html.

UNITE (2012) http://www.unite-students.com/accommodation-for-students/about+us?#. Accessed 3 May 2013.

United States Liberals About.com (2012) http://usliberals.about.com/od/education/a/PublicLibraries.htm. Accessed 3 May 2013.

Universitas 21 (2012) http://www.universitas212.bham.ac.uk/TandL/Presentations/LSB.pdf. Accessed 3 May 2013.

University College London (UCL) (2007) 'Office Space Utilisation Part 1 April 2007', UCL. Retrieved from: http://www.ucl.ac.uk/estates/space/UCL%20Office%20Utilisation%20Study.pdf.

University College London (UCL) (2008) 'Information behaviour of the researcher of the future: a ciber briefing paper', UCL/ JISC, January. Retrieved from: http://www.jisc.ac.uk/media/documents/programmes/reppres/gg_final_keynote_11012008.pdf.

University of Cape Town (UCT) (2012a) University of Cape Town Research Commons, http://www.lib.uct.ac.za/rc/index.php?html=/rescomm/carnegieproject.htm&libid=110. Accessed 3 May 2013.

University of Cape Town (UCT) (2012b) University of Cape Town Student Affairs: sport clubs http://www.uct.ac.za/students/recreation/sports/overview/. Accessed 3 May 2013.

University of Dayton (UD) (2012) Artstreet. http://artstreet.udayton.edu/about/index.html. Accessed 3 May 2013.

University of Michigan (UM) (2012) University of Michigan North

Quad housing http://www.housing.umich.edu/north-quad-tour-brochure. Accessed 3 May 2013.

University of Minnesota (UM) (2007a) 'Office of Classroom Management. Active Learning Classrooms (ALC)', UM. http://www.classroom.umn.edu/projects/ALCOverview.html. Accessed 3 May 2013.

University of Minnesota (UM) (2007b) 'Active learning classrooms pilot evaluation: Fall 2007 findings and recommendations', University of Minnesota. Retrieved from: http://www.classroom.umn.edu/projects/alc_report_final.pdf.

University of North Florida (UNF) (2012) http://www.unfospreys.com/sports/2008/9/23/AthleticTrainingFacilities.aspx. Accessed 3 May 2013.

University of Otago (2012a) Hunter Centre, Health Sciences Faculty http://www.odt.co.nz/on-campus/university-otago/21213/officials-pay-tribute-opening-centre http://www.duffillwatts.com/Project_Profiles/Structural_Engineering/The_Hunter_Centre. Accessed 3 May 2013.

University of Otago (2012b) Information Services Building http://www.library.otago.ac.nz/services/admin/isbnews.html#building. Accessed 3 May 2013.

University of Oxford collegiate system (2012) http://www.ox.ac.uk/colleges/the_collegiate_system/index.html. Accessed 3 May 2013.

University of Phoenix (UP) (2011) http://en.wikipedia.org/wiki/University_of_phoenix. Accessed 3 May 2013.

University of Santa Clara (2012) Information commons and library. http://www.scu.edu/newlibrary/. Accessed 3 May 2013.

University of Stirling (2011) Gannochy Sports Centre. http://www.sportingexcellence.stir.ac.uk/about-us/news-archive/2011/february/scottish-athletes-to-benefit-from-sports-science-investment-at-stirling. Accessed 3 May 2013.

University of Virginia (UV) 2002) 'Faculty Senate. Feasibility Study for a Graduate Professional Student Studies Center at UV', 11 April. Retrieved from: http://www.virginia.edu/facultysenate/warnerstudentctr.html.

Unwin, L. (2009) *Connecting Workplace Learning and VET to Lifelong Learning,* Institute of Education, Beyond Current Horizons project, Futurelab (commissioned by DCSF).

Urban Renaissance Institute (2010) 'UniverCities Starterpack', Academy of Urbanism, April. Retrieved from: http://www.academyofurbanism.org.uk/projects/unv/univercities_starterpack.pdf.

US Department of Education (2011) 'The American jobs by the numbers', Homeroom, official blog of the US Department of Education, 18 October. Retrieved from: http://www.ed.gov/blog/2011/10/the-american-jobs-act-by-the-numbers-40/.

US libraries (2010) 'Quotable facts about America's libraries 2010', Office for Library Advocacy, American Library Association, January. Retrieved from: http://www.ala.org/offices/sites/ala.org.offices/files/content/ola/quotablefacts/QF.3.8.2010.pdf.

USA Today (2009) http://www.usatoday.com/news/education/2009-02-01-libraries_N.htm. Accessed 3 May 2013.

Van Meel, J. and Vos, P. (2001) 'Funky offices: reflections on office design in the "new economy"', Journal of Corporate Real Estate, 3, 4: 322–34. Retrieved from: http://www.cfpb.nl/fileadmin/cfpb/images/publicaties/artikelen/2001/Meel_2001_FunkyOffices.pdf.

Van Note Chism, N. (2006) Challenging traditional assumptions and rethinking learning spaces', in Oblinger, D. (ed.) Learning Spaces, Educause. Retrieved from: http://net.educause.edu/ir/library/pdf/PUB7102.pdf.

Venturi, R. (1972) Learning from Las Vegas. Cambridge, MA: MIT Press.

The Village at Penn State (2005) 'Life care'. Retrieved from: http:// www.villageatpennstate.com/lifecare.htm.

Voigt, C. (2008) 'Educational design and media choice for collaborative, electronic case-based learning (e-CBL)', PhD thesis, July, University of South Australia.

Virtual Worlds (2012) http://virtualworlds.nmc.org/. Accessed 3 May 2013.

Wall, E. (2011) 'Want 10pc? Try student housing investment', Telegraph, 5 Sept. Retrieved from: http://www.telegraph.co.uk/finance/personalfinance/investing/8741937/Want-10pc-Try-student-housing-investment.html.

Ward, H. (2010) 'School libraries refuse to be shelved', TES, 17 September. Retrieved from: http://www.tes.co.uk/article.aspx?storyCode=6058191.

Warner, M. (2011) 'Apollo Group 4Q net soars on fewer charges; enrollment falls', Dow Jones News Plus: North American Equities, 19 October. Retrieved from: http://www.djnewsplus.com/rssarticle/SB131902434067897972.html.

Wasonga C., Rari, B. and Wanzare Z. (2011) 'Re-thinking school-university collaboration: Agenda for the 21st century', Educational Research and Reviews, 6, 22: 1036–45. Retrieved from: http://www.academicjournals.org/ERR/PDF/Pdf%202011/19Dec/Wasonga%20et%20al.pdf.

Watch, D. and Tolat, D. (2010) 'Research laboratory', Whole Building Design Guide 2010. Retrieved from: http://www.wbdg.org/design/research_lab.php.

Watch, D., Tolat, D. and McNay, G. (2010) 'Academic laboratory', Whole Building Design Guide. 2010. Retrieved from: http://www.wbdg.org/design/academic_lab.php.

Watson, L. (2006) 'The Saltire Centre at Glasgow Caledonian University', SCONUL Focus 37 Spring. Retrieved from http://www.sconul.ac.uk/publications/newsletter/37/2.pdf.

Wawrzaszek, S. and Wedaman, D. (2008) 'The academic library in a 2.0 world', Educause Center for Applied Research Bulletin, 2008, 19 (16 September). Retrieved from: http://net.educause.edu/ir/library/pdf/ERB0819.pdf.

Webster, K. (2010) 'The library space as learning space', Educause Review, 45, 6 (November/December): 10–11.

Welsh Assembly Government (2010) 21st Century Schools Information Document, Welsh Assembly Government.

White arkitekter (2010) 'Future learning environments – how the environment impacts on learning', Karolinska institutet & the Stockholms läns landsting. Retrieved from: http://ki.se/content/1/c6/12/35/72/Final%20report%20Future%20Learning%20Environments_White%20arkitekter_low%20res.pdf.

White House (2011) The American Jobs Act Fact Sheet, The White House. http://www.whitehouse.gov/the-press-office/2011/09/08/fact-sheet-american-jobs-act. Accessed 3 May 2013.

White, D. (nd) 'Closing public libraries – a death knell of democracy: shutting homework, literacy & citizenship centers', About.com. Retrieved from: usliberals.about.com/od/education/a/PublicLibraries.htm. Accessed 10 May 2013.

Whiteside, A. and Fitzgerald, S. (2009) 'Designing spaces for active learning', Implications, 07, 01. Retrieved from: http://www.informedesign.org/_news/jan_v07r-pr.2.pdf.

Whiteside, A., Brooks, C. and Walker, J. (2010) 'Making the case for space: three years of empirical research on learning environments', Educause Quarterly, 33, 3. Retrieved from: http://www.educause.edu/EDUCAUSE+Quarterly/EDUCAUSEQuarterlyMagazineVolum/MakingtheCaseforSpaceThreeYear/213681.

Whiteside, A.L., Jorn, L., Duin, A.H. and Fitzgerald, S. (2009) 'Using the PAIR-up model to evaluate active learning spaces', Educause Review, 32, 1. Retrieved from: http://www.educause.edu/EDUCAUSE+Quarterly/EDUCAUSEQuarterlyMagazineVolum/UsingthePAIRupModeltoEvaluateA/163845.

Whitespace (2012) http://www.abertay.ac.uk/About/WhitespaceFacilites.cfm. Accessed 3 May 2013.

Whole Building Design Guide (WBDG) (2010) http://www.wbdg.org/design/academic_lab.php. Accessed 3 May 2013.

Williams, D., Wavell, C. and Coles, L. (2001) Impact of School Library Services on Achievement and Learning. School of

Information and Media, Faculty of Management, The Robert Gordon University.

Williams, J. and Wilson, T. (2010) 'Work and learning: IFLL Thematic Paper 7', National Institute of Adult Continuing Education. Retrieved from: shop.niace.org.uk/ifll-work-learning.htm.

Wilson, K. (2011) 'Staffroom improvement', Facebook page comment Katie Wilson, 21 Feb 2011. http://www.facebook.com/staffroomforimprovement. Accessed 3 May 2013.

Wilson, N. (nd) *Boots and the Novel: The Circulating Libraries and their Readers, c. 1900-40.* http://www.reading.ac.uk/web/FILES/DEAL/BootsandtheNovel.pdf. Accessed 3 May 2013.

Wineki, A. (2010) *The Makeup and Utilization of University Student Unions: A Comparative Analysis*, The Martin School of Public Policy and Administration, 15 April. Retrieved from: http://www.martin.uky.edu/Capstones_2010/Wineki.pdf.

Winterbottom, M. and Wilkins, A. (2009) 'Lighting and discomfort in the classroom', *Journal of Environmental Psychology* 29: 63-75.

Wooden, R. (2006) 'The future of public libraries in an internet age', *National Civic Review*, Winter, pp. 1–7. Retrieved from: http://www.ncl.org/publications/ncr/95-4/0107libraries.pdf.

Woolner, P., Hall, E., Wall, K., Higgins, S., Blake, A. and McCaughey, C. (2005) *School Building Programmes: Motivations, Consequences and Implications,* CfBT Research and Development, Newcastle: University of Newcastle upon Tyne.

Worldarchitecture (2006) 'AHMM architects design state-of-the-art student digs in Kings Cross.' 27 September 2006. Retrieved from: http://www.worldarchitecturenews.com/index.php/index.php?fuseaction=wanappln.projectview&upload_id=536. Accessed 3 May 2013.

Worthington, J. (2007) 'Enabling place-making: the role of the school in supporting the community', *Building Excellence: Exploring the Implications of the Curriculum for Excellence for School Building*. The Scottish Government, p. 14. Retrieved from: http://www.scotland.gov.uk/Resource/Doc/207034/0054999.pdf.

Wright, S. (nd) 'Look what you can do in five days', *21st century schools*, 2.3: 48–53 (at 50). Retrieved from: http://www.bigschoolmakeover.org.uk/documents/Liscard_Article.pdf.

YouMedia (2012) Harold Washington Library, Chicago: YouMedia. http://youmediachicago.org/10-philosophy/pages/37-youmedia-layout. Accessed 3 May 2013.

Young, J. (2009) 'When computers leave classrooms, so does boredom', *Chronicle of Higher Education,* 20 July. Retrieved from: http://chronicle.com/article/Teach-Naked-Effort-Strips/47398/.

Index

Note: Page numbers in **bold** type refer to **figures**
Page numbers in *italic* type refer to *tables*